DIARY OF A COMMON SOLDIER IN THE AMERICAN REVOLUTION, 1775–1783

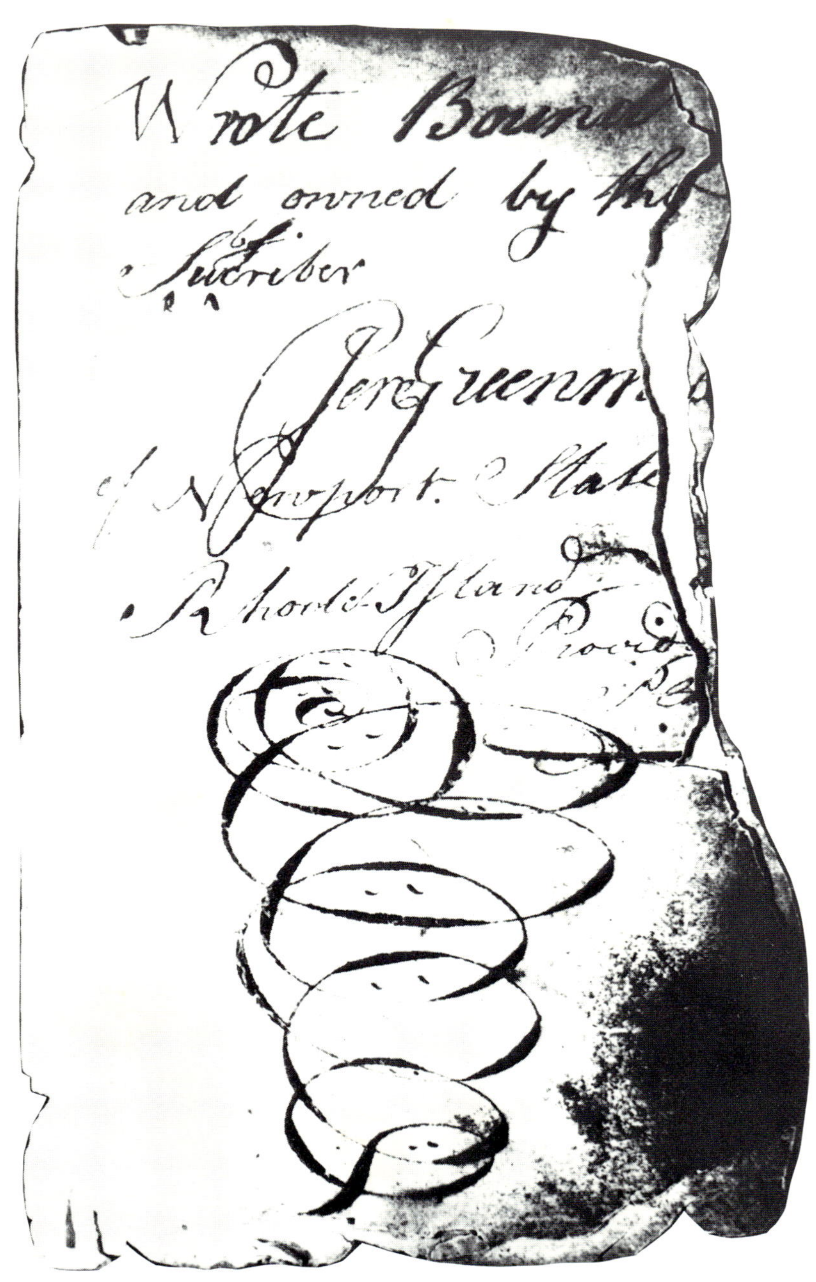
Wrote Boun
and owned by th
Sucriber
Jer Greenm
of Newport Stat
Rhode Island
Provid

The first page of Greenman's diary.

Diary of a Common Soldier in the American Revolution, 1775-1783

An Annotated Edition of the Military Journal of JEREMIAH GREENMAN

Edited by
Robert C. Bray & Paul E. Bushnell

Published by the Northern Illinois University Press
with the assistance of a grant from The Rhode Island
Bicentennial Foundation.

DeKalb, Illinois

1978

Library of Congress Cataloging in Publication Data
Greenman, Jeremiah, 1758–1828.
Diary of a common soldier in the American Revolution, 1775–1783.

Bibliography
Includes index.
1. Greenman, Jeremiah, 1758–1828. 2. United States—History—Revolution, 1775–1783—Personal narratives. 3. United States. Army. Continental Army—Biography. 4. Soldiers—United States—Biography. 5. United States—History—Revolution, 1775–1783—Campaigns and battles. I. Bray, Robert C. II. Bushnell, Paul E. III. Title.
E275.G78 1977 973.3'3'0924 [B] 77–18528

ISBN 0-917012-04-6

Published by the Northern Illinois University Press,
DeKalb, Illinois 60115
Manufactured in the United States of America

Designed by Gerard A. Valerio

For

Lorena Grace Bray

and

Mildred S. Bushnell

ACKNOWLEDGMENTS

We want first to express our gratitude to Mrs. Edwin R. Lederer, direct descendant of Jeremiah Greenman and gracious owner of his journal; she and her husband are good neighbors to Illinois Wesleyan University. The Lederers had laboriously begun the work of transcribing the journal when one of the editors, Paul Bushnell, was first introduced to them by Professor Bunyan Andrew, former chairman of the History Department of Illinois Wesleyan University. Work on authentication of the document and bibliography began immediately, but the size and scope of the Greenman journal were so great that soon a collaboration begun in the classroom was happily extended to this project. From the beginning of our editorial collaboration more than three years ago, we have been fortunate in enlisting the interest and support of a number of persons and institutions we want gratefully to acknowledge here.

For grants that provided substantial support for research or publication we want to thank the Rhode Island Bicentennial Foundation, the National Endowment for the Humanities, the Newberry Library of Chicago, and the Penrose Fund of the American Philosophical Society. Early support in the form of Newberry Library fellowships opened to us the vast resources of their collections and enabled us to utilize them. Special thanks go to Richard Brown, Director of Research at the Newberry, to his able colleagues and staff, and especially to John Long and Gordon DenBoer of the Atlas of Early American History Project, who generously listened to our many questions about places and place-names and pointed the way to sources we would otherwise probably have missed.

It is particularly appropriate that this project has received a large measure of support from Jeremiah Greenman's native Rhode

Island, and it is a special pleasure to record here the debt we owe to the Rhode Island Bicentennial Foundation. The Rhode Island Historical Society graciously gave us firsthand access to their whole range of New England genealogical records, Revolutionary War materials, and Customs House papers, for which the editors wish especially to thank the director of the Rhode Island Historical Society, Albert T. Klyberg, and the Manuscript Curator of the Society's library in Providence, Nathaniel N. Shipton.

One of the first institutions to aid our work was the Illinois State Historical Library, which took an interest in the preservation of the Greenman manuscript. Advice and valuable help in the microfilming of the journal came from Roger D. Bridges, Director of Research, and Paul D. Spence, late Curator of Manuscripts there. The National Archives in Washington, D.C., cooperated in making available to us the military and pension records of Jeremiah Greenman, of which the latter proved to be a most valuable source of information for his later life. The collections of the Ohio Historical Society in Columbus, Ohio, yielded additional materials pertaining to Greenman's later life. In Marietta, Ohio, the records of the Ohio Company of Associates and of the early history of Washington County, Ohio, were kindly made available to us by Special Collections librarian Patrick J. Mullin of the Marietta College Library. We also value the cooperation of the Public Archives of Canada, which made available copies of some manuscripts in their collections.

While we depended upon our travels for uncovering vital sources and answering many of our most puzzling questions, the great majority of our textual work had to be done at home. For that reason we are grateful for the encouragement and support of our work from colleagues and students at Illinois Wesleyan University and from its President, Robert S. Eckley. We also want to thank the libraries of Illinois Wesleyan and Illinois State University for responding to our many needs, whether for books, microfilm reading facilities, or interlibrary loans. For her expert and painstaking labor in the preparation of the bibliography, we are grateful to Janette Bray. We also wish to acknowledge the timely and careful assistance of Lynn Lehman in the preparation of the index.

Among the scholars who have taken an interest in this project we wish especially to thank Professor Alfred Young of the Department of History at Northern Illinois University for his many helpful suggestions about editorial procedure and his help in putting us in touch with important work in progress.

Finally, the editors wish to acknowledge their gratitude for the many contributions to this project of Jerry Israel, Chairman of the Department of History of Illinois Wesleyan University. Urging us over the initial obstacles in our path, Jerry got us to begin editing the Greenman journal in earnest and then continued to work indefatigably to help us find the means to complete our work and bring the manuscript to publication. Completion of this project finally affords us an opportunity publicly to offer our thanks to Jerry, whose good counsel, energy, and wit have helped us to prevail.

CONTENTS

JEREMIAH GREENMAN, 1758–1828

It seemed as if the war not only required, but created talents. Men whose minds were warmed with the love of liberty, and whose abilities were improved by daily exercise, and sharpened with a laudable ambition to serve their distressed country, spoke, wrote, and acted, with an energy far surpassing all expectations which could be reasonably founded on their previous acquirements.

David Ramsay, *The History of the American Revolution* (1789)

I. The Elusive Ancestor

In the best American tradition, Jeremiah Greenman undoubtedly came from "a long line of plain people."[1] Yet who these were and where they came from will probably never be known. The Greenmans with whom we are concerned—because they must be seen from a vast distance in time, because they were common folk, and because such records as they kept have atrophied with the centuries—seem simply to have appeared in Massachusetts in the middle of the seventeenth century. No ship passenger lists announce their arrival, no town records have them paying taxes or being put into the stocks. The solitary source is a family Bible register page. It speaks of one "Wm Greenman," said to have been born "at Plimoth Mass" in 1652. Usually the staunchest of genealogical records, this family Bible would seem a hopeful sign for the tracing of the early Greenmans, but it is an eighteenth-century Bible, and the note on William Greenman, Jeremiah's grandfather, was obviously inserted a century or more after his heyday—nothing definitive there.[2] All that is known with certainty about William Greenman is that he settled in Swansea, Massachusetts, early in the eighteenth century, married a woman named Esther, and began a family. In the old Swansea record books, five births are noted for William and Esther Greenman, and the third of these was Jeremiah senior, born on 11 February 1719/20.[3] Not one thing further is known about the life and times of William Greenman of Swansea.

Of course, this paucity of records and sources gives the lie to the continuity of living that the Greenmans had. The years, to our eyes, pass unnoted: a Swansea boy grows up and goes down to Newport, Rhode Island. And there, in 1749, Jeremiah Greenman, Sr., married Amy Wiles.[4] He was one of many Greenmans in Newport before the Revolution, and he has managed to retain his anonymity. The supposition that Jeremiah senior followed the sea is attractive, given the maritime essence of that thriving city, and in fact there is one tantalizing mention of a "——— Grinman" serving as boatswain on a Newport privateer during the Seven Years' War,[5] but the connection with any particular Greenman cannot be made. Yet he came from Swansea, lived in Newport until the British occupation in 1776, and finished his life in a coastal village called Acoaxet, within the town limits of Dartmouth, Massachusetts: living always by the sea strongly suggests a vital relationship with it.

Jeremiah junior was born in Newport on 7 May 1758, apparently the only child—or only surviving child—of Jeremiah and Amy Greenman, for one searches in vain for any mention of brothers or sisters. Concerning his childhood only one sentence has ever been recorded, and with that we are obliged to sum it up: He "received in his native town such an education as the Common Schools afforded."[6] Depending upon school and schoolmaster, this meant a more or less elementary induction into the mysteries of literacy. Probably it was not much at all, for Newport—indeed all of Rhode Island—lagged behind the rest of New England in the establishment of free public education for its children. "The public schools of Newport were tuition schools, with special provision for free education for poor children."[7] Jeremiah junior might well have echoed the sentiments of fellow Rhode Island soldier Stephen Olney, who ruefully remarked of his own education, "What I had learnt was mostly rong."[8] It was the institution of war and not the common school that taught Greenman to write, though the latter deserves a measure of credit for giving him the rudiments of literacy in those prewar years.

There is no indication that the young man was actively preparing for a trade or career. To be sure, the Revolution began at just about the time he would have been making serious decisions about his life. Nearly half a century later Greenman would recall that "having Devoted my youthful days to the service of my country I was deprived of the opportunity which young men generally possess of acquiring any mechanical art of perfecting my self in any profession."[9] Yet this does not alter the probability that the war came opportunely—came, that is, at a season when nothing else was offering and gave prospect both of patriotic service and a livelihood. It would be temporary, full of vicissitudes, and dangerous, but it was surely something to do that was worth doing. Here was a practical and time-honored reason for joining an army, and so, just after his seventeenth birthday, Jeremiah Greenman went to war "to make a man of himself" and help in the birth of a nation. His military service was long and varied: it included treks as far north as Quebec in Canada and as far south as Philadelphia; there were two separate and lengthy sojourns in British prisons; and there was frequent enough advancement in rank to hold his interest in the protracted drama of the American army. After a season as a private on Benedict Arnold's expedition to Quebec, followed by a term as a prisoner of war, Greenman reenlisted in the Rhode Island Continentals as a sergeant for the campaign of 1777, and by its end he was first sergeant of his regiment. In 1779 came promotion to ensign; in 1781, first lieutenant; and in 1782 he assumed the duties of regimental adjutant for the Rhode Island troops, remaining on active service until after the definitive treaty of peace was signed and most of his fellow soldiers and officers had already been mustered out.[10]

II. "Settled Myself as an Inhabitant of Providence"

Unquestionably the American Revolution transformed the life of Jeremiah Greenman, as it must have done for thousands of its soldiers, especially the younger ones. But among the war's manifold influences, the cardinal effect upon Greenman was to increase dramatically his expectations for the future. With the concluding of peace in 1783 he found himself hopeful and invigorated. After all, had he not served long and faithfully, rising steadily through the ranks from private soldier to commissioned officer? Was he not, at war's end, certified as a competent and energetic officer, loyal and dependable beyond the average? He was, in fact, a member of an officer cadre that had all the appearances of an elite. It was an aristocracy of worth within the young democracy, a natural growth, its proud members felt, from the political sentiments underlying the new nation they had helped to found; and now, still young, they were eager and expectant in their desire to finish "growing up with the country." They wished nothing so much as to continue to serve America by instituting themselves into a variety of civil and semicivil positions which they felt they had earned by their blood and loyalty and for which they were undeniably and preeminently qualified. Not all the retiring officers felt this way, of course: here and there was a man who asked nothing more from the country than the privilege of resuming his private business.[11] But such officers were generally affluent enough to afford such strict republican virtue, reminiscent of the best of the Romans, having land or other property awaiting their attention, and consequently scorning government sinecures. For every one of these, however, there were a dozen or two who very much needed a civilian stage upon which they might continue their progress towards a competency.

Greenman was a good case in point. Utterly without skills when he entered the Continental army, he had learned in his regimental life to keep rolls and accounts, to write as well as a middling scrivener, to give orders and take them, to judge and manage men. These abilities had been developed over a period of years, at a considerable investment in time by the soldier himself and in money by the fledgling state. But now the war was over, and what was to become of these really remarkable attainments? In 1783 Greenman was twenty-five years old and one of the officers that the nation—with the inevitable deemphasis on and reduction of the army—could no longer use. As the country got going with its peacetime economy and government he would see what it could do for him. In the meantime he wisely proposed to try doing for himself.

The ex-soldier's "Revolutionary expectations" were highest in the decade between the treaty of peace with Britain and the end of Washington's first administration. It was predictably an expansive era, and many of the Revolutionary veterans were already looking westward to redeem both congressional promises of bounty lands and their sagging fortunes as well. But Jeremiah Greenman chose not to participate in this first phase of what would later become an American habit of starting over out west. Instead he determined to settle in Providence, Rhode Island. To a man with his eye on the main chance in the 1780s, Providence must have looked promising. For the city was alive and growing, beginning to assert a postwar commercial dominance over Newport that would become more pronounced in succeeding years. The latter town had lost fully one-half of its population with the British occupation in 1776 and was never able to recover as a metropolitan center of trade.[12] Now it was Providence's turn to prosper. But what was the town like at the time Greenman settled there? The Marquis de Chastellux, an accurate observer of the American scene at the time of the Revolution, visited Providence late in 1780, saw it for what it was and would be, and noted the town's salient features in his journal:

> *The town of Providence is built on the bank of a river only six miles long, which empties into the same bay in which Rhode Island, Conanicut and Prudence Islands, etc., are situated. It has only one street, which is very long; the suburb, which is rather extensive, is on the other* [*western*] *side of the river. This town is handsome, the houses are not spacious, but well built and well appointed within. It is pent in between two chains of mountains, one to the north, and the other to the southwest, which causes unbearable heat in the summer; but it is exposed to the northwest wind, which rakes it from one end to the other, and renders it extremely cold in winter. It may contain twenty-five hundred inhabitants. Its situation is very advantageous for commerce, which accordingly was very considerable in peacetime. Merchant ships may load and unload their cargoes in the town itself, while ships of war cannot approach the harbor. Their trade is the same as that of Rhode Island* [Newport] *and Boston; they export lumber and salt provisions, and bring back salt and a great quantity of molasses, sugar, and other products from the West Indies. . . .*[13]

It was this thriving commerce that initially drew Greenman to Providence. In one of his rare journal entries set down after the war he notes: "entered into a contract with Mr. Masury formely an officer of the Regt to put our small interest together (which we had been fighting, bleeding, and all most dying for,—for the space of 8 long years in the Army of the United States,) in order for to trade and try for a lively hood." He had known Joseph Masury for most of the war. Both men had risen through the ranks, becoming friends and fellow officers, and now they decided to throw their lots together in some sort of retail store. The "small interest" of which Greenman speaks consisted of the five years' full pay that Congress had authorized for officers in lieu of half pay for life. The sum in Greenman's case was not insignificant, for at the time of his discharge he was a first lieutenant serving as regimental adjutant, drawing thirty-nine dollars a month.[14] Thus his separation pay would have been something like twenty-four hundred dollars—a tidy nest egg, though certainly not all that impressive in view of the horrendous depreciation of money during the war. Yet with this sum, and whatever other capital he may have been able to raise, Greenman in April of 1784 moved himself and his mother to Providence from Swansea, Massachusetts (his father had died in 1781) and started life as a shopkeeper.

The firm of Greenman and Masury, if such it was called, was established on "the west side of the river," in a section of Providence which was just beginning to be developed. He settled in a house on Broad Street (now part of Weybosset Street) owned by "Decon" Barzillai Richmond, but the exact location of the store is unknown, though a Broad Street address is probable.[15] The partnership in retail trade, however, did not prosper. So little is known about the nature of Greenman's and Masury's store—one is not even aware of what they sold—that it would be absurd to speculate on the causes of their failure. All Greenman says on the subject is that, scarcely five months after they began, "buisness grow'd very dull," and he left Mr. Masury to try it on his own. But the retail trade, he soon found, was not for him, and by September of 1785 he had called it quits.

In his season as a struggling merchant, Greenman had something else on his mind. He was courting a woman named Mary Eddy, also known as Polly. She was the daughter of Esek Eddy—one of the ubiquitous Providence Eddys, a family which came in those postwar years to dominate the shipwright's craft on the west side of the river. "When the John Field farm was opened for settlement at Cowpen point, the Eddy family established a shipyard there, and so many of this name were engaged in building vessels and houses that soon the 'Point' was called 'Eddy's neighborhood' or 'Eddy's Point.'"[16] Jeremiah Greenman and Mary Eddy were married on 23 October 1784 at the nearby Second Congregational Church. The minister was the Reverend Joseph Snow, a local patriarch and almost as much an institution on the west side as the Beneficent Meeting House itself.[17] Jeremiah and Mary probably set up housekeeping at the Richmond house, though it is just possible they moved in with the Esek Eddys. At any rate the newly-married Greenman now faced more directly than ever the dilemma of getting his living. How much of his capital he had lost in the failure of the store is not known, but that he found himself in reduced circumstances on the verge of starting a family seems certain.

III. "I Followed the Seas as a Nautical Commander"

Perhaps it was the valuable connection with the Eddy family that suggested to Greenman a life at sea. True, he had begun his study of navigation during the war, but now the intimate contacts with shipbuilders, traders, and sailors must have caused him to look down the salt river towards Narragansett Bay and the beckoning Atlantic. He set his sights on earning a captain's or master's position in the growing American merchant marine, and of course he needed more than navigational treatises to qualify: he needed to sail. In the New England merchant marine "the great majority of masters came in through the hawse-hole, and the vast majority of seamen had sufficient command of the three Rs to post a log, draft a protest, draw up a manifest, and, with a little instruction on shore or shipboard, find a position at sea."[18] From this it is clear that Greenman entered upon his new calling with qualifications considerably above the average. His first voyage—not as a master but as a seaman—was on board the *Active* from Boston bound for the West Indies in the autumn of 1785, not to return until June of the next year. He left his wife Mary with child, and while he was at sea his only daughter, Mary Eddy Greenman, was born on 26 November 1785. He saw home again for less than a month in 1786, scarcely time enough to get to know his daughter and reacquaint himself with his wife, before sailing again—this time on the *America* for the coast of Guinea and the Cape Verde Islands. On this voyage he was absent for nearly two years and did not make port in Providence until May of 1788. At some indeterminate time during these apprentice sailings he got his master's certificate and began to captain the vessels on which he sailed.

The customshouse records for the port of Providence, in which Greenman's name appears from time to time, provide the facts of a career at sea but not the feeling. The legal details of the sailings are there: the owners of the ships, the bonds, the cargo manifests, the ports of call, and the dates of departure and arrival at Providence.

But they do not begin to imply the dangers and excitements of piloting vessels ranging in size from small to tiny, often by dead reckoning, to Africa or the West Indies and back. "Quaint and interesting the ships of the Federalist period certainly were, with their varied coloring (bright lemon, or orange waist against black, blue or dark green topsides, and a gay contrasting color for the inside of bulwarks); their carved 'gingerbread work' on stern, and 'quick-work' about the bows; their few, well-proportioned sails . . . and their occasionally graceful sheer. But strip off their ornaments, and you find . . . a chunky, wall-sided model."[19] While Greenman was not the caliber of captain to be entrusted with one of the imposing East Indiamen that were opening the far-flung China trade for Providence, he did enjoy his measure of the overall social prestige attached to the New England merchant marine, where "American shipmasters [*were*] received into the upper bourgeois society of the seaports where they traded."[20] It was Greenman's lot to sail sloops and schooners and an occasional brigantine in the employ of small trading firms or even individual owners. Yet this was the backbone of the Providence trade, and the lot that fell to him was not a bad one.

The first voyage on which he is listed as the master was that of the schooner *Alice*, for the Cape Verde Islands, in the fall of 1790.[21] And so he began a fifteen-year career as a sea captain in the American merchant marine. It was to be a career punctuated by periods of home life, as his family grew,[22] interrupted by a period of government service, crowned by part-ownership in a vessel, and ultimately destroyed by the disruption of ocean commerce during the Napoleonic Wars.

Jeremiah Greenman, no matter what else he might be doing, never relinquished his goal of obtaining some sort of government appointment. In the seagoing years he still thought much about it, and as the 1790s opened, two circumstances appeared to favor his chances: in the first place "His Excellency Genl. Washington" was the first president of the United States under the new Constitution, and surely his old commander in chief would lend a sympathetic ear to the request of a faithful veteran like himself. Then, too, his regimental commander, Jeremiah Olney, was firmly installed as collector of customs for the port of Providence. And had not Olney, on the occasion of disbanding the Rhode Island Regiment, promised to use his influence to further the aspirations of his officers in civilian life?[23] Greenman, nothing loath, took Colonel Olney at his word, and applied to him several times in the early 1790s for letters of recommendation to the federal government.

His initial idea was to get in on the ground floor when the United States Army was to be bolstered and new companies formed in each state. Greenman asked Olney to sponsor him for a captaincy, and accordingly the latter wrote Secretary of War Henry Knox in April of 1791 that "the long experience of his Millitary Tallents, and the particular knowledge I have of his perservering Fortitude and abilities . . . give me every reason to believe he will do honor to the Appointment. . . ." Olney also remarked that "a Millitary Life" would be "more Congenial to his wishes" than that of the sea—a clear and suggestive indication of Greenman's career predilections.[24] But the appointment was not forthcoming. Did Greenman realize that he was in competition with hundreds of other, equally hopeful veterans of the Revolution? Perhaps, but this daunted him not at all. The next enterprise, again with Olney's second, was seeking the first mate's berth on a revenue cutter being built in Connecticut for duty in Long Island Sound. Olney initially wrote Secretary of the Treasury Alexander Hamilton sometime in late 1790 or early 1791 (the letter has not survived), but nothing was heard in response for more than six months, and when word finally did arrive it was not what Greenman wished to hear: he was offered only the position of second mate. Now Olney, who was certainly doing all he could and considerably more than Greenman should have expected, wrote Hamilton again, this time noting that "Mr. Jeremiah Greenman [*was*] exceedingly mortified after throwing himself out of the best Imploy in this Town and waiting four or five months with a reasonable expectation of receiving an appointment to the office of first mate of the Cutter, to which he was early recommended, to find that he must now accept the Station of Second Mate, or continue out of business. . . ." The letter goes on to speak frankly of Greenman's economic necessity and his desire for public service.[25] If the career of shipmaster was indeed "the best Imploy in this Town," Greenman's decision to stay ashore for almost half a year is an eloquent testimony both to the formative nature of his earlier military experience and to the persistency with which he saw public service as a desirable and fitting part of his self-definition.

Having little choice, Greenman accepted and was eventually

confirmed in the second mate's position. Late in 1791 he assumed his duties in the Sound. Just how long he continued on the cutter *Argus* is not known, but the fact that there are no records of any voyages for him between 1791 and the end of 1795 suggests a tenure of several years. Greenman does not seem to have resumed his shipmaster's career on an active basis until 1799, when once again frequent trips through Providence customs are noted. In the year 1794, however, he made one final effort to get back into the United States military. The depredations of the Barbary corsairs in the early 1790s awakened the nation to the need for a navy, and the plans for its reconstitution filled the air in 1794. Greenman saw a chance for a lieutenancy on one of the frigates that were to be built. As usual, he called upon his old commandant to recommend him; as usual, Jeremiah Olney did his part; and, as usual, it was all to no avail.[26] Finally, the hard and repeated lesson had been learned, and Greenman would wait almost twenty-five years before asking his country for anything again.

But despite all the uncertainty of employment and the disappointed expectations, there were some real strides in these years towards a competency for the Greenman family. In 1793 they became proprietors, buying a lot and house on the Pawtuxet Road (now Broad Street) between Ship Street (now Chestnut) on the east and Claverick on the west.[27] For the "sum of One hundred and thirty five pounds Silver Lawful Money" paid to one Edward Hawkins, Greenman got "One House of Wood—2 Story's 18 feet front and 23½ back" with six glass windows.[28] Here the family—by now numbering five, with the son Jeremiah yet to come—located and remained for thirteen years, improving the property and making it more livable for an active and ever-increasing group. The Greenmans were soon to be joined by William Williams Dunham, who, according to a family tradition, was a cousin of Mary Greenman and, after being orphaned, came to live with them in Providence in the late 1790s.[29] Later he completed the story pleasantly by falling in love with the daughter Mary, marrying her, setting up as a Providence printer, and editing for a time the *Phoenix*, a short-lived Jeffersonian paper.[30] After their marriage, the Dunhams continued to live with the Greenmans, and the little house on the Pawtuxet Road must have fairly bristled with activity, what with the two elder Greenmans, four children, a son-in-law, and, very soon, a grandchild.[31]

Jeremiah Greenman, of course, intermittently left the crowded home-place for the expanses of the Atlantic Ocean, and as the old century gave way to the new, he was busier than ever as a shipmaster. How proud he must have been when, in 1799, he became half-owner of the schooner *Jerushia*, a ship built in Rehoboth, Massachusetts, in 1794 (burthen 49 45/95 tons, dimensions 51 ft. by 17½ ft. by 6½ ft.).[32] Here was a rewarding command indeed—his own ship. He sailed her often in 1799, sometimes to the West Indies, sometimes in the coastal trade. But for some unknown reason his ownership was all too brief: he was obliged to sell his share in the *Jerushia* near the end of the year, though he continued as her master for most of 1800. His interest in the *Jerushia* is the only recorded instance of a proprietorship for him in some twenty years as a mariner. Probably Greenman had had dreams of emulating the prosperous merchants of Providence, but these were not to be.

As he got older, Greenman more and more felt the toll that the sea and its sailing exacted from the human body. Yet could there be anything else for him? Finally he determined that there could be: sometime in 1805 or early 1806 the momentous decision was made to emigrate to Ohio. As with so many other aspects of Jeremiah Greenman's life, both the reasons for this fundamental change and the details surrounding it are obscure. It might seem astonishing that an established and respected citizen, with deep New England roots, surrounded by friends and relatives, would suddenly "light out for the territory"; and when one adds to this the fact that Greenman was well past forty and apparently tied by nature and long familiarity to the sea—having never farmed a day in his life—the prospect of removal to the agrarian, landlocked West becomes even more difficult to understand. This time there is no journal or other record of family deliberations to help explain. One can only imagine the long discussions that led to the decision. What was said in favor of emigration? The sons' overriding motif must have been land. By 1805 the magic of the West was beginning its work on easterners in earnest. The land was waiting for such as the Greenmans, all but illimitable and just about free, for the elder Greenman still held his Revolutionary land bounty. Now the sons urged their father to make good his hard-won claim. They, after all, were not seamen and more likely than not held the typically naive American view that farming might be done with ease by anyone, if only the land might be had. Mrs.

Greenman, hard as it was for her to contemplate leaving home, here must have raised her voice in support of her boys: she had spent too many days and months alone, anxious, gazing out to sea and wondering if Jeremiah would return safely home. Her sons should not go to sea.[33] Greenman listened to them, perhaps thinking too of his own disability, the result of a war wound that never properly healed and that appeared to be worsening with age.[34] He also knew that the situation with ocean commerce was bad and not apt to improve soon. There was no embargo yet, but the European wars were creating havoc with American shipping, and the little sloops and schooners, the *Pollys* and *Jerushias*, no longer felt even a measure of safety on the high seas, caught as they were between British impressment and French letters of marque. The sea had made its timeless call to Greenman, but that had changed. Now the land beckoned to another generation with a similar power. He contemplated a life change of tremendous import, and one can imagine his taking pause to see the parade of postwar years from the eminence of bittersweet experience. Disappointed as a merchant, repeatedly denied the opportunity of government service, destined to be a master of ships but not their owner: much that he had confidently expected had not come to pass. To a man getting older, Rhode Island and New England themselves must have seemed old. Yet some of the Greenmans were young. They would go to Ohio.

IV. That "Night Would Overtake Me in the Wilderness of Ohio"

In the autumn of 1806 the Greenman family pulled out of Providence and by October had reached Marietta, Ohio, a young town with high hopes planted at the confluence of the Ohio and Muskingum rivers. The home ties were broken, the uprooting complete. Before leaving, Jeremiah had bid good-bye down at the old State House to those of his Revolutionary brethren who yet attended the meetings of the Society of the Cincinnati. Then he had sold the home on Pawtuxet Road for "1,000 Spanish milled dollars," a nice sum to take west, even considering the many improvements the Greenmans had made on the property over the years.[35] With this capital, a wagon load or two of possessions, and a new set of expectations, the family

—father, mother, the sons John and Jeremiah, daughter Mary with her husband and infant son—[36]took leave of Rhode Island and struck westward. None of them ever returned.

It seemed natural to them to head for Ohio. Recently admitted to the union, the state had been for years and would continue to be the goal of New England emigrant trains. In fact, Ohio—or at least the corner of it to which the Greenmans journeyed—probably owed its existence to the energy and opportunism of Rufus Putnam and his Ohio Company of Associates; for these men, wishing to establish an agrarian empire for Revolutionary soldiers and make money in the process, had twenty years earlier convinced Congress to sell them and their subscribers a tract of land which turned out, after all the surveys were in, to be almost 1,800,000 acres in the Muskingum Valley at a cost of eight cents an acre![37] The Reverend Manasseh Cutler, the astute chief lobbyist for the Ohio Company, likewise persuaded the Confederation Congress to adopt his plan for the settlement of the "territory North West of the Ohio." The result was the famous Northwest Ordinance of 1787, guaranteeing statehood and civil rights for the colonies if they prospered.[38] While Greenman had been following the sea, the Ohio Company was busy surveying and platting, laying out towns and mills and forts, and giving free land to "Warlike Christian Men" who would settle on the frontiers of their tract close to the Indians. "Here . . . was a New England village transplanted bodily to the Ohio wilderness, with a paternalistic colonizing company playing the same valuable role that town proprietors played in seventeenth-century Massachusetts."[39]

The model of these transplanted villages was Marietta, often called Ohio's first town and named by the Ohio Company after none other than Marie Antoinette—it was 1788, and though the French were on the eve of a revolution of their own, the town planners in far-off Ohio could not have known. By the time Greenman and family arrived, Marietta was thriving as the commercial hub and county seat of Washington County. Under the Ordinance of 1787 sixty thousand inhabitants were required for statehood, and by 1806 the goal had been reached and passed, with the Ohio Company lands in the neighborhood of Marietta solidly settled. To the Yankee skipper it seemed truly "the wilds of Ohio," but in reality the frontier had established itself further westward, and the tide of migration had moved on down the river to Cincinnati by the time the Greenmans looked upon Marietta for the first time.

In his pocket Greenman carried one of the most important possessions the family had brought with them. It was his bounty land warrant for Revolutionary service. He was entitled to 200 acres for his lieutenancy, but the land in question was not a part of the Ohio Company tract. Rather, it was located further north, in the United States Military Reserve, Franklin County, Ohio. Greenman had registered his claim in 1796 as part of a 4,000-acre parcel near Columbus,[40] but whether he ever seriously contemplated settling there is not known. Probably he held on to the land for speculative purposes, for very soon after the family's arrival in Marietta, the elder Greenman was diligently searching for local property. In early November of 1806 he was able to buy a small farm near the village of Waterford, some fifteen miles up the Muskingum from Marietta. He bought it fee-simple, paying one Nathan Cole "four hundred dollars lawfill money" for 100 acres "N W of Wolf Creek."[41] This was the property he came to call his "upland hilly farm" and was to be the Greenman homestead until his death.[42] In no sense was it desirable farmland: rocky and hilly, with little topsoil, unimproved, perhaps even uncleared when he bought it, it was part of that land which the Ohio Company had given away in 1788 and was not likely to produce the best crops or the most. But the Greenmans were not *yet* farmers, and the sons, John and Jeremiah, were eager to try *any* land, however niggardly and inaccessible.

If it was a change Jeremiah Greenman wanted, a change he decidedly got. After living for twenty years and more in the urban ambience of Providence, so delightfully flavored with the cosmopolitanism that was in the air of all busy American seaports, Greenman —a provincial who was something of a cosmopolitan himself, having seen Canada and the middle states during the Revolution and Europe, Africa, and the West Indies as a seaman—now looked out over a windswept ridge at an unending forest, with the Muskingum Valley and the tiny village of Waterford below. As a view it was superb, though it must have appeared lonely indeed. With the farming of the "hilly upland" left largely to young Jeremiah, the father was on his own to make the best of the new life of a retired and "landed" Revolutionary veteran and sea captain. He passed many days at home, reading and taking walks, but now and then he would saddle one of the two old family horses and ride the tough two or three miles to Waterford, there to visit with the townspeople—some of them he knew from old New England; most he did not—or sit awhile on the veranda of the guesthouse his son John was managing.[43] Waterford was one of those now-forgotten towns that even in their youth seem already old, passed by, destined never to "boom" the way their few vocal boosters were always predicting. Waterford was somehow devoid of the life-principle of its blooming sister village Marietta. The still-sharp eyes of Jeremiah Greenman took all this in. He saw where he was. If the prospect occasionally brought on a certain despair in the man, the compound of age and situation, there was reason enough for it. On his lowest days he was apt to remark, "I have not one Solutary friend or acquaintance that knows or ever heard of me."[44] But this was an exaggeration. Greenman was anything but antisocial, and before too many months had passed in Waterford he was well-known to the locals. Two or three times he was elected township justice of the peace, and between 1812 and 1816 he was able to return to that official service he dearly loved but had so rarely been given the opportunity to perform. He would ride about the township or set up his office on the farm or in town to transact the homely business of his position: marrying, witnessing lesser legal documents, and keeping the "estray book" of lost and wandering horses.[45]

> State of Ohio, Washington County,
> July 12, 1815
> TAKEN up by John Beach of Waterford, a black Mare with large saddle marks, a white spot on the left side of the mane betwixt her ears, dim star in her forehead, twelve years old, natural trotter, fourteen hands high, four white feet, and the appearance of her left rib being broken and falling in, a few white hairs on her left hip:—Appraised at twenty-five dollars by Stephen Gates and Samuel Nott.
> I do hereby certify the above to be a true extract from my Estray Book.
> JERE. GREENMAN, J. P.

Such was the notice he published in the Marietta *American Friend* for 21 July 1815, one among dozens the newspaper carried every year, for horses were important to the agrarian community, and keeping track of them was not the least demanding duty of a justice of the peace.

Through these years of increasing poverty and loneliness, Jeremiah Greenman managed to carry himself with much of his old New England upright dignity, and it is probably not too much to say that because of it he won the respect of the people. "Captain" Greenman became a regular feature of the Waterford landscape, and plenty of Ohio afternoons must have seen him slowly riding westward out of town, down to the Muskingum, or perhaps to Wolf Creek Ferry, run for a time by his son-in-law William Dunham, there to cross and head up the ridge to the cabin. And on important holidays one could expect to see him engrossed in the pomp and circumstance of Mount Moriah Lodge, for he assiduously kept up his Masonic connections after removing to Ohio, helping in fact to found the Freemasons in Waterford.[46] On 27 December 1817 he was observed at the local Masonic celebration of the "Antient St. John"—thirty-six years after he had mentioned in his wartime journal keeping the same holiday in Providence:

> *The members paraded to the church with music. This was the common practice of the time. . . . The rites of the order were at that time observed with the greatest precision. The periodical performance of ceremonies threw around the order an air of mystery, which affected both those within and without the mystic circle.*[47]

Inevitably, the clichéd image springs to mind of the parading Revolutionary veteran—was there another in Waterford?—with his patriarchal status in the ascendant, as the events he represented receded into myth and the infirmities of age made themselves apparent to the curious onlookers. What did Greenman, this man who in other years had known his own worth, had set a decently high value on his talents, and had entertained significant aspirations both for his own future and for that of his country, think of it all? Did he feel now the irony of being, far past his prime, the *newest* American institution, the "Old Revolutionary Soldier?" If it bothered him he was not saying. He was not ordinarily a reflective person, and in any case he kept no autobiography of the Ohio years. Yet as he passed his sixtieth year, events were approaching that would force Jeremiah Greenman to take up his pen for one last time.

V. "I'm Nothing but a Plain Old Soldier"

Early in the year 1818 Congress decided it was about time to do something for the surviving soldiers and sailors of the American Revolution. Indeed, it was long past time in the minds of many, although the Pension Act was not without its controversies, as Greenman himself unhappily discovered. The bill passed in March 1818 provided a life pension of twenty dollars monthly for officers (eight dollars for private soldiers) "who served in the War of the Revolution until the end thereof, or for the term of nine months . . . on the continental establishment" and who needed the assistance of their country.[48] The old soldiers were required to depose before a court in their locality, summarizing their service and stating necessity. To this end Greenman, on 16 April 1818, appeared before Judge Ezekiel Deming of the Court of Common Pleas, Washington County, was duly sworn, and offered a straightforward narrative of the highlights of his more than eight years' service. As to being in need of "the assistance of his country" due to "reduced circumstances," Greenman merely deposed that he was—for the time being he was spared giving the galling details. His deposition was certified and sent on to the secretary of war in Washington.[49] Before too long he was placed on the pension rolls and began receiving his allowance. This ought to have ended Greenman's dealings with the War Department, and he should have been allowed to collect his twenty dollars monthly to the end of his days. Instead, the document of 16 April was to be but the first in a correspondence that would last more than three years and embroil Jeremiah Greenman in an exasperating debate with the bureaucrats over his qualifications for the pension. The surviving documents, four in number, are eloquent and moving glimpses into the life and mind of Greenman in his final years, and form the only autobiographical testimony after the journal. Because these letters and declarations are retrospective, they provide a fascinating parallel to certain events of the journal: the Revolution viewed from the "wilds of Ohio" thirty-five years after its finish.

By 1820 Congress apparently thought it was being imposed upon by some of the pensioners. The act of 1818 had not required any real proof of "reduced circumstances" to qualify for the pension, but the amendatory act of May 1820 forced the soldiers to return to court and submit a "schedule" of personal property and income, this to be reviewed by the secretary of war, who would decide the merits of each case individually.[50] Accordingly, on 24 July 1820 Greenman again made the trip down to Marietta to have his day in court. He carefully listed his personal property, farm and household, and a curious enumeration it was! The list of "things" gives a quaint impression of pioneer life, but also sadly speaks to the poverty of the Greenmans. Here are the household belongings:

> . . . *one three feet poplar Table, one Bureau one light stand a portable writing desk, four common chairs, one pair of fire dogs, one pr of tongs & shovell, one looking glass 14 by 20 Inches one Monumental engraving of the memory of Washington 12 by 14 Inches, Six Silver Table spoons, six ditto of Teaspoons 3 old case Knives & forks, Ten volumes of old books and Pamphlets on different subjects, two pewter platters, Six pewter plates, twelve earthen Ditto, two earthen Teapots, one sugar bowl & creampot five china cups & saucers, four Liverpool Ditto, one castor containing four glass pieces, five wine glasses, one earthen pitcher Two Iron Kittels 10 Gals each, one dinner pot, one Cake Oven without a cover one frying pan One Small Skillet One small Spider, an old tin bake oven & several other articles too trifling to mention.* . . .

In his declaration Greenman went on to say that he and his "very much debilitated" wife Mary had "about sixty dollars" to their name —and that only because of two years on the pension rolls—and were reluctant to look to their children for subsistence, for they too were burdened with marginal farms and burgeoning families;[51] moreover, the Greenmans were trying to sustain at least a measure of personal pride.

In the final paragraph is a statement that makes clear, all these years afterward, the notion of his "Revolutionary expectations" in the first hopeful seasons after the war. Speaking of his casting about for something to do in those days, he comments, "And where [*sic*] it not for the leasure hours I spent while in the army in the Study of Navigation under the pupilage of Major Genl. Schuyler, at the close of the War I should [*have*] been plunged on the world destitute of employment or been Obliged to have resort to some business ill becoming a person who for more than eight years had [*merited* ?] the attention and approbation of the best men of his country." Greenman was far from having forgotten. Those early expectations were etched in his memory as distinctly as ever, and now hardened rather than softened by the retrospective light of what might have been. Congress did not have this sort of declaration in mind when they passed the act of 1820, but here was a rare platform from which Greenman could speak, a chance to say some things he had kept within until old age, and the righteousness of his claims matched the occasion. He did not know to whom he was talking in Washington, for the days of intimacy with "the best men of his country" were long over. Yet that hardly mattered, since he was speaking for the record. It was a justification that he in all justice should not have been asked to make. Still, if they asked, he would tell them.

Unfortunately, the result of this second declaration was that Jeremiah Greenman in the summer of 1821 was stricken from the United States pension roles.[52] Somewhere in the offices of the Department of War was someone who deemed him self-sufficient, the possessor of a competency. The tenant of the "upland hilly farm," with its two cows, two old horses, a few sheep, and indifferent crops—which in any case he was able neither to plant nor gather—was understandably deeply disturbed by the news, and he determined to make another effort. On 14 October 1820 he wrote directly to John C. Calhoun, secretary of war, noting "with diffidence" that he supposed "Eight years & siven months service together with three wounds received whilst in that service, & one of them rendering me incapiable of *hard* labour, that it would have some weight in the decision. . . . " Here was characteristic Greenman understatement! He ended the short letter with a reiteration of the plea that a continuation of his pension would afford him "some degree of support, without thowing myself on the charrity of my Children, which has been the case for five years before I received the bounty of my Country. . . . " The letter was endorsed by the local pension officer, who had, he said, "perused a very voluminous Journal" which "[Capt Greenman] . . . kept during the War," and had no doubt "but he ought to be continued on the principle which has governed in deciding on others from this County."

But all this latest appeal elicited from Washington was a formal letter confirming Greenman's fears: he had been stricken. At this point he might have been forgiven for quitting the field; he was clearly losing his little private war with Washington. Instead, the situation inspired Greenman to write a longer, more energetic, more eloquent and detailed letter, partly in defense of his claim, which he knew to be just, and partly to redeem his character, which he took to be under attack. His was a righteous anger now, one that aroused something of his old martial spirit. In his letter of 20 September 1821 he made a conscientious effort to juxtapose his pitiable contemporary state with past glories: "I can say that duering 8 years & 7. month service in the Revolutionary War & some parts of that time before the enemy of my Country, that duering that period of *time* . . . I never felt my heart recoil or my Spirit more dejected, than on reading the Secrateries oppinion on my schuidel [schedule] of property. My hopes & prospects to a future residence on this Terestiacal Globe, it seams are to be filled up with mortification of spirit & attended with hard labour what few remaining yea[r]s I am permited to tarry on it, being prosc[r]ibed by the Laws of that Country I had faithfully served 8 years. . . . " His need was real and his service extraordinary, but a particular sore point with him was the dubious nature of some of the other claims:

> *Amongst many I could mention, I will take notice of Mr.* [illeg.],[53] *whose farm joins on the one I returned & is called superior to the one I reside on, his service . . . was of short duration, but long enough to come under the period of time allowed by Law to intitle him to a pension, but he hath frequently told Me that, he was tired of the Service & that he had hired a substitute, & for all I know both receive the bounty of their Country.*

Worse yet, "Mr. ————'s" estate had been adjudged about equal in value to Greenman's, yet only the former qualified for the pension rolls.

Greenman wrote a remarkably various letter, surely one of the most interesting documents of its kind. Garrulous and unstructured, it even contained some touching bits of humor. Recalling the courtroom scene in 1820 when he had made his schedule of personal property, Greenman noted that "when my old horses where to be aprised, that the Judges Unanimously said *Nothing*, but on my observeing they where like their Master worn out in Service but was Yet worth something, the Court then ordered $20 to be put down." And as if further proof of reduced circumstances were needed, he confided to his correspondent that "since the stoping of my pension that one solletary pound of Tea hath not entered my Cabbin," nor "many other Articles of the necessaries of life."

By this time he was guilty of rambling and admitted as much when he said, "I cannot stop my pen when I reflect on a number of circumstances that took place duering an 8 years War." He was no longer merely trying to document his military service: it was a question of spending the emotional momentum generated by the acts of writing and retrospection. He recalled his wound during the brave stand at Springfield Bridge in 1780, then cast his mind back further to Quebec Prison in 1776: the youthful declaration before his captors that he would continue in the American cause "untill our rights was declared," and the derisive laughter this aroused in the British officers. So many things he could have mentioned, but who cared about an old man's wordiness? Still, he mustered a neat parting shot as a conclusion to his "lengthry rhapsody": "A little merrit where tis due might mitigate the Mistaken notion of my being *rich* because *I formely wore desent Cloathing. . . .*"

This was a kind of last testament, transmitted to the War Department by the Washington County pension agent, although whether it led to the reinstatement of Greenman's pension its author probably never knew. But reinstated he certainly was (in February 1822), and Greenman no doubt took pleasure in his last years from the thought that his old pen, warmed up once again after so many years of inactivity, had done the convincing. The twenty dollars, plus arrears, began coming again every month, and Mary and Jeremiah were relieved and grateful. The old soldier, though failing in health, was content.

VI. "The Tomb and the Battle Have Laid Them Low"

Of all the conspicuous gaps in the biography of Jeremiah Greenman, none, perhaps, is so puzzling and disappointing as the absence of politics. Was he in his younger days a Jeffersonian or Federalist? In the Ohio years, a Democrat or Whig? From his humble origins and implicit belief in liberty one might assume the former, but his New England roots and the fact that he lived the discipline of the army both as private and officer and knew the autocracy of the sea from a captain's stern perspective[54] just as strongly imply the latter. Almost no source, however, speaks on the subject. The military journal tells us only that he was superlatively loyal; nothing of a personal nature has survived from the middle years; and even the otherwise revealing correspondence with the War Department is silent when it comes to politics. Yet it goes against the grain of even a partial portrait of the man to consider him, based only on lack of positive evidence, politically indifferent. Fortunately, one splendid reference to his political predilections has survived, and it is a source which, though brief, sketches the politics of Greenman in a memorable fashion.

The presidential campaign of 1828, a warm one throughout the United States, was incandescent in the West. Marietta and Washington County were for months, even years, prior to the election afire with the contentious rhetoric and carnival antics of the Democrats. From the moment of John Quincy Adams's election in the House of Representatives early in 1825, the Jacksonians, who had won the popular vote, vowed revenge and began planning for 1828. Locally, they went so far as to establish a second newspaper for little Marietta, one that could be counted on to trumpet the glorious cause of the people and Old Hickory, while maliciously taunting the whiggish sedateness—at least for the West—of the older *American Friend*. The newcomer was the Marietta and Washington County *Pilot*, which began issuing in 1826 with a masthead motto of "*vox populi* and no concealment." And so it went right up to the election: the established *American Friend* deprecating "Jacksonian levelling" and "mob-rule," the young but puissant *Pilot* raucously proclaiming a "Western Rovolution."[55] The Washington County scene was a microcosm of the confrontation across the country at large, for "the election of 1828 was the first presidential one that really smelled . . . altogether . . . the most degrading presidential election the United States had ever experienced."[56] It was also a campaign which featured by far the most intense polarization around party standards yet seen in America. One was either for the incumbent and what he symbolized or for Jackson and popular democracy—including the "spoils system." Absolutely no middle ground was allowed to an electorate that, surprisingly, soon found itself intoxicated by the frenzied western style electioneering—intoxicated and liking it. In the spring of 1828, when the campaign really got rolling, there were the ubiquitous parades, rallies, and "Grand Barbecues" with which the Jacksonians hoped to warm the hearts of the voters. Only those "who fear to grease their fingers with a barbecued pig or twist their mouths away at whisky grog, or start at the fame of a 'military chieftan' or are deafened by the thunder of the canon . . . may stay away."[57] It was quite a spectacle, nothing remotely like it having been seen by the people before. And they were impressed.

At 71 Jeremiah Greenman might have thought himself too old for such celebrations, though he could count on being courted by the agents of both parties. He was more of a Revolutionary patriarch than ever, and these venerables, dwindling rapidly in number, were of supreme symbolic importance to the politicians who wished to hitch their cart to the sacred history of 1776. But Greenman apparently was not having any of the "Grand Barbecues" of the Jacksonians. It might have been mere political feeling that put him off, though he was likely to be revolted by the tawdry sensationalism of the ridiculous rhetoric and patriotic exhibitionism. To a man who had seen more than one wartime supper of boiled squirrel skin and brackish water, scores of roast bullocks and rivers of whisky must have seemed wretchedly excessive and not at all what he had fought for. There was little he could do to stem this new political tide, but just the same he would do it.

On polling day for Waterford Jeremiah Greenman went down to town. It was early in October, but balloting in some states was already finished, though it had not yet begun in others. Ohio was regarded by both parties as a pivotal state, and the Jacksonians, with their superior party organization in the West, were pushing hard in the state. Waterford was small enough and out of the way enough to insure relative quiet at its polling place, but it could not hope to escape the noise of the contending factions altogether. When Greenman crossed the river and came down the main street he could see a small crowd gathered around the polls. Perhaps it was then that he knew his duty after thinking about it all the way to town. He stepped up a bit to get a better view of the people, many of whom knew and recognized him at once. Then Greenman made a speech. He urged in a firm voice the reelection of John Quincy Adams of Massachusetts. He spoke "with the ardor of younger days—endeavoring to convince the ignorant and confirm the wavering."[58] We can guess that he appealed to the essential New England character of the Waterford enclave, emphasizing the old virtue of self-reliance. Had they left it behind when they came to Ohio? Could they of all people, with their fine tradition of the best doing the most in society, now turn the government over to the untutored and the indiscriminate? And could they, whose very village was patterned on the New England plan, now forswear the mother region? The irony was that these were the same questions asked half a century before by earnest loyalists on the eve of the Revolution, but one could not blame Greenman for believing that to have been a very different case. And if he had long ago entertained sanguine expectations of political patronage, was it not fitting and proper that a country be administered by those who had bled for its establishment? For the rest, such schemes were the fancies of his youth and had long since come to nothing. With a clear conscience he took "the bounty of his country" and used it to shore up the infirmities of age. And that was all he took. His speech made, his vote cast—neither put Ohio in Adams's column—the old man made his way back home to the farm. A month later he was dead.

Jeremiah Greenman died at his home on 15 November 1828 of what was then known as "a billious colic." Two days later Waterford saw the funeral of one of its best-known citizens. The Reverend John Pitkin of the local Presbyterian congregation preached the sermon before "a large concourse of citizens and the Members of Mount Moriah Lodge."[59] He was buried atop the highest hill on his "upland hilly farm" and the grave headed with a sandstone marker. It carried this inscription: "Revolutionary Soldier—in memory of Jeremiah Greenman Esq an active officer in that army which bid defiance to Britons power and established the independence of the United States." The words were carved opposite the weather side of the stone, and the grave has been carefully tended for a century and a half by the successive owners of the farm, who, knowing little if anything about Jeremiah Greenman, recognized the ground as inviolable. To the occasional pilgrim who journeys there today, the grave looks much as it must have in that late autumn of the year 1828.

VII. The Illinois Country: Scatterings and Descendants

The remainder of the story is soon told. The Greenman family, not long after Jeremiah's death, determined to move westward once again, and their departure from Ohio was to be as complete and irrevocable as that from Rhode Island twenty-two years before. They sold their land—"except so much as is now enclosed for a grave yard"[60]—to a local speculator and prepared to head for the Illinois country. The exodus was in two phases: John Greenman led his part of the family out of Ohio in July 1829, traveling overland with teams. "They camped and cooked by the wayside, and the journey, especially through Indiana, was slow and tedious. In places the sloughs were so bad that all the animals were required to pull one wagon through."[61] On 29 August, John, his wife, Ruth, his children, and another Waterford family reached a place called Blooming Grove (later Bloomington), McLean County, Illinois, where he rented a house and took up schoolteaching. John Greenman put up a log house, only the second permanent dwelling in what would become the town of Bloomington, and got his wheat into the ground for the following season.[62]

In the meantime, Jeremiah, the youngest son, but the one with most of the continuing family responsibilites, stayed behind in Ohio. An overland journey would have been too much for his mother, and so in June of 1830 Jeremiah took the rest of the family—including his wife Letitia, the Dunhams, and all their children—down the Ohio on a flatboat to Cairo, where they took steamboat passage up the Mississippi and Illinois rivers to Pekin, Illinois. By the spring of 1831 they were settled in Old Town Timber (McLean County, near Bloomington).[63] Jeremiah was the ablest farmer among the Greenmans, and he found the Illinois land miraculous after the rocks and hills of Ohio. In Illinois the Greenman family at last became farmers in more than name.

Those were early days for McLean County, Illinois, closer to the real frontier than had been the case in Ohio in 1806. And the Greenmans seemed to "take" better in Illinois than they had in Ohio. Widow Greenman, watched over by Jeremiah, lived on in Old Town Timber, drawing her husband's pension until her death in 1839.[64] By that time the days of the sons and daughters of Jeremiah Greenman of Newport and Providence Plantations, Rhode Island, and Waterford, Ohio, were themselves passing, and the grandchildren were moving to the front of the scene. John and Jeremiah, the sons, had thought of the War of 1812 and not of the Revolution when they remembered war, and the grandsons would before very long be involved—at least one of them to the death[65]—in the Civil War, whose bounty lands were to be the plains of Kansas and beyond. In such a typically American fashion did the Greenmans scatter and thin, all the way to California.

Yet here and there a few dim memories of talk of the Revolution and old Jeremiah's business in it survived, metamorphosed, and finally became family tradition. Hadn't he been a lieutenant colonel? Wasn't he a "warm friend and associate of Gen. Washington"?[66] And, oh, yes, he was an aide-de-camp to the commander in chief. True, the old journal, its hand-binding moldering and cracking, did not say *just* that, but then it was less and less consulted. Gradually it assumed the aspect of some mysterious and slightly forbidding relic; in the family it must by all means remain, but the Greenmans left it alone. There was one, however, who did read it, who made a career of reading it, one might say. This was Esek Eddy Greenman, John's son, who settled in LeRoy, Illinois, and became a fixture of that town.[67] He was fond of taking his grandfather's journal gingerly from its box of a summer afternoon and opening it, sometimes at random or again with design, to some campaign or other. He read slowly, now and then underlining what he took to be important passages and penciling in a marginal comment in a crabbed hand. What a character his grandfather had been! It was 1875 and the events of the Revolution had that golden-age aura about them. Perhaps Esek Eddy knew that someday people other than a few Greenmans would want to see this plain record of a plain old soldier's works and days, and he was the man to see to it that the record would be there when the time came. Back on that Illinois shelf went the Revolutionary War journal of Jeremiah Greenman, where it remained for another hundred years, waiting and weathering, its words with passing generations increasing in quaintness, its author becoming a family legend without a family. Now, two centuries after the writing, the Greenman journal is about to be read once more. But where are the Greenmans to read it?

NOTES TO JEREMIAH GREENMAN

1. The phrase is Edgar Watson Howe's, in his autobiography *Plain People* (New York: Dodd, Mead & Co., 1929).

2. This Bible register page, torn from the Bible, survives in the National Archives. Jeremiah Greenman apparently sent it to the War Department in 1818 as part of his Revolutionary War pension application.

3. Marian Pearce Carter, ed., *Swansea Vital Record Book "B,"* (Attleboro, Mass., 1930). Esther Greenman's maiden name may have been Wilson (see inquiry no. 9486, *Boston Evening Transcript*, 6 Feb. 1922).

4. James Arnold, *The Vital Record of Rhode Island*, 1636–1850, 1st series, 21 vols. (Providence, R.I.: Narragansett Historical Publishing Co., 1891–1912), 4:236.

5. Joseph J. Smith, *Civil and Military List of Rhode Island* (Providence, R.I.: Preston and Rounds, 1901), p. 699.

6. Gardiner MS, in Asa Ward Gardiner, "Biographies of the Original Members of the Rhode Island Society of the Cincinnati," (Rhode Island Society of the Cincinnati Archives, Rhode Island Historical Society, Providence, Rhode Island), p. 332.

7. Charles Carroll, *Public Education in Rhode Island* (Providence, R.I., 1914), p. 27.

8. Olney Narrative, Shepley Collection of Revolutionary War MSS, Rhode Island Historical Society, Providence, Rhode Island, p. 2. (Hereafter cited as Shepley Papers, RIHS.)

9. Jeremiah Greenman Pension Document of 24 July 1820, National Archives, Washington, D.C. (See appendix.)

10. Details of Greenman's military career may be found in the introductions to the several parts of the journal and in the notes accompanying the journal text.

11. One such was Capt. Stephen Olney, who resigned his commission soon after Yorktown, having "served my Country through all her dark Days of adversity and in all situations of Danger that fell to my lot, having acquitted myself much better than I could have expected to the sattisfaction of my superiors, and expecting no other reward but the Independence and Liberty of my Country. . . ." Olney went so far as to refuse his due of half-pay for life (Olney Narrative, Shepley Papers, RIHS, p. 26).

12. Carl Bridenbaugh, *Cities in Revolt* (London: Oxford University Press, 1971), p. 216.

13. Marquis de François Jean Chastellux, *Travels in North America*, ed. Howard Rice, 2 vols. (Chapel Hill: University of North Carolina Press, 1963), 1:66–67.

14. "Return of the Officers of the Rhode Island Regmt. Intitled to the Commutation of Five Years Full Pay in lieu of half pay," Shepley Papers, RIHS.

15. Richmond was at this time the deacon of the Second Congregational Church and the owner of several pieces of property in the area, including one building on Broad

St. rented as a store. (See Henry R. Chace, comp., *Maps of Providence*, R.I., 1650–1765–1770 (Providence, R.I.: N. E. Osterberg, 1914), plate xi; Henry Chace, *Owners and Occupants of the Lots, Houses and Shops in the Town of Providence, Rhode Island in 1798* (Providence, R.I.: Livermore and Knight, 1914), plate xi; and Arthur E. Wilson, *Weybosset Bridge in Providence Plantations, 1700–1790* [Boston: Pilgrim Press, 1947], p. 150.)

16. Chace, *Owners and Occupants*, introduction.

17. The Rev. Joseph Snow is one of the most interesting figures of eighteenth-century Providence. He was largely responsible for breaking off part of the "flock" of the First Congregational Church and establishing a new church on the west side of the river in 1743. He continued in the pastorate of what came to be called "the Beneficent Congregational Church" for fifty years (see Wilson, *Weybosset Bridge*, especially chap. 8, and James G. Vose, *Sketches of Congregationalism in Rhode Island* [New York: Silver and Burdett, 1894], pp. 88–98).

18. Samuel Eliot Morison, *The Maritime History of Massachusetts, 1783–1860* (Boston: Houghton Mifflin, 1921), p. 107.

19. Ibid., p. 99.

20. Ibid., p. 113.

21. *Ship Registers and Enrollments of Providence, Rhode Island, 1773–1939* (Providence, R.I.: Works Projects Administration, 1941), p. 40. This W.P.A. compilation, while incomplete and not always accurate, is the only index to the Providence Customs House papers in the Rhode Island Historical Society.

22. According to the family Bible register page, John Greenman was born on 1 January 1790, Esek Eddy Greenman on 21 February 1792, and Jeremiah Greenman on 8 August 1794.

23. See the copy of his speech to the Regiment, 13 June 1783, in the Shepley Papers, RIHS, 10:68.

24. Letter of 25 April 1791. Olney's correspondence in behalf of Greenman is in the Shepley Papers, RIHS.

25. Letter of 11 June 1791, ibid.

26. Letter of 20 November 1794, ibid.

27. See Chace, *Owners and Occupants*, plate xi.

28. Town of Providence Land Evidences, 23:202, Providence City Hall, Providence, R.I. (hereafter cited as Deed Books); and Town of Providence Tax Records (Direct Tax List of 1798), RIHS.

29. See inquiry no. 8711 in the *Boston Evening Transcript*, 14 March 1921.

30. "The Providence *Phoenix* was begun 11 May 1802 to help the organization of the Democratic-Republican party, under the leadership of Thomas Jefferson, then President of the United States, and further the political interests of Hon. Theodore Foster, whose term as United States Senator from Rhode Island was about to expire." *Printers and Printing in Providence* (Providence, R.I.: n.d.), p. 21.

31. William Greenman Dunham was born 24 November 1805.

32. *Ship Registers and Enrollments of Providence, R.I.*, p. 574.

33. See Edward Duis, *The Good Old Times in McLean County, Illinois* (Bloomington, Ill.: McKnight and McKnight, 1968), p. 746.

34. See Greenman's pension declaration of 24 July 1820, reproduced in appendix 2.

35. Town of Providence, Deed Books, 31:211.

36. The son Esek Eddy Greenman did not make the trip westward with the rest of the family. At some undetermined time he settled in Cheraw, South Carolina, where he died in 1825 (Arnold, *Vital Record of Rhode Island*, 21:221).

37. Ray Allen Billington, *Westward Expansion*, 2d ed. (New York: Macmillan, 1964), pp. 212–14.

38. Ibid., pp. 216–17.

39. Ibid., p. 218.

40. The speculator who collected 4,000 acres worth of land-patents was Theodore Foster, the Rhode Island politician with whom Greenman's son-in-law William Dunham had been associated in Providence. The details of Greenman's claim in the U.S. Military Reserve may be found in Clifford N. Smith's *Federal Land Series, A Calendar of Archival Materials on the Land Patents Issued by the United States Government, with Subject, Tract, and Name Indexes*, 2 vols. (Chicago: American Library Association, 1972), 2:xi–xix, 70, and the plat map on p. 353. Greenman never realized much from his bounty lands: in October 1816 he transferred ownership of half the property to his son John and gave the rest to Jeremiah in May 1819 (see Washington County Tax List, 1810–1824, Washington County Courthouse, Marietta, Ohio, p. 58).

41. Washington County Land Evidences, 9:458–59, Washington County Courthouse, Marietta, Ohio. (Hereafter cited as Deed Books.)

42. The old Greenman homestead is now owned by Neal Davis (Rt. 2, Waterford) and may be reached by driving out the Wolf Creek Mills Road from Waterford. The property has been in the Davis family for a century, and the white frame house in which the Davises live—built, Mr. Davis says, in 1905—is on the exact location of the double-log cabin the Greenmans erected shortly after they took possession. The original hand-dug well still survives in remarkably good condition, testifying to the care with which it was made. The well is forty-seven feet deep and stone-walled to within four feet of the bottom. The water is as sweet as ever.

43. Duis, *Good Old Times in McLean County*, p. 539.

44. See Greenman's Pension Declaration of 24 July 1820, appendix 2.

45. See Jeremiah Greenman's obituary, appendix 3, and William Jennings, "Marriage Record of Washington County, Ohio," *Old Northwest Genealogical Quarterly* 4 (1901): passim.

46. The Waterford Lodge was founded 28 September 1816, with Greenman as an original member (*History of Washington County, Ohio*, Cleveland: H. Z. Williams & Bro., 1881. p. 543).

47. Ibid., p. 543.

48. *Debates and Proceedings of the Congress of the United States*, 15th Congress, 1st Session, pp. 2518–19.

49. The documents in Greenman's correspondence with the War Department are reproduced in appendix 2.

50. *Debates and Proceedings*, 16th Congress, 1st Session, pp. 2582–83.

51. John Greenman, for example, had nine children living at the time of his father's death.

52. A note on Greenman's pension file (now preserved at the National Archives) says "off July 26, 1821."

53. The name of the person has been blotted from the ms., either by Greenman himself, or, more probably, by "L. Barbour," the local pension agent to whom Greenman was writing.

54. As Morison so aptly puts it, "The sea is no wet-nurse to democracy. Authority and privilege are her twin foster-children. Instant and unquestioning obedience to the master is the rule of the sea; and your typical sea-captain would make it the rule of the land if he could" (*Maritime History of Massachusetts*, p. 24).

55. For example, see the article on "Jacksonian Mobs" in the *American Friend* of

29 November 1828. The *Pilot* predictably went out of business as soon as Jackson's election was effected, but not before blaring the news of the "glorious triumph" in the largest point and boldest type it had. The *Pilot*'s editor, A. V. D. Joline, was rewarded for his loyalty with the postmastership of Marietta.

56. Samuel Eliot Morison, *Oxford History of the American People* (New York: Oxford University Press, 1965), p. 422.

57. Robert V. Remini, *The Election of Andrew Jackson* (Philadelphia: J. B. Lippincott Co., 1963), p. 110.

58. See the Jeremiah Greenman obituary, appendix 3.

59. Ibid.

60. Washington County, Ohio, Deed Books, 22:302–3.

61. *Portrait and Biographical Album of McLean County Illinois* (Chicago: Chapman and Bros., 1887), p. 303.

62. Duis, *Good Old Times in McLean County*, p. 540.

63. Ibid., pp. 746–47.

64. Military Pension Records, National Archives, Washington, D.C.

65. Henry Clay Greenman, son of Jeremiah, was killed at the Battle of Prairie Grove (Duis, *Good Old Times in McLean County*, p. 747).

66. Reported in Charles P. Merriman, *The History of McLean County, Illinois*, Containing a History of the County, its Cities, Towns, etc. . . . (Chicago: W. LeBaron, 1879), pp. 882–83.

67. In 1887 he was known as "the oldest male settler of Bloomington now living" and got his picture in ibid., p. 764

EDITORIAL PREFACE

We have transcribed this journal according to one basic editorial principle: remain faithful to the original. Thus, while keeping in mind that manuscripts and books are different, we have tried to render the manuscript literally. We believe that the distinctive flavor of Jeremiah Greenman's prose—and even some of the peculiarities of his journal-keeping format—ought to be preserved. Our departures from the literal page as Greenman penned it serve, we hope, only to enhance his style and clarify the substance of his notes.

Jeremiah Greenman took the usual eighteenth-century license with both capitalization and spelling. We have generally gone along with him—with several exceptions. Greenman consistently failed to distinguish between certain upper- and lower-case initial letters (for example, *s*, *c*, and *d*). We have *sometimes* regularized, using capitals when Greenman's intent appears clear (as when the word forms part of a noun phrase or begins a sentence). Consistent misspellings have been silently changed when meaning may be a problem: thus, "of" in "this morn set *of*" becomes "off," and "*mad* a small halt" becomes "made a small halt." Uncharacteristic misspellings, on the other hand, have been changed—again, only where meaning seems to demand it—through the use of interpolated letters in square brackets: "recev'd" becomes "rece[*i*]v'd." Past participles written with the so-called hanging *D* will be printed with an apostrophe; we have retained "ye" for "the" because of its flavor.

Greenman's journal is only infrequently punctuated, and such marks as occur may seem capricious to the modern eye. We have strictly followed the text except to add a period to the conclusion of each journal entry and to add appropriate punctuation within square brackets where meaning would otherwise be impaired. In the former case, in those rare instances where the author *did* finally punctuate, his marks, whether periods, dashes, or commas, have been retained. Within journal entries two spaces and a / designate the end of one sentence element and the beginning of the next. Although this device is a slight concession to the reader, it does not significantly detract from the matter-of-fact, often elliptical flavor of the original.

We have made interpolations in syntax only when meaning is clearly jeopardized. In cases where crucial words have been omitted by the author, they have been supplied in italics within square brackets, as in "This [*morning* (or *morn*)] set off. . . ." Likewise, material which is illegible or indecipherable: "the firing lasted 'till 2 oClock PM. with [*rel*]entless fury." Where the meaning is obvious, words or phrases which have disappeared due to edge wear in the manuscript pages will be silently reconstructed; conjectural readings will appear italicized in square brackets. Such textual reconstructions occur on three levels: the silent, as indicated; the bracketed, where the editors' rendering is probable; and the bracketed with question mark and textual footnote [*fore* ?],[1] where the material interpolated is at best a decent guess. Bracketed interpolations in Roman type are intended to clarify the meaning of the previous word or phrase.

We have also routinely regularized slips of the pen, double-writings, and other repetitions. Canceled miswritings have been ignored unless they contain pertinent information, in which cases they have been footnoted. Superscriptions have been brought to line level and inserted in their proper places within sentences.

We have tried not to encumber the text with a barrage of scholarly annotations, but for a number of reasons this has proved a principle difficult not to betray. The main problem we have faced, of course, is the essentially *private* character of Greenman's journal: he was, as he thought, writing for himself, and what he wrote was a highly *un*circumstantial account of his works and days, a kind of written remembrancer which years later would—through a brief and, to us, almost cryptic allusion—unlock his much fuller memories of the Revolution. In this sense the journal is materially as well as syntactically elliptical. We have tried to provide the reader with sufficient information and explanation to follow young Greenman's military progress over the eight-year period and to do so without overwhelming his own rather tentative voice.

PART ONE

The Quebec Campaign, 1775–1776

INTRODUCTION

THE EXPEDITION to conquer Quebec offered to American soldiers maintaining the seige of Boston in the summer of 1775 an opportunity for relief from what had become largely a war of sentries and skirmishes. This initiative and the shroud of secrecy drawn around the launching of the expedition seem to have alerted the soldier volunteers to the historic importance of this military undertaking, the outcome of which might bear heavily upon their future relation to England. Expectations were high enough to stimulate what seems an unusual diligence in the keeping of diaries and journals among soldiers on the march.[1] Among these men was young Jeremiah Greenman, who procured pen and paper for the keeping of a journal, in all probability the first serious daily writing effort of his life. As his journal now stands, it begins rather abruptly on the eve of embarkation, 18 September, in Newburyport, Massachusetts. There is no account of how they marched to Newburyport nor of how the first volunteers were ordered to parade on Cambridge Common near midday on 6 September to be issued tents by the quartermaster general.[2] Indeed, the origins of this expedition were probably unknown to this common soldier who enlisted a week after that parade on Cambridge Common, but they are worth a brief exploration here, for they vitally affected the lives of the participants and the odds they would struggle against.

Mid-September was late in the season for marching an army through the Maine wilderness to the south shore of the St. Lawrence River opposite Quebec, but the idea for this sudden offensive does not seem to have arisen until late in the summer, when General Washington brought it quickly to a head. This is not to say that the northern approaches to the colonies had been ignored in the strategic thinking that summer, for from the moment information reached Philadelphia on 17 May that Fort Ticonderoga had been taken by Ethan Allen and Benedict Arnold, the Continental Congress began to be affected by what Edmund Burnett called "the Canadian temptation."[3] Moreover, Congress had taken an additional step in pursuing these interests by naming as major general and commander of the Northern Department Philip John Schuyler, member of a substantial and respected New York family who had gained valuable experience during the French and Indian War as a deputy commissary in the northern lake country. But the expedition that attracted seventeen-year-old Greenman was only a daring thought entertained by General Washington even as late as August of that year, while he anxiously awaited the delivery of enough gun powder to enable his troops to defend themselves from an anticipated British attack.

The idea behind the expedition was not new, as Justin Smith has ably demonstrated,[4] but it remained untried and intriguing. The idea was to launch an attack along an overland route between Quebec and New England by following the courses of two rivers that nearly meet, the Kennebec and the Chaudière, hiking over the high land that separates them along the Quebec boundary to arrive by this cunning means at the enemy's door. Indians of the Abenaki tribe frequented these waterways and forests, but the military potential was not seriously studied until the time of the French and Indian War, when Gen. James Murray at Quebec ordered the British military scout and engineer John Montresor to map the route in 1761. With the revival of hostilities it is not surprising that new proposals for an expedition against the British, "a Diversion of the Provincial Troops into that part of Canada . . ." were made by Col. Jonathan Brewer to the Massachusetts Congress about May of 1775.[5] It is possible that this proposal led to discussion of the idea in Washington's presence at about the time he was beginning to contemplate seriously what moves he might make to support General Schuyler in the North. The idea must have grown more attractive when he received reports of the weakness of British garrisons in the principal forts of the region: according to the information of Gov. Jonathan Trumbull of Connecticut there were no more than 700 men from the settlements at St. John's and Chambly on the Richelieu River to Quebec on the St. Lawrence.[6] Not until 20 August, however, did Washington propose an expedition to General Schuyler. The purpose of this expedition "which has engaged my Thoughts for several days," explained Washington, would be to

> *make a Diversion that would distract* [*Gen. Guy*] *Carleton, and facilitate your Views. He must either break up and follow this Party to Quebeck, by which he will leave you a free Passage, or he must suffer that important Place to fall into our Hands, an Event, which would have a decisive Effect and Influence on the publick Interests.*[7]

By dividing the already thin resources of the enemy, Washington believed he might win on either the western or eastern point of this dual thrust toward the St. Lawrence and quite possibly on both. He wanted to hear immediately from Schuyler whether he was prepared soon to send a force against the posts at St. John's and Chambly and whether he had recent intelligence from Canada on three points: the size of British forces, the likelihood of their bringing reinforcements by sea, and the probable attitudes of the inhabitants, including the Indians, toward Americans "upon a Penetration into their Country. . . ." Washington cautioned: "There may be some Danger that such a sudden Incursion might alarm the Canadians and detach them from that Neutrality, which they have hitherto observed. . . ."[8] But that and other risks soon appeared to him worth taking.

No amount of scheming, shrewdness, or secrecy could assure success for this expedition if Washington could not find a leader equal to its demands. He would have to find somewhere in that not very large pool of uneven and relatively untested talent an officer who could plan and act decisively enough to put his plans in motion before winter foreclosed all his options, a man who was frontiersman enough to march his men through a wilderness and an officer equal to the task of organizing and leading an assault upon a fortified city. An officer who might possess these qualities suddenly became available when Benedict Arnold resigned a Massachusetts command he had held and returned to Watertown, Massachusetts, to settle his accounts. It is not entirely clear when Washington first discussed the possibility of the Quebec expedition with Arnold, but it seems clear that Washington soon believed that he had found in Arnold a leader of demonstrated courage and audacity, an active mover who could pull together the necessary supplies for an expedition and who could win the respect of his men. Moreover, Arnold was probably the only available candidate who had previously seen Quebec. The speed with which Arnold would have to move is made dramatically clear to us by a letter of 25 August from Maj. Gen. Horatio Gates to Arnold which reveals that Washington had not even then made the final decision to give this command to Arnold.[9] But both men were working together toward that decision, which seems to have depended primarily upon positive replies from two directions: one from Schuyler and a second from one Maj. Reuben Colburn, landowner on the Kennebec River and the owner of a shipyard. Colburn and his shipyard were vital factors in the developing scheme. On 21 August, Arnold had addressed Colburn on behalf of Washington, asking how soon he could have ready two hundred light bateaux, each built to carry six or seven men with baggage and provisions. Colburn was asked to inquire into the quantity of fresh beef that could be had on the Kennebec and was required to furnish intelligence about the proposed route—"get particular Information from those people who have been at Quebec, of the Difuculty attending an Expedition that way, in particular the Number, & length, of the Carrying Places, wheather Low, Dry land, Hills, or Swamp."[10] Such basic questions asked less than a month before the expedition marched out of Cambridge for Newburyport reveal lingering uncertainties about the route.

Provided all the replies were positive, where would the officers and men come from for this campaign? The answer, given the shortness of time and the secrecy with which it was being conducted, would have to be to recruit them from the camps about Boston. As Washington said when he broached the idea to Schuyler, "I can very well spare a Detachment for this Purpose of one Thousand or twelve Hundred Men, . . ."[11] The detachment was first announced in General Orders on 5 September, and three days later orders went out to remove the names of those going with Arnold from duty rolls; they were to join the detachment at Cambridge by the morning of Saturday, 9 September. Some of the officers for this expedition were carefully chosen, but probably most of the 676 privates called for in General Orders of 5 September were volunteers. General Orders read: "as it is imagined the Officers and Men, sent from the Regiments both here, and at Roxbury, will be such Volunteers, as are active Woodsmen, and well acquainted with batteaus; so it is recommended, that none but such will offer themselves for this service."[12] Those who volunteered were probably young men tired of fighting a holding action or soldiers chafing under camp discipline and regulations. The orderly books for early August reflect the condition of the army; officers tried to combat drunkenness, men going on guard without cartouche box or bayonet, laxness in exercise and drill, wasteful firing of guns in and about camp, complaints of bodily "indisposition" used as an excuse to avoid duty, and ignorance of the proper duties of sentries.[13] The men were rapidly assembled who wanted to leave all this behind for the excitement of detachment under Arnold, whether they were skilled in the ways of active woodsmen or not.

Jeremiah Greenman may have been typical of the soldier volunteers in that he was certainly not an experienced woodsman, though he was able-bodied enough. Although at seventeen only just old enough to make a successful show of bearing arms, as a native of Newport, Rhode Island, he would have been as well acquainted with boats as any native of the Narragansett shores, but not necessarily with the flat-bottomed bateau of the upland freshwater streams. Inexperience aside, the hardy spirit of such young men as Greenman would be invaluable, as they had proved from the first when numbers of them aroused by the Lexington alarm of April 1775 had hastened to the defense of Massachusetts without even bothering to enlist. The same spirit might help them at the carrying places and bogs along the trail to Quebec; it would help them stand their ground in combat. Their most persistent enemies in this campaign would be rocky river beds and tangled forests on and above the Kennebec. There they battled fatigue, hunger, and the desires of the weak-willed to return home. Washington had thought that colonial forces betrayed weakness in the numbers of "Boys, Deserters, and Negroes" they enlisted in their ranks, but he realized there was strength there too, strength easily overlooked but demonstrated, as Washington observed, by those whose "Spirit has exceeded their Strength."[14] The Quebec expedition required such reserves of strength and spirit that in effect it became a great testing ground for devotion to the cause of the American colonies.

We do not know how seventeen-year-old Jeremiah Greenman came to the point of commiting himself to the colonial cause, but we do know he joined early and never abandoned the cause. He made it his career. What we have learned about his life suggests that the army provided him not only a cause in a political sense but larger opportunities, since he had not found a trade or profession for himself when the hostilities began. His service as a "hard core" Continental veteran fits the socioeconomic pattern of those who bore the heaviest share of the soldiering, according to a study made by John Shy. These men "were something *less* than average colonial Americans. As a group, they were poorer, more marginal, less well anchored in the society."[15] "Less well anchored" is an apt phrase to describe Greenman's condition in relation to others, for on 20 May, less than two weeks after his seventeenth birthday, he joined a Rhode Island company before Boston, commanded by one Colonel Church.[16] For the next eight years an army would provide more of a home for him than for most young men of his generation.

The force that young Greenman joined that spring of 1775 was not yet a colonial army in rebellion; it was Rhode Island's Army of Observation. That army had come into being by an act of the Rhode Island Assembly on 25 April 1775 in the aftermath of the Lexington alarm. The act provided that

> *a number of men be raised and embodied, properly armed and disciplined, to continue in this Colony, as an Army of Observation; to repel any insults or violence that may be offered to the inhabitants; and also if it be necessary for the safety and preservation of any of the Colonies, that they be ordered to march out of this Colony, and join and co-operate with the Forces of our neighboring Colonies.*[17]

It is possible that Jeremiah Greenman received his monthly pay in advance—forty shillings, as authorized by the Assembly—and that he brought along his own blanket and knapsack as required. The oath he was required to take upon joining the Army of Observation neatly embodied the two loyalties that were in contention: "I, . . . hereby solemnly engage and enlist myself as a soldier in His Majesty's service, and in the pay of the colony of Rhode Island, for the preservation of the liberties of America, . . ."[18] So far as we can determine in the absence of any writing from Greenman during those summer months, he served in this army during the seige of Boston in the vicinity of Prospect Hill, under the command of Brig. Gen. Nathaniel Greene. If his looks betrayed his youth, Greenman may have helped to inspire an exclamation from a southern rifleman, who also served on Prospect Hill—"Such Sermons, such Negroes, such

Colonels, such Boys, & such Great Great Grandfathers."[19] On 13 September he enlisted as a private in a company commanded by the son of one of Rhode Island's delegates to the Continental Congress, Capt. Samuel Ward. This was the beginning of an expedition from which he would not return for more than a year and then only as a barefoot captive in a prisoner exchange.

NOTES TO INTRODUCTION

1. The most valuable collection of these diaries that has been published is that edited by Kenneth Roberts, *March to Quebec: Journals of the Members of Arnold's Expedition*, 2d ed. (New York: Doubleday, Doran & Co., 1940), which includes the journal of John Pierce, surveyor to the expedition and an excellent keeper of a journal. See the bibliography for other editions of the journals of Dearborn, Henry, and Senter.

2. General Orders, 5 September 1775, in John C. Fitzpatrick, ed., *The Writings of George Washington from the Original Manuscript Sources, 1754–1799*, 39 vols. (Washington, D.C., 1931–44), 3:473.

3. Edmund Cody Burnett, *The Continental Congress* (New York: Macmillan, 1941; reprint ed., New York: W. W. Norton and Co., 1964), p. 68.

4. Justin H. Smith, *Our Struggle for the Fourteenth Colony* (New York and London: G. P. Putnam's Sons, 1907), 1:497–98.

5. Ibid.

6. Douglas S. Freeman, *George Washington*, 7 vols. (New York: Scribner, 1948–57), 3:530.

7. Washington, *Writings*, 3:437–38.

8. Ibid., p. 438.

9. Freeman, *Washington*, 3:535n.

10. Justin H. Smith, *Arnold's March from Cambridge to Quebec, A Critical Study together with a Reprint of Arnold's Journal* (New York: G. P. Putnam, 1903), p. 76.

11. Washington, *Writings*, 3:437.

12. Ibid., p. 473.

13. These problems are mentioned in the manuscript orderly books for Capt. Daniel Hitchcock's regiment under entries of 20 June and 6 July and for Brig. Gen. Nathaniel Greene's regiment on 3, 4, 5 and 8 August. These orderly books are preserved in the collections of the Rhode Island Historical Society in Providence.

14. Washington to the President of Congress, 10 July 1775, in Washington, *Writings*, 3:327.

15. *A People Numerous and Armed; Reflections on the Military Struggle for American Independence* (New York and London: Oxford University Press, 1976), p. 173.

16. G. M. Saltzgaber, U.S. pension commissioner to Milo Custer, 22 June 1918, in Milo Custer, ed., *A Few Family Records, No. 7* (Bloomington, Ill.: privately printed, 1922), n.p.

17. Peter Force, ed., *American Archives*, 4th Series, 6 vols. (Washington, D.C., 1848–53), 2:390.

18. John R. Bartlett, ed. *Records of the Colony of Rhode Island and Providence Planta-*

tions in New England, 10 vols. (1856-65; reprint ed., New York: AMS Press, 1968), 7:317, 319.

19. Quoted by Charles K. Bolton, *The Private Soldier Under Washington* (New York: Scribner, 1902), p. 43.

GREENMAN'S PREFACE

The following Journal contains the *Ma*terial Transaction of [*Events?*] as they fell under my observations, or came to my Knowledge—and the Incidents [*of*] my private Life—T[*hese*] commence from the thir[*teenth*] of September. 1775—soon [*after*] my Entering the Service [*of*] the United States and wer*e* penn'd intirely for my Own Amusement at the time of writing and as a Memorial of Facts which, I suppos'd might [?]elt me Some Pleasure [*in?*] Recollection—This being the case—if by any Accident I should loose them, I request they may [*be*] conveyed to me, if alive / If I am not, I wish them to be transmited to my Friends, as I dont look upon them of Suffeceint Consequence to merrit the Public View—

I am yours—
J—Greenman

THE QUEBEC CAMPAIGN, 1775–1776

SEPTEMBER 1775 CANNABECK [Kennebec]

M 18. had orders for to be in readiness for to imbarck.[1] In the evening wint all on board our fleat consisting of a[*bout*] eleven in Number / our troops consist of 13 hunderd 11 [*companies*] of musquet men 3: of rifle[2] / we lay in the river on b[*oard* ?] of our Shiping.

T 19. Early this morn. waid anchor with the wind at: SE a [*fresh* ?] gale our Colours fliing Drums a beating fifes a plaing the hils and warfs a Cover [*with people*] biding thair friends fair well. at Night fogey / h[*ove*] two till next morning then Sot Sail went into the mouth of Cannabeck river and came to an anchor.

W 20. this day the rest of the transports came in to [*anchor* ?].[3]

T 21. this morn no wind / we was oblig'd for to tow our Ship in morning tide with our boat / we came 15 milds & came to an anchor at george town.[4]

F 22. this morn proceded up the river as far as Coberconta[5] and thare came two.

S 23. this day pushed to hollo wils[6] ware we landed a Lieut and 20 men ordered to stay hear to see that thee flower was baked into bread to proceed up the river with.

S 24. this morn marched up to fort weston[7] wich was about fore milds ware incampt 48 milds up the river / So far this river is Navigabel with good pilots.

M 25. Continuing at fort weston getting in readyness to imbarck on board of our boats.

T 26. Continuing at fort weston / In the after noon a man belonging to Capt goodri[*ch's*] Company, James Mcarn[8] being [*in*] liqour shot Serj't Bishop belonging to Capt Williams Company /

he was set upon [*the gallows* ?] 10 minits then was taken down [*sent* ?] to Cambrige to have another tryal.

W 27. this morn fitting to go on board of our battos[9] / Imbarked in my batto 4 barrils & a tent for fort hallefax[10] / had to git out and draw our batto over rips and roks[11] in the room of rowing / up to our arm pits in water and very cold.

T 28. this morn proceeded on with the battoes / very swift water indeed and rockey / came over two pair falls[12] / got forward 12 milds and incamped in the woods ware we made up fires to dri our Selvs by.

F 29. this morn proceeded on fore [four] milds / got to fort hallefax ware thare wass a pair of fals 600 rod[13] ware we carried our battoes and provision then we incampt the other Side of the Carring place wich was Nothing but rock and roots and a Swamp.

S 30. this morn set out from fort halefax[14] / came 8 milds / the water very swift indeed / we ware obliged to draw our boats up over the S[*hoals* ?] in many placs up to our arms in water an so swift that we could hardly stand / Incampt at the river side at winserlow.[15]

OCTOBER 1775 CANNEBECK

S 1. October ye 1st 1775 / this [*morn*] we proceeded on [*6 mi. through*][16] very bad rips and incampt in the woods in Goshen.[17]

M 2. Set out this morn / got forward [*9* ?] milds / the water being Strong & being very Swift we w[*ere*] obliged to git out and [*draw* ?] our boats over the rock to a carring place called Cowhigens / Camp at C[*anaan* ?][18] by the fals ware we bu[*ilt* ?] up fire as us[*u*]al.

T 3. Carried our battoes & provision a 100 hundred [*rods* ?] & put them in to the river again / got forward 5 milds / one of Capt. hendricks Company[19] killed a yong mo[*o*]se waing 200 wait.

W 4. this morn smoth water / about 4 milds came ware I got a break fast / then set off came to Norigewalk[20] and incampt by the carring place.

T 5. Continuing at Norigewalk mending our battoes fitting to carry over ye falls.

F 6. this day carried over Norigewalk carring place 1 mild and a quarter over roots & rocks and mud / here we got sum oxen to carry a few of our barrels over the caring place / after we got all a crost we pushed on 2 milds. & incampt &c.

S 7. Set out this morn very early / came 7 milds / came ware was [*a*] small river [*that*] led in to [*the*] main[21] / this branch we tooc[*k*] / No Inhabitance being here to inquire of we wen[*t*] up two milds before we found we w[*ere*] rong / then the river was so r[*ocky* (L)] we was oblig'd to turn back / this day left all Inhabitance & enter'd an uncultervated co[*untry* ?] and a barran wildernes[22] / the [*trees*] hear for the most part Bi[*rch* ?] pine hemlock / there [*are*] sum [*places* ?] on the river ware mapel tree[*s*] grew ware the Inhabitance made Sugar / got forward 7 mild to day.

S 8. this morn it began to wrain. Continuing raining all day and part of the night / this day I went on the land thro the woods 8 mild & incampt &c.

M 9. this morn went with the battos 3 milds / came to tintucket or hell gate falls[23] / carri'd our battoes & barrils 86 r[*o*]ds over the carring place / then proceeded on 4 milds / very rockey and swift water so that we was obliged to wade and draw our boats.

T 10. this morn found a place ware thare was troves [*troughs*] made of burch barck and two old wigwans and a Number of small bowls wich we supposed thay cuked [cooked] thair mapel juse in to make Sugar of / we brought a number of ye bowls a[*way* (L)] with us: this day got forw[*ard*] 12 milds up to the great carring place[24] & got sum of our provision part way a crost.

W 11. this day implying our Selv[*s*] in making a sort of a roud [road] thro the woods so that we might git our battoes and provision a long / we got [sum (L)] of our bagage a crost / this day a man was pasing [*when*] a tree that sum of ye men was cutting fell on him & wounded him so that he dyed / we buried him thare / this carring place 4 mild 40 rod.[25]

T 12. this day gitting over our battoes and provision to ye first pon [pond].[26]

F 13. this day got all acrost and incampt ye west Side of ye carring place / Sum small Spits of Snow fell to day.

S 14. this morn carr[*i*]ed a crost a pon a half mild over / then carried our battoes & provision a half mild and incamp upon low land towards the S[*e*]cond pon.[27]

S 15. Carried a half a mild / came to the Second pon crost the pon wich was one mild over. then carried 2 milds very bad going to the third pond[28] / crost the pond wich was two milds over / came to carring place 3 mild 3 quarters long / carri'd part of ye way then incamp upon very high land and made sum flower cake &c.

M 16. This morn carri'd all acrost wich was very bad going / in sum plac[*e*]s half leg deep with mud and mire / ware it was[*nt* (L)] mud and mire it was roks and hils as steep as a hous Side a most / we got all a crost put our battoes into [*a*] Small Stream that led in[*to*] dead river[29] / this river runs SE. and so still you cant but jest procive wich way it runs / its black and very deep now / betook to our ours [oars] / rowed up six milds and incampt.

T 17. we set out this morn very early / came ten milds over took capt tophams comp[*any*][30] / came to a carring place carri'd a crost then incampt [*illeg.*] provision: short.[31]

W 18. Remain'g ware we incampt till 12 oClock then set off / came 8 milds[,] 4 milds very bad rips and roks / one batto over sat and lost / rain & sum hungry.

T 19. this morn set off / came 7 milds / came to a carring place wich was ten rod / got forward 17 milds / the water groing swift and the river groing shole [shoaly] we put by our owers [oars] & took our seting poles [32] a gain.

F 20. this day we proceded on[33] / came to two carring places the first 40 rod the second 60: came a few milds / came to another a half a mild / we carried the battoes a crost. a freshet arose in the night overflowed ware we incampt:[34] carried away part of a barrel of pork and a barrel of powder: very cold.

S 21. this morn I came by land: ware I and sum more got lost in the woods ware we stayed all night / in the morning sum battoes come to us [*illeg.*][35] / came to one carring place 20 rod: a crost.

S 22. proceded on this fore or five milds / came to a carring place 30. [rods ?] ware we incampt.

M 23. this [*morn*] the water very swift indeed / a number of battoes over sat & lost a number of packs / then came to a carring [*place*] wich was 30 rod ware we held a Coun[*sel of War* ?].[36]

T 24. our provision growing scant sum of our men being sick held a Counsel / agreed to send the Sick and we[*a*]kly men back & to send a Capt and 50 men forward to get in to the Inhabitance as soon as posabel that thay might send back provision / accordingly the sick wass sent back & a capt and 50 men sent forward to make the Inhabitance as quick as posibel: before this Colo Enoss with 3 Companys turn'd back[37] [*and*] took with them large Stores of provision and amunition wich made us shorter than we was before [*illeg.*].

W 25. Set off this morn / came one mild / came to a carring place which was 3 rod. acrost / came 40 rod / came to a nother wich was 4 rod / then came 3 milds & came to a nother wich was 3 quarters mild long. came to the first pon on ded river[38] / Incamp[*t*] on a hill / very cold and [*some* ?] rain / sum hungery for our provision is very short.

T 26. this morn set off from the first pond / came to the second the carring place 8 rod / carri'd into the third pond wich [*is*] 3 quarters of a mild acrost / the ground covered with Snow and very Cold and our provision very [*low*] so that we expetckit to kill sum of our dogs to eat—

F 27. Set out this morn very early / from the third pond carred into the forth wich was one mild a crost / then into the fifth wich was 60 rod / hear the people [*were*] cuting up the tents for to make bags to put what small provision thay had in / here it was agreed to leave our battoes and to fut [foot] it after being gratly fateg'd by carring over such hils mountain & Swamps such as men never pased before[39] / we carried two or thre battoes over this carring place to carry ye Sick down ye river Shedo[40] in but could not go down in a batto so raped [rapid] and [*last line missing*].

S 28. early this morn set out for Shedore pon[41] / took our provision on our backs and went thre milds / Stopt by a Small Stream runing in to Shedore pond ware we had delt out 4 or 5 oz of pork 5 pints of luse flower / came 5 milds & incampt.

S 29. this morn set out for the head of Shedore river / took provision on our back wich was but very small quanterty / this day we suffer'd gratly had to wade [*6* ?] rod & came to another [*stream*] wich was 6 rod acrost / we was ferried a crost hear and came a few rod / had to wade 20 rod more then pushed on very briskly / came to an old hut that they sed was a guard house but nothing [*was*] thair but the house[42] / came this day got [*line missing*].

M 30. Set out this morn by day light / came 15 [*rods ?*] thro Seader Swamp up to our neas and Cold / got to Shedore river / this river is very swift water rockey & shole / over took Liut Shaw[43] that went forward with that batto [*which*] was to carry Sick in but the river [*was*] so raped and swift thay could no batto go down the river / thare was one man lost by the battow a quanerty of amunition and guns with sum money.

T 31. Set out this morn very early / left 5 sick men in the woods that was not abel to march[44] / left two well men with them but what litel provision thay had did not last them [*very long ?*] / we gave out of our little / every man gave sum but the men that was left was obliged to leave them to the mercy of wild beast / this day as we ware pasing along the river we saw 3 Cannows that went forward with the advance party stove against ye rok[*s ?*] / we pased 2 pair of fall / we had very bad traviling th[*ro ?*] ye woods and Swamps / our provision being very Short hear we killed a dog[45] / I got a small peace of it and sum broth that it was boyled with a great de[*al*] of trubel / then, lay down took our blancots and slep[*t*] very harty for the times.

November 1775 by Shedore

W 1. Set out by day & left ye comp[*any*] / travel'd all day very very briskly / at night incamp 5 milds a hed of ye company / In a very misrabel Sittiuation / nothing to eat but dogs / hear we killed a nother and cooked / I got Sum of that by good [*luck*] with the head of a Squirll with a parsol of Candill wicks boyled up to gether wich made very fine Supe without Salt[46] / hear on this we made a nobel feast without bread or Salt thinking it was the best that ever I eat & so went to Sleep contented not noing what to [*remainder missing*].

T 2. this morn when we arose many of us so weak that we could hardly stand / we stagerred about like drunken men / how sumever we made shift to git our pack on[,] them that did not thoro them away / we marcht off hoping to see Sum Inhabitance by night / I hap to git a pint of water that a partrig was boyled in / about ten o Clock then I set out Strong hoping to find the Inhabitance by night but Sum of them so weak that a Small Stick as big as mans thumb would bring them to the ground / In the after noon w[*hen* ?] we came in Sight of the Cattle wich the advanc party had sent out[47] it was the Joifulest Sight that I ever saw & Sum could not refrain from crying for joy / the men that came with the Cattle told us it was yet 20 milds to ye Nearest Inhabitance / hear we killed a creatur and Sum of ye men [*were*] so hungrey before this Creater was dressed thay had the Skin and all entrels guts and every thing that could be eat on ye fires a boyling / we had ate meat with Staws [*straws* ?] in an inch or two long served out in the rom[48] of bread but that was very good [*so we slepped* ?].

F 3. this morn thick raining wea[*ther*] / we set out for to reach the Inhabitance it being 20 mild ware we was obliged to wad[*e*] several small river Sum of [*them* ?] up to our midels & very cold / we met Sum Indians on the march that had sum flower kakes & sum potatoes wich we bout of them giving a very great price. then we came in Sight of a house the first I had seen 27 day ware thare was beaf and brea[*d*] for us wich we cooked very plenty of / Sum of the men made thair Selvs Sick eating so much / at night Snow but we Slep very harty in the woods.

S 4. Continuing at Setigan[49] in the province of cannada / very Cold & snowing / only one hou[*se*] hear; & sum Indians wigwan.

S 5. this morn march down the river on the frosen ground bare footed[50] and very Cold till at last I came to a french house ware I [*blank*] a pair of Seal Skin maugerson and had Sum fine Supe made out of cabage and bread / hear in this house I sleep by the fire.

M 6. Set off this morn / came up with Colo arnold[51] ye advanc party marcht off to gether / the rodes very bad half leg deep with mud and water / marcht till 2 o Clock at night / march 17 milds.

T 7 to S 11. this morn set out / came a few milds / came to Saint mareys ware I continued with Lieut Shaw till Satterday ye 11 giving out provision to the rear as thay come up &c forth.[52]

S 12. to day travel'd a few or twelve milds to point leve[53] / took up quarters in french housand 1 mild from ye river Saint Lawrence till our troop could all git up / Continuing Near head Quarters 4 mild from ye City / during the time we stayed this Side of ye river we took a mid ship man belonging to a Ship in the harber who came a Shore with sum others to carry sum flower away from this Side of ye river[54] / ye river hear is about 1 mild wide / thare layeth in the harbour 1. 28 gun frigat with a Slupe of war with sum marchent men[55] / the men moun[*t* ?] Spears to storm the city the first word.

M 13. at point livey on guard by the river Side. ye hole guard ordered to turn out to make oar and p[*ad* ?]els for to cross the river Saint Lawrance. at night we crost the river with Cannoes and bo[*ats* ?] / Sum of the Cannoes over S[*et* ?] crosing the river nothing Lost olney [only] a few po[*les* ?] and guns / we got all over / Landed our men at wolefs Cove ware landed his army[56] / marcht up the bank wich was very Steep / came on abrahams plains ware wolf had his battle. ware we formed marcht back and forth to keep from freasing wills [while] the officer held a Counsel ware to storm the Cyti or not & the most part sed not storm[57] / then we march about [*a*] mild to sum very good housand wich was forsaken by the owner[*s*], major Colwils house for one[58] / he had jest gone as we got to the house / hear was a number of teems loaded with patoes [potatoes] for to carry in to the cyti / we took the teems and delt out the patoes to the Solgers &c.

T 14. Continuing at french vilage called Saint foies[59] / a guard we had stayshened by the river was fired upon by a Small Ship that lay in ye river / about ten oClock we was peraded / marched up clost by the wals of the City gave three Chear[60] / the enimy not being fixed we stayed thair a Small Sp[*ell* ?] till thay fixed a Cannon but was obliged to g[*o to* ?] a barn to get wort bef[*ore*] they could fire at [*us*] then thay fired a few Shot amung us but did no damage / then we return'd to our Quarters again.

W 15. this [*day*] very plesant but Cule / we ware plesantly [presently] alarmed but proved to be a false one / we mad an atemp to sent a flag in to the City but they fir'd at the flad [flag] & would not recive it.[61]

T 16. we took this day a quanerty of flower belonging to the inemy & Sum Sheep / thay keep a continual fire at our guard / a Serjeant of ye rifel men had leg shot off and died with the wound.[62]

F 17. Continuing at Sain foies ware we was informed that thare ware not more than 100 Regular in ye City with a number of Saylor that came from on board ye Ships wich thay compell'd to fight / in all not exceding 6 hunderd und: arms[63] / very cold & blustering weather.

S 18. this day thare was a Counsel held ware we should storm the City or retreat back till genl Mountgomery forcs could join us.[64] thay consulted to march 20 milds back in ye Countery / orders came out at night for every man to be in readyness to march in ye morn at 3 oClock.

S 19. this morn very early march 20 [*milds*] up the river to small town point auxtrumbel[65] our a[mmunition ?] being almost exspended to [*illeg.*] with.

M 20 to T 23. Continuing at point axtrembel ware we [*are*] continuing till the 23 fitting our Selvs for to go to Quibeck as ever genl mogemry joyned us / News came from genl Silow[66] that genl Mogemory was on his march with 15 hunderd men for our assistance.

F 24. this day thare was a counsel held consirning our alowance / we ware order'd to have one pound & a quarter of beaf & the same of flower[67] / hear we got morgasons made of half tan'd leather wich made us comfertable for we was very bad off for Cloths &c forth.

S 25. Continued at point a trembel / 3 Ships from quebeck agoing up the river came two againts our quarters & lay all night.[68]

S 26. this morn the Ships waid anchor / went up 9 milds & one of them got a ground and damaged her Sum. News came that genl Mogomerys Cannon was landed / orders was given for a hunderd men to be atacht as queck as posabel for to meet genl Mogomery.[69] very Cold and poor off for Colthing.

M 27. this day the french Inhabita[*nts*] sent to Colo Arnold for asistance to prevent the kings troops for [from] burning and plundering thair housan / a Capt & to men sent down to Saint foies.[70]

T 28. Continuing at point axtrembel / very cold. at a french house ware I fair very well for victual &cf.

W 29. the Ships that went up the other day return back to Qubeck again / a quanerty of Snow fell / very Cold.

T 30. this Day the men that went forward to meet genl Montgomery returned back / a Comp of french came with them & a quanerty of amunition.

December 1775 point aux

F 1. December the 1st 1775 / this day 4 vessels came from mountreall with genl Montgomery with the York forces who had taken Saint Johns[,] Shamberl[71] & mountreall / in the [these] placs thay took a quanerty of Clothing amunition & provision with 950 prisoners.

S 2. this day genl Montgomery made a present to most of Colo Arnold Detachtment[,] a Coat blankit vest & soforth / about 8 oClock at night Josiah Carr dyed belonging to our Company.

S 3. this morn very Cold / in the after noon the Company a[*t*] funeral / ye Chaplin of our d[*ivision* ?][72] made a prayer over the Corps / then we carried him 2 milds & enter'd a buring yard at point axtrumble ware we got lia[*ve*: leave] to bury him.

M 4. Set out this morn from point atrembl & marcht 15 milds / came to Saint ories ware I put up in a french house ware I [*ate*] bread & milk &cforth.

T 5. Set out this morn from Saint ories / came to the Subburb of Quebeck ware we pu[*t up*] at a french house by the river Saint Charles.

W 6 to 8. Continuing at Saint Charles river / ye Inhabitance imply'd in carring fashshuns[73] for to build a battery / very Cold.

S 9. a pleseant morn but Cule / in the after noon thare was orders given for 440 men to be in readyness / it [at] night thay wass all peraded / march't uppon the plains ware thay built a batery with Snow and fasheens & sum earth.[74]

S 10. this day we began ye Sige on quebec / to day thare was 5 morters set in a town[,] cal'd Saint Rox[75] near quebeck / at night our people sent in to the city very plenty of Sells / ye enemy keep a continual fire all day / Set a number of housan on fire / killed a french woman.

M 11 to the 21. during our time we stayed we took several prisoners and cannad & bumbarded each other both night & day / during ye tran[*s*]action we hear that the two men that was left back with Leut MCeland and other Sick return / Inform'd that Capt MCeland was [*buried* ?] at the first french Inhabit and the others died in the w[*oo*]ds[76] / Continuing fire both Sides / a number of men kil'd & wounded / made another attemt to send a flag into the city but thay would not recive it / the small pox very plenty

Map of Quebec and environs, published in London in 1776 by William Faden. Courtesy of The Newberry Library, Chicago.

Greenman's drawing of a ship that he called the *Liberty*. Possibly this is one of the ships he saw on the St. Lawrence River.

among us / preparing to storm the city / making pike and Spears / nothing very meteral [material].

F 22. the enemy set two housas on fire / very still on both Sides / we prepared to storm the city at night but ye Genl thought it to light an so ajurn'd it.

S 23. the small pox very breaf[77] amung our troops / a very brisk cannading / our Detach't was drawed up and and form'd a Square ware genl Mountgomery asked us if we ware wiling to storm the city & the biger part of them seam willing for to s[*t*]orm the city[78] / the enemy thoeth [throweth] Shells in to Saint rox and very plenty kill and wound a few / we return as many back to them.

W 27. this day being snowey and very stormy the genl thought best to storm the City at night[79] / we prepared / got all in readynes / turn'd at 2 o'Clock / marcht to head Quarter / we recieved orders / marcht clost to the wals of the City / the Genl thought it to light / we return'd to Quarters for ye first dark Night.

T 28 and 29. very plesent / Sum of our Company dieth with ye small pox / a very brisk cannading both Sides.

S 30 and S 31. this day it began to thicken / towards night we got in readyness / Snowed and blowed very plenty / we ware order to be in the greatest readyness for to [*storm* ?] the city / at 2 oClock at night we turn'd out[,] it snowing and blowing very hard / got all in readyness with our laders Spears and So forth / with hearts undanted to scale the wals marcht down into Saint rox a town near the City or jest under ye wals ware we sent off an advance guard of 50 men wich soon alarmed the town at wich all the bels rang / thay soon turn out ware thay formed them Selvs along the rampers[,] keep a continual fire on us but we got up to thair two gun battery after loosing a great number of men[80] / we soon got into thair battery wich was two Nine pounders / we got in[,] took 70 prisoners / then our men['s] arms being wet we could not do much / howsumever we tryed to forcs the gate to git into the uper town but all in vain / Genl: Mountgomery being killed all the men retreated and left us to fight for our Selvs.[81] then thay sent a flag to us to give up / our Colo A[*rnold*] wounded Colo Green took Command[82] / then the officers held a Counsel / agreed to give [*up*] / thay marched us into a french Jessewit Collage[83] after taking away our arms. hear we [*were* ?] very much crowded / No room for us to stur and very cold.

JANUARY 1776 IN QUEBECK

M 1. we ware put all in to a french Covint[84] ware thay gave us a gill of rum for a New years gift & sum bisquit / we ware aloued by the genl: 1 pound of bread and a half a pound of meat[,] 6 ozenes of butter a weak[,] a half a pint of boyled wrice in a day / we had a Cask of porter gave to us by sum jentel man of the town.

T 2. this day ye Genl sent for all our names placss of abodes and our ocupations and List of ye old Countery men by them Selvs.[85] a flag sent out after our Cloths[86] / most of ye prisoners had then sent in to very our provision Salt meat. but don git half so much as is a lowed by the Genl.[87] we live very uncomfertable for we have no room / Not a nuf to lay down to sleep.

T 9 to S 21. this day to pleas us we ware shot [shut] up in a smaller part of ye house than before / Stinking Salmond is provision we have / the biger part of it tho very Small is the Same / ye biger part of ye old Countery men listed out into the kings Service / the Small pox very breaf among us / our people burn down Saint rox / we git sum of ye old board to burn wich we m[*ade* ?] up cabins to lay in wich maketh sum room to wha[*t we* ?] had before / two of our men put in Irons for talken of desarting / got over heard / hubard died with his wound that was in his heal.[88]

M 22 to W 31. thare was three vessel and a Still house sat on fire by our people[89] / the garrisen people goeth into Saint rox gitteth ye remaind of ye buildings for woods is very Short in town / 8 of ye old Countery men that listed out ran away. 2 of our men taken that was a going to sat fire to thair Shiping / we live very happy & conteded tho we are in such a dismal hole hoping the first dark night that our people will be in & redeem us / hear we continu very lousey making wooden Spoons & one notion [*and*] a Nother to imply our very disagreeable time.[90]

FEBRUARY 1776 IN QUEBECK PRISONER

T 1 to T 15 / this day we had a nother Cask of porter gave to us by sum jentel man of ye town wich was very kind & very exseptful for we wanted sum thing of liquid nator. to revive our Spirits we had sum fresh beef wich we made very fine [*illeg.*] of / we are now implying our Selvs in picking of ochum[91] for sum marchant thinking to get sum present but wass very much mestaken / the Small pox very breaf amung us / 40 men Sick in prison with it now. very Cold & a very heavy Storm of Ice / thare was 3 men perished on Sentry / Sum more of ye old Country men that listed out ran away / we live very Cold and desag[*reeable*] but imply our Selvs in all of plays [games] that we can think of.

F 16 to T 29. very Cold indeed / we git sum wheat that is [*in*] bags below ware we go after wood and burn it wich makith very good Coffe and selling sum of our thing we git sum money & so we have once in a wile Sum Caffe. Sum more of ye old Countery men desarted that listed out of prison and the rest of them wass put into prison again[92] / the enemy went out after our Cannon that was on abrahams plains but return'd without them faster than thay went out. thare layeth 60 men Sick in prison. thay ware all sent to the aspital ware thay was used very kindly / thare was not more than 4–5 died with the Small pox out of all that went to the aspital.

March 1776 Quebec prisoner.

F 1 to T 14. this day we had a nother Cask of porter gave to us / I had a present gave me by Capt frost[93] of Sum Sugar & tea & sum money wich maket me very Comfertabl / we had Codfish 2 day in a [*illeg.*] / 1 of ye prisoners was put [*in*] irons for talkin with one of ye Senterys / we are plised with a notion we hear that the enemy is left Boston & 2 thousand men on ye march for hear[94] / the carpender order'd to nail Slabs of bords a cros[*s ?*] our windors to keep us from loocking out of ye & thay are very Strickt amung us.

F 15 to S 23. very Cold this night / thare was an alarm in the City at wich [*a*] large guard was set by the pr[*ison ?*] and field peacse set before ye pris[*on*] dore. for thay was very much afraid of us / Nothing more rema[*rkable*] the days.

S 24 to T 28. a flag sent out to our people but did not hear what the business was / the emigrants that is the old Countery men that listed out of prison ware moved from amung us & put into sum other place and we are orderd to pack up our things to move / thay moved us into a Stone jayl[95] ware it wass all boonprofe [bomb-proof] & then we went so Many in a room ware we gave a list of our names in each room / ware we live sum confertable to wat we lived before but the Stones is very cold indeed / hear we can see our peoples Colour[96] & a small breast work thay have heft up &c.

F 29 to S 31. we being in Sight of our people and Clost to the wals & a guard of old french and boys we throut it a Shame to be keep in prison by them / So the Serjeants consul'd to be best to sent out a man to our people to inform them & acordin[*g*] we sent a man out in ye night[97] / if he got clear he was to set a Signal on the flag Staf according / in the morn we see a nother flag histed below the other / then most of the prisoner tho[*t*] best to try to get out then / our names we gave in to ye Serj[*eants*] / we divided our Selvs in fore partys 1 to go to the train[98] and turn that apon the town a nother p[*arty*] to Saint John Guard[99] another [*to*] take ye guard of french men that was over us another [*to* ?] set fire to sum housan [*illeg.*] the jayl / by this time we ware in hopes that our people would come to asist us by sending out one of ye Spryest we could git to inform them we ware out / but one of ye prisoners taking an acks going into the Lower boom profe ware thare was a door that we was to go out at[,] he began to cut the ice to try to git the door open / a boy that was standing Sentry see him / he informed the officer of the guard / the officer come in went down Seller [*and*] asked what we was a cuting the ice from that door for / we told we did not know / Neither did we know who it was but thay mistrust'd that we was agoing to try to git out but thay did not know [*it* ?].[100]

April 1776 Quebec prison

M 1 to T 30. this day one of the prisoner an old Countery man that did not enlist out[101] told that had Carry'd on [*in*] prison / then sum officers came [*and*] sirched every mans pack and the room to see if thay could not find sum arms or amunition / thay mistrusted that the people of the town aquiped us with arms but thay found nothing / then thay put us [*in*] Irons sum leg bolts & sum hankufs wich was very uncumfertable / the officers of ye Jayl or povost master count us twise a day / it is very Sickly among us rease[*ent*]ly / Such provision as thay give us thay give us warm bisqu[*its*] wich we think was poysined for the doctors would cure us jest as thay pleased / Say or do what you would thay would give such phisick as thay thought [*missing*] / Complain of ever so deferent an ayl[*ment*] thay would serve us all a like and give one sort of phisick wich proved that we was poysoned but we soon got better / our people keep a Continual a fire in the lower town wich we are very glad to see hoping we shall be redeem'd very soon but almost ready to give up fearing thay will not come / but we keep up our hearts with a puter fife that we made out of all the button that we could git off our Cloths wich made us sum mery / So we pased away the long teatedus [tedious] time.

MAY 1776 IN QUEBEC PRISON

W 1 to M 6. the City was alarmed in the night by a Ship that came in to the lower part of the town wair thair Shiping lay but did no damage[102] / thay took the Captain off her / this morn about Sunrise 3 Ships came into the [*harbor*] with a reing foresement with about 1 thousan men at wich all the bels in ye City rang:[103] thay marcht out upon abraham plains to give our people battle but thay retreat'd as fast as posable / left a number of Sick in ye aspital with sum war lik Stores[104] & we see our people retreat wich made us all feel very bad wishing our Selvs tha[*ir*] to ingage them / if thay had o[*nly*] known how bad it wass to be a prisoner thay never would [*have* ?] retreated anought giving battle.

T 7 to S 25. the general order'd all the irons to be taken off thank god / the biger part of us could take them off without thair help / the genl gave the emegrants thair Liberty again / a number more of Ships come up the river / a number of troops gone up to mountreall by land / 6 or 8 men braught into prison that was taken who inform us that our people was very unhealthy / thare arived a very great number of Shiping every day / 13 or 14 of our men lis[*t*]ed out into ye Service / 1 of our men went out to work / thay requir'd him to swear Legons to the king but he would not / then he was put in Irons & [*they*] yoused him very bad &cforth.[105]

S 26 to F 31. Continue in prison / hear we live very discontented and quite out of hope of ever being reliv'd but keep up our hearts all we can / 20 or 30 Sail more of Shiping came up the river with Genl Burguine [Burgoyne] & his army who brought up with him a parsol of hasans about 6 or 7 thousan.[106] a Number of ye troops marcht off for moreall / the hasans put on the povost guard over us ware thare is Sentinels no less than 5 set round the prison / [*They*] hardly give us liberty to look out of ye windows

/ we can't see no Snow but plenty of Ice in our bumprofe / keep o[*u*]r Selvs ha[*r*]ty in playin ball in ye yard [*illeg.*]

JUNE 1776 IN QUEBEK PRISON

S 1 to T 4. these [*days*] very Contented hoping we shall go home in a litle wile / genl Calton [Carleton] with a number more of officers with a parsol of hasan officer came into prison to see us / inquir'd if we had fared well / we told him we had fared well for ye Stayshon we was in. he asked if we had fared as he promised / we told him yes / he then asked if we had behaved as we promised / we told him know / we began to think wat was coming.[107] then he asked us if he let us go ware or no we thought we could lay at home & not come thair to trubel him / he like wise said he did not take us as enemy & hoped we [*would not take up arms* ?] any more and if he could Religh on our honours he would send us home / he talked very prity indeed / we made him answer that we would go home & remain peasful till we ware interupted, well saith he I will leave to you to think and so send me an answer to morrow[108] / then we bagan to write petision / Sum one Sort & Some a Nother Sort / Sum thank for his goodness & other to know upon what terms he would send us home upon / this one was writ & a Nother / then thare was a dissturbence wich should go / we went out into ye yard and so we aturm'd [determined] it by a vote wich should go.

W 5 to W 12. this mor[*n*] very plesant indeed / after the provost Master came in we gave this as follrs to him May it pleas you Excellincy we the prisoner in his Majesty gail return your excellency our most hearty & unfeigned thanks for your goodness & Clemency to us since our Imprisonment / being Sensible of your humanirty we return your excellincy thanks for your offer made to us yesterday & having a desire to return to our friends & families again will promis not to take up arms againts his majesty but remain peacefull & Quiet in our respetive placs of abode & we further asure your Excelincy that you may depend on our fidelity So we remain your excellincy['*s* ?] humble Servants / Sighned in behalf of ye prisoner

13 or forteen prisoners ware takin out to go fishing / governer Calton gone to Montreall / Solger march off from ye garrison every day [*and*] leave ye town allmost bayr of Solders / only

a few hasan to keep guard over us. the enimy forses a number of Troops to go out of every parrish, & cforth.

W 12 to S 16. very plesant / we are told every day that we shall be sent on board the transports / a list of all our names was sent for[109] Likwise our ages & the province & town ware we was born & ocupation / Some of the prisoners that went out to work wran [*away* ?].

M 17 to S 30. very raining weather thurndering & lightning / the Solders in the garrison are cut off thair provision a half a pound of bread in week and all the prisoners the Same / we begin to think that we are not to be sent home / we are put off from one day to another and next week but we keep our hearts up all we can for our cituasion for we are very unhealthey by keeping us in such a hole not fit for dogs much more for men / thay march off for Mountreall every day.

July 1776 in Quebeck prison

M 1 to S 21. more Ships ariv'd. Sum pris[*oners* ?] put in [*who were*] taken up to the lak by Indians who inform us that our people is all gone over the lake & that all ye Cannadean Indians is joyned burguines army[110] / capt frost came into prison to see me / asked me if I wanted any thing either money or Cloths / he would help me to them and would have me send: I sent to him / he gave me a Coupel of Shirts & a pair of trowses with Sum Sugar & tea wich I was very glad of for we had Nothing but beaf & bread & but little of that[111] / Now I live well and my pardener he that was put in Irons I mean with me our hands ware put in one hankuf & so we marched together.

M 22 to W 31. [*this*] day we are told by the provost Master that we are to be put on board ye transports in a weak or ten day at wich we are all very glad / 5 more of the prisoner that went out to work wran away & thay have sent a Scout of Indians after them / we hear wen the Ships comes down that is to convoi us we are to be sent on board. then agin to comfort us we hear that the militia oficers of the town with sum others held a Counsell consern-ing our going away & thay think is best not to send us home / then agin we hear that we are not agoing to day / we hear by sum jentelman of the town that Lord how is taken[112] / one of our prisoner taken Craz[y] so that we are obliged to wait with him night

& day / the barrack master & sum other officers came into prison to day to [*tell*] us that we ware all to be put on board of ye transport & all that wanted a Shirt should have one given to them for sum of [*them*] had no Shirt to put on. the biger part of us had Shirts gave to us a present / We ware told by the provost Master that we should have 12 pound of bread in a week & 2 pound of beef in wich kill'd sum of them / After being So Short of provision then giving on such a plenty / we hear that our officer have thair Liberty of ye town &cfort.

AUGUST 1776 IN QUEBECK PRISONER

T 1 to S 3. We hear that all the old countery men that did not enlist out amung ye emegrants [*blank*] / Now we are wating for some more prisoner to come down the river.[113] thay let sum of us go out into the town to by Seastores them that hath money / to day capt frost came into prison to see me to [*tell*] me if I wanted any Sea Stores to send to him & I should have Sum &cfir [forth].

S 4 to M 5. this day I had sent into me ten pound of Sugar & two pound of tea / Now we are in Great Spirits fixing to go on board the transports / 35 prisoners sighned the parole / our door not locked up / Sum of us out of prison wich was a very great Liberty.

T 6. this day I had some more money gave me [by] capt frost / all the prisoners signed the parole wich we was glad to see / we would sign'd any thing thay braught to us if that would carry us home / hear is what we signed—We whose names are under writen do sollemnly promis unto his Excellingsy Genl calton that we will not say or do any thing againts his parson or goverment but will repair wenever his excellingcy Genl or any other of his Majestys Commander shall say or see fit to call for us.
this we all sighned.[114]

W 7 to S 10. this day we imbarked on board of the John & Christopher wich was a very great chang of life aftr being in prison 7 month in a stone jayl / here we lied in the river Saint Lawranc till 11 day / hear our alowanc is meat twice in a weak about two ozences & a quart of brandey a mung six men and three pound of molde bread & the rest of ye day in the weak we have about half a point of boyl'd wrise a day.

S 11 to S 18. this day we set Sail from Quebeck with the wind at NNE / came down the river a little ways / Come two agains the river Sain charles[115] / in ye morn waied anch'r / proceed on our pasage as fast as we could down the river Saint Lawranc / we have sum contrary wind & rainin weather / the river very wide down this way & the land very high indeed / we got into the river Saint Lawrance ware we spok with a brig capt rogers from providence / left bonaventure[116] barring SWbW / the wals [whales] very plenty around.

M 19 to S 31. very plesant / made the Island of Saint Johns ware we was detained a day by Carring sum letters / then we proceeded on our pasage / we made Novoscotia Shore / we spock with 3 or fore vessels / left Novoscotia barring NW / very stormy weather so that we was obliged to strike our topgallon-mast / very foguy / then cleared up / we got our topgallon mast up again / we ar[*e*] very healthey indeed / our alternation of Weathar & Climate suits us very well &c / Nothing very [*illeg.*].

September 1776 on pasage for New york

S 1 to S 8. very stormy but not much damage to us / we keep below / Nothing very Remarkeble more than proceding on our pasage wich we want to be made soon for we are almost tir'd out being prisoners so long / No[*w*] we are in lattitude of Rhode Island / one of our transports are run out of sight & thay think that the prisoner is carried her into Rhode Island &c.

M 9 to T 10. this morn plesant / Sounded got botton [bottom] black & white Land wich we was very Glad to see hoping we should now see the land very soon / at night sounded again / got botton very much as before / halled our Cours more to the Southward and westward.

W 11. this morn very pleasant / halled our Cours up to west / gain about 5 or Six not [knots] at night / we made the land baring WNW wich we was very glad to see.

T 12. this morn ran in for the land wich we found to be amboy[117] / we ran in amboy bay & came to an anchor till 12 o'Clock then ran up to Stanton Island ware we came too & [*were*] very Glad to see that aftr along & tidious pasage.

F 13 to F 20. this day we see 4 or 5 Ships go up by the town / thay keep a very constant fire at the Ship but thay soon got up the north river[118] out of our Sight. thare came on board of our Ship a jentel man [*who*] told us we need not be concerned for we should be landed in a few days. for what ever Genl Calton had promised we should be priformed / more Shiping went up by the town ware thay keep a very heavy Cannading on both Sides the Grand battery from New York & a nother battery from ye jersey Side[119] / thare came on board a boat told us that our people had left new york / very plenty of Shiping gone up to wards the town / we see Ingish Colours fliing at the town wich we did not like very well / thare is orders given out death for any Saylor cetched ashore / we hear that a flag is gone to genl washington to see ware we shall belanded / we hear that ye inmy [enemy] is kil'd & taken great numbers of our people / an officer came on board to git all our names & told us we should go home in a few days / 2 of our prisoners in the night stole a bote & ran away[120] / our time seen to be very long staying hear on boar[d] of this Ship all most out of patince.

S 21 to S 22. thare came on board an officer told us we should all be landed a munday at Night / a very great fire broke out in the town and by looks of it burnt the biger part of the town[121] / the river & harbour full of Shiping going up to the town / we hear that the 200 housand burnt down in ye City / we hear that ye man was cetched that set the housend on fire by the Sentry and run throu by a bayinet & then the next day he was hung.[122]

M 23 to T 24. this morn we got in readyness to go a Shore / we pasported to be landed very soon but ware disapinted again. the Stuard of ye Ship gone ashore by wich we could not have any provisions for 24 howers / we are told that the boats that was to land us was taken up in landing the enimey on red hook[123] / thare comes on board of us 190 men from other prison Shipt / we ware to be landed to Elisebeth town point / about 12 o'Clock we heft up our anchor came to elisebeth town ware we land one boat / Lord we lay hear drinking grog &c that we got out of the Stuard room / all hands on deck dansing & Courrousin all Night.

W 25. this morn very early remainder of us was landed to the greatest of our joy after being prisoner almost 9 month / hear we was carried to the barracks ware we drawed 1 pound of bread & the same of beef / we ware order'd by our officers to be in readyness to march in the morn up to head Quarters.

T 26. this morn very Cold / two or three of us went about 2 milds into the Countery ware we got a fine breakfast of bread & milk &c / then return'd to the barracks took our packs wat smalls ones we had & came to New work [Newark] ware we made a small halt / then to Seconnector[124] ware we put up / came all the way bare footed.

F 27 to M 30. this morn set off from Seconnetor / very plesant but very hard without Shoes / came [*to*] fort Constitution[125] ware ye rhode Island Regiments ware / he[*re*] stopt a little while then crost ye north river / came to fort washington / Stayed thay [there] till almost night then came to East Chestor[126] / Stop't thays all Night ware we was hansomly entertained / in the morn came to new rochel [New Rochelle] ware ye paymaster genl was but could not git our money till then / we was payed off 9 month pay / then I proceded on / came to New rochel thro weschester Newrake [New York ?] [*stopt*] in Grinage [Greenwich] in Coneticut ware I got me a pair of Shoes.

October 1776 on a march for Newingland

T 1 to T 3 and W 16. this morn I started very early / came to Stanford ware I stopt a few moments / then came Norwalk ware I got my breackfast then marched on / came redding ware I stayed all night / in the morn came to danbery ware I got my breakfast / then came as far as New milford ware I dined / proceeded on as far as Judear in wodbury.[127] in the morn I came to Bethelem in woodbery ware I continued till thee 16 at one of my Relatons ware I began to live well & have on Clean Cloth wich was a rareity after going Lawsey [lousy] & durty almost 9 months.

T 17. this morn from bethleham came to Litch field ware I oated my hores / then came to harrington[128] ware I made a small halt / then came to farmington ware I dined then came to hartford ware I put up all night.

F 18. this morn from hartford came to bolton ware I got my breakfast / then to anderver ware I made a small halt / then to lebenoncrank[129] ware I dined / then into windom ware I was hansomly yoused.

S 19. from windom came to New Scotland & thro Canterbury

and to plain field ware I got breakfast / then to volling[130] ware I put up at a privot house.

S 20 to M 21. this morn from Volentown came to Coventry[131] in ye State of [*R*]hode Is[*land*] and then into west grinage ware I got breakfast / then into exeter ware I made a small halt / then came to Northkingstown ware I continued till ye 22 / Nothing very remarkible.

T 22. from Northkingstown threw Newtown[132] ware I got a passage in a barge for Rode Island &cforth.

W 23. from Newport to portsmouth ware I crost ye fery / came to tivertown ware I made a small halt then proceded on my march / came to accoxet[133] in Dartmouth in ye State of ye Masechutes Bay.

T 24 to T 31. Continuing in Dartmoth to fair haven Bedford[134] & round ye Countery / Nothing Remarkeble. 16 Sh3739gs.[135]

NOVEMBER 1776 IN DARTMOUTH

F 1 to F 8. Nothing Strange onley fleing News &c. Laide out Six pound five Shilings and eight pence.

S 9. this day went to Rhode Island / Colo Ritchmonds Rigement return'd from long Island who in form us of killing & taking a number of tories on long Island with Los[*s*] of one man and one or two wounded[136] / very Cold for ye time of year.

S 10 to T 12. Continuing in Newport untill the 13 / Nothing Strange. 13. Shiling.

W 13. to day crost the fery at portsmouth / came to dartmouth.

T 14 to S 30. Continuing in Dartmout, about the head of Coxet river[137] down below to wards the point to bedford and around dartmout, went down to Litle Compton from thair to tivertown & to Dartmouth 'gain gitting sum walnut to eat / we hear that they exspetakt the fleat[138] in to Newport every day / Implying my Self in gitting some board from a mill clapboard to make a hen house.

DECEMBER 1776 IN DARTMOUTH

S 1 to T 31. Very Cold / the enimeys fleet ariv'd at Rhode Island[139] / ye Militia pasing to ye fery every day / the inhabitance of ye Island gitting off what Stock thay can / ye Solgers gitting off all that thay can / went to the fery / Nothing Remarkebl / Implying my Self in keeping Scholl [school] / very Cold & Snowery weather / we hear that Genl Calton is sent for all his prisoner that he took at Quebeck 31 of December 1775[140] / C[*a*]rousing around / Nothing very remarkebl.

NOTES TO DIARY

1. Newburyport, Mass., on the south bank of the Merrimac River about three miles from the sea, was the point of embarkation and the setting for the events described in the first two diary entries, despite the heading "Cannabeck," referring to their destination, the Kennebec River in what is now Maine. Since the preface indicated that Greenman had begun keeping his diary earlier, probably the thirteenth of September, it is clear that the first page of the diary recording the march from Cambridge to Newburyport has been lost.

2. Greenman's estimate of the number of troops enlisted for the expedition to Quebec is probably high, since the number of troops carefully compiled by Justin H. Smith totals only 1051. *Arnold's March*, pp. 56–57. Greenman was correct in his observation of the number of sloops and schooners ("dirty coasters and fish boats" said Simon Fobes, Roberts, ed., *March to Quebec*, p. 581) employed to transport the expedition to the Kennebec River. Confusion has arisen because one of them, the *Swallow*, lodged on some rocks, had to be unloaded to be worked free, and was late in joining the expedition (ibid., p. 289). The rifle companies referred to by Greenman were one from Virginia under Capt. Daniel Morgan and two from Pennsylvania, commanded by Capt. Matthew Smith and Capt. William Hendricks. It is harder to understand why Greenman said there were eleven musket companies, for there were two battalions, each composed of five companies as detailed by Henry Dearborn in Lloyd A. Brown and Howard H. Peckham, eds., *Revolutionary War Journals of Henry Dearborn, 1775–1783* (1939; reprint ed., New York: Da Capo, 1971), pp. 36–37. There was also a small company that General Washington asked Reuben Colburn of Gardnerston (now Gardiner, Maine) to form "consisting of Artificers, Carpenters, and Guides . . ." (*Writings*, 3:471).

3. It is possible that they anchored in a place identified by Justin Smith as Parker's Flats, about four miles from the mouth of the Kennebec (*Arnold's March*, pp. 69, 290).

4. Perhaps the laborious business of towing the ship made it seem farther, since according to Smith, Georgetown lay upstream only about six miles (ibid., p. 69).

5. Coberconta appears to be Greenman's rendition of the name of a river, the Cobbossee Contee, that flows into the Kennebec from the west near Gardiner. The route Greenman took must have been similar to Dearborn's: "we all proceeded up the River to Cabisaconty, or Gardners Town, . . ." (Brown and Peckham, eds., *Dearborn's Journals*, pp. 39–40.)

6. Hallowell was on the west bank of the Kennebec River about two miles below Fort Western, four miles by Greenman's calculation in the next entry. See the map in Smith,

Arnold's March, p. 67, and the description by John Hayward, *The New England Gazetteer*, 5th ed. (Boston, 1839).

7. Fort Western, on the east bank of the Kennebec, was the head of navigation as this entry suggests and is, according to modern calculation, about forty-three miles from the sea. Today it is within the bounds of Augusta. Fort Western was the staging point where men, supplies, and boats were collected for the assault upon the wilderness trail to Quebec. Greenman was part of the last group to arrive.

8. This was James McCormick, identified by Arnold in a letter from Fort Western to Washington, 27 September, as "a peaceable fellow . . . drafted out of Col. Scamman's regiment, . . ." (Roberts, ed., *March to Quebec*, p. 67.) He served under Capt. William Goodrich of Massachusetts and shot Sgt. Reuben Bishop from another Massachusetts company commanded by Capt. Thomas Williams. According to Dearborn, the incident occurred after an argument that arose in a private house (Brown and Peckham, eds., *Dearborn's Journals*, p. 40). The simplicity and former peaceable reputation of McCormick seem to have induced Arnold to avoid carrying out the death penalty and to pass the problem up to General Washington (Fort Western, 25 September 1775, in Jared Sparks, ed., *Correspondence of the American Revolution* [1853; reprint ed., Freeport, N.Y.: Books for Libraries Press, 1970], pp. 48–49). Dearborn wrote his account of this incident in his journal for 23 September, the night the shooting took place according to Dr. Isaac Senter, *The Journal of Isaac Senter* (Philadelphia: Historical Society of Pennsylvania, 1846), p. 7, while Greenman entered it on 26 September, the day of the trial, according to the copy of Arnold's journal of that date made by his secretary, Capt. Eleazer Oswald (Roberts, ed., *March to Quebec*, p. 44b).

9. Bateaux were the 200 special boats ordered for the expedition by General Washington from Capt. Reuben Colburn, whose shipyard was located just below Gardiner on the Kennebec. Washington had specified that Colburn was to "proceed to The Constructing of Two Hundred Batteaus, to row with Four Oars each. Two Paddles and Two setting poles to be also provided for each Batteau." (Letter to Reuben Colburn, Cambridge, 3 September 1775, *Writings*, 3:471.) These bateaux were probably flat-bottomed boats with flaring sides and tapered ends, designed for carrying loads on rivers (Smith, *Arnold's March*, p. 293; Mark M. Boatner, *Landmarks of the American Revolution* [Harrisburg, Pa.: Stackpole Books, 1973], p. 121).

10. Fort Halifax, a decaying relic of the French and Indian War, was located about eighteen miles north of Fort Western on the east side of the Kennebec. It lay on a plateau that bordered the Sebasticook River on the north near the point where it flowed into the Kennebec from the east. It should be noted that, as he informed General Washington in a letter of 25 September, Arnold had divided his forces into four divisions and staggered their departures from Fort Western to facilitate travel along rivers and trails (Sparks, *Correspondence*, 1:47). Greenman was part of the third division led by Maj. Return Jonathan Meigs of the Second Connecticut Regiment; his company was commanded by Capt. Samuel Ward of the First Rhode Island Regiment, son of one of Rhode Island's representatives to the Continental Congress.

11. Broken water, or rapids and rocks.

12. Probably the stretch of river referred to by Arnold in his journal entry for 30 September as "the 3 mile Falls" (Roberts, ed., *March to Quebec*, p. 46).

13. The modern Ticonic Falls in the Kennebec above Fort Halifax; at that time they extended a half mile, according to Justin Smith (*Arnold's March*, pp. 99, 323), not the nearly two miles indicated by Greenman when he wrote "600 rods." But perhaps the carry was farther than the rough water. Captain Thayer records this as the first carrying place of the expedition in his journal (Roberts, ed., *March to Quebec*, p. 250).

14. Greenman evidently considers himself close enough to Fort Halifax to count it as his starting place, even though the previous entry indicated that he had carried around the falls and camped at the upper end of the carrying place.

15. A town named Winslow lay along the east bank of the Kennebec River opposite present Waterville. It was named after Gen. John Winslow, who designed a defense for this strategic tongue of land on which Fort Halifax was built and commanded there (Smith, *Arnold's March*, pp. 97, 322 (map), 323). Whether or not the area of the town extended eight miles up the river, Greenman spoke as though it did.

16. A piece of the page now missing, the distance is supplied from an earlier transcript of this section of the journal made by its owner, Mrs. Edwin R. Lederer. Other reconstructions derived from this source will be accompanied by an *L* in parenthesis.

17. Goshen has not been located, but it might have derived its Biblical name from the fact that it lay on a rough stretch of the river one day's travel from Canaan, at the rate Greenman was proceeding up the river.

18. The camp referred to must have been at Skowhegan Falls, twenty-one miles above Fort Halifax, a place name spelled differently by nearly every one of the diarists. For example, Major Meigs referred to it as Scohegin Falls (Roberts, ed., *March to Quebec*, p. 176). The falls were so high and the river so narrow and rapid below the falls that the boats were probably drawn by the painters (bow ropes) to the point where the portage began. Canaan was the name of this place, as Captain Thayer noted: "The people call this place Canaan; a Canaan, Indeed! The land is good, the timber large and of various kinds, such as Pine, Oak, Hemlock, and Rock Maple . . . The land is very fine, and am thinking if worked up, would produce any grain whatsoever" (ibid., p. 250).

19. Capt. William Hendricks of Thompson's Pennsylvania Rifle Battalion commanded a rifle company in the advanced division, two or three days ahead of the third division of which Greenman was a part. Evidently the moose impressed Greenman as well as the others who commented on them: see Thayer's journal, Roberts, ed., *March to Quebec*, p. 252, and John Joseph Henry's *Account of Arnold's Campaign against Quebec* (Albany, 1877; reprint ed., New York: Arno Press, 1968), p. 16.

20. Norridgewock Falls, around which the expedition carried, and old Norridgewock village are not on the site of modern Norridgewock but are in the area of the town of Starks (Smith, *Arnold's March*, pp. 108, 332). Old Norridgewock lay on the east side of the Kennebec, opposite the mouth of Sandy River (Meigs's journal, Roberts, ed., *March to Quebec*, p. 176) and about a mile below the falls. The settlement had once been the site of a large Indian village and a mission to the Indians, but only the ruins, a cross marking the grave of a priest, and large tracts of land that the Indians had cleared remained for the men to see. Most of the oxen used at the portage were probably those herded along by the soldiers in order to provide fresh meat for the future. Major Meigs, for example, on 18 October "ordered eight men to kill two oxen, which we had drove with great difficulty to this place, . . ." along the Dead River (ibid., p. 178).

21. Probably this was Seven Mile Stream, the Carrabassett River, which was about six miles from the Norridgewock carrying place, according to Dr. Senter (*Journal*, p. 10), and flowed into the Kennebec from the west.

22. A wilderness barren of permanent inhabitants or of what Dr. Senter termed "improvements" (*Journal*, p. 11).

23. Tintucket or Hell Gate Falls must be Greenman's version of Carratunkas Falls, now Solon Falls (Boatner, *Landmarks*, p. 131). Hell Gate finds an interesting parallel in Thayer's journal of 5 October, where he refers to "the falls called Carrytuck, otherwise Devil's Falls. They fall about sixteen feet" (Roberts, ed., *March to Quebec*, pp.

251–52). Here the river was "confined between two rocks, not more than 40 rods wide," according to Major Meigs, who camped at the falls in the rain on 8 October and watched Greenman's company pass by the next day at noon. Then the weather cleared enough so that Meigs, who camped like Greenman four miles above the falls on 9 October, was able to report seeing "high mountains rise to our view" (Meigs's journal, Roberts, ed., *March to Quebec*, p. 177).

24. The Great Carrying Place was a traditional way to shorten the route up the Kennebec by traveling along a chain of ponds with carrying places in between to reach the west branch of the Kennebec or Dead River at a point where mountains force it north and eastward before it flows into the Kennebec. The beginning of the Great Carry was at a point where a stream from the first pond flows into the Kennebec, and there they beached their bateaux. For present locations see Boatner, *Landmarks*, pp. 126–28, as well as Smith, *Arnold's March*, pp. 113–14 and map, p. 119. Discovery of the sugar camp, not mentioned by the other diarists, suggests that Greenman was traveling by land this day.

25. Major Meigs, who was in the vicinity, did not record this death in his journal, but did note on 14 October a possibly fatal injury to a man in his division from a tree blown down in the night (Roberts, ed., *March to Quebec*, p. 178). Two days before, Arnold had recorded with obvious gratitude that "only one death has happened, & very few accidents by water, . . ." (ibid., p. 50).

26. This is known as East Carry Pond. A sketch map showing the location of this and the other ponds on the Great Carry appears in Smith, *Arnold's March*, p. 119. Access to the ponds and trails of the Great Carry and present efforts to preserve these sites are described by Boatner in *Landmarks*, pp. 127–28. Though they arrived on the Great Carry on 10 October, Greenman's group from Ward's company took until the fourteenth to cross this first pond. Probably this was because in addition to improving the road some of his division was employed in building a log house for provisions and invalids, as ordered by Arnold (Roberts, ed., *March to Quebec*, pp. 50, 177), a "blockhouse," wrote Abner Stocking, to which they gave the name Fort Meigs (Roberts, ed., *March to Quebec*, p. 550). Captain Dearborn said they could not cross the pond on 12 October "by reason of the winds blowing very hard" (Brown and Peckham, eds., *Dearborn's Journals*, p. 45).

27. Second Pond is also known as Little Carry Pond or Middle Carry Pond.

28. West Carry Pond. Greenman's estimates of distances along the ponds on the Great Carry correspond rather closely to those of Dearborn (Brown and Peckham, eds., *Dearborn's Journals*, pp. 45–46) or those reported to Colonel Arnold by Lieutenant Church of the advance party, sent ahead to survey the route to the Dead River (Arnold's journal for 11 October, Roberts, ed., *March to Quebec*, p. 49).

29. This was Bog Brook (Smith, *Arnold's March*, p. 108). The portage to Dead River had begun on fairly firm ground, but it descended into what Dearborn said was for "the last mile a Spruce Swamp Knee deep in mire all the way" (Brown and Peckham, eds., *Dearborn's Journals*, p. 46). The last part of this entry describes Dead River, which derived its name from its black depth and seeming stillness (Smith, *Arnold's March*, pp. 360–61).

30. Capt. John Topham, commissioned a captain-lieutenant in the Third Rhode Island Regiment, commanded a company in Arnold's second division under Lt. Col. Christopher Greene, which had left Fort Western a day ahead of the third division in which Greenman marched (Arnold's journal in Roberts, ed., *March to Quebec*, pp. 44b–45).

31. The "carring place" mentioned in this entry is probably the portage around the

rough rapids now called Hurricane Falls (Smith, *Arnold's March*, p. 139). The final words indicating that provisions were short signal a condition that was becoming acute, particularly among those in the advance division under Colonel Greene, whose men had passed Morgan's riflemen along the ponds of the Great Carry and finally halted by the Dead River to wait for provisions from the rear. On 15 October Major Meigs, leading the third division, of which Greenman was a part, ordered that the food "allowance should be ¾ lb. pork and ¾ lb. flour per man per diem" (Roberts, ed., *March to Quebec*, p. 178). The next day Captain Thayer cut the allowance per man in his division in half and recorded that they had "but 5 or 6 pounds of flour for 60 men" (Roberts, ed., *March to Quebec*, p. 254).

32. Two setting poles with four oars and two paddles were presumably standard equipment for each of the bateaux, as General Washington had requested (*Writings*, 3:471). Poles were useful in water too shallow for paddles or in swift rapids to hold the boats off rocks.

33. Greenman and the other men of the third division here began to move ahead under new orders from Arnold to Meigs, issued 19 October: "to proceed with my division, with the greatest expedition, to Chaudière River, and when arrived there, to make up our cartridges, and wait for the rear division, and furnish a number of pioneers, under command of Mr. Ayres, to clear the carrying-place" (Meigs's Journal, Roberts, ed., *March to Quebec*, p. 179).

34. Probably Greenman has mistakenly placed the "freshet" in his journal a day too soon, for both Meigs and Haskell of his division place that event on the night of 21 October (ibid., pp. 179, 476); Meigs says "the water rose 8 feet perpendicular," and Haskell agrees on the loss of powder and pork.

35. "A number of our men that marched on the shore, marched up a river that came in from the westward, mistaking it for the main river, which as soon as we discovered, we despatched some boats after them," Meigs's journal of 23 October, ibid., p. 179.

36. "I ordered a counsell of warr summoned of such officers as were Present," wrote Arnold in his journal of 23 October (ibid., p. 55).

37. Like Arnold, Greenman records the decisions of the council in his journal entry of 24 October. The sick, in several boats, were sent back to New England, and Capt. Oliver Hanchett of the Second Connecticut was chosen to strike out immediately with fifty able men, including some from Captain Ward's company, to reach French inhabitants along the Chaudière River in Quebec as soon as possible and send back provisions to feed the advancing expedition (ibid., pp. 55–56). Possibly the failure of the men in Col. Roger Enos's division to come up with the main body at the time of the council was interpreted by Greenman to mean that they had already turned back. The journal kept by Pvt. Ephraim Squier of Connecticut, who marched in Capt. William Scott's company of the division led by Enos, indicates, however, that he turned back on the afternoon of 25 October, after the various councils (ibid., p. 624).

38. The first of a chain of ponds at the upper end of the Dead River, which provided for the Indian or voyager a water route by which to approach the Height of Land, a ridge along the Quebec boundary.

39. The last pond mentioned here must have been Arnold Pond, where in preparation for the hike over the Height of Land they cut up their tents to make packs and abandoned their boats. Rather uncharacteristically, Greenman allows himself an allusion to the heroic dimension of the expedition when he refers to their passage over terrain "such as men never pased before." Perhaps it was a thought that occurred to him as he looked back from the Height of Land over to the wilderness from which they had emerged. George Morrison, a rifleman from Hendricks's company, said they called it "the Terrible Carrying Place; a dismal portage. . . ." Probably because of the snow

underfoot and the boats Morgan insisted upon carrying over, Morrison found it "inconceivably difficult" (ibid., pp. 522, 523). Later companies were spared that ordeal when word came from Arnold on the twenty-seventh: "I think the whole will get forward much sooner by leaving all the batteaux. If there are any people sick you will perhaps be under a necessity of bringing on some batteaux" (ibid., p. 77). The route they followed here took them through "a rather low saddle" in the mountain (Boatner, *Landmarks*, p. 129).

40. "Shedo" and more frequently "Shedore" are Greenman's efforts to spell the French name of the river, Chaudière, a name which suggests that the river boils as it descends through its rocky twisting course to the St. Lawrence.

41. Chaudière Pond is the pond at the head of Chaudière River known as Lake Megantic. Captain Thayer identified it in his journal as "the great Ammeguntick Lake, otherwise Shadeur Pond, fourteen miles in length and six Broad" (Roberts, ed. *March to Quebec*, p. 258). The distance from the heights of the carrying place to Chaudière Pond as Arnold recorded it was less than fifteen miles, but numerous streams and treacherous bogs caught many of those who left early on 28 October, before Arnold's letter of the previous day arrived. He warned them "by no means keep the brook, which will carry you into a swamp, out of which it will be impossible for you to get" (ibid., p. 79). For a careful effort to reconstruct the route and a detailed account of the difficulties of the army in this segment of the expedition, see Smith, *Arnold's March*, chap. 13, pp. 196–216.

42. Possibly this was the "very considerable wigwam" discovered by Arnold on the east side of Chaudière Pond (Roberts, ed., *March to Quebec*, p. 58). Pvt. James Melvin of Dearborn's company appears to have slept in the hut the previous night, for on 29 October he wrote: "I lay at a bark house, and this morning went in the canoe to ferry the people over the two rivers. . . ." Ibid., p. 439. Melvin may have ferried Greenman across the stream and showed him where to find the hut.

43. Lt. Sylvanus Shaw of Newport, Rhode Island, member of the Third Rhode Island Regiment, served in Captain Ward's company. The loss of the bateau reported in this entry appears to be that described by Melvin: "A batteau was stove, with four men, and one man drowned, named George Innis" (ibid., p. 439). Attempts to navigate the Chaudière River proved unexpectedly hazardous and cost the expedition a significant proportion of their already seriously depleted military supplies and food. The next day Dearborn came upon ten boats overturned at a fall in the river and found that "a great Quantity of Baggage and Guns were lost" (Brown and Peckham, eds., *Dearborn's Journals*, p. 52).

44. Caleb Haskell, also of Ward's company, corroborates (31 October) that "at sunrise we set out, leaving 5 of our company behind," and added, "There is scarcely any one who has any more than one day's provision, and that small, and a great number none at all. Some have had none at all for two days" (Roberts, ed., *March to Quebec*, p. 478).

45. In their extremity they were forced to take the step they had contemplated on 26 October, and by 1 November several of the diarists report the eating of dogs that had accompanied the expedition. The incident described by Greenman was not the first in his company: "Captain Ward's company killed another dog," according to James Melvin of Dearborn's company (ibid., p. 440). Most of the diarists reported the killing and eating of dogs by others before admitting to it themselves.

46. As a last resort, the eating of candlewicks appears to have been more profitable than the boiling of moccasins (Henry, *Account of Arnold's Campaign*, p. 72) or the roasting of a leather shot pouch (George Morison's journal, Roberts, ed., *March to Quebec*, p. 528), perhaps as a substitute for salt. Dr. Senter discovered Col. Christopher

Greene's division using them as early as 24 October: "I found them almost destitute of any eatable whatever, except a few candles, which were used for supper, and breakfast the next morning, by boiling them in water gruel" (*Journal*, p. 15). 1 November was a miserable and precarious day for many. Dr. Senter seemed to speak for all the men who had reached "almost the zenith of our distress" (*Journal*, p. 22). Some felt a moral revulsion at an order passed that day by the officers "for every man to shift for himself and save his own life if possible" (George Morison's journal, Roberts, ed., *March to Quebec*, p. 526).

47. The advance party led by Arnold reached the first French village on the Chaudière the evening of 30 October, procured provisions of live animals, ground meal, mutton, and tobacco early the next day, and sent them upstream toward the approaching army with a party of French Canadians under Lieutenant Church (Arnold to Officers of the Detachment, 31 October, and Arnold to General Washington, 8 November, Roberts, ed., *March to Quebec*, pp. 80, 84–85). John Pierce, surveyor for the expedition, was one of the first to encounter the relief party (1 November): "Met Church and 3 Frenchmen with 5 cattle 2 horses 2 Sheep 11 Bushels of Flower for the army" (Journal, ibid., pp. 669–70). Meal, mutton for the sick, and tobacco are mentioned by Dr. Senter (*Journal*, p. 23).

48. Room, meaning that straw served in place of bread.

49. *Sertigan* or *Sartigan* are the accepted spellings of this name, which the Americans applied to the first settlement of French and Indians they came to on the Chaudière River in Quebec. Justin Smith, with his usual thoroughness, which included questioning the oldest inhabitants along the Chaudière, determined that this term, which among the Indians signified "shady river," was applied by the inhabitants to a large region watered by the Chaudiere, rather than to a particular village (Roberts, ed., *March to Quebec*, p. 236). Smith concludes that the settlement mentioned lay about seventy to seventy-five miles from Quebec and "on the northern side of the Riviere la Famine" (ibid., p. 240), which enters the Chaudière from the northeast, four miles north of the Du Loup, a river probably among those Greenman says he waded in the previous entry.

50. This was not a unique condition. Melvin wrote in his journal of 2 November, "I had gone barefoot these two or three days, and wore my feet sore" (ibid., p. 441). Almost a week later, Abner Stocking observed that "few of us had any shoes, but moggasons made of raw skins," (ibid., p. 558) and John Pierce found the majority, or the "Chief of the army is almost Barefoot" (journal of 10 November, ibid., p. 673).

51. Abner Stocking of Captain Hanchet's company of riflemen, George Morison of Captian Hendricks's company of riflemen, and Caleb Haskell with Greenman in Captain Ward's company all recorded catching up with Colonel Arnold this day, 6 November, but only Stocking says that the meeting occurred at St. Mary's (journals in ibid., pp. 557, 531, 479). Arnold, who had addressed an oration to Indian leaders and recruited "about fifty of them" two days earlier (Senter, *Journal*, p. 24), was organizing his advance. On 5 November Arnold learned from an express that his courier sent from Sertigan had been captured by the British: "This put the people in a great panic, as they heard the English were determined to burn and destroy all the inhabitants in the vicinity of Quebec, unless they came in and took up arms in defence of the garrison" (Senter, *Journal*, p. 25). On the sixth, according to Dr. Senter, Arnold ordered "every captain to get his company on as fast as possible, and not to leave a man behind unless unfit for duty" (*Journal*, p. 25). The sense of urgency imparted by Arnold may account for the fact that so many of the men who kept journals recorded marching until late that night.

52. Ste. Marie on modern maps of Quebec province. The route of Arnold's expedition on the Chaudière River appears on a map in Smith, *Our Struggle*, 1:582, and is

described in modern terms by Boatner in *Landmarks*, p. 31. Greenman's duties with Lieutenant Shaw are likely to have been carried out under orders to the engineer, John Pierce, who recorded in his Journal (4 November): "I am ordered to Tarry at a French House and act as Commisary and Quartermaster for the 5 Companys now behind" (Roberts, ed., *March to Quebec*, p. 671).

53. Point Levis referred to an area on the heights opposite Quebec, on the south side of the St. Lawrence, near the modern Levis, a major link in communications with the city of Quebec. For a discussion of the problems of its location and a map drawn in 1759, see Smith, *Arnold's March*, pp. 450–52. Anticipating capture of Point Levis by Arnold's men, the defenders of Quebec had, as Arnold reported to Gen. Richard Montgomery, "destroyed all the canoes at Point Levy, to prevent our passing" (Letter of 8 November 1775 in Sparks, *Correspondence*, 1:476). But on 9 November Capt. John Hamilton of H.M. Frigate *Lizard* informed Vice-Admiral Samuel Graves that "the Rebels are now in possession of Point Levi, which stops all Communication, and I am afraid the Town of Quebec will be invested in a short time." William B. Clark, ed., *Naval Documents of The American Revolution*, 5 vols. (Washington, D.C.: U.S. Naval Department, 1966), 2:942.

54. The capture of the midshipman impressed even journalists like Greenman, who could not have witnessed it, though he was wrong about the purpose of the party from the ship. Captains Thayer and Topham correctly thought it was to remove oars (Roberts, ed., *March to Quebec*, p. 263). The incident provided dramatic material for the storytelling of rifleman John J. Henry (*Account of Arnold's Campaign*, pp. 79–81), but he mistakenly records it under the date of 14 November. In contrast, the journals of Thayer, Topham, Haskell, Meigs, and Senter agree with what must be regarded as the most reliable source, the journal of H.M. Sloop *Hunter*, whose captain, Thomas Mackenzie, was the brother of the captured midshipman, George Mackenzie (Smith, *Arnold's March*, p. 253). The *Hunter's* journal places the incident on 9 November: "At 10 A M sent the Cuttr to Lower Mile to bring off Boats Oars to look at a Schoonr that lay there / seeing that the Rebels had come down on which we made the Signl for an Enemy and fired 10 Guns loaded with round Shot at them which drove them into the Woods on the Cuttrs returning on Board found the Rebels had taken Mr Geo Mackenzie Prisoner" (Clark, ed., *Naval Documents*, 2:944).

55. The sloop of war was the *Hunter*, mentioned in the previous note, which according to official ratings mounted ten guns and carried a crew of eighty; the frigate was the twenty-gun *Lizard* with a complement of 130 ("Disposition of Ships Under the Command of Vice Admiral Samuel Graves," 3 December 1775, Clark, ed., *Naval Documents*, 2:1251). Colonel Arnold's report to General Washington of 8 November said he was "Informed by a Friend from Quebec that a Frigate of 26 Guns & two Transports With 150 Recruits Arivd there last Sunday [5 November], which with another small Frigate [meaning the Sloop *Hunter*] & 4 or 5 Small Armed Vessells up the River is all the force they have except the Inhabitants, . . ." ibid., p. 923. The "marchent men" or transports included the *Elizabeth*, a store ship which, as Lord Dartmouth had wished, was brought to Quebec under convoy by the *Lizard* and arrived on 5 November (ibid., pp. 722, 942). The *Jacob*, a "Store Ship with Arms and military Cloathing and Stores for Quebec," (said Vice Admiral Samuel Graves, ibid., pp. 947–48) was convoyed also by the *Lizard*, but "having parted Company in a thick Fog" did not arrive until 9 November (ibid., p. 942). Another transport, the *Dorothy & Isabella*, probably lay at Quebec at this time, for it attempted to sail for Boston on 28 November but was turned back by ice in the river.

56. Though the sloop *Hunter* and the frigate *Lizard* were stationed to prevent it, Arnold's men, as Dr. Senter described it, "crossed between the two vessels, notwith-

standing the armed barges were plying every hour from ship to ship . . . Landed above the Cove, without being discovered," despite the "bursting asunder" of a birch canoe (*Journal*, p. 27). Stocking, who very possibly crossed in the same group as Greenman, said "several of the bark canoes in crossing upset, by which accident we lost some muskets, and baggage, but no lives, though some of us very narrowly escaped" (Roberts, ed., *March to Quebec*, p. 559). Maj. Gen. James Wolfe's daring assault upon Quebec in the French and Indian War began with the scaling of the heights in the dark of 12 September, 1759; thus his name was given to the Cove where Arnold's men gathered after their crossing and "where, since the French war, a fair road had been constructed to the plains above" (Smith, *Arnold's March*, p. 256; the Cove is the "Landing Place" shown in the 1759 drawing by a British officer and printed by Justin Smith in *Our Struggle*, 1:11).

57. Judging by the end of this confused sentence, the question was whether to storm the city, not where to storm it. None of the other diarists records a council of war being held that night, but Captain Thayer reports that such a council took place on the night of 12 November, and it is possible that Greenman has misleadingly added his account of it to his next entry. Thayer wrote that "a council of war was held, whether we were to attack or not after crossing, being carried in the negative, to the mortification of the opposite party being informed of they having no cannon mounted, cartridges made, and even the Gates of the City open. Col. Greene, Arnold & the Rhode Island, with some other officers, were for attack" (Roberts, ed., *March to Quebec*, p. 264). Not surprisingly, it is from Rhode Islanders Thayer and Greenman that we have a record of this disagreement.

58. Maj. Henry Caldwell, commander of the Canadian militia, leased this property where he lived from a former governor of Canada, Gen. James Murray (Brown and Peckham, eds., *Dearborn's Journals*, p. 57n.). Greenman's characteristic "housand" refers not just to Caldwell's large house, *Sans Bruit*, but to adjacent farms and outbuildings or what Haskell called "some Tory houses" (Roberts, ed., *March to Quebec* p. 480). Major Caldwell, in a letter of the following 15 June, says that Arnold's men marched from Wolfe's Cove and Sillery "directly to *Sans Bruit*, where he surprised some of my servants, who were busy loading some of my carts and waggons for town. They got there before day, seized on all my working bullocks, about 20, and 4 or 5 fat ones, with all my horses; and there they lived on my beef and potatoes about a week, . . ." ("The Invasion of Canada in 1775," *Manuscripts Relating to the Early History of Canada*, 1st ser., no. 5 [Quebec: Literary and Historical Society of Quebec, 1866], pp. 5–6. Hereafter cited as Caldwell, "Invasion".)

59. Ste. Foy, a village about four miles from Quebec from which supplies might be brought along roads leading across the heights. See the "Plan of the City and Environs of Quebec," (facing page 22), published by William Faden in 1777 and reprinted in Kenneth Nebenzahl, *Atlas of the American Revolution* (Chicago: Rand McNally, 1974), pp. 52–53.

60. "The Enemies sallied out and surpris'd one of our sentries, whereon we immediately turn'd out our men and march'd within 80 Rods of the walls, giving 3 Huzzas, and marching in such a manner that they could not discover our numbers," wrote Captain Thayer (Roberts, ed., *March to Quebec*, pp. 264–65). Arnold wrote Captain Hanchet that he was "in hopes of their coming out" (ibid., p. 88), apparently adopting the tactic of General Wolfe.

61. A flag of truce carried by a messenger was ordinarily honored by an enemy according to military standards of the time, but not invariably during the Revolution (Bolton, *Private Soldier*, p. 149). The governor of Quebec refused to receive even Colonel Arnold's letter (14 November), protesting that an officer bearing the flag of truce

"was, contrary to humanity and the laws of nations fired on, and narrowly escaped being killed" (Roberts, ed., *March to Quebec*, p. 88). This was no mistake. As one of the defenders, supposed to be Hugh Finlay, wrote in his journal that day, General Carleton "would not admit them into town, neither would he hear them, nor receive any letter from them, . . . he would have no communication with the Rebels" ("Journal of the Siege and Blockade of Quebec by the American Rebels, in Autumn 1775 and Winter 1776," *Manuscripts Relating to the Early History of Canada*, 4th ser., no. 4 [Quebec: Literary and Historical Society of Quebec, 1875], p. 6. (Hereafter cited as Finlay, Journal."

62. Sergeant Dixon of Capt. Matthew Smith's company of riflemen (Topham's journal, Roberts, ed., *March to Quebec*, p. 265) has the last few hours of his life preserved in the narrative of John Henry followed by additional words of tribute (*Account of Arnold's Campaign*, pp. 87–90, 115–16).

63. Greenman's information on the numbers of men defending Quebec is incorrect; there were more than 600 men under arms, and better information was available to the Americans, but apparently not to many. Stocking tells how a servant of Arnold's, who had been taken prisoner, had escaped and brought back word that "the inhabitants and King's troops exceeded 800 under arms" (Roberts, ed., *March to Quebec*, p. 559); Topham put their strength at "8 or 900 Men," after weighing the accounts he had heard (ibid., p. 266). On 20 November, Arnold wrote General Montgomery that "their force is about 1900 men," a force which his breakdown makes clear was composed of 900 able and willing to bear arms and 1,000 who were unwilling or neutral (ibid., p. 91). Actual returns of men available for the defense of Quebec, drawn up for a British Council of War on 16 November, listed 1,116 men and 52 officers (Clark, ed., *Naval Documents*, 2:1038). Of this number 200 belonged to the Royal Emigrant Regiment, and over 300 were seamen or ship carpenters. The journal of Capt. Thomas Ainslie, a British militia officer who was collector of customs for Quebec, provides a different breakdown of figures, but a similar total of 1,126: see Sheldon S. Cohen, ed., *Canada Preserved* (New York: New York University Press & Copp Clark Publishing Co., 1968), p. 23. But Ainslie does list 1,800 garrison men as under arms by 30 November (ibid., p. 24).

64. The decision to retreat was based upon two considerations reported to General Montgomery by Arnold on 20 November. These were a persistent rumor that Lt. Col. Allen McLean would sally forth from Quebec with his Highlanders to attack the beseigers and Arnold's discovery on the eighteenth that a "great part of our cartridges proved unfit for service, and to my great surprise we had no more than five rounds for each man, and near one hundred guns unfit for service" (Roberts, ed., *March to Quebec*, p. 90).

65. Pointe Aux Trembles on the north side of the St. Lawrence River is now Newville, about 20 miles, just as Greenman thought, above Quebec (Boatner, *Landmarks*, p. 38). The road from Montreal, along which General Montgomery's forces would march to join Arnold, passed through this village on the way to Quebec.

66. Maj. Gen. Philip John Schuyler, as commander of the Northern Department, was Gen. Richard Montgomery's superior but was forced by ill health to withdraw from the field that fall to headquarters at Ticonderoga leaving to General Montgomery the leadership of the invasion of Canada from the west.

67. This represents an increase of one-quarter pound each of beef and flour in the daily allowance decided upon by a council of officers in response to growing numbers of complaints aimed perhaps not just at the meager diet but at the lack of vegetables and the money to procure any (Journal of John Pierce, Roberts, ed., *March to Quebec*, p. 682).

68. The journal of H.M.S. *Lizard* for 23 November explains the appearance of the ships: "Sailed Hence up the River, H'M: Sloop *Hunter* and the *Full* [*Fell*] Armed Snow to Prevent the Rebels bringing Down Cannon in the *Gaspy* and some other Vessels they had taken of ours" (Clark, ed., *Naval Documents*, 2:1124).

69. "Capt. Goodrich with 2 subalterns, 4 Sergeants and 64 men, were detach'd to meet Gen. Montgomery's advanced guard with necessary stores, &c., and to watch the Vessels" wrote Captain Thayer in his journal of 28 November (Roberts, ed., *March to Quebec*, p. 269).

70. Some houses had been burned, including the fine house of Major Caldwell in which many of Arnold's men had found comfortable quarters, but Caldwell attributed that fire to a stray ember from the pipe of his caretaker ("Invasion," p. 7). Much of the destruction was purposeful, as we learn from the journal of an unidentified officer defending Quebec; he wrote (on 27 November) that he was "employed in reinforcing the different out-posts, and destroying out-houses, which might shelter the beseigers" ("Journal of the Principal Occurences during the Siege of Quebec . . . ," in Fred. C. Wurtele, ed., *Blockade of Quebec in 1775–1776 by the American Revolutionists* [1906; reprint ed., Port Washington, N.Y.: Kennikat Press, 1970], p. 66). Reacting quickly, Arnold ordered Morgan, the captain referred to by Greenman, "to go before Quebec to watch their motions" (Thayer's journal of 28 November, Roberts, ed., *March to Quebec*, p. 269). Greenman's statement that two men were to accompany the captain must be a slip in which he substituted "to" for "do," an abbreviation for ditto, which he might have used to indicate that the number of men sent with Morgan was the same as that sent with Goodrich to meet Montgomery on the twenty-sixth, as Thayer said it was (ibid.). Thayer indicates, however, that the number of troops in each case was seventy, not one hundred, and indicates that both detachments were formed on the twenty-eighth, which seems likely.

71. Greenman's rendition of Chambly, a fortified site in the province of Quebec. Like St. Johns, Chambly was the location of a fort originally built by the French at a strategic site along the Richelieu River in an effort to control this water route between the St. Lawrence and Lake Champlain. A convenient sketch map of this area may be found in Mark M. Boatner, *Encyclopedia of the American Revolution*, Bicentennial ed. (New York: David McKay, 1974), p. 175.

72. Chaplain to the expedition was Samuel Spring, a graduate of the College of New Jersey (now Princeton University), who had spent three years in theological study and preparation for the ministry under such worthies as John Witherspoon at Princeton, Joseph Bellamy, and Samuel Hopkins. Quite possibly as a result of his experience with the expedition, Spring accepted a call as a minister to what was then the North Congregational Church of Newburyport (later Central Church), Mass., where he was ordained in August 1777 and ministered the rest of his life (*Dictionary of American Biography*, 21 vols. [New York: Scribner, 1943], 9:481–82, hereafter cited as *DAB*).

73. Plural of fascine, "a long, cylindrical bundle of brushwood or the like, firmly bound together, used to fill ditches, construct batteries, etc." (Christopher Ward, *The War of the Revolution*, 2 vols. [New York: Macmillan, 1952], 2:928.)

74. The technical term Greenman needed here was "gabion," used on 8 December by the engineer Pierce (Roberts, ed., *March to Quebec*, p. 690) and later by Dr. Senter. The gabion was "a cylindrical wicker basket open at both ends, to be filled with earth and used in fortifying a position or erecting a battery" (Ward, *War of the Revolution*, 2:928). Dr. Senter, on 14 December, described this process in more detail: "The gabions were filled with earth and snow, little, however, of the former, as it was almost impossible to procure any, as the ground was very hard frozen. After the fabric was sufficient in magnificence to cement firm, large quantities of water were poured thereon. This

freezing, soon formed into a heterogenous body, not, however, sufficient to repel the monstrous force of their 32s and 42s, as sad experience soon proved," *Journal*, p. 30.

75. St. Roch, sometimes St. Roque, a suburb of Quebec northwest of the walls of the fortified upper town, is clearly drawn on William Faden's map, facing page 22.

76. John McClellan, commissioned a 1st lieutenant in Thompson's Pennsylvania rifle battalion, marched in Capt. William Hendrick's company of riflemen as long as he could and then was borne by his friends until his death (Henry, *Account of Arnold's Campaign*, pp. 69–70, 75–76).

77. "Brief" used to describe an epidemic disease meant "rife," "common," or "prevalent" (*Oxford English Dictionary*, s.v. "brief").

78. The democratic expectation among the troops that they would be consulted as well as ordered is explicit in the journal of Abner Stocking, who was referring to General Montgomery when he wrote that "before he undertook . . . this hazardous and daring project, it was necessary to have the approbation of all the officers and soldiers" (Roberts, ed., *March to Quebec*, p. 561). Contradicting what Greenman says, however, Stocking adds that "many . . . appeared unwilling to attempt so daring an enterprize; especially those of us who belonged to Arnold's corps." One possible explanation is that some may have disagreed with specific tactics to be employed, such as scaling the walls of Quebec. But surely Stocking, who belonged to Captain Hanchet's company, reflected some of the unhappiness and dissent brewing there and in the companies of captains Hubbard and Goodrich, for which the best evidence is the journal of engineer John Pierce, ibid., pp. 698–700. It is Pierce, in the passage just referred to, who says the council occurred the night of 22 December at Menut's Tavern, Arnold's headquarters, but clearly that was a meeting only of commissioned officers, as Major Meigs said, "to compose some matters" (ibid., p. 187), before meeting with the men.

79. "I propose, the first strong northwester," General Montgomery had informed Brig. Gen. David Wooster (left in command at Montreal) on 16 December, "to make two attacks by night, one with about a third of the troops on the Lower Town, having first set fire to some houses, which will in all probability communicate their flames to the stockade lately erected on the rock, near St. Roc suburbs; the other upon Cape Diamond bastion, by escalade" (Sparks, *Correspondence*, 1:496). But as deserters informed the defenders of Quebec of these plans, "the General was induced to alter his plan, . . . to make two different attacks upon the Lower Town; the one at Cape Diamond, the other through St. Roc" (Arnold to Wooster, 31 December 1775, ibid., p. 500.)

80. Arnold with the advance guard "passed through St. Roc, and approached near a two-gun battery, picketed in, without being discovered" (ibid.), but by the time Greenman with Ward's company got there the situation had obviously changed. British militia Captain Ainslie said the attackers were "obliged to pass close under the pickets behind the Hotel Dieu & Montcalms house, where they were exposed to a dreadful fire of small arms which the Sailors pour'd down on them, as they passed" (Thomas Ainslie, *Canada Preserved, The Journal of Captain Thomas Ainslie*, ed. Sheldon S. Cohen [New York: New York University Press, 1968], p. 34). Justin Smith, who has composed the most careful and detailed account of this battle, says that the guns in the battery mentioned in this sentence were twelve pounders, not nine pounders (*Our Struggle*, 2:131).

81. The soldiers in Arnold's column carried their attack to a second barrier, under the precipice of the *Sault au Matelot* (see Faden's map, facing page 22), where their attack bogged down. The gate in this second barrier, mentioned by Smith (*Our Struggle*, 2:134, 136), may have been what Greenman referred to as the gate to the upper town. One reason the attack stalled was that General Montgomery, rounding Cape

Diamond to attack the lower town from the southwest at the *Pres de Ville* (also shown by Faden), was killed at the first discharge of a cannon there (*Our Struggle*, 1:142–43) and Col. Donald Campbell, who assumed command, ordered a retreat, enabling Gen. Guy Carleton to concentrate his forces on Arnold's men, who felt let down and abandoned and left to fight their way out.

82. The role of Capt. Daniel Morgan in leading the assault on the first barrier is stressed in the journals, and Henry indicates that it was Morgan who ordered the men to occupy the houses (*Account of Arnold's Campaign*, p. 111). Not specifically documented, but based on his careful study, Justin Smith said that after Arnold was wounded "the soldiers then called on Morgan to lead them, and Greene—since Morgan knew something of war—cordially assented" (*Our Struggle*, 2:132–33). Rhode Islanders Greenman and Thayer give a more prominent place to Lt. Col. Christopher Greene, who was the ranking officer. Col. Donald Campbell, in his report of the battle to Gen. David Wooster on 31 December, singles out for praise such men as Colonel Greene, Maj. Timothy Bigelow, and Major Meigs, but strangely does not even mention Captain Morgan.

83. The Jesuit College, which stands opposite the cathedral, is marked "Jesuits" on the map of Faden, facing page 22.

84. Probably the convent of the Recollects, a branch of the Franciscan order, which had a large monastery overlooking the square marked "Place of Arms" on Faden's map of Quebec, facing page 22.

85. The provost marshal of the Quebec garrison, according to diarist Simon Fobes, "called out all the prisoners born in England or Ireland, and told them that, according to the letter of the law, they deserved nothing but death; for they had taken up arms against their own country; but, if they would take the oath of allegiance, and enlist in the British service until the first of the following June, they should be reprieved" (Roberts, ed., *March to Quebec*, p. 591). The casualty list published by Roberts indicates that this threat was effective, for out of the forty captured from Lamb's artillery company sixteen enlisted to serve the King, while the greatest number, thirty-six, enlisted from among the sixty-one well or wounded from Hendricks's company that were captured (ibid., pp. 29, 31–32). Later entries show that so many of these old-country men or emigrants pressured into enlistment took advantage of their liberty to escape that in February they were returned to prison.

86. "Major Meigs was allow'd to go out on his parole and get our Baggage, and to return on Friday," according to Thayer's journal of 2 January (ibid., p. 278).

87. The reason for this was that a quartermaster sergeant named Dewey (Melvin informs us) defrauded the prisoners so that they got "not above three ounces of pork a day, and not a half-pint of rice and two biscuits a day" (ibid., p. 443). The general mentioned in Greenman's entry was the governor of Quebec and commander of British forces in Canada, Gen. Guy Carleton. See Boatner, *Encyclopedia*, p. 182, and *Dictionary of National Biography*, 66 vols. (London: Smith, Elder, 1885–1901), 3:1002ff. (Hereafter cited as *DNB*.) Gen. Guy Carleton's "Return of Rebel Prisoners Taken at Quebec" is available in the Public Archives of Canada, series Q, 12:159–68.

88. This was Capt. Jonas Hubbard of Worcester, Mass., the time of whose death may be more accurately reflected by Greenman's entry than by Thayer's rewritten entry of 1 January (Roberts, ed., *March to Quebec*, p. 278), and the certainty of whose death casts an eerie light across the record of the supposed meeting with "Captain Hubbard" in September 1776, recorded by Simon Fobes (ibid., p. 612).

89. Haskell, down with the smallpox during the assault, remained against his wishes among the besiegers and in his journal of 22 January supplies evidence of the essential

accuracy of Greenman's record: "Last night some of our guards at St. Roche's set a number of vessels on fire that lay against the village" (ibid., p. 488).

90. The prisoners lacked spoons according to Henry, who tells how he used a concealed knife to carve out spoons, a commodity with which he conducted a brisk trade for extra biscuits (*Account of Arnold's Campaign*, pp. 140–41).

91. Loose fiber used to caulk the seams of wooden ships. "The picking of oakum was formerly a common employment of convicts and inmates of workhouses" (*O.E.D.*, s.v. "oakum").

92. A "Journal of the Siege and Blockade of Quebec . . ." believed to have been kept by one Hugh Finlay records on 16 February this corroboration: "On this day all the Rebel Provincials in Col. Maclean's corps were ordered into confinement, and their arms and clothes given them, taken from them by order of General Carleton" (p. 13).

93. Capt. James Frost, we now know on the basis of a letter from Greenman to the Pension Office of the War Department after the war (20 September 1825, Military Pension Records, National Archives, Washington, D.C.) and of Simeon Thayer's journal for 10 November 1775 (Roberts, ed., *March to Quebec*, p. 264), was a Rhode Islander and partner of Newport loyalist Simeon Pease (L. Sabine, *Biographical Sketches of Loyalists of the American Revolution* [Boston: Little, Brown and Co., 1864], 2:156). He commanded what Thayer called "a Sloop of War," but it may have been a privateer sailing, as Greenman said, "in the British Service." The meeting with Frost, who "came into prison with a Number of British officers," must have made a profound impression upon the seventeen-year-old Greenman, for some of its details were better preserved in memory than in his journal. He revealed that Frost, "forme[r]ly an intimate with my Farther [*sic*] . . . called me out of prison and made me a present of mony & solicited me to sign the Kings pardon, & [*said*] that he would have me entered as a midshipman on board his Ship & put me immeadeatily under pay / this I refused telling him I had entered the Cause of my Country & ment to continue in it untill our rights was declar'd." Typically, there is no hint of his feelings upon this encounter with Captain Frost in his journal, but they surge across the page of his letter written when his name had been struck from the pension lists. For the complete text of the letter, see appendix 2.

94. Two Canadians, Lamotte and Papinot, managed to get through American lines and into Quebec on 8 March, according to the journal of Captain Ainslie, bringing fresh intelligence and no doubt inspiring a fresh round of rumors (*Canada Preserved*, pp. 60–61). Nevertheless, there is credibility in these, for the British were preparing to leave Boston and would embark on 17 March. What John Hancock called "the reduction of Quebec" was deemed of such importance that before the end of March, Hancock, on behalf of Congress, requested Washington to detach four battalions (over 3,000 men as they were then constituted) from eastern service for duty in Canada (Sparks, *Correspondence*, 1:176).

95. Called by Henry the "Dauphin jail" (*Account of Arnold's Campaign*, p. 143), this was a barracks "capacious and well supplied with berths or bulks," and located "may be three hundred yards from St. John's gate, . . . " (ibid., p. 145). The date of this move to the Dauphin barracks may be questioned, since both Ainslie of the garrison and James Melvin among the prisoners record the move on 13 March (*Canada Preserved*, p. 63; Roberts, ed., *March to Quebec*, p. 446). Moreover, there was a clear reason for this move—fear that the prisoners would find some way of cooperating in an attack they expected from the Americans on the fifteenth. A Canadian had brought word from behind American lines that "the common talk among them [*is*] that they will storm the Town on the fifteenth of this month" (Ainslie, *Canada Preserved*, p. 61).

Thus they were put into the more secure building, but one which ironically strengthened the prisoners' "notions of escape" (Henry, *Account of Arnold's Campaign*, p. 144).

96. Their colors, that is, their flag. The flag was first raised before Quebec on the morning of 5 March and was understood even by staunch loyalist Ainslie as commemorating the Boston massacre (*Canada Preserved*, p. 57). The flag flown was red with a black border and was an ominous sign to those expecting attack, but it also provoked derisive comment: "Some say tis a Squaws blanket border'd with black tape —others say, wringing their hands, *Mon Dieu c'est la Pavilion Sanglante*" (ibid., p. 60). Fobes's journal tells how they climbed into the garret of the Dauphin barracks at night and raised a trap door to gain the roof from where they could "see our American flag" (Roberts, ed., *March to Quebec*, p. 593).

97. Greenman neglects to record the reason for sending a man to the American camp, which was to try to coordinate an escape from the jail with an attack on the city. The elaborate attempts to arm themselves, the choosing of leaders (their officers were imprisoned elsewhere) and targets for each squad, and plans for escape are most fully reported by Henry (*Account of Arnold's Campaign*, pp. 145–57) and Fobes (Roberts, ed., *March to Quebec*, pp. 593–95).

98. The artillery mounted on the walls of Quebec. With expert help from some of Lamb's company of artillerists among them, the prisoners would signal those outside the walls by the burning of houses and "the firing of the guns of the ramparts towards the city" (Henry, *Account of Arnold's Campaign*, p. 149). Fobes says they were divided into three divisions (Roberts, ed., *March to Quebec*, p. 594), but fails to mention the plan to fire houses in the vicinity of the jail.

99. To attack the guard stationed at St. John's gate. Their object was to throw the gate open to American forces they hoped would be advancing to attack there.

100. A well-intentioned but fatal mistake made by young lads whose chopping at the ice was heard (Henry, *Account of Arnold's Campaign*, p. 157) rather than seen, as Greenman says. Henry explains that the "two lads from Connecticut or Massachusetts," were not privy to the details of the escape plan, which no doubt contributed to innocent disclaimers of knowledge of any such design all around. But they must have known the sally would proceed through this door, which was sealed by a bed of ice formed from the overflow of a spring in the cellar (ibid., pp. 148, 156–57).

101. We are told that John Hall was the man who betrayed their plans, both by Fobes, who says he was a "British deserter" (Roberts, ed., *March to Quebec*, p. 595), and Melvin, who says that then "all the sergeants and corporals were put in irons" (ibid., p. 447). The implication is that many of them had served as leaders in the absence of their officers. Henry indicates, however, that all were shackled except those whose services were required or for whom there were no irons because there were not enough to go around (Henry, *Account of Arnold's Campaign*, pp. 158–59). Greenman's entry for 1–21 July indicates that he was handcuffed to a partner.

102. Warned as early as 9 April that the Americans were "preparing a fire vessel to burn the shipping in the *Cul de Sac*" (an inlet, shown on the map, facing page 22, where ships were pulled up for winter protection, repair, and refitting), and again on 20 April that "the Gaspe, armed schooner taken last fall, they have prepared as a fire ship," the defenders still were not prepared for its appearance from downstream on the night of 3 May (Finlay, "Journal of a Siege," pp. 20, 21, 23–24). Ainslie tells how "those who saw her wish'd one another joy of the 1st ship from England." Then Quebec's batteries "play'd briskly on her," and she caught fire or was set afire too soon, so that her sails were consumed and the tide carried her clear of the shipping (*Canada Preserved*, pp. 87–88).

103. This was the expected relief, the frigates *Surprise* and *Isis* with the sloop *Martin,* which turned Point Levis on 6 May, the first of fifteen ships that had already entered the St. Lawrence for the relief of General Carleton. (Finlay, "Journal of a Siege," pp. 24–25; Ainslie, *Canada Preserved*, pp. 88–89; letter of the Commissioners in Canada to General Schuyler, 10 May, in Sparks, *Correspondence*, 1:512–23.)

104. The Americans "fled most precipitately . . . they left cannon, mortars, field pieces, muskets & even their cloaths behind them. As we pursued them we found the road strew'd with arms, cartridges, cloaths, bread, pork, &cc. Their confusion was so great, their panic so violent, that they left orderly books & papers, which for their own credit shou'd not have been left" (Ainslie, *Canada Preserved*, p. 89).

105. Among those working on ships in the harbor this may have been Thomas Boyd from Pennsylvania, sergeant in Matthew Smith's company of riflemen, who, according to Fobes, provoked his commanding officer by boldly declaring "he would not take up arms against his country." Consequently, Boyd was clapped back "in irons and sent back to prison" (Roberts, ed., *March to Quebec*, p. 597).

106. In the vocabulary of the time all Germans were Hessians, and in Greenman's customary usage they appear not in a regiment or company, but in a "parsol." Rumor has exaggerated their number, which was 4,300 under General Von Riedesel (Boatner, *Encyclopedia*, pp. 178, 933). The flotilla also brought Gen. John Burgoyne, who would lead the offensive southward in 1777.

107. The sudden appearance of Gen. Guy Carleton accompanied by several British and German officers was obviously an awesome event that might signify a change in their condition. But probably the men guessed than an offer of parole might be forthcoming on the basis of the grant of parole already made to Major Meigs and Captain Dearborn in May (Brown and Peckham, eds., *Dearborn's Journals*, pp. 83–84), which they had learned about by 18 May (Melvin's journal, Roberts, ed., *March to Quebec*, p. 449).

108. The date of this visit from General Carleton and the offer of parole is not absolutely certain, although Greenman seems to indicate that it was on 4 June. His accuracy is called into question by Melvin, who places this event in his journal on 5 June, and both Morison and Stocking, who record it under the date of 6 June (Roberts, ed., *March to Quebec*, pp. 449, 539, 567). Some circumstances tend to support Greenman; for example, the information about this offer to the men may have been delayed in reaching the officers, who were kept in separate confinement; thus, the fact that Capt. Thayer heard about it on 6 June (ibid., p. 287) makes that date less likely. Moreover, Thayer also received a visit from the Hessian officers on 4 June, although that fact does not fully confirm the accuracy of Greenman's date. What Thayer says about foreigners in the British army may help to explain Greenman's treatment of the "hasans": "This Army consists of Britains, Irish, Hanoverians, Hessians, &c. Oh! Britain, Britain, how art thou fallen, that thou dost hire Foreigners to cut thine offspring's throats!" (Ibid.)

109. This may be the British return of prisoners published in the Canada Archives, series Q, 12:37, mentioned by Justin Smith (*Our Struggle*, 2:128n.).

110. Unlike so many of the other rumors that alternately raised and dashed their hopes, this discouraging report was largely true. The Indians were being drawn to the British side, and despite the high hopes held out for the capture of Trois Rivierès in their assault begun 8 June with "2,000 of the best Americans" under Brig. Gen. William Thompson, these men were bogged in swamps, scattered, hunted down, "routed . . . and completely demoralized" by a far larger British force. (Ward, *War of the Revolution*, 1:198,200.) This American army and other forces under Brig. Gen. John Sullivan by 19 June had retreated to Ile aux Noix in Lake Champlain (probably the lake re-

ferred to by Greenman), and in the first week of July stragglers from that army had begun to appear in Crown Point (Boatner, *Encyclopedia*, p. 178). They were in the process of completing their withdrawal "over the lake."

111. Captain Frost, a loyalist shipmaster from Newport, was first mentioned in the entry for 1–14 March 1776 and is identified there. In July and August, on the eve of Greenman's parole, Frost seems to become more solicitous about his welfare.

112. A baffling and wholly false rumor of the capture of Adm. Richard Howe, who had, in February 1776, secured a dual appointment as commander in chief and peace commissioner to North America (see Ira Gruber, *The Howe Brothers and the American Revolution* [New York: Atheneum, 1972], pp. 60–71). Lord Howe arrived in America on the afternoon of 12 July aboard the *Eagle* and anchored off Staten Island. While news of the Declaration of Independence was being discussed on every side, he began his immensely difficult mission of reconciliation by addressing his initial letter to "George Washington, Esq.," ignoring the military title bestowed upon him by the Continental Congress and suffering the rejection of his letter. These negotiations and his activities in July are discussed in some detail by Gruber, ibid., pp. 91–100.

113. American prisoners on the St. Lawrence River fell into two categories. Some, like diarist Simon Fobes, were working on British storeships for wages and had been released from prison for that purpose, beginning probably sometime in May to judge from his journal (Roberts, ed., *March to Quebec*, p. 597). When Fobes's commanding officer would not release him to sail with the other prisoners on parole, Fobes jumped ship and hiked back to New England the way he had come with Arnold (ibid., 600ff.). Much more numerous were those prisoners taken upstream, particularly at Trois Rivières, where if Carleton had wanted to, according to Ward, he might have captured more men; still he "found he had 236 prisoners on his hands, men who had given themselves up rather than attempt a seemingly impossible escape" (Ward, *War of the Revolution*, 1:200).

114. Allowing for minor differences resulting from the peculiarities of Greenman's spelling and the fact that he was probably trying to reproduce a formal document from memory, this statement of parole conforms closely to that which Henry reproduced from the original paper, which he says was dated 7 August 1776 (*Account of Arnold's Campaign*, p. 170).

115. The St. Charles River winds its way around the north side of Quebec and empties into the St. Lawrence there.

116. Bonaventure Island lies off the eastern tip of the Gaspe Peninsula and seems to be the point from which they took their bearing for St. John's.

117. This was Perth Amboy, N.J., described on a contemporary map as "the provincial town of the East Jersey, . . . delightfully situated on a neck of land, included between the rivers Raritan and Amboy and a large open bay." See "The Theatre of War in North America" (London: R. Sayer & J. Bennett, 1776); reprinted in Nebenzahl, *Atlas*, p. 207.

118. The Hudson River.

119. The battery on the Jersey side was located at Paulus (Powles) Hook near Bergen and is clearly shown on William Faden's map of 27 August 1776, "A Plan of New York Island with part of Long Island, Staten Island & East New Jersey," (facing page 182), reprinted in Nebenzahl, *Atlas*, pp. 86–87.

120. No amount of reassurance seems to have been enough for these prisoners, brought so far and so close to freedom but afraid of being left to languish aboard floating prisons. As Henry said, they were afraid that Gen. William Howe would detain them despite the promises of Sir Guy Carleton; they were "tantalized every day with reports that to-morrow we should be put on shore." The escape of Dr. Thomas Gibson

and John Blair is recounted in detail by Henry, who adds that General Washington "disapproved of their demeanor" (*Account of Arnold's Campaign*, pp. 177, 178).

121. The "town" where the great fire broke out was New York City. The fire began late during the evening of 20 September and burned well into the next day, consuming about one fourth of all the houses in the city, some 493, rather than the 200 reported to Greenman. See O. T. Barck, Jr., *New York City During the War for Independence* (New York: Columbia University Press, 1931), pp. 80–81.

122. From the time of the fire there were stories of arson similar to that told by Greenman and Henry, *Account of Arnold's Campaign*, pp. 178–80. The New York *Gazette and Weekly Mercury* of 30 September told a sinister story of a New England captain of the Continental Line "discovered with large bundles of matches, dipped in melted rosin and brimstone," with £500 on his person and other villains caught by an outraged populace (reprinted in Frank Moore, comp., *The Diary of the American Revolution*, abridged ed. [New York; Washington Square Press, 1967], p. 161). Undoubtedly, suspicion of arson fed upon rumors that preceded the event and had a basis in fact—Washington had considered putting the torch to the city to deprive the British of its use as a base, and he had consulted the Continental Congress about it. The decision was not to destroy the city (Ward, *War of the Revolution*, 1:239–240). But the rumor persisted that "if the American Army should be obliged to retreat from this City, any Individual may set it on fire" (Washington, *Writings*, 5:477). Washington denied there was any truth in the rumor, but after the conflagration he was inclined to view it as an act of Providence (Douglas S. Freeman, *George Washington*, 7 vols. [New York: Scribner, 1948–57], 4:205). Barck discounts the rumors and concludes the "inception of the fire was accidental" (*New York City*, p. 82), but one cannot lightly dispose of Henry's feeling that Americans bent upon thievery and devastation started it (*Account of Arnold's Campaign*, pp. 179–80), though investigations afterwards did not produce credible witnesses.

123. Red Hook, the location of Fort Defiance, lay on the western end of Long Island below Governors Island within present Brooklyn. It is easily located on Faden's map of New York (facing page 182). Although the battery there had engaged the British ship *Roebuck* on 27 August 1776 (Boatner, *Landmarks*, p. 285), the area had subsequently been evacuated in the withdrawal from Long Island, 29–31 August (Freeman, *Washington*, 4:171–79).

124. Probably what is now Secaucus, N.J.

125. Fort Constitution, N.J. (later called Fort Lee) lay opposite Fort Washington on the heights above the east bank of the Hudson; "they were built to cover a line of obstructions across the Hudson River to bar the movement of British ships" (Boatner, *Encyclopedia*, p. 381). These positions seemed strong but proved ineffective, and both were captured by the British in November; only the garrison of Fort Constitution escaped capture. See Faden's map, "New York and East New Jersey," in Nebenzahl, *Atlas*, pp. 88–89, and his more detailed map of the forts, p. 91.

126. East Chester lay in "Pelhams Mannor" and almost midway on a road leading from West Chester to New Rochelle. (It is shown on Faden's maps, facing page 182, and in Nebenzahl, *Atlas*, p. 89.) Part of the remainder of this entry is confused since it seems to indicate that Greenman came to New Rochelle twice without ever leaving. It is likely that after receiving his pay, Greenman took the road through Mamaroneck and Rye in Westchester County, N.Y., to Greenwich, Conn.

127. From Norwalk, Conn., Greenman had turned north on the road to Danbury, taking a direction that would bring him to the well-known "upper route" across Connecticut, from Fishkill on the Hudson through Litchfield to Hartford. There it connects with a good road through Andover, Windham, Scotland, Canterbury, and Plain-

field to Coventry, R.I. Taking this route home, he turned east at New Milford and found his way to Woodbury Township in Litchfield County. There he stopped overnight at Judea and then spent nearly two weeks in Bethlehem with relatives, his "Relatons," where he lived well and reveled in clean clothes. Who these relations were we do not know. Bethlehem, just eight miles south of Litchfield, was in 1787 set apart as a separate township. Hayward, *New England Gazetteer.*

128. Harwinton, Conn.

129. Not then a town but the Lebanon Crank Tavern, which in the words of the Marquis de Chastellux was "a solitary little tavern, kept by Mrs. Hill" (*Travels*, 1:71). The place where the house in which Mrs. Hill kept tavern stands has since been incorporated as Columbia, Conn. (ibid., p. 256).

130. Not the present Voluntown, though the next entry suggests it, but another one on the site of what is the modern Sterling Hill in Windham County, Conn. (ibid., pp. 251–52).

131. Coventry and West Greenwich are more clearly defined on the older maps, such as "A Map of the State of Rhode Island" by Caleb Harris (Providence, 1795), facing page 131.

132. Now Wickford, R.I., it was known in Greenman's time as Updike's Newtown or Updike's Harbour, as on the fine map of 1777 available in Nebenzahl, *Atlas*, pp. 94–95. There he boarded a boat for Newport on Rhode Island.

133. Why should this weary young veteran returning from his Canadian odyssey arrive in his native Newport and immediately leave town for Dartmouth, Mass.? The answer is that during his absence, unknown to him, his family had moved to the village of Acoaxet in Dartmouth, perhaps in response to the growing threat that the British fleet would bring an army to occupy Rhode Island. So Greenman followed, crossing from Portsmouth to Tiverton by Howland's Ferry (see Nebenzahl, *Atlas*, pp. 94–95) and making his way by land to Acoaxet, which was at the end of a finger of land on the west side of the west branch of what is now the Westport River and is known as Westport Harbor. John Hayward, *A Gazetteer of Massachusetts*, rev. ed. (Boston: John P. Jewett & Co., 1846), p. 306.

134. Fairhaven and Bedford were both villages within the territory of Dartmouth; they were situated at the head of Buzzard's Bay and later connected by a bridge over the Acushnet River (Hayward, *Gazetteer of Massachusetts*, p. 147). Bedford is now New Bedford.

135. Part of an expense record which is more extensively displayed in the next entry. For the sake of privacy or perhaps curiosity about such things used in the intrigues of war, he has expressed these in simple code. This entry records an expenditure of of "16 shilings." Using the same values, the next entry reads: "Laide out six pound five shilings and eight pence." It may be the kind of thing with which he amused the school children he faced in December.

136. Col. William Richmond commanded a regiment of Rhode Island militia, part of which served on Long Island with New York troops under Lt. Col. Henry B. Livingston, who led this detachment "in all amounting to 250 men" to "Setalket Harbour" (now Port Jefferson Harbour near Setauket) in Suffolk County, Long Island, to attack a company of loyalist troops belonging to Oliver DeLancey's famous brigade. In a letter written about 25 September 1776, Henry described to his father, Robert, the action which followed their crossing to the Island during "prodigious Rough weather" and their arrival wet and numb with cold: "We found them up and in Arms expecting us / they began the Fire and killed one of the Rhode Island men and wounded Another." Clark, ed., *Naval Documents*, 6:983.

137. Head of Acoaxet was at the head of the east branch of Acoaxet River; it is now

Westport, about eight miles above Westport Point: Hayward, *Gazetteer of Massachusetts*, p. 306.

138. The British fleet.

139. A fleet under Com. William Hotham brought 7,000 British and Hessian troops under the command of Sir Henry Clinton into Weaver's Cove on the western side of Rhode Island on 7 December. The next day they landed unopposed and "pushed the Americans from Weaver's Cove to Bristol Ferry, at the northern end of the island, whence they escaped with the loss of only a few prisoners and two cannon" William B. Willcox, *The Portrait of a General: Sir Henry Clinton in the War of Independence* (New York: Alfred A. Knopf, 1964), p. 122. The ferry landings from the first sighting of British sails must have been teeming with people and stock leaving the Island and militia mustering to block British efforts to cross to the mainland.

140. Possibly writing on the cold and snowy anniversary of the attack on Quebec, Greenman cannot entirely discount this nightmare rumor that Carleton is recalling his prisoners. In fact, amid all his other duties, Washington was trying to work out an orderly exchange of prisoners with General Howe, as he wrote Gov. Jonathan Trumbull, "beginning with those taken at Quebec under Generals Montgomery and Arnold" (21 December 1776, *Writings*, 6:410).

PART TWO

Defense of the Delaware, 1777

INTRODUCTION

As THE new year opened uneventfully at home in Dartmouth, Massachusetts, young Jeremiah Greenman could scarcely have foreseen the months of intense activity that lay ahead in the campaign of 1777. For him the war was already an old one: He had endured the march to Quebec, the abortive assault, prison; then had come his repatriation and the barefoot walk homeward from New York. At eighteen he was as distinguished a veteran as any who had persevered throughout Arnold's Canada affair. The difference now was that he was a civilian. And, not surprisingly, his first interest was in collecting his long overdue wages from "ye late campaign." Reenlistment might wait awhile. In search of his pay, he spent a good deal of January walking all over Rhode Island: he visited Providence time and again and even walked over to Westerly to wait upon his Quebec captain, Samuel Ward, at the Ward home in Weekapaug, And eventually he got his due:

> *Providence, Jan. 25, 1777.*
> *The Officers and Soldiers belonging to Capt. Samuel Ward's Company, in Gen. Arnold's Detachment, are desired immediately to attend him in Providence, to receive Pay due to them, from the time they marched from Cambridge (First of September, 1775) to the first of January following.*[1]

Here was the offer of four months' pay for prodigies of human endurance and deprivation which had lasted considerably more than a year. Still, it was ready money—though whether Continental or specie is not mentioned—and could not have been more honestly earned. He had struggled and learned on the Quebec expedition; indeed he had been lucky to return. But from the strong sense of so little with which to "imply" himself conveyed by the diary entries of early 1777, it is perhaps predictable that Greenman soon determined to be a soldier once again.

Moreover, Rhode Island never seemed to have enough soldiers. To be sure, the center of the war was far away in New Jersey, but its reality was brought home almost daily to the Rhode Islanders through the incursions of British raiding ships into towns all along the shoreline of Narragansett Bay. Recruiting efforts were insistent in the winter of 1776–1777 and must have been considerably aided by the British occupation of Newport at the end of the year: "6,000 troops and a large supporting fleet" had entered the city in December 1776.[2] Even if Newport was, in the minds of many Rhode Island patriots, a Tory enclave, it was still a part of the homeland, now being violated, and there was good reason to believe that Providence would be next. The fact was that the most autonomous colony in the happier years before the rebellion was being ignominiously invaded, and the call for fresh militia and continentals was ringing out across the land. Then, too, there were the patriotic columns of John Carter's Providence *Gazette*, offering "freshest Advices, Foreign and Domestic" and doing what could be done to further the American cause. On 25 January 1777 a recruiting notice for the imminent campaign appeared in the *Gazette*, "by order of Congress, John Hancock, President," requiring the state "immediately to inlist into the service of the United States all able-bodied men" (or at least those who were free, white, under fifty, and not deserters from His Britannic Majesty) "to serve three years, or during the continuation of the present war." If Greenman saw this notice, or perhaps one of the handbills proclaiming the same thing, he undoubtedly also saw the inducements Congress was offering for continental enlistments: a twenty-dollar bounty, a "new suit of clothes," and the promise of one-hundred acres of land in some unspecified place at some equally vague time after the war was won.

Whatever his reasons, Greenman reenlisted at Coventry, Rhode Island, on 22 February 1777. For this campaign, however, he would be serving under Capt. Sylvanus Shaw, and instead of a private he would be a sergeant in Shaw's company, Col. Israel Angell's Second Rhode Island Regiment.[3] The return to active service must have looked good to a young man who had been initiated into the Canadian wilderness and had known a British prison-ship before his eighteenth birthday, but now was back home, tradeless, with nothing much offering.

Because his regiment was still recruiting and could not march to join Washington until the weather moderated and the ranks were reasonably filled, Greenman records that he "took barracks in ye Collage" and drilled for the coming campaign. Rhode Island College (not yet Brown University) had suspended its academic business when the British occupied Newport. According to college President James Manning, when "the Royal Army landed on Rhode Island . . . the Country flew to Arms & marched for Providence, there, unprovided with Barracks they marched into the College & dispossessed the Students, about 40 in Number."[4] This was doubtless the only tenure in any university for Jeremiah Greenman, who needed a war and garrison duty to pass through the gates of Rhode Island College.

The Rhode Island troops finally marched "to the westward" the second week of April with Greenman in the rear with the baggage guard. Their way lay across Connecticut into New York, then south into New Jersey. It was for many days the same route that would be traversed in 1781 by the French army under Rochambeau, as they marched to join Washington at Yorktown. The Rhode Islanders' goal was the encampment at Morristown, New Jersey, with an intermediate stop in the Hudson Highlands.

Greenman's regiment arrived in camp on 24 April, and soon after the diarist began to comment on the pitiful condition of the American army: discipline was a problem, small pox was rampant, and the men were in rags and tatters. His account of the condition of the army conforms with the attitude of the commander in chief himself, who complained to Congress that he was in "the situation . . . of scarce having any army at all" and saw those yet remaining in camp ill, hungry and "absolutely perishing for want of clothes."[5] Yet ill-provisioned as the American army was, it was slowly showing signs of becoming an army in more than name after the low point of the winter of 1776–1777. Fresh troops—units like Greenman's, recruited all over the Colonies—were steadily reinforcing the main camp at Morristown: "thare arrives Continental troops into town every day."

Many of the diary entries for May and June deal—though typically in the confusing fashion of one not in a knowledgeable military position—with the American responses to the series of British maneuvers that were designed to lure Washington out of his strong defensive positions, first at Morristown and then at Middlebrook.[6] All of the activity on both sides was indecisive, no general engagement was brought on, and Sir William Howe soon evacuated all his troops to Staten Island. New Jersey was free from the British presence by the end of June—"the regulars is quited the Jersies."

With the departure of the British from New Jersey, Washington looked apprehensively to the north. He understandably thought Howe and his troops would be sailing and marching up the Hudson to link up with Burgoyne's expeditionary force coming down from Canada. This seemed so likely that when Washington learned that Howe had sailed his army *south*, he was mystified, almost incredulous: "Howe's in a manner abandoning General Burgoyne is so unaccountable a matter that till I am fully assured it is so, I cannot help casting my eyes continually behind me."[7] The American commander compromised by sending a portion of his army to reinforce Gen. Israel Putnam in the Hudson Highlands, while keeping his main body ready to move to Philadelphia if that city proved to be the British object. The detachment to the north was under the command of Brig. Gen. James Mitchell Varnum and included Greenman's regiment. Greenman was apparently in the vanguard of this force, for he arrived at Peekskill on 6 July, well before the rest of the troops.[8]

The Hudson Highlands were of vital strategic importance to the Americans throughout the war, allowing them to monitor closely the British movements in and about occupied New York City. These Highlands "are a topographical curiosity of the valley in that they cross this strategic avenue [the Hudson River] a mere 45 miles north of N.Y.C. to constitute a natural barrier of easily defensible terrain."[9] Greenman's three months in the area were largely filled with desultory camp activity punctuated now and then with foraging or raiding parties into the so-called neutral ground in Westchester County, executions or other highly ceremonial military punishments, and minor disturbances among the men "concerning thair wages" and the fact that the clothing bounty promised by Congress months earlier had yet to be delivered. The men certainly had a point. Colonel Angell wrote in desperation to the governor of Rhode Island, detailing the wretched condition of the men in his Second Rhode Island Regiment:

> *Not one half of them can not [sic] be termed fit for any duty in any immergency; of those, who of them went with me on a late expedition near to Kings bridge many were bare foot, in consequence of which its probable they won't be fit for duty again for man week[s] / 5 of them deserted to ye enemy which I have reason to believe was principally owing to ye non fulfillment of engagements on ye part of ye State. . . . In fine ye Regiment is scandalous in its appearance in ye view of everyone—and has because of this incurred from surrounding regiments [and] from ye inhabitants of Towns thro which they have lately passed, ye disagreeable & provoking Epithets of the Ragged Lousey Naked Regiment.*[10]

But for the time being the men could only complain and make shift while waiting for marching and fighting orders.

Their orders came near the end of September. The major defeat at Brandywine and the British occupation of Philadelphia moved Washington to order Varnum's brigade back to the main army outside Philadelphia. By 8 October Varnum had reached Coryell's Ferry (now Lambertsville, New Jersey) and had crossed to what is now New Hope, Pennsylvania. There they were met by an express from the commander in chief with orders for Christopher Greene's and Angell's regiments to proceed at once to Fort Mercer, on the Delaware at Red Bank, New Jersey. Greene's troops arrived at Mercer on 11 October. Angell's regiment, delayed by conflicting orders, did not reach the fort until the eighteenth.[11]

Now began the series of engagements that constituted for Jeremiah Greenman the most momentous events of an eight years' war. The defense of the Delaware River forts, Mifflin and Mercer, hardly remembered in modern histories of the Revolution, was in its own time and for the generation following the war a major source of national pride. Against much greater fire- and manpower the Americans were asked by Washington to hold the forts and retain control of the lower Delaware, thus preventing the British from supplying occupied Philadelphia by ship. It was fervently hoped that the interruption of regular provisioning by water would force Howe to evacuate the city (at best) or would lead at least to severe deprivation of the British army as it wintered in the city. Though the American resistance in the lower river ultimately accomplished neither of these things, the effort was tenacious and came very close to succeeding.

Leonard Lundin has pointed out just how near the Americans were to their goal when forced to give up: "It was indeed an open question whether, if the Americans held out, Howe would be able to stay in Philadelphia until his guns had battered Fort Mifflin to pieces. There were rumors that the British were discouraged and about to evacuate the city. Such supplies as could be brought up by the small boats did no more than cover the bare necessities of the army, and beef had become so scarce and so expensive that the soldiers were put on reduced rations."[12]

Perhaps because of the intensity of the fighting and the emotive potential of a "last ditch" defense, something of a tradition has grown up around the fight for the Delaware. Charles Stedman, British officer under Howe and author of one of the early histories of the war, helped establish the notion that possession of the Delaware meant everything to the Americans and was crucial as well to the British: "the subsistence of the British troops in Philadelphia depended so much on the surrender of this fort [Fort Mifflin], that Washington exerted every nerve to preserve it. He offered one hundred pounds extraordinary bounty to every soldier who should serve in defending it during the seige."[13] The hundred-pound bounty appears to have been entirely Stedman's fancy, but the felt importance of the defense is corroborated by the American soldier, physician, and historian David Ramsay, who uses precisely the same metaphor to tell us that "the British were well apprized, that without the command of the Delaware, their possession of Philadelphia would be of no advantage. They therefore strained every nerve, to open the navigation of that river. . . ."[14] The point here is not to establish the strategic military importance of the Delaware defense—modern military historians do not often concern themselves with it—but to suggest the disproportionate stature that this "minor" engagement assumed in the minds and hearts of the participants. And that stature is quite plainly heroic.

There are several things in the diary's account of the defense which indicate that the month Greenman spent at Forts Mifflin and Mercer was his definitive military experience. Foremost among these, to be sure, is the radical departure in style: from the usual clipped, formulaic, elliptical list of dates and places toward (if not actually reaching) fully fleshed eighteenth-century sentences—sentences that exhibit a measure of accurate punctuation, significantly improved grammar and spelling, some image words, and even a rhetorical flourish or two. There is also evidence that the author took particular care in composing this section of the diary. In fact, internal features in the prose and on the physical diary pages suggest that Greenman rewrote the entire account of the Delaware action at some later time during the war. If this surmise is correct, it would both account for the strength and amplitude of the prose and attest to the importance of the battle in the eyes of the author. In the record of the Delaware defense we see, perhaps uniquely in the entire diary, Greenman the deliberate chronicler and stylist. For once he apparently had both the time and the inclination to transcend his own stated purpose in keeping a journal ("penn'd intirely for my own Amusement"), and the result is a solid and engaging attempt at history.

That the author was himself convinced of the historical importance of the defense—and of the Rhode Islanders' dramatic role in it—should be apparent to all who read this section in the context of the whole journal. In his belief Greenman was representative of a Rhode Island regimental pride extending from the highest officers to the rawest recruits.[15] Greenman's colonel, Israel Angell, wrote that the Delaware action "was an event, which, by producing consequences of great importance, threw a new appearance on the face of the affairs of both the contending powers."[16] Congress voted commendation and a sword to Col. Christopher Greene for his command in the devastating victory (22 October) over the Germans at Fort Mercer. Maj. Simeon Thayer's reputation was made for his determination at Fort Mifflin, and the Rhode Island regiments solemnly celebrated 22 October as an anniversary for years to come.[17] From that time onward, they would be regarded as crack regiments and would be employed as such at Monmouth, Newport, Springfield, and Yorktown. It is interesting to note that Sgt. Jeremiah Greenman, an untutored writer without access to the deliberations of the field officers has handed down to us the most circumstantial record of the Delaware defense written by a Rhode Islander.

With the abandonment of Forts Mifflin and Mercer, Greenman's regiment had little fighting to do in 1777. The troops participated in the skirmishing around Whitemarsh, Pennsylvania (5–8 December), but their object was the same as that of the entire army: to get into winter quarters. Greenman's year closes with a tired and hungry army gathering for food and fuel a providentially unharvested field of corn, then drawing axes "to build huts for ye winter" in a place called Valley Forge.

NOTES TO INTRODUCTION

1. Providence *Gazette*, 1 February 1777.
2. Boatner, *Encyclopedia*, p. 788.
3. Gardiner MS, Shepley Papers, RIHS, p. 333.
4. W. C. Bronson, *The History of Brown University* (Providence, R.I.: The University, 1914), p. 67.
5. Washington, *Writings*, 7:29.
6. Boatner, *Encyclopedia*, pp. 857–58. For a full description of these maneuvers, see Freeman, *Washington*, 4:428ff.
7. Washington, *Writings*, 8:499.
8. According to the Angell Orderly Book, the Second Rhode Islanders marched northward on 12 July, and the first camp entry for Peekskill is 15 July.
9. Boatner, *Encyclopedia*, p. 530.
10. Angell, Israel. *Diary of Colonel Israel Angell Commanding the Second Rhode Island Continental Regiment During the American Revolution, 1778–1781*, trans. and ed. Edward Field (Providence, R.I.: Preston and Rounds Co., 1899), p. xii.
11. Samuel S. Smith, *The Battle of Monmouth* (Monmouth Beach, N.J.: Philip Freneau Press, 1964), p. 6, and Smith, *Fight for the Delaware* (Monmouth Beach, N.J.: Philip Freneau Press, 1964), p. 16. Smith's *Fight for the Delaware* is both the most recent and the most exhaustive analysis of the defense of the river. Other important sources include Leonard Lundin, *Cockpit of the Revolution: The War for Independence in New Jersey* (Princeton: Princeton University Press, 1940), chap. 11; John W. Jackson, *The Pennsylvania Navy, 1775–1781: the Defense of the Delaware*, 2d ed. (New Brunswick, N.J.: Rutgers University Press, 1974), chaps. 8–12; and William S. Stryker, *The Forts on the Delaware in the Revolutionary War* (Trenton, N.J.: J. L. Murphy, 1970).
12. Lundin, *Cockpit of the Revolution*, p. 365. In his recent study, *The Howe Brothers*, Ira Gruber, using many British sources, comes to about the same conclusion: "Keeping Philadelphia without uninterrupted access to the sea was difficult, if not impossible" (p. 246). Gruber's book includes an excellent map (p. 245) of the lower Delaware around Forts Mifflin and Mercer, showing the land route from Chester, Pa., to Philadelphia over which the British tried to supply the occupied city.
13. Charles Stedman, *The History of the Origin, Progress, and Termination of the American War*, 2 vols. (London: J. Murray, 1794), 1:301.
14. David Ramsay, *The History of the American Revolution*, 2 vols. (1789; reprint ed., New York: Russell and Russell, 1968), 2:17, 19.
15. And, of course, to the people of the state. Said Henry Marchant, Rhode Island delegate to the Continental Congress in 1777, "It is with peculiar pleasure that I re-

flect upon the honor which the Rhode Island battalions have acquired to themselves and their state. Their reputation is high. The fort [Mercer] was defended by them alone, and to their bravery under heaven, and not to the sufficiency of the works, is that victory to be attributed" ("Revolutionary Collections," RIHS *Collections*, 6:202).

16. Israel Angell, letter to the Providence *Gazette*, 14 March 1778.

17. See, for example, Greenman's entries for 22 October 1778 and 1779.

DEFENSE OF THE DELAWARE, 1777

JANUARY: 1777 AT DARTMOUTH

W 1 to S 18. raining raw cold weather / we hear a very brisk Cannading / this [*morning*] I wen to little Comton[1] ware I got Intiligence of my last Campaigns wages / from Litele Compton to the pond / from thair to the head of ye river / from thair to poniganset[2] / very blustering weather / Snow abot 4 Inches high & cold / Spent nine shilings.

S 19. this morn cule / from acoxet crost Slaids fery / came to Swansy ware I dined / then crost Seconk fury[3] and came to providence: six pence.

M 20. this morn clowdy / Continuing in providance till 12 oClock then set off came to grinadge[4] ware I made a small halt / then I came to north kingstown.

T 21. this morn from north kingstown came to little rest ware I made a small halt and then came to south kingstown ware I put up all night.

W 22. this morn from south kingston ware I got a hores [horse] came to Charlestown ware I made a small halt / then came to Westerly to Capt wards.[5]

T 23. this morn from westerly came to little rest ware I made a small halt / then came to north kingstown / tarri'd all night.

F 24. this morn from north kingstown came to warrick[6] ware I halted sum time / then came to providence / very stormy & raining weather.

S 25. this morn clear & very warm / rece[*i*]v'd my back wages of capt ward for ye Lat[*e*] Campaign.

S 26. this morn from providence came to Swansey ware I dined

& then into acoxet in dartmouth / very bad traviling & mudey / twenty one & nine pence.

M 27 to F 31. Continuing in dartmouth / Sum Snow & warm wich soon carry away ye Snow / Nothing very Strange / Spent twenty shilings.

FEBRUARY 1777 LITTLE COMTON

February 1777: S 1 to M 3. Continuing in Dartmouth / a small mater of wrain then clear'd off warm. Went down to little Compton / at night return'd. [*cipher*].

T 4. this morn clear / Slung my pack / went to little Compton to stand guard for one month to the point[7] / Sixteen shiling and nine pence.

W 5 to S 9. Continuing in little Compton about a half a mild from the Shore 3 quarters of a mild from head Quarters / on guard every other night. one and nine pence &c.

M 10. this morn from little comton came to dartmouth ware I tari'd all night / [illeg.] shilings.

MARCH 1777 IN DARTMOUTH [*illeg.*]

S 9 to S 16.[8] Continuing in dartmouth and from Little Compton marching back & forth & to tiverton / very heavi cann[*a*]ding at the fery / the galley burnt / nothing very remarkeble / 31 dollars and 3 shilings &c.

M 17 to W 19. this morn from Little Compton came to providence ware I took barracks in ye Collage[9] ware I staye till ye 20th: [*This*] day drawe Cloths Regimental Coat & other Cloths in this time / 7 dollars and three & eight pence.

T 20. this day from providence about 12 oClock raining weather / came to Swansy ware I got sum victols [victuals] / then proceded on as far [*as*] the pond in freetown ware I put up.

F 21 to S 22. this morn from the pond came to dartmouth ware I stayed all night / in the morn set off for providence again / 15 shilings &c / lodged providence.

S 23 to T 25. very pleasant weather / Continuing in providance till ye 26 / nothing very Remarkeble / Spent 22 shilings & six pence.

W 26 to S 30. this morn from providance came to Swansy ware I dined / then proceeded on as far as Dartmouth ware I continued till the 31 / very blowing snowing and stormy weather / three and 3 pence &c.

M 31. this morn from dartmouth came to freetown ware I made a small halt / then proceded on as far as taunton ware I stayed all night / Nothin Remarkeble.

April 1777 in providance

T 1. this morn from taunton came to providance ware I tari'd all night / two and six pence.

W 2 to M 7. Continuing in providance ware we was order['*d*] for every man that had had the small pox to bee in readyness for to march to the westward:[10] hear we continued till the 8th. / three dollars.

T 8. Continuing in providence / this morn all the men that had had the small pox peraded with thair guns & packs / marcht off for Washingtons head Quarters[11] I con. in providence till jest night / then was order'd to go with ye bagage guard / Set off / Came as far as Cituate[12] ware we put up.

W 9. this morn from Cituate with the bagage Guard / came to Cranston ware we dined / then proceeded on as far as Coventre ware we tari'd all night.

T 10. this morn from Coventre came to plainfield ware we dined / then we came to Canterbury ware we made a small halt / then pr[*o*]ceded on as far as New Scotland ware we taried all night.

F 11. this morn from Scotland came to windom[13] ware we taried all day & got sum bread baked.

S 12. this morn from windom came about 6 mild ware we f[*l*]oged a man 30 lashes / then proceded on as fas[14] lebenon ware we dined then we pushed on as far as boltan ware we halted / rain & cold.

S 13. this morn from bolton came to east harford ware we put up / very raining & stormy weather.

M 14. this day marcht from east hartford / came down to ye fery[15] / ye wind blowing so hard that we could not cross with the waggons / then we return'd to east harford again. One dollar &c.

T 15. this morn from east hartford came down to the fery / Crost then came 5 milds ware we [*got*] sum prok & bread for fore days / then came to falmingtown[16] ware we halted / very bad going.

W 16. this morn we set off from falmington / came to harrington[17] ware we din'd / then we set off / came to litchfield ware we continued all night / very bad road all this day / one dollar &c.

T 17. Continuing in Litchfield / drawed provision to carry us to ye fish kilss / two days allowance.

F 18. this morn about eight oClock came from Litchfield / came to new p[*r*]eston ware we dined / then two kent ware we put [*up*] / very high mountain and mudy all the way.[18]

S 19. this morn from kent came over one or two very large mountain / then came into oblong in dutches county in hopewill[19] ware we made a small halt to mend one of ye waggons that broke coming over ye mountains / then came on a few mild & halted.

S 20. this morn from hopewill came to fish kilss ware we put up in the barracks[20] / drawe provision hear to carry us to morristown / one shiling &c.

M 21. this morn from fishkilss barracks came down to the landing ware we crossed ye river / Landed to new winsor[21] then proceded on as far as bethelem[22] ware we dined / this day left the waggon guard / then came three mild ware we put up to the high lands of york [*at*] John house.

T 22. this morn from bethelem came to Chester ware we got breakfst / then pushed on as far as Starlings Irons works[23] ware we put [*up*] and very hilley Country.

W 23. this morn from ye Iron works came to ringwood ware we made a small halt then came to wanacke ware we dined / then to pumton / very good going / lodged in pequamet in a barn / thick weather & cold for the time of year & so forth[24] / two dollars.

T 24. this morn from pequanet / very cold & raining weather / cam to bonetown[25] ware we made a small halt / then came to morristown / the town being fool [full] of troops we went about 3 milds out of town.

APRIL–MAY 1777 MORRISTOWN

F 25 to S 25. Continuing in morristown till the 25 of may 3 milds from head Quarters / our men all most ye biger part of them old

Country men wich are very bad / we are [*forced* ?] to flog them night & morning a hunder[*d*] lashes a piece / Sum will git drunk stab the genl horses wen [when] on Sentry at the door[26] / others wen on Sentry at the Comesery will leave the[*i*]r post and git drunk / atten[*d*]ing Court martial / Nothing else to day.

[*Undated entry.*] Sum Small Spits of Snow & cold / we hear that the Regular[*s*] landed up the Sound went to danbury & burnt a great Quanerty of provision & return['*d*] with the loss of a great many men[27] / fixing up our arms fit for action drawe cartirges and flints / floging 3 or 4 men every day / going to morristown / Nothing to do but walk around the Countery / thare arives Continental troops into town Every day / we hear a Cannonnading towards boun bruck[28] / very cold / we hear that head Quarters is to be moved in a few days nigher the enemy / [*an*] order for all our arms to be carried to town to have them stamped US— in this time spent eleven dollars.[29]

May–June 1777 Morristown

M 26 to T 3. very hot sultry wether / head Quarters moved from morristown towards the lines / [*A*] very unwholesum time very sickly. the men comes into town from head Quarters / very plenty small pox very brief[30] / moved our Quarters into town / Stays[*i*]oned in a Scholehouse / Nothing very Remarkeble / went to Bottle hill[31] ware I laid out two dollars / the jayl full of tories & sum other prisoners of war / a number of hasons taken.

W 4 to F 13. this day Major ward ariv'd with a number of troops[32] / we incamp this day in our tent on very dry land & durty raining weather / we ware order'd to be in readyness for to march / Spent five dollars / Nothing very remarkeble.

S 14. this morn at ye beet of ye Genl[33] struck our tents / marcht off from morris town / came to pluckemin ware we took quarters in a Church ware we was order['*d*] to lay on our arms / one dollar.

S 15 & M 16. Continuing in pluckemin ware we turn'd out about day light / exersised with our packs on then grounded our arms for about three owers / then it began to wrain & [*so we*] took them up again / very hot weather & c forth.

T 17. this morn very early slung our pack march[*t*] from our Quarters with 2 days provision / marcht about 6 milds & grounded our arms till late in the afternoon / then took them up march[*t*] toward our Quarters then ware order['*d*] to turn back again / we turn'd back went on a large hill called rockey hill ware we grounded our arms[34] & [*were ordered*] to lay by them & not be from them / Spent two dollars & four Shillings.

W 18. this morn arose very early / marcht jist below ye hill ware we exersised sum / then at night marcht on ye hill again & lay on our arms / three Shillings.

T 19. this morn moved below the hill on a very rockey piece of land ware our tents was braut to us and we pitched them / drawed provision & was order'd to cook it all up / part of a rigement joyned our brigade this afternoon / we hear that the regulars is remov'd from Sumer Set[35] after setting a number of housan[36] on fire as they wen[*t*] back / two dollars.

F 20. this morn after drawing [*provision*] & cooking it ware order'd to hold our Selvs in readyness for a march / we was about 4 milds from head Quarters / in ye afternoon struck our tents / marcht down to brige water in Sumerset County ware we incamped in the woods & C.[37]

S 21. this morn remov'd from ye woods into a pease of plain land and pitched our tent a mild & a half from head Quarters / in the afternoon struck our tents again / marcht off about 2 mild on very livel pease of land ware we pitched our tents / about 12 oClock at night was alarmed / march[*t*] off left our tents standing / marcht as far as milstone[38] ware we made a small halt then came thro boun bruck ware we made a small halt till day light.[39]

S 22. at Sun rise this morn marcht towards brumswick[40] but the enemy being all peraded ware we was to go in we retreated back again about 2 milds / about 12 oClock march[*t*] into brumswick / we advanced towards the enemy but our men being very much fateagued we could not follow after them but the light hores had a small brush with them / we lay in a duch Church all night / lay['*d*] on our arms.

M 23. Continuing in brumswick / sarching the town all over / drawe 3 days provision / Cooked it all up / four shilings and eight pence.

T 24. this morn at day light left Brumswick / marcht to Bolington ware we mad a small halt / then we marched towards the enemy a bout 6 thousand of us / then at night march[*t*] to Samptown ware we lay in an orchard / very cold & C.

W 25. this morn from Samptown came to quibeltown[41] ware we incamp a half a mild from town in a very thick woods ware we drawed sum provision / Spend two Dollars and four pence.

T 26. Continuing in the wood till about eleven oClock / then we was alarmed & left a mos [almost] all our provision / hear it was order['*d*] for all ye Sick to be sent away / we march[*t*] from Quibeltown / came to a very thick wood ware we were order'd to lay on our arms / our light hores ingaged the enemy & took one or two.

F 27. Continuing in the wood cal'd linkkins Gap we marcht in to a plain peace of land ware the Chaplin went to prayer[42] then return'd to ye woods again.

S 28. Continuing in ye wood / very plesant / holding our Selvs in readyniss to ingage ye enemy not being more than 3 milds from them / about 10 oClock at night was alarmed / marcht about a half a mild & return'd to the woods again

June–July 1777 on a march

S 29 to T 1. this morn rain / moved out of the woods into our ten[*t*]s jist below the hill / the bagage ariv'd but lost almost all my Cloths / we hear that the regulars is quited the Jersies & we are order'd to be in readyness for a march in ye morn[43] / two or thre men desarted.

W 2. this morn at ye beet of ye Genl struck our tents slung our packs from linkkins gap came as far as bown bruck ware we got our breakfast / then proceeded on as far as Barskinrige[44] ware we dined / from thence came to morristown ware we pitched our tents / we hear a Number of ye enemy is imbarked from New York.

T 3. this morn from morristown came to Cituate ware we eat breakfast / then proceeded on as far as pumton ware we put up / had orders to be in readyness for to march in ye morn at 2 oClock.

F 4. this morn very early marcht from pumton / marcht as far as yapor [?] ware we halted a little while / then came to the Clove or Quantrom ware we pitched our tent[45] / draw'd sum provision & cooked it / then struck our tents jist at night / came as far as kearkreart[46] ware we put up being fatiagued very bad / 1 or 2 men draped dead with heat wen marching.

S 5. this morn from kearkreart marcht about 3 milds / made a halt till ye after part of ye day / then marcht as far as haverstraw[47] ware we put up in a barn / very hot sultry weather & C.

S 6. this morn turn['*d*] out very early / grounded our arms / very cold indeed & blustering till about Sun rise / then proceeded on as far as kings fery ware we continued till most night / then crost ye fery / went on [*a*] hill jist by peekskills ware we pitched a few tents & lay all night.[48]

M 7. Continuing in peekskills ware we drawed provision / Sum of ye Regiment come up who informs us that the rest of ye rigment is on the march.

T 8. Continuing at ye peekskills about 1 mild from ye North river[49] very raining and squaly weather.

W 9 to M 21. Continuing in peekskills / a Scouting party return'd that took a Number of Cattle & Sum Cann[*on* ?] / Sum Shoes came into camp / very clowdy and sultry weather / Sum Continental troops ariv'd / Implying myself[50] in making a coat / Sum men desarted / took off three horses with them / a very great disturbance among ye men conserning thair wages / went to Nomber two[51] / Spent one Dollar / Sum vessels came almost up to ware our camp [*was*] / the bigger part of ye Rigement marcht off for kings brige[52] Sum more of our men return'd / we ware order'd to be in readyness for a march.

T 22 to S 27. this morn from peekskils came about 6 milds / came to a hill ware Sum Troops had left ware we pitched our tents at a place called Crumb pond[53] ware we continued till the 28th ware we hear that the Regulars landed in the State of Conaticut & did a great deal of damage thair[54] / a party of men sent on Command two fort Montgomery / two men hanged at fishkils / we hear that ye regular is got up to providence / our Stores is ariv'd ware we drawed Sum Sugar & Coffie / we ware order'd to be in readyness for a march / in ye after noon marcht off as far as N 2 [Number Two].

M 28 to T 31. Continuing in Nom two / very unhealthy in camp / the mesals very plenty.

August 1777 on a march

F 1 to T 19. Continuing in No 2 untill ye 19th / we exspect the inemy up the river / Colo Greens rigmt mov'd to fort Montgomery / we hear a number of french vessels is in ye bay of Saint Lawrance bound for Quebeck / a man hanged for being Spy by order of genl putnam[55] / we hear that ye enemy is almost got down to alberny[56] / very raining weather / our [*blank*] ariv'd who inform us that the rest of ye regiment is on ye march. a Comman[*d*] of men about 50 gone out of our Rigement / we keep hear in readyness for the enemy movement / we ware order'd to be in readyness for to march / packed up our things / drawed 2 days provision.

W 20. this day very raining wether / about 8 oClock marcht from Nom: 2 / Came to New Caswill ware we put up in a barn.[57]

T 21. this morn set [*out*] very early for the white plains / a large Nom of Militia set off with us and lite hores[58] / came to white plains ware we made a small halt til Night / then pushed on as fas mild Square[59] / made a halt.

F 22. this morn marcht from mild Square to East Chester ware made a halt / very hot wether / the Inhabitance left the biger part of ye housand / hear a detachment of our men marcht towards the enemy lines / took a number of fut men & two or thre lite hores / then retreated back from the ground / came thro New rochel / lodg['*d*] in maneck[60] / spent one shiling.

S 23. this morn from manneck came a small distance / came to ry neck[61] ware we made a halt a few moments / then came to king Street ware we put up and drawed sum provision[62] / very raining weather / at night we was alarmed by sum tories that fir'd at our Senterys but could not find them & so f.

S 24. this morn thick clowdy weather / marcht from king street / at Night came to North Caswill ware we taried all night / 1 shilling.

M 25. this morn from North Caswill came to Crumbpond ware we made a small halt then proceeded on as far as Nom 2.

T 26 to S 31. Continuing in Nom 2 / we hear that we lost 100 men on Stranton Island & 14 hunderd of ye enemy taken prisoners / Great Confuson in Colo Green['*s*] Rigmt about Clothing &C[63] / we had a field day / hole of ye brigad appear'd on ye grand perade [&] fir'd a number of Cannon and small arms / very cold weather and no Clothing.

SEPTEMBER 1777 NOM. 2

M 1 to S 28. Continuing in Nom 2 wating for a movement of ye enemy / thare was a man sat on ye gallos 50 minuits then taken down & floged 50 lashes[64] / we hear a Number of ye kings troops desarted & a Number more taken prisoners / Genl Putman order'd all ye old Country men that had desarted from ye kings troops to appear on ye grand perade ware thay was order'd to be sent to georgy to keep garrison[65] / the men that was in ye provost gua[*r*]d that was condemned this day was [*taken*] to gallos hill to be executed & was reprieved by the genl[66] / colo onley['*s*] party ariv'd from Norwalk[67] / a party of ye rigement ariv'd from Coventry / we hear that genl washington['*s*] army is [has] killed a great Number of the enemy.[68] we hear that ticontiroge is taken again by our people / we hear that philadelpha is taken by how[*e*] / we hear very good News from ye Northward army / our Rigement past muster / we ware order'd to pack up all our things to be ready for a march.

M 29. this day at the beet of ye Genl struck our tents / from Nom 2 came to peekskils ware we made a small halt / then we came to the landing at fish kills ware we stay'd.

T 30. this morning marched down to the Landing / Crossed the North River and came to Haverstraw where we floged a Man 30 Lashes for Desertion / went on to kearkeart where put up—

OCTOBER 1777

W 1. Continuing in kearkkeart till 3 oClock / then came 5 miles where we pup.[69]

T 2. this morning came to the Clove where we made a halt, then came to Pumton where we halted.

F 3. this morning from pumton came to pequamet where we made a halt to execute but he made his Escape from the Guard, from hear set out / Came to Morristown where we drawed Provision.

S 4. Continuing in Morris Town till 3 oClock / then came to Veal Town[70] where made a halt in the woods.

S 5. this morning from Veal Town came as far as jarmantown[71] where we made a small halt / then set off came to Badmister[72] where put up in the woods—

M 6. this morn from Badmister came as far as Flemton[73] where made a small halt / then proceeded on our March to Amwell where we drew Provision,[74] then pushed on to Mount fair where we put up [,][75] the Brittish Army being in possession of Philadelphia. but the Comunication was not oppen with their Fleet & when Genl Washington left the Town he took care to poste a Garrison in Fort Mifflin, not as strong as the importance & exigence of the place did require but such as the Army could afford / Colo Green & Angells Regts. was ordered to Read Bank opposite Mifflin—[76]

T 7. this morning from Mount fair came to Correlis ferry where we crossed the Dilleware[77] & drew Provision / then marched the biger part of the Night and stopped in Plumstage in the woods—[78]

W 8. this morning from Plumstage came 8 miles where mad a halt in a thick woods in hiltown where we received orders to march back / Stayed on the ground 'till Sun Set / then came to Plumstage where incamp[*t*] the Night Before.

T 9. this morning from Plumstage / very raining & stormy / came to Newtown where we halted / had two barrels of Cyder and delt them out to the Regiment.

F 10. this morning from Newtown came to Middle Town[79] where we made a halt & received orders to march Back to join the Grand Army[80] / hear lef Colo Greens Regt and came 4 miles where made a halt and cooked sum provision / then came thro Newtown from where came to wrights Town where halted.

S 11. this morning from wrights Town came to Newbritton[81] where we drew provision & washed our Cloathing—

S 12. Continuing in Newbritton washing our Cloathing—

M 13. this morning from New Britton came to Head Quarters where we continued untill the 16th in which time we are informed of the Sucksess of our army to the Northward / the Army gave the Chears & fired 13 Cannon—[82]

T 16. this morning at the beet of the Genl. struck our Tents / Marched to New Britton where made a small halt then went into a wood where we incamped.

F 17. this morning impresed sum Waggons at writes Town, came as far as Bristol where a Gentle[*man*] treated the Regiment, then crossed the Dileware at Burlington[83] where we drew sum Provision and marching half a mile from Burlington to a wood where we halted and kooked our Provision / about 11 o'clock we proceeded on to Mount Holley where we drew sum Lequor and pushed on till day Break / on our March to this place kicked a posson, a very strang kind of a Creature having a falce belly or place to carry its yong in / hear continued till Sun wrise.

S 18. this day pushed on to Hattonfield[84] where we halted and drew sum Provision / then pushed on to Read Bank at Fort Mercy[85] / we lodged on our tents, & very cold—

S 19. we are informed on our arrival hear[86] that two Bomb batterys which the Enemy had erected on fort Mifflin, which they left unsupported gave an oppertunity to Colo. Smith to order a sally above & below, & the two partys supported by the gallies under Commodore Hazlewood[87] they landed on the Beach of Province Island & stormed the Batterys, which was defended by two officers & 60 Brittish, who surrendered themselves and where carried into the Fort before the Enemy's Guards could attack the party but not before the Guns where spiked up / this small check caused the Enemy to be more cautous, & the guard of their Trenchment was afterwards so strong that it became imposable to make any other attempt. we keep very Constant Fire one [on] batterys which the Enemy was erecting to reduce for[*t*] Mifflin, and indeed it was very weak[,] Nothing more than a wooden fort especilly on the Side which we wanted for Defense, on the Side of New Jersey very dangerous for the Splinters[88]—& quite unfit to support a Sige / the enclosure was of Pallsades,[89] on the Side of Province Island; and in front opposite to Hog Island a Water Battery [*of*] 10-or a dozen guns, 18 pounders / The Enemy where not unaquainted with the Miserable Situation of the Fort and their Chife Enginear Montresor, who had been imploy'd in its Constructions, knew its weakness, & the most proper means to reduce it,[90] Accordingly the Enemy employed a Great Number of men on Povince Island to raise more Batterys againts the fort, and covering works on the Hights in their Rear, for their Protection againts the attack that might possibly happen from Genl. Washington by the Side of Derby[91] / the Garrison of the Fort was quite inadequate to its extensiveness & the heavy duty, which required 1500 men in stead of the 500 which had been left for the Defense of the place & two thirds of these whare Jersey Militia / in the mean time the Enemys Batterys had got ready to play very smartly on the Fort, two bomb Battrys[92] three 3 Gun Batteries, one of Six Guns 24 pounder between the two lower block houses, the other at the Hospital Warf of 5-24 pounders & one intermediary upon the Little Warf of Communication between Province Island and Mud Island,[93] a Bridge of Boats was built at the lower ferry, for the Communication between the division at the Trenches & the Main camp Philadelphia / two other Batterys were likewise raised on the point of land, at the Mouth of the Schuylkill, to cut off the upper Navigation of the River, we all this time ware not inactive[94] for we raised two 18 pounder batterys againts the Enemys Main Battery a nother of two 9 pounders to annoy the Batterys on the warf, we [*had*] our Magazine secured againts Shells, we endeavoured to cover ourselves againts the Shots of Province Island and diged in the inside of the Fort a Square Intrenchmt, but could not find any Means to secure againts the bombs & Carecases,[95] except under the wall which faced the Jersey Shore, & that lay all open to the Shipping and it was very much to be feared that a Storm would be attempted, we surrounded the fort with wolf holes and Vertical Pickets[96] to render the approach more difficult and wake up the Defenders[97] / a sevear fire was keep by the Enemy on us, the two west block housan were ruined & the north one blew up by the fall of several Shells by which two or three men was killed & two or three more wounded, the enemy seeing this hoped to soon be in possession of the Fort & as it was very important, for their remaining in Philadelphia to have the Communication open to their Shipping.[98]

M 20. this day we hear that Burgines Army is all captured at which this fort and fort Mercy fired 13 Cannon[99] & all the Shipping, the Gallies went down to the Chevaux Defrizes[100] & drove one or two Ship that was trying to get up to have fore play on the Fort / we took 6 men & a Serjt. that was in a boat going to Province Island from the Shipping.

T 21. Continuing at fort Mifflin / the duty very hard indeed / keep a continual fire on the Enemy & they on us with hot Shot & Shells, & building a Nother Battery to open on the fort.

W 22. this morning are informed that a party of the Enemy crossed Cooper fery[101] last Evening and was on their way thro Haddonfield for this Fort / Came a crost this morn from Fort Mifflin / had scarce an opportunity to git into the Fort, before a

Flag came to Colo. Green,[101] who commanded the Fort threatning to put the Garrison to [*death* ?] if he did not surrender it immediately, Colo. Green answered with disdain, that he would defend it 'till the last drop of his Blood—as soon as the Flag had returned they oppined 7 field peaces & 2 Howitzers on the fort and played very smartly for about ten moments then rushed on very Rash that even Success could not justify its temerity / they attacked on the North & South Sides, the North Side was a brea[*st*] work within a nother which we cut off and made the Fort small as we had but few men to man it especially the Bigness it was wen we first arrived,[102] the Parapet was high the Dikes deep / a row of strong pallesaids sallied out from the parapit on the gate on the South Side / we had a small place big enough for eight men to fight in which overlooked all the ground round the Fort which was surrounded with double abattis[103] / Both of the attacks where such as was expected / the artillery & Musquetry of the fort Great Slawter / they advanced as far as the abbatis, but they could not remove it (tho sum few got over) being repulsed with great loss / they left their Command'g officer dying on the Ground in his glacis, and retreated with hurry & Confusion[104] / they rallied in the woods and leaving thear Dead wounded & a few prisoners (which was under the walls of the Fort that could not handely retreat) in all amounting to about three hundred in our hands they returned to Philadelphia that Night—we feched in to the fort all the Wounded & dressed them shewing as [*much*] humanity as posable.[105] Colo. Donop was attended with care / in the attack we lost 7 of our Regiment killed & 14 Wounded / [*One*] of the Killed proved to be my Capn. Shaw who was shot thro the Neck[106] / in all Killed and Wounded it amounted to 31—[107]

T 23. the fore part of this day implying ourselves in burying the dead 73 buried in one grave 4 or 5 in [*an*]other & C[108] / about 9 o'clock the Ships Eagle, Summersit, Isis, agusta, Pearl Leverpool & Several Fregates with a Galley, came up to the Chevaux de frize 500 yards from the fort, at the same time the Land Batteries & our gallies, & the Brittish S[*q*]uadron engaged and one of the Most Solumest Actions commenced, that may be seen by a soldiers eye, the Spectacle was magnificent, to see at once, the river covered with Ships, four great fire ships, in a blase, floating on the Water / the Island & Main covered with Smoak & fire / part of the English

Army drew up in battle array on Province Island ready to th[*r*]o them selves into boats, to storm the Fort, which appeared involved with fire & was the prise of the day, the firing lasted 'till 2 o'clock PM. with [*rel*]entless fury. The Fort frequently fired red hot balls / Likewise one of the floating Batterys & either by chance or good luck one of these shot set [*afire*] the Augusta,[109] a 64 gun Ship, the nearest to the Chevaux de frize / [*She*] suddenly took fire at the stern, and in a moment She wass in a blase, & soon after blew up, with a thundering noise, before the Enemy could take out all their hands (our gallies was so nigh her at this time that several peaces fell on board of them in which one officer & a number of men [*were*] wounded[)] / a Moment after the Merlin, a 22 gun Frigate ran a shore below the Agusta nigh to this shore[110] so that she was reached by Genl. Varnum's Battery,[111] and as she could not be moved from the explosion, took fire & also blew up,[112] the other ships frightened by the fate of those two retired below hog island, & the Land Batteries (which had hoised the Blody flag to warn the garrison that they were not to expect any quarter) continuing the firing from Province Island 'till Evening & then a plenty of Shells / the troops that where to storm did not attempt & the Victory yet remained to the fort and gallies.

F 24 to T 30. we hourly expect a nother visit from the Enemy, a flag went to Philadelphia / Sum hasan Doctors returned to take care of their wounded,[113] ordered to lay on our arms—Nothing more Remarkable only the Enemy keep a very constant fire on fort Mifflin & on[*c*]e in a while give us a shot from a 32 pound at Hospital.

F 31. this day buried the Hasan Colo. [*von Donop*] who said previous to his Death I fall a Victim to my own ambition & to the avarice of my prince; but, full of thankfulness for the good treatment I have received from my generous Enemy, he was buried with the Honours of War,

November 1777

S 1. this day we hung two who piloted the hasans to this fort,[114] the Enemy crossing the Schoolkill River with a large Number of Waggons / rain & cold.

S 2 to S 9. Genl. Varnum's Brigade with about eleven hundred men went about 3 miles below this fort[115] / Colo. Smith by his being absent by sickness was superceeded by the Barron Detrand a prusan officer [*who*] joined us again[116] / the garrison by this time was very much reduced by the Dead, Wounded, Sick, and it was thought proper to relieve part of it / Some Pennsylvania & Virginia Troops took place of the Militia / the fetigue in a place where no body could sleep on account of the numerious shells, & the Garrison not having any covering was as great as the Danger [*to*] the Salt Provision [*from*] the water which was obliged to be waided into up to the knees, the cold nights & especially for the want of sleep, turned the men to the Hospital & the inclemency of the Wether almost insupportable in the Fort / in the beginning of the Sige the Garrison had opened the beach of Province Island, in ord[*er*] to overflow it[117] / the Enemy filled up the Trench again, but with not sufficient Care; for a heavy Wind at NE raised the Water so high and increased its Strength so much that it brock [broke] the Beach, & almost overflowed the Island, Mud Island was drowned as much as the opposite shore, the water was two feet deep in the fort & all the barracks that yet remain where filled with it, at this time the fire was neither heavy no[*r*] continual—[118]

M 10. this day the Enemy set out a new, resolving if posable to reduce the fort, knowing if it was not done they would be obliged to evacuate Philadelphia, [*they*] oppened three more batteries upon it & keep up an incessant fire on the Fort, all the pallisades where broken dow[*n*], the Diches filled up with Mud by the strong tides, Capn. Treet,[119] who distinguished himself by his bravery, and his Lieut, was killed / the Garrison exhausted & almost reduced.

T 11. this morn cule / We burst an eighteen pounder which was got from the wreck of the agusta, and killed one Many & by the Scales & peaces of the Carrage Eighteen More where slightly wounded—[120]

W 12. Colo. Smith was wounded and went out of the [*fort*] with the old Garrison, being relieved by Major Thare with sum of our men,[121] the Enemy now began to doubt the promises of their Enginer Montresor who had constructed the Fort & had bosted at the beginning that he would reduce it in a few days, but thought all invain expecting very little from their Land Batteries.

T 13. but this morn we found a New Battery opened on the Fort, but as long as the Shipping keep below the Chevaux defrize we where in hopes, the c[*h*]annel between Hog Island & Tinicut had been stopped,[122] the tides by the Chevaux defrize in the main channel had opened a new current, and the River was deeper than it was thought to be & several sail of Vessels passed the Fort with Provision to Philadelphia this Evening—

F 14. this day the Enemy sem to be very buisey on hog Island & Tinicut, we burst a 24 pounder this day that was got from the wreck of the agusta / they keep a very constant fire from the Batteries on the Fort.

S 15. this morning about 8 oClock the Enemy made a furious attack, by the River, & land / the Ships came as near to the Fort as posable in the Main Channel, & a large East Indiaman they cut down & mounted 20 24 pounders on her.[123] She came up under the protection of the Land Batteries, behind Hog Island & anchored four yards from the Angle of the SW Battery, the Fort had been very much exposed on this side / than [then] on it, did not remain one Single Gun excep those that was dismounted / Major Thayer ordered a 32 pounder to be carried thare, which was effected with great trouble & danger, this was done before the Ship got up / this single gun put 14 Shot into her bow but as soon as She was farly at anchor she began to play, all resistance became imposable, in 3 or 4 Broad Sides and from the tops with Cowhorn filled with Grape Shot so that it was almost imposable for a man to move without being killed,[124] not only the parapet & the carrages, but even the Iron of the guns were broken the platforms destroyed an[*d*] in half an hour, not a Gun in the fort was able to fire, Soon after this the Vigilant a Sloop carring 18 guns[125] came up & anchor'd above her, played againts the Fort all the afternoon (with her Cannon & bombs) / the gallies at the same time employed againts the ships, & shells poring from Province Island, we was not able to give them any assistance (the Ships laying so nigh the Chevaux defrize that it was almost imposable to pass with boats from us to them in this critical situation[)] / a storm was expected all the afternoon / the Garrison buried in ruins unable to retreat during the day & unwilling to do it, as long as they could expect a reingforsment, had not much expectation but to sell their selvs as dear as they could, however the Enemy did not profit this moment / Major Thayer asembled a Counsel of War in the midst of the firing a little before Night,[126] it was imposable [*to*] defend the fort with so small a Force & it was determined to call for a Reingforcement from Fort Mercy & if they could not reingfors to evacuate the Fort, Before the Counsel of War broke up Major Fleury who commanded the Infentry Battery that day was wounded by the bursting of a shell & an officer of Artilery killed / at ten o clock [P.M.] no Reingforcement went from us but was sent with boats to fech them off / it was become imposable [*to defend*] the Fort any longer / open on all sides, without a single gun, it was no longer a Defence for the River, during the Transaction of ye day Major Talbert[127] was wounded with a Musquet ball —Major Thayer evacuated the Fort with a Degree of fermness equal to the Bravery of his defence, he set fire to the Remains of the Barracks & with less than two hundred men carried off all the wounded & most of the Stores / he arrived hear about 12 oclock in the night.

S 16 & M 17. this morning we had a few 32 pounder sent among us from the Hospital Battery, the Colours was left flying which we saw in the morning halled down by the Enemy—[127]the Field officers holding a Counsel of War, which we suppose is concerning the evacuation of this place—[128]

T 18 & W 19. we hear a number of the Enemy is marching for this post, at 10 oclock at night we received orders to march & struck our tents, loading them into waggons & took what provision we liked / destroyed the remainder, then proceeded on to Haddon Field where we made a halt.

T 20. Continuing in haddonfield / a party of men sent back to ye fort with a Serjeant to stay thair till ye enemy appeared then to blow ye fort up / Sum waggons ariv'd this afternoon with sum clothes / a quanterty of flower came in from the fort / order'd to lay on our arms.

F 21. this morn about 4 o clock slung our packs march[*t*] from haddon came to morestown[129] ware made a small halt / then proceded on as far as moun halle[130] ware we made a halt / lodged in a barn & very cold.

S 22 & S 23. Continuing in mount hole / this day ye biger part of ye Rigement drawed Clothes &c / we ware ordered to be in ready ness for a march / about ten oClock order'd to sling our packs / we marcht to the uper end of the town ware we made a halt / was orderd to bring in the returns of each company what men was fit for duty. then return'd to our quarters again / drawed 50 rounds of carteriges & C.

M 24. this morn ware ordered to get our breakfast very soon

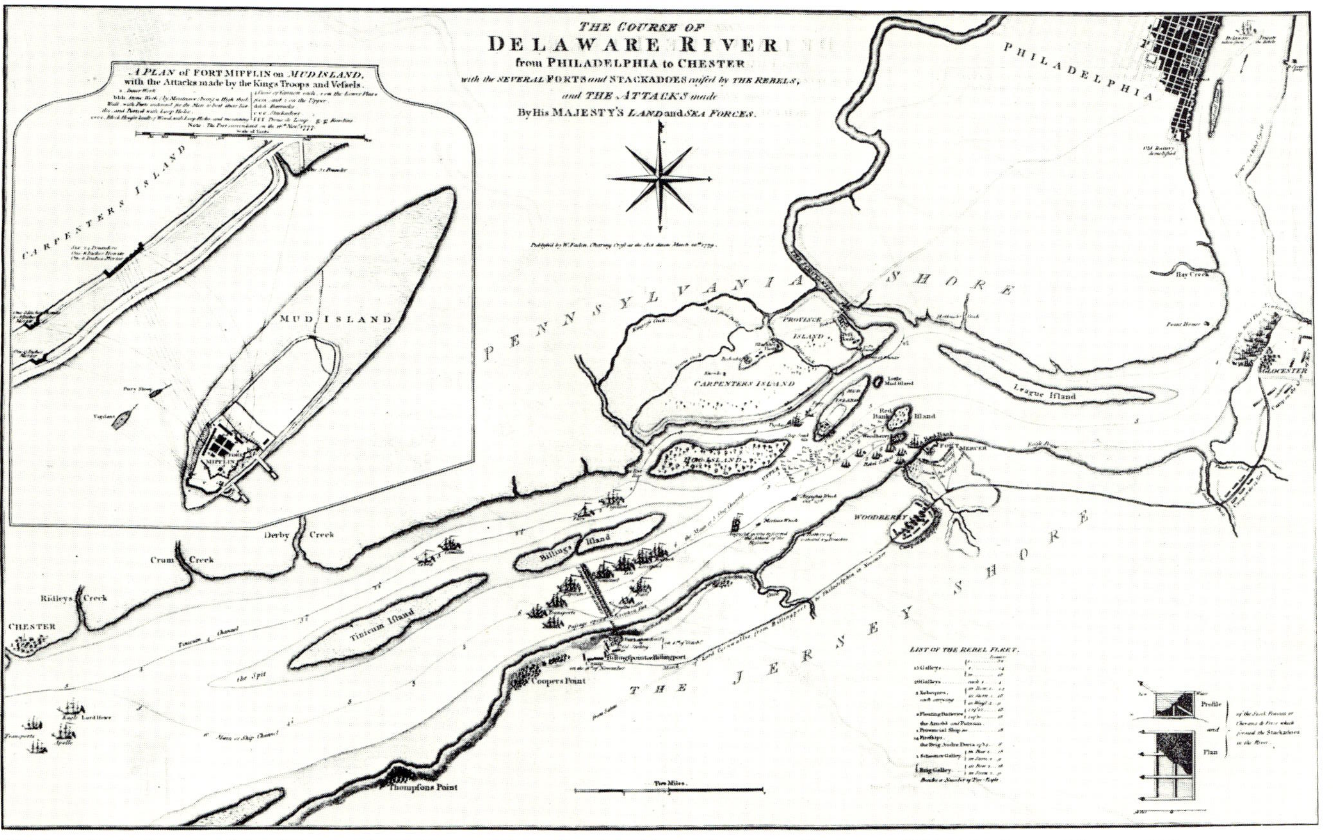

William Faden's map of the fight for the Delaware River, October–November 1777. Courtesy of The Newberry Library, Chicago.

[...] in Dartmouth

Continuing in Dartmoth
to fair haven Bedford &
round ye Cauntery Nothing
Remarkeble 16 Sh3739go

Novembr friday 7 1778
Nothing Strange onley
flieing News &c. L13d2.
05t S3x p439d f302 Sh3739go
and eaght peqee

this day went to Rhode Island
Cols Ritchmonds Regement
Returned from long Island
who Inform us of killing & taking
a number of tories on long Islan
with Los of one man and one
or two wounded very Cold
for ye time of year

Entries showing one of Greenman's ciphers, used mostly to record expenses.

to go to incamp / we fixed our things / marcht about half a mild & piched our tents on a hill ware [*was*] ordered to draw a days provision & be in readyness for a march & C.

T 25. in mount holey on ye hill in our tents / very cold / drawed 3 day[*s*] provision / marcht from mount holey / came to mores[*town*] ware we built up fiers and made a small halt / then again we proceeded on our march to haddonfield / went about a mild from town & encampt in a thick woods & C.

W 26. Continuing in ye woods near haddonfield / two hasans desar'd from ye enemy [*and*] came to us at night / we built buth to lay in[131] very cold.

T 27. this morn we marcht from the woods / came to morestown ware we made a small halt & then proceeded on as far as mount holey ware our tents was / ordered to be in readyness for a march.

F 28. this morn at ye beet of ye genl struck our tents came as far as burlington ware we made a halt / then crost ye Diliware / came to bristol ware we grounded our arms in a field about a mild from town / then we march[*t*] about two milds from town on ye other [*side*] ware we grounded our arms. then went to town / draw'd provision for ye Rigement / then came back / delt it out / then proceeded on our march as far as ye [*illeg.*][132] ware we incamped in ye woods very cold & clowdy wether.

S 29. this morn about 5 oClock very cold & raining turn'd out from among our leavs / very wet & cold / marcht all day in ye rain / at night incampt in ye woods near Crucked billet ware we drawed sum mutton & flower & C.[133]

S 30. Continuing in ye woods near crooked billit till 4 oClock in ye after noon / then marcht off for head Quarters[134] / very muddy & bad marching / at night came to wite ma[*r*]sh ware we built up housan of branchis & leavs to keep ye rain off but not much good.

DECEMBER 1777. WHITE MASH

M 1 to W 10. this morn turn'd out very cold / slung our packs marcht off about two milds on a hill ware we built up buth ware we continued until ye eleventh in wich time we was alarmed a number of times & ordered to cook our provision & fit for a march / we see great lights to the Northward more than common.[135] we marcht down on a plain peas of ground jist below the hill ware we incamped

& formed a line ware we continued a few owers / then came to our buths again / we hear that ye enemy is advancing towards ye hill / we soon paraded our selves & formed on top of ye hill & sent out guards Colo morgan[136] atacked them at the left of ye army / killed & took a few of them & [*at*] night they went on a hill / both army incamped in sight of one a nother / in ye morn discharged a few volleys at each other / then the enemy retreated in to Philadelphia again taking all ye cattle they could carry with them & forrages / we hear they are bound for halifax / we hear a number of shiping is gone down the river / we ware ordered to be in readyness to march in ye mor[*n*] very early.

T 11. this m[*orn*] turned [*out*] very early / marcht up to the grand perade grounded our arms till light / the[*n*] we marcht off / came about 5 milds towards Scoolkills / then turn['*d*] back / came to a cros road / came 2 milds then incampt / we heard a very brisk firing. Snow Sum Small Spits.

F 12. Continuing ware incamped, till Night / then marcht off / came near Scoolkill river ware that our people was crosing. hear we lay till morn / rain & cold / then crost ye river.

S 13 to T 18. came about 5 milds and incamped in a thick woods ware we drawed sum provision and ordered to cook it / in ye morning we was peraded ware we heard prayers / we ware order'd to lay on our arms [*and*] be in reddyness for to march in ye morn / our order was countermanded / very short of provision / drawed a gill of wrise[137] / raining weather / boyled sum cattles feet and dined & C.

F 19. this morn ye hole camp moved about 6 milds & stoped in a thick woods[138] ware a corn field stud by / about 10 acres not gethered / in 5 minits it was all gethered & sum of it to the fire.

S 20 to W 31. Continuing near vally forg / we drawed axes to build huts for ye winter / we began our huts / order'd to build them with logs 14 feet one way & 16 ye other / Continuing building our huts / nothing very Remarkeble & C / mov'd in.

NOTES TO DIARY

1. Little Compton, R.I. The towns mentioned in this section of the diary are in the area of eastern Rhode Island and adjacent Massachusetts, or across Narragansett Bay in southwestern Rhode Island.

2. The Aponiganset River (Massachusetts), also known as the Pamanset.

3. Greenman indifferently spells "ferry" as "fery," "fury," and "phery." The Seaconk Ferry (upper and lower) was a much-used communication between Providence and points in Massachusetts, while Slaid's Ferry (Massachusetts) crossed the Taunton River (see Nebenzahl, *Atlas*, pp. 94–95, and Anna A. Chapin and Charles V. Chapin, *A History of Rhode Island Ferries, 1640–1923* [Providence, R.I.: Oxford Press, 1925], pp. 126ff.).

4. East Greenwich, R.I.

5. Samuel Ward, Jr., had commanded Greenman's company on the march to Quebec in 1775 (see part 1). His father was "three times Governor of Rhode Island, and for a year Chief Justice of the Supreme Court." The Ward homestead was "in the Weekapaug district, about five miles south east of the present town of Westerly" (Bernard Knollenberg, ed. *The Correspondence of Governor Samuel Ward, May 1775–March 1776* [Providence, R.I.: Rhode Island Historical Society, 1952], pp. 3, 5, 35).

6. Warwick, R.I.

7. That is, he was assigned to watch for British naval activity in the East Passage, probably near Sakonnet or Warren Point.

8. Two pages are here missing from the bound fascicles of the diary; hence the gap between 11 February and 9 March.

9. Rhode Island College, now Brown University (see the introduction to this chapter).

10. Greenman does not mention here or elsewhere that he has had the smallpox nor that he has been inoculated for it, but as he does accompany the troops "to the westward," one or the other must have been the case. If he escaped the ravages of the disease while in Canada, that fact strongly implies a childhood exposure, for the chances of being exposed to the smallpox during an epidemic are practically 100 percent. On the other hand, doctors at this time were regularly holding inoculation clinics in the area, and Greenman may have gone to one of these without setting down the fact, as did Capt. Stephen Olney of the Second Rhode Island Regiment. He records that he was "inoculated for the small pox at Coventry in April 1777" (Olney Narrative, Shepley Papers, RIHS, p. 13). The process of inoculation or variolation was considered far less dangerous than natural exposure and involved transplanting the infection from the sores of a victim into an incision in the skin of a healthy person. This was followed by a period of quarantine, while the milder form of the disease ran its course (John Duffy,

Epidemics in Colonial America [Baton Rouge: Louisiana State University Press, 1953], pp. 24, 41, 56).

11. Their goal was the American encampment at Morristown, N.J. The route through Connecticut was the so-called upper road to the Hudson, followed by the French army under Rochambeau in the march (1781) to Yorktown. The splendid route-maps drawn by the French topographers are the definitive representations of the way taken by Greenman and his regiment several times during the war (Howard C. Rice, Jr., and Ann S. K. Brown, eds. and trans., *The American Campaigns of Rochambeau's Army, 1780, 1781, 1782, 1783*, 2 vols. [Princeton: Princeton University Press, 1972], 2:9–39, and maps 14–25). The famous French soldier and traveler the Marquis de Chastellux has amply and engagingly described the route's points of interest in his *Travels* (1:78–87).

12. Scituate, R.I.

13. Windham, Conn.

14. Abbreviation for "as far as."

15. Across the Connecticut River from East Hartford to Hartford.

16. Farmington, Conn.

17. Harwinton, Conn.

18. The baggage train apparently crossed the height now known as Mt. Bushnell (Conn., elevation 1100 ft.) between New Preston and Kent.

19. "Hopewill" is now Hopewell Junction in Dutchess County, N.Y. The Oblong was a narrow strip of land on the Connecticut-New York border ceded to New York in 1683 and now part of Dutchess County (Chastellux, *Travels*, 1:84, 263–64).

20. Fishkill, N.Y., on the east bank of the Hudson, was at various times during the war an American supply depot, barracks, and encampment.

21. New Windsor, N.Y., opposite Fishkill Landing by the ferry (Freeman, *Washington*, 5: map, p. 117).

22. Greenman's characteristic way of spelling "Bethlehem." In this case he is referring to Bethlehem Meeting House, on the road southward from New Windsor to Chester (ibid).

23. Throughout the war there was activity along the Ramapo River at forges such as Sterling's and at the furnace in nearby Ringwood, N.J. "The Ringwood works furnished the American armies a variety of iron products from miscellaneous hardware, camp stoves, and ordnance items to major components of the great chains used to obstruct the Hudson." The master of Ringwood Ironworks was Robert Erskine (1735–1780), who became chief geographer and mapmaker for Washington in 1778 (Boatner, *Landmarks*, pp. 213–14).

24. The three New Jersey towns Greenman struggles with here are Wanaque, Pompton, and Pequannock.

25. Boonton, N.J.

26. Although Greenman's reference here is obscure, the context indicates that discipline in camp was problematic and had to be enforced by severe corporal punishment. Charles Knowles Bolton has pointed out the public and ceremonial nature of military punishments: flogging was at first restricted to the thirty-nine lashes sanctioned by the mosaic law, but this amount proved quite insufficient for the edification either of offender or audience and was soon increased by Congress to fifty, and eventually to one hundred (*Private Soldier*, pp. 169ff). Greenman's figure of a hundred lashes, while the legal limit, is still far short of the enormity of British practice, which Trevelan says not infrequently allowed a thousand strokes—resulting in death, disability, or at the very least disfigurement for the victim (George O. Trevelyan, *The American Revolution*, 3 vols. in 4 [London: Longmans, Green, 1899–1907], 1:128–29).

27. The Danbury, Conn., raid took place 23–28 April 1777. A 2,000-man British force under New York's governor William Tryon destroyed most of the stores (including 1,700 tents) at the American depot there. In the skirmishing attendant to the British withdrawal there were about 100 American casualties and 150 British. Greenman's report of the loss of "a great many men" is the typical exaggeration of camp rumor (Boatner, *Encyclopedia*, pp. 315–16).

28. Bound Brook, N.J.

29. This is a good example of Greenman's personal expense code, variants of which occur intermittently throughout the diary, but especially in the years 1777–1779. The phrase says "in this time spent eleven dollars." More often the code will be in shillings and pence. For convenience, all the other expense-code material has been deciphered whenever possible and omitted otherwise.

30. Brief: "prevalent," "rife" (*OED*, s.v. "brief").

31. About four miles east and south of Morristown (Freeman, *Washington*, 5: endleaf map).

32. Greenman's former captain was promoted to major on 12 January 1777. (Heitman, Francis B. *Historical Register of Officers of the Continental Army During the War of the Revolution, April, 1775 to December, 1783*, rev. ed. [Washington, D.C.: Rare Book Shop Publishing Co., 1914]).

33. According to Bolton, the "General" was beaten to announce the striking of tents and the preparation to march; as such it followed "Reveille" but preceeded the "Troop," which was the signal to march. This was the generally accepted pattern, but there were many variations to it (*Private Soldier*, pp. 195–96).

34. About five miles north and east of Princeton, N.J. (Freeman, *Washington*, 5: map, p. 21).

35. Somerset, N.J., near New Brunswick.

36. Greenman variously spells the plural of "house" as "housan," "housand," and "housen."

37. Bridgewater was on the road some ten miles west of Quibbletown (William Faden, *The North American Atlas, Selected from the Most Authentic Maps, Plans, &c.* [London: 1777], map 20, "Province of New Jersey" [hereafter cited as *NAA*]).

38. Millstone, N.J., just west of New Brunswick.

39. Bound Brook.

40. New Brunswick, N.J. All this marching and maneuvering culminated in the minor engagement here described in the entry for 22 June. The city had been a British stronghold for over a year, and Greenman's estimate of six thousand British troops encountered between New Brunswick and Bolington does not seem to be an exaggeration. Washington issued elaborate orders to strike at the British as they were evacuating New Brunswick on 22 June, but the plan was not well executed, and little damage was done (see Boatner, *Encyclopedia*, pp. 118–19; and Freeman, *Washington*, 4:432).

41. Quibbeltown and Samptown were old settlements a few miles apart, located south and a bit east of Morristown (Lundin, *Cockpit of the Revolution*, map, p. 418). The former of these is now New Market, N.J. (Boatner, *Encyclopedia*, p. 1006). Greenman's regiment was camped with the main body of Washington's army, while a few miles to the eastward a detachment under "Lord Stirling" (Gen. William Alexander) was fighting the engagement known as Short Hills (Freeman, *Washington*, 4:433).

42. The chaplain to Angell's Second Rhode Island Regiment was Ebenezer David of Providence, whose own account of the 1777 campaign survives in a series of letters to Nicholas Brown, of the prominent Rhode Island merchant family. David's letters have been collected and published as *A Rhode Island Chaplain in the Revolution* (Providence: The Society of the Cincinnati, 1949).

43. The British evacuation to Staten Island was completed by 30 June (Boatner, *Encyclopedia*, p. 858).

44. Basking Ridge, N.J.

45. The place Greenman calls "yapor" has not been identified, but "the Clove," also known as "Smith's Clove," refers both to a passage through the mountains on the east side of the Ramapo River and to the mountains themselves. According to the editors of *Rochambeau's Army*, "'clove' is a regional word of Dutch origin (cf. English 'to cleave,' 'cleft,' 'cloven hoof,' etc.) roughly equivalent to such terms as 'gulf,' 'notch,' and 'gap' " (2:51n.). The French topographers in their route survey for the march of 1781 reported that "this part of the Upper Jerseys is no less extraordinary than the [Hudson] Highlands and seems to be a continuation of them. . . . The Clove is less extensive than the Highlands, but the mountains are higher and steeper" (Rice and Brown, eds., *Rochambeau's Army*, 2: 53).

46. Greenman was obviously puzzled over the spelling of "Kakiat," now New Hempstead, Rockland County, N.Y. "Kakiat . . . was a pivotal point on the eighteenth-century routes leading from the Hudson into northern New Jersey" (ibid., p. 142).

47. Now Stony Point, N.Y. (ibid.).

48. Washington sent Varnum's Brigade on a rapid march to the Highlands because he feared Howe would try to join Burgoyne in the north (see the introduction to this chapter; also Ward, *War of the Revolution*, 1:328; and Freeman, *Washington*, 4:433–34).

49. The more common name in the eighteenth century for the Hudson.

50. Greenman's characteristic malapropism for "applying."

51. Probably refers to the "Continental Village," just north of Peekskill, an American "camp and supply center." On 9 October, soon after Greenman and his regiment marched southward to the Delaware, the base was destroyed by British raiders (Boatner, *Landmarks*, p. 234; see also Boatner, *Encyclopedia*, map, p. 531; Reginald P. Bolton and William L. Calver, *History Written with a Pick and Shovel* (New York: New York Historical Society, 1950) map, p. 38; David, *Rhode Irland Chaplain*, pp. 38–39 and Angell, *Angell Diary*, entry of 27 July 1777).

52. "The point at which the Post Road crossed Spuyten Duyvil creek—which separates Manhattan from the Bronx—Kings Bridge was strategically important in the N.Y. Campaign and subsequently in the British defense of N.Y.C." (Boatner, *Encyclopedia*, p. 575).

53. Crompond, now Yorktown, N.Y., was about midway between Peekskill on the Hudson and Pine's Bridge (also Croton Bridge or Point's Bridge) across the Croton River (Rice and Brown, eds., *Rochambeau's Army*, 2:35, and map 48).

54. Apparently this was an unsubstantiated rumor, for no record of any such raid is found in Heitman, Boatner, or Peckham.

55. This was Edmund Palmer, who had claimed he was a lieutenant in the British service. The "infamous Tory and Robber" had been captured on 18 July, tried and convicted on 27 July, and sentenced to be hung "by the neck until he is dead, dead, dead" (Angell Orderly Book, Shepley Papers, RIHS). When Gen. Henry Clinton sent a flag of truce from New York City asking for Palmer's exchange, he received this answer from Israel Putnam: "Edmund Palmer, an officer in the enemy's service, was taken as a spy lurking within our lines; he has been tried as a spy, condemed as a spy, and shall be executed as a spy, and the flag is ordered to depart immediately. Israel Putnam. P.S.—He has been accordingly executed" (Worthington C. Ford and George Billias, eds., *General Orders Issued by Major-General Israel Putnam, When in Command of the Highlands, in the Summer and Fall of 1777* [Brooklyn, N.Y.: Historical Printing Club, 1893], p. 49. Hereafter cited as *Putnam Orderly Book*).

56. Burgoyne's expeditionary force had penetrated southward nearly to Albany, N.Y.

57. Probably Newcastle Township, N.Y., in the general area around Crompond, also called by Greenman "North Caswill."

58. The activity around White Plains here described was part of an American feint, while the real fight consisted of Gen. John Sullivan's unfortunate raid on Staten Island (22 August) (Boatner, *Encyclopedia*, p. 1054) to which Greenman alludes in his entry for 26–30 August.

59. Mile Square, N.Y. (also Miles Square) was midway on the road between King's Bridge and East Chester (Nebenzahl, *Atlas*, pp. 88–89).

60. Probably Mamaroneck, N.Y.

61. Rye Neck, N.Y.

62. Northwest of Rye Neck (cf. Christopher Colles, *A Survey of the Roads of the United States of America, 1789*, ed. Walter W. Ristow [Cambridge: Harvard University Press, 1961] plate 3).

63. There was considerable disaffection at this time in Col. Christopher Greene's First Rhode Island Regiment—as in so much of the Continental army—over broken promises of pay and clothing. Many of the enlistment bounties had not been paid, nor had the "new suit of clothes" been forthcoming. The men were sullen, even embarrassed, about their condition (see the introduction to this chapter), and a "mutiny"—in fact a term applied to most spontaneous complaints among the soldiers—is said to have occurred at about this time. A court-martial was held at Peekskill on 2 September 1777 at which nine sergeants and three corporals were "try'd for Raising a mutiny"; however, they were convicted not of mutiny but of disorderly conduct and were suspended "During the Pleasure of the Colo or Commanding Officer of the Regt.," namely, Christopher Greene (Ford and Billias, eds., *Putnam Orderly Book*, p. 70). The suspension lasted until 21 October when, on the eve of the German assault on Fort Mercer (see below), Greene thought it politic to reinstate the offenders, with hopes that they would "demean themselves as becomes brave Serjeants" (Angell Orderly Book, Shepley Papers, RIHS).

64. Gen. Putnam's *Orderly Book* for 5 September 1777 reports on the court-martial of "James Duggins of Colo. Charles Webbs Regt." who "was tryed for firing his gun at a party of fatigue men as they was coming from Work and uncaping another Cartradg to fire again / are [*sic*] found Guilty of the charge / But are of Appinan that the Prisoner Ment to fire at one Barns who had thretned to kill his wife / the Court therfore Sentance the Prisoner to set upon the gallos half an hour with A halter Round his neck and then to receave 50 Lashes on his naked Back at the gallos" (p. 69).

65. By "old country men" Greenman means both British deserters and first-generation emigrants from England, though obviously the former is referred to here. Putnam's general orders for 6 September 1777 command the parading of these men as Greenman reports, and the following day's orders mention that they are to be formed into a separate regiment. But whether they were ever "sent to Georgy" is not made clear (ibid., pp. 71–72).

66. The execution of Amos Rose and Samuel Ackerly was scheduled for 9 A.M. on Tuesday, 9 September. Rose had been convicted of shooting a fellow soldier (orders for 22 July), and Ackerly was convicted of spying (orders of 31 July). The *Putnam Orderly Book* does not report their reprieves.

67. This was a group under Lt. Col. Jeremiah Olney. Throughout the summer, recruiting continued in Rhode Island, and the two regiments gained strength as men trickled into the Highlands.

68. The Battle of Brandywine, in Pennsylvania, had been fought on 11 September. It resulted in a solid defeat for the Americans. As Freeman put it, "Washington conducted the Brandywine operation as if he had been in a daze" (*Washington*, 4:488). The way was now open for Howe to occupy Philadelphia, which, as Greenman notes, he did on 26 September (Ward, *War of the Revolution*, 1:361). Actual casualties at Brandywine were quite different from what is implied in the camp rumor Greenman reports: Boatner makes the total American losses about 1,300 and the British, 577 (*Encyclopedia*, p. 109); Howard Peckham says only an estimate is possible of American losses (1,100), while the British are reported to have lost 544 (*The Toll of Independence* [Chicago: University of Chicago Press, 1974], p. 40).

69. Abbreviation for "put up."

70. Vealtown, N.J., was on the main road south and a little west of the Morristown (Lundin, *Cockpit of the Revolution*, map, p. 418).

71. Germantown, N.J., about 10 miles west of Bedminster (Faden, *NAA*, map 20, "Province of New Jersey").

72. Bedminster, N.J.

73. Flemington, N.J.

74. Amwell Township, Hunterdon County, N.J.

75. Probably Mt. Airy, N.J.

76. General Varnum actually received his orders from Washington on 8 October: "detach Colo. Greene's and Colo. Angell's Regiments with their Baggage" and send them to Fort Mercer at Red Bank, N.J., on the Delaware (Washington, *Writings*, 9:326–27).

77. Coryell's Ferry crossed the Delaware between the places now called Lambertsville, N.J., and New Hope, Pa. (Smith, *Monmouth*, p. 6, and map, p. 4).

78. Plumstead Township, Pa. (Faden, *NAA*, "A Map of Pennsylvania . . .").

79. Hilltown, Newtown, and Middletown are all towns and townships on the road from Coryell's Ferry to Bristol (ibid.).

80. Washington recalled Angell's troops because of intelligence of British activity around Peekskill. By 16 October, however, he felt those reports to be exaggerated and sent the Second Rhode Islanders on to Red Bank (Smith, *Delaware*, p. 16).

81. New Britain Township, Pa. (Faden, *NAA*, "A Map of Pennsylvania . . .").

82. Headquarters at this time was at Pawling's Mill, Pa., now Schwenksville (Smith, *Delaware*, p. 16). The good news concerning Gates's battles with Burgoyne had been filtering down from the north for almost two weeks, although Freeman shows that Washington did not receive definitive reports of the Saratoga surrender until 18 October (*Washington*, 4:524). Greenman's recollection that the celebrations were on or before the sixteenth is clearly mistaken—perhaps further evidence that this section of the diary was recomposed at a later date.

83. The ferry was from Bristol, Pa., to Burlington, N.J.

84. Haddonfield, N.J.

85. Fort Mercer at Red Bank, N.J., facing page 86 (see also Nebenzahl, *Atlas*, pp. 124–25) was always known to Greenman as "Ft. Mercy." Smith has calculated that Angell's regiment made a seventy-mile march from Schwenksville to the fort in just two days (*Delaware*, p. 16).

86. The "sally above & below" described by Greenman occurred on 11 October. The "arrival hear" refers to Fort Mifflin, for Greenman was part of a detachment from Angell's regiment sent over from Mercer on 19 October to strengthen the Mifflin garrison (Smith, *Delaware*, p. 16).

87. Lt. Col. Samuel Smith, of the Fourth Maryland Regiment, was at this date the commandant of Fort Mifflin. Com. John Hazlewood commanded both the Continental

and the Pennsylvania State Navies (Smith, *Delaware*, p. 64; and Jackson, *Pennsylvania Navy*, chap. 9).

88. Greenman refers here either to fragments from exploding cannon balls—what we would call shrapnel—or to splinters from wood shattered during bombardment, or perhaps to both.

89. Pallisades: pointed wooden stakes forming the outer walls, or parapets, of a fort.

90. Capt. John Montresor, chief British Engineer in the colonies since 1775, had directed the building of Fort Mifflin in 1772 (it was unfinished in 1777) and now was assigned the task of "reducing" it (Smith, *Delaware*, p. 13). Montresor's journals, including his eye-witness account of the Delaware action, have been edited by G. D. Scull and published by the New York State Historical Society (1882).

91. Greenman here alludes to what might have been a nice piece of strategy, but one which never happened; the defense instead centered on holding and reinforcing Fort Mifflin, and there was no serious attempt to attack British batteries on Province Island "by the side of Derby [, Pa.]."

92. Greenman probably had in mind here either howitzers or mortars—both of which were types of cannon ideally suited for the short-range, high-trajectory firing from Province and Carpenter's islands into Fort Mifflin. When well aimed, their shells would have fallen almost vertically into the middle of the fort (Smith, *Delaware*, p. 13).

93. The island upon which Fort Mifflin was built was known as both Fort Island and Mud Island.

94. The task of constructing new defenses for Fort Mifflin was entrusted to the French volunteer, Maj. François Louis de Fleury, a capable engineer (Smith, *Delaware*, p. 13). Fleury's journals covering the period of the Delaware defense and recording his plans for Fort Mifflin are in the Washington Papers, Library of Congress, Manuscript Division, vol. 58. His drawing of the fort is reproduced in Smith, *Delaware*, p. 30.

95. Carcases were incendiary shells (round, made of iron, and full of holes for the flame) fired from mortars (*OED*, s.v. "carcase"; Ward, *War of the Revolution*, 2:927).

96. Vertical pickets were pointed sticks driven into the ground and used to retard the advance of soldiers storming a fort; wolf-holes, or wolf-traps, were holes dug in the ground within which were placed sharpened sticks. In the last days of Fort Mifflin's defense, these wolf-holes were under water and would have served their purpose well if a storm had been attempted by British troops (Smith, *Delaware*, pp. 30–31).

97. That is, to alarm them.

98. The main strategic value of Forts Mifflin and Mercer—namely, to keep the British from properly provisioning Philadelphia by the river—is discussed above in the introduction to this chapter.

99. The Orderly Book for the Rhode Island regiments at Forts Mifflin and Mercer mentions Colonel Greene's having got word of Burgoyne's defeat (but not of his surrender) on 16 October and then gives the orders for a celebration of the victory on the same day. The sixteenth, however, was fully two days before Greenman's regiment (under Angell) arrived at Red Bank. This could hardly be a lapse of memory on the author's part, for he is claiming to remember something he could not have witnessed, which suggests either that there was a subsequent celebration when news of the *surrender* became generally known (not mentioned in the Orderly Book) or that perhaps Greenman was recounting something told to him or copying from another source.

100. *Cheavaux de frise* (literally "Friseland horses") were an integral and sometimes effective part of the defense of the Delaware. For description and pictures see Smith, *Delaware*, p. 8; and Jackson, *Pennsylvania Navy*, pp. 354ff. For their placement in the river see map, facing page 86.

101. The British officer who delivered the ultimatum was Lt. Col. Alexander Stewart,

who "was of the opinion that the fort would be easily taken" (Smith, *Delaware*, p. 20). According to another eye-witness, Capt. Stephen Olney of the Second Rhode Island Regiment, it was his kinsman, Lt. Col. Jeremiah Olney, who was deputed to meet the flag, carrying Greene's message of no surrender, no quarter expected (Olney Narrative, Shepley Papers, RIHS, pp. 13–14).

102. The ingenious plan for a fort within a fort which so confused the Germans during the attack was the work of Capt. Mauduit du Plessis, a French volunteer engineer-artillerist, whose drawing of the revamped fort and the manner of the German attack is reproduced in Smith, *Delaware*, p. 17. Three years after the battle, du Plessis recounted it for the Marquis de Chastellux, who recorded the story in his *Travels* (1:154–60).

103. Abattis are felled trees with their branches—sometimes sharpened—towards an advancing enemy (Ward, *War of the Revolution*, 2:927).

104. That is, the mortally wounded Count von Donop was abandoned by his retreating men on the sloping ground, or glacis, before the parapet of the fort (see ibid., 2:928).

105. Capt. Stephen Olney asserts on the contrary that the wounded were left outside the fort on the night of the twenty-second: "I had charge of the guard that night / my Centrys were placed round the whole fort, that part evacuated was cover'd with dead, Dying and wounded Hessians, the groans and cries of the two latter were quite solitary musick. . . . several of the wounded and about dying appeared to suffer with the cold. . . ." (Olney Narrative, Shepley Papers, RIHS, p. 15).

106. Sylvanus Shaw.

107. Ebenezer David reports the American casualties as totalling 32 (*Rhode Island Chaplain*, p. 53), and Stephen Olney makes them about the same (Olney Narrative, Shepley Papers, RIHS, p. 14). Peckham lists 14 Americans killed, 23 wounded, and 1 captured (*Toll*, p. 44).

108. Estimates of the German dead have been as high as 151, but this figure includes those who died in the days following the battle—nearly as many again as died the first night (Smith, *Delaware*, p. 23). Peckham records German dead at 153 and wounded at more than 200 (*Toll*, p. 44).

109. The naval engagement Greenman describes, with his characteristic fascination for the "Shipping," was actually the continuation of what the British had planned as a combined army-navy assault on the twenty-second (Smith, *Delaware*, pp. 24–25). Unfortunately for them, the *Augusta* ran aground and could not materially aid in the attack. Com. Hazelwood saw her plight on the morning of the twenty-third and ordered his galleys to open fire, which may have started the fire on board. The *Augusta* exploded "at 2 p.m." (ibid., p. 25, quoting British Admiralty records). For a complete list of the British ships involved in this action, see ibid., p. 46. Smith maintains that the *Somerset* did not come up river until 5 November and was therefore *not* among the British ships engaging on 22–23 October (ibid., pp. 27–28).

110. That is, the New Jersey shore.

111. According to Smith, there were no American land batteries in position until 5 November. The *Augusta* and *Merlin* were assaulted mainly by gallies assisted by floating batteries (ibid., p. 27). See n. 115 below.

112. Although it may have appeared to the onlooking Greenman that the Americans set fire to the *Merlin*, it was in fact the decision of the commander to abandon ship and destroy her (ibid., p. 25).

113. Ebenezer David was among the truce party: "A few days after the Battle I accompanyed Majr Thayer on a Flag to the City bearing Letters from their wounded officers. . . . we were brought too at the hither end of the Town—where they eagerly received the Letters & spedily provided the Surgeon who was wrote for. . . ." (*Rhode Island Chaplain*, p. 55).

114. The Fort Mercer garrison orders for 31 October report the court-martial: "At a Court Martial held by Order of Colo. Greene of which Lt. Colo. Olney was President, Jno. Mucklewain, and Dick Ellis, were tried for conducting ye Enemy thro the Country, for being Spies & Traitors . . . found guilty of ye former Charge, & sentenc'd to suffer ye pains of Death . . . The Colo. approves ye above Sentences of ye Court Martial, and orders that Jno. Mucklewain, & Dick Ellis . . . be hang'd tomorrow Morning 10 oClock . . . A Gallows will be erected this afternoon for that Purpose . . . .The Garrison will attend the execution of ye Criminals . . . under Arms at ye time appointed. . . ." (Angell Orderly Book, Shepley Papers, RIHS).

115. There had been increased British activity around Billingsport, N.J., and General Varnum was dispatched both to counter this and to build artillery batteries to harass the encroaching British ships (Smith, *Delaware*, p. 27).

116. Col. Henry D'Arendt, commander of a German-American regiment (hence Greenman's reference to him as "a Prusan [Prussian] officer") and one of the first commanders of Fort Mifflin. Lt. Col. Smith was actually wounded and relieved a few days after this (see entry below for 12 November and Smith, *Delaware*, p. 29).

117. Both Fort Mifflin and Province Island were mostly below the water level and had to be diked to fend off flooding during high tides and storms.

118. At some indeterminate day and time during this siege of Fort Mifflin, Greenman apparently returned to that fort from Fort Mercer. Although the writing makes it appear to have been during the week of 2–9 November, the return might have been earlier. An alternative, of course, would be that he remained at Fort Mercer and observed the plight of Fort Mifflin. There is no definite evidence external to the diary.

119. Capt. Samuel Treat, Second Continental Artillery. His death occurred in a freakish manner and was damaging to the American cause because of the scarcity of skilled artillerists at Fort Mifflin: Treat and Col. Smith were " 'conversing near the 32 pounder, when a ball from the enemy came. . . . Captain Treat tottered, and was upheld by the Colonel. A slight squeeze of the hand, and he expired. No wound was apparent; and the question is, was it the sensation from the ball that caused his death?' " (Smith, *Delaware*, p. 29).

120. This cannon was retrieved by the garrison at Fort Mercer, not Fort Mifflin (see ibid., p. 31).

121. Maj. Simeon Thayer of the Second Rhode Island Regiment volunteered to relieve the exhausted troops at Fort Mifflin, and Smith reports that General Varnum was "rejoiced to hear [him] offer himself" (ibid., p. 32). The tenacity of the defense he made was praised by many, including his colonel, Israel Angell (see his letter to the Providence *Gazette*, 14 March 1778). If Greenman was at Fort Mifflin (see note 118 above), it is likely that he was among those relieved by Thayer's detachment, for subsequent entries are clearly written from Fort Mercer.

122. Tinicut was another name for Carpenter's Island, adjacent to Province Island.

123. This was the *Vigilant*, a converted transport of "120 ft. length on the keel and . . . a 36 ft. beam." Her armament—not the "20 24 pounders" Greenman reports—was "one '24 pounder, nine 2 pdr, six 4 pdr,' all on one side." After repeated tries she had finally made it across Hog Island Bar and came to anchor at 11:30 on the fifteenth. Her position was " 'about 200 steps from the fort' " and safe from the guns on the southwest end of Fort Mifflin (hence Greenman's "four yards from the Angle of the SW Battery") (Smith, *Delaware*, pp. 33–34).

124. The *Vigilant* was so close to the fort that Marines in her round top were able to pick off men with musket shot and threw a good many hand grenades directly into the fort (ibid., p. 36).

125. This was not the *Vigilant*, but the *Fury*, which carried according to Smith "three 24 pounders" (ibid., p. 34).

126. With reinforcements Major Thayer, "'most firm and unshaken,'" was convinced that he " 'could & would hold the Fort.' " But instead of support, General Varnum sent " 'a number of boats with discretionary orders to hold or evacuate the fort.' " (ibid., p. 37).

127. According to John Montresor, "at half past seven . . . a boat with some sailors landed at the Fort on Mud Island and took down the rebel colours" (*Journals*, ed. G. D. Scull (New York: New York State Historical Society, 1882), p. 477). On their arrival at Fort Mifflin the British were astonished to see that "nothing surely was ever so torn and riven by cannon-Balls. A more dismal Picture of Ruin can scarce be conceived. . . . every gun [was] dismounted, and a great many dead bodies were found, scarce covered . . ." (Smith, *Delaware*, p. 37).

128. Though the evacuation did not take place until two days later, the garrison was very much aware of increased British activity in New Jersey—manifested in a huge force (7,000 troops) under Cornwallis sent from Philadelphia towards Fort Mercer. The evacuation on the nineteenth was ordered by Colonel Greene after hearing rumors of the British being only a few miles from the fort (ibid., pp. 38–39).

129. Moorestown, N.J.

130. Mount Holly, N.J.

131. buth: booth(s)—a temporary dwelling covered with boughs, canvas, or other slight material (*OED*, s.v. "booth").

132. The words appear to be "fore lain end," which could be a place name.

133. Crooked Billet is now Hatboro, Pa. (Smith, *Delaware*, p. 39).

134. Washington had decided to move his headquarters from Whitemarsh to Valley Forge, Pa., and to winter there (Boatner, *Encyclopedia*, p. 1199), and the tired American army was harassed all along the way by British raiders from Philadelphia. The minor engagement Greenman mentions in his entry for 1–10 December is known as Whitemarsh, but it really consisted of a series of skirmishes around that area between 5 and 8 December (Boatner, *Encyclopedia*, p. 1199).

135. Greenman refers to a weather phenomenon rather than to any military activity or conflagration. Joseph Plumb Martin, of the Connecticut Continentals, was in the same camp and noted: "While we lay here, there happened very remarkable northern lights. At one time the whole visible heavens appeared for some time as if covered with crimson velvet. Some of the soldiers prognosticated a bloody battle about to be fought, but time, which always speaks the truth, proved them to be false prophets" (*Private Yankee Doodle* (Boston: Little, Brown, 1962), p. 99).

136. Col. Daniel Morgan (later brigadier general) of Virginia, commander of the renowned Virginia Riflemen and another famous veteran of the march to Quebec. His corps had recently rejoined the main army after the victories at Saratoga (Boatner, *Encyclopedia*, p. 736).

137. A gill was commonly either one-fourth or one-half of a pint.

138. The heading for this page of the diary ms. reads "Chester Woods"; this is apparently the area near Valley Forge in which Greenman's regiment was to quarter for the winter.

PART THREE

Valley Forge, Monmouth, and the Battle of Rhode Island, 1778–1779

INTRODUCTION

No SOONER does Sgt. Jeremiah Greenman get settled in his hut at Valley Forge than he is sent home to Rhode Island—to rest, certainly, but also to recruit. For the chronic problem in the Rhode Island Line, as with so many elements of the Continental army, was an abundance of officers and a scarcity of enlisted men. Brig. Gen. James M. Varnum was very much aware of the dilemma, and on 2 January 1778 he wrote to Washington proposing a novel solution:

> *The two batallions from the State of Rhode Island being small, and there being a necessity of the State's furnishing an additional number to make up their proportion in the Continental army, the field officers have represented to me the propriety of making one temporary batallion from the two, so that one entire corps of officers may repair to Rhode Island in order to receive and prepare the recruits for the field. It is imagined that a battalion of negroes can be easily raised there. Should that measure be adopted, or recruits obtained upon any other principle, the service will be advanced.*[1]

Washington acceded to the plan, which Varnum then put before the Rhode Island Assembly.[2] The result was the notable act authorizing the recruitment of slaves for the American service: "every able-bodied *negro*, mulatto or *Indian* man slave in this State may inlist into either of the said two battalions to serve during the continuance of the war with Great Britain . . . every slave so inlisting shall be entitled to, and receive all the bounties, wages and encouragements allowed by the Continental Congress to any soldier inlisting into their service . . . every slave so inlisting shall, upon passing muster before Colonel Christopher Greene, be immediately discharged from the service of his master or mistress and be absolutely FREE."[3] The owners, of course, were to be suitably indemnified by the state for their property loss: an expensive manner of raising an army, but one which, if it accomplished nothing else, gave freedom to a number of men who did not have it before.[4]

It was this group of freedmen whom Greenman had the task of drilling into something like a fighting unit before the campaign of 1778, a business that did not get well underway until late in March. The training camp was at East Greenwich ("peraded our Slaves for to march to Grinage"), which allowed the seasoned troops to keep one eye on the British in Newport while they exercised their raw recruits. Greenman gives no indication as to how well the training got on, but it was only a matter of five weeks before the Rhode Islanders were called back to the main army at Valley Forge.

Back in camp—having missed the worst part of the winter—Greenman got a taste of serious military drill himself. "Baron" von Steuben had begun to work his remarkable transformation of the American army in February, and the "Prusand Genl.," as Greenman calls him, made quite an impression on the diarist then and later.

Because the British tarried so long in Philadelphia, Washington kept his army in their unwholesome winter quarters well into the month of June. But when the enemy did evacuate the city, the commander in chief was decisive in putting his army in motion: they pursued the British through New Jersey and eventually brought on "the last important engagement in the North,"[5] the Battle of Monmouth. This battle is famous for a number of reasons: it was protracted and intense; it was fought in almost unbearable heat; it precipizated the court-martial of Gen. Charles Lee; and it remains to this day the hardest battle of the war to chronicle, let alone to analyze.

Our diarist's account of the action is, not too surprisingly, somewhat muddled. Greenman did not—as he had done with the defense of the Delaware—take the trouble to recompose the entries dealing with Monmouth. Nor was he in much of a position to comprehend the totality of the fight. To read his description of the battle is to be reminded of the truth of what Charles K. Bolton says about the vantage of the common soldier in battle: "Until a soldier acquired sufficient education to fit him for an officer's commission he was not thrown with men who heard the current news at head-quarters; his horizon, therefore, was limited, and a battle, far reaching in its influence upon events, meant no more to him than a chance encounter."[6] To be sure, Monmouth was a kind of midpoint of Greenman's evolution into a realized soldier, but he had yet to be given a privileged place to stand which would allow him to understand what was happening around him.[7] Still, when one sees that Charles Lee lost his reputation, then his rank, and finally his human dignity because he was unable to find out just what was happening in the battle at Monmouth, and that historians have yet to reconstruct the fight in any convincing fashion, Greenman's confusion is understandable indeed.

After Monmouth, the Rhode Island troops were part of a detachment sent on to their native state to reinforce Maj. Gen. John Sullivan, who had command of the Rhode Island department. The British occupation of Newport—they had been there now over a year and a half—grated not only on the inhabitants of the state but on the commander in chief, who very much wished to dislodge them from their comfortable seat. The entry of the French into the war and the arrival of a French fleet under Comte D'Estaing appeared to make an assault on the island feasible. And feasibility quickly turned into the "most flattering hopes of success":[8] a combined land-sea invasion of the island simply could not fail. Perhaps the arrival of the French thoroughly swept aside the native caution of the New Englanders, but for whatever reason the operations culminating in the Battle of Rhode Island (29 August 1778) were approached with what now appear to be laughably inflated expectations: Sullivan himself was bouyantly confident, Washington guardedly so. But the generals who were to support Sullivan ran to the operation like boys to the carnival. Nathanael Greene, itching to get down to Rhode Island from the main camp at White Plains, wrote Sullivan on 23 July: "You are the most happy man in the World. What a child of fortune. The expedition you are going on against Newport I think cannot fail of success. . . . I wish you success with all my Soul and intend if possible to come home to put things in a proper train in my department and to take a command of part of the Troops under you. I wish most ardently to be with you."[9] And Lafayette, always eager for the glories of the field, wrote Sullivan the day before begging him, "for god's sake, my dear friend," not to "begin any thing before we arrive."[10] All this set a *mise-en-scene* of "too good to be true." And so it was.

The embarrassing failure of this first venture under the Franco-

American alliance is well known. Gen. Robert Pigot and his garrison were not dislodged from Newport, and in fact Sullivan's troops were driven from the island and only just managed to get off without losing both army and baggage. The Americans, of course, blamed D'Estaing severely for what they took to be the abandonment of the troops on the island, and in their consternation, many—especially the local Rhode Islanders who were the most immediately affected—thought Sullivan's leadership had failed them and the American cause. No doubt Sullivan had offended the French, who were, as Washington put it "a people old in war, very strict in military etiquette and apt to take fire where others are scarcely warmed,"[11] but the American general was not without his warm defenders.[12] The best that could be done was to put the failure behind and try to patch things up with the French.

With the British still in firm possession of Newport and unlikely to be soon removed unless they wanted to go, it was thought wise to leave the Rhode Island regiments in their own territory for a while. Dispositions were made on all three landed sides of the Island—to watch the British in every area of Narragansett Bay and to strengthen the defense of Providence should the British threaten it.[13] Thus the campaign of 1779 was spent at home, though the defense of the homeland and the proximity to friends and loved ones did not appear to gratify the soldiers as might be expected: Greenman reports no less than three separate mutinies in his regiment alone during 1779. Two of these appear to have been serious. The reasons for the disturbances were those that would become troublesome in the army at large in 1780 and 1781—misunderstanding over the term of enlistment ("3 years or the War"), depreciation of the currency with which the men were paid, and lack of proper outfitting and provisioning of the army. In one of his last general orders (5 February 1779) before resigning his commission, General Varnum expressed his disappointment that after "the amazing pains he has taken to make every corps in this Army comfortable, the exertions of the Officers to obtain for the Soldiers . . . satisffaction for ther Service . . . those non Commissioned Officers who without complaining to the Officers or saying a word to them upon the subject of greviences should cause a whole regiment to rise in opposition to the Officers who have thus been exerting themselves to obtain redress."[14] Throughout all the turmoil—the marches out of camp, the seizure of cannon, the arrests and courts-martial—

Greenman refers to the mutineers as "the biger part of the Regt.," making it plain that he is not numbered among them. The tenor of the journal for this period suggests that Greenman (especially after he assumes his duties as an ensign on 1 May) is considered by his superiors as solidly loyal, for he is called upon during the most serious mutiny to bring his command back from a guard outpost to help subdue the mutineers. It is likely that Greenman owes his advance through the ranks as much to steadfastness as to anything else.

In the autumn of 1779 Col. Israel Angell's Second Rhode Island Regiment was ordered to return to the Grand Army, then quartered in and around Morristown, New Jersey. The men upon arrival fell to the familiar work of hut-building, preparing for the fifth winter since the war began. What they did not know was that this one (1779–1780) would prove far worse than the celebrated winter at Valley Forge two years earlier. The journal for the year 1779 ends with a pleasant little piece of unintentional irony: Greenman, at last a commissioned officer pulls rank on some sergeants, dispossessing them of their cozy (and completed hut) until his own is finished.

NOTES TO INTRODUCTION

1. "Revolutionary Correspondence," RIHS *Collections*, 6:209–10.

2. Washington wrote to Rhode Island governor Nicholas Cooke the same day he received Varnum's letter, asking the governor to give the Rhode Island officers all the assistance in his power to advance the plan for filling the Rhode Island regiments. Sidney Rider points out, however, that Washington did not *specifically* endorse the scheme for recruiting slaves (Sidney S. Rider, *An Historical Inquiry Concerning the Attempt to Raise a Regiment of Slaves by Rhode Island During the War of the Revolution* [Providence, R.I.: 1880], pp. 10n., 34–35).

3. Quoted by Rider, ibid., pp. 10–11.

4. "Against the passage of this law, six members of the General Assembly recorded their protest," on the grounds that there was an insufficiency of blacks in the state who would enlist, that the measure was prohibitively expensive, and that the irony of having slaves fight for the civil rights of their masters was overwhelming (ibid., pp. 17–18). But the measure was approved and put into prompt operation, with some seventy-five slaves being enlisted by early spring of 1778 at a cost to the state of over £10,000 ($50,000 at par) (ibid., pp. 53–56). While it is fairly clear that the black soldiers never constituted a regiment in and of themselves, but were incorporated into Christopher Greene's First Rhode Island, they did fight together at Monmouth, Newport, and Springfield. Their behavior in these fights was cast heroically during the years of the abolitionist movement in New England, but Rider's monograph throws much of this into question—claiming in fact that the whole attempt to recruit blacks was a sad mistake and one dearly repented of by Rhode Island (ibid., pp. 33–50; see also Benjamin Quarles, *The Negro in the American Revolution* [Chapel Hill, N.C.: University of North Carolina Press, 1961], pp. 55–56, 80–82). But the subject requires further study. Research is now going on in Rhode Island, sponsored by the Rhode Island Bicentennial Commission, aimed at placing the so-called Black Regiment in its proper historical context.

5. Boatner, *Encyclopedia*, p. 725.

6. Bolton, *Private Soldier*, p. 224.

7. For example, compare Greenman's account of Monmouth with that covering the Battle of Springfield (see part 4) two years later—two years of soldierly growth for the young officer.

8. Washington, *Writings*, 12:277.

9. John Sullivan, *Letters and Papers of Major-General John Sullivan*, 3 vols. (Concord, N.H.: New Hampshire Historical Society, 1930–39), 2:103.

10. Ibib., pp. 101–2.

11. Washington, *Writings*, 12:385.

12. Concerning Sullivan's military conduct in the Rhode Island operation, there was a spirited exchange of letters between John Brown of Providence and Gen. Nathanael Greene. Brown had cast aspersions not only upon Sullivan's strategy but upon the man's character as well—upon Greene's, too, for that matter—and in a lengthy, point-by-point response, General Greene refutes the other with a frankness that reveals nothing of the pandering to opinion often found in letters to rich and influential merchants. The document is eloquent and altogether to the credit of Greene, offering as it does a rare glimpse of the relationship between civilian and soldier in Rhode Island, a relationship the amicability of which was sometimes strained by the presumption of powerful civilians in military affairs. Of Greene's defense of Sullivan, only a small segment can be quoted here: "I have seen as much service, almost, as any man in the American army, and have been in as many or more actions than any one; I know the character of all our general officers, as well as any one; and if I am any judge, the expedition has been prudently and well conducted; and I am confident there is not a general officer, from the Commander-in-chief to the youngest in the field, that would have gone greater lengths, to have given success to the expedition than General Sullivan" (Sullivan, *Sullivan Papers*, 2:317).

13. This plan for the defense of Rhode Island appears to have originated with Gen. James M. Varnum. He described it in great detail in a communication that has been printed as part of the *Sullivan Papers* (2:175–78).

14. Sullivan Orderly Book, Shepley Papers, RIHS.

VALLEY FORGE, MONMOUTH, AND THE BATTLE OF RHODE ISLAND, 1778–1779

JANUARY 1778: VALEY FORG

T 1 to T 8. Continuing in our huts or little town 12 men in each hut / we hear that sum french privateer is [has] taken sum of ye kings shiping off by the capes of Philadelphia. this afternoon a ball of fire fell from heaven / apear'd as big as a mans head / fell as far as ye tops of ye trees then burst into a Number of peaces / Sum Small Spits of Snow / both our Rigements turn'd into one / Colo Greens turn'd into Colo angells / all ye spayr officers sent home to recrute a nother regiment & sum on furlow.[1]

F 9. this morn left ye camp / cross'd Scoole kill river & then proceed'd on as far as washester[2] ware we put up with our waggons wich was about 8 mild [miles] from Camp.

S 10. this morn started after eating breakfast / proceeded on / came to frankolness[3] ware we put up / very muddy & bad traveling.

S 11. this morn impresed a horse / went about 2 milds. came to a village cal'd Quaker town & impresed 2 more hores / then proceeded on / came as far as Richland[4] the men that came with ye hores stole them away in ye night wen we was sleping wich detained us the next day till late.

M 12. this morn from Richland after presing 2 horses came to uper Sockenit ware we made a small halt / then proceeded on as far as lower Sockenit ware we made a nother halt for a few moments[5] / then pushed on / Crost lahio river[6] then came to Bethelem ware ye moravin liveth.[7]

T 13. this morn very pleasant but cold / proceeded on as far as Easttown[8] ware we ariv'd about 2 oClock & drawed provision / then crost ye River Diliware came about 4 milds to Greenwich town

Ship ware we put up in a Duchmans hause / very cold wether.

W 14. turn'd out early this morn & impresed two horess to go 8 milds / then releast them at Mr. Wm. Cons. Tavern in oxford ware we presed 2 more horses and proceeded on to a widow woman['s] house / halted to get quaters but thay ware full / then we pushed on [*to*] a Small Village called hope or moravins town inhabited by duch Moravins / here we taried all night ware we was kindly entertain'd / this town [*is*] 22 milds from easttown & 16 from Sessex.

T 15. from mount hope came to hardwick ware we presed 2 horses & proceeded on to new town[9] in Sessex County ware we drawed provision & C.[10]

[*T 20*]. [*blank*] paulings precinct in dutchess County wich was about 8 milds from ware we dined.

W 21. this morn from paulings precinct in dover came to kent ware we made a small halt / then proceeded on as far as raw mug in Newpreston ware we dined[11] then pushed on as [*far as*] Judear ware I made a small halt / then came as far as Litchfield ware I halted, 4 mild from Bethelem in Woodbury.[12]

T 22. this morn from Litchfield came to Bethelem ware I continued till the 27[*th*][13] / then set off / came to harrington ware I dined / then pushed on as far as farmington ware I put up.

W 28. this morn warm & thick cloudy weather / came in to farmington ware I got my breakfast / then pushed on as far as har[*t*]ford ware I got my diner. then came 8 milds ware I put up in harford township.

T 29. this morn set off from ware stayed last night / came to bolton ware I made a small halt / then came to anderver[14] ware I dined / then pushed on as far as Lebenan crank ware I put up[15] / very raining wether &c forth.

F 30. this morn pushed on as far as Windom ware we got our breakfast / then came to Scotland ware we made a small halt / then came to Canterbury ware we dined / then came to plainfield ware we made a nother halt / then proceeded on as far as vollingtown[16] ware we put up / this morn we waded 40 rods to git to a bridge up almost to our wasbunss[17] & very cold.

S 31. this morn from vollingtown / very muddy & raining wether / came to Coventry ware we got our breakfast / then we pushed on as far as Cranston ware we dined / then came to

Johston ware we stopt a few moment[*s*] / then came to providence ware we put up / very stormy weather & soforth.

FEBRUARY. 1778 FROM PROVD

S 1. Continuing in providence till ten oClock / then set off crost Seconk fery / came to Swansey ware I dined / then pushed on / crost Slaids fery[18] came to freetown ware I put up very muddy walking and warm &C.

M 2. this morn very cold / came from freetown ware we put up / then came about 3 milds got my breakfast / then pushed on as far as acoxet in Dartmouth ware I continued till Satterday ye 14 / Nothing very Remarkeble / [*illeg.*] dollar.

S 14. This morn from Dartmouth crost Slaids fery / came to Swansey ware I put up not being very well able to travel.

S 15. this morn from Swansey came to providence wich was 12 milds ware I put up Nothing very Remarkeble more than Cold.

M 16 to T 17. this day drawed provision & c forth & wood / went in to Barracks / very cold.

W 18. this afternoon a very sad ascedince[19] hapened / a woman falling down hurt her Self so that She died in a Nower afterward & a Negro fell off hiss hores and wounded himself so that he died.

T 19 to M 23. this morn very pleasant / draw'd B Cloath to made us Cloaths we [*hear*] our rigement to the westward is very sickly / we beet thro the town for vollingteers / Sum Small Spits of Snow.

T 24. this morn very pleasant / from providance came to petuxet[20] ware I made a small halt / then I pushed on as far as Warwick ware I drawed sum wages / then came as far as munketown[21] ware I dined / then came to providance ware I put up at ye Widdow Olney:[22] at my Quarters: eighteen dollars and 3 shillings for board &C altering a Coat.

W 25 to S 28. Continuing in providance / nothing very Remarkeble oney [only] implying our Selves in Recruting as fast as posable / wrain & warm.

MARCH 1778

S 1 to T 3. Sun March ye 1st 1778 / this morn Snow and Cold at Night Supt on o[*y*]sters . . . gitting my Regimentals made / very blustering wether Lay'd out this day for my board &C twelve dollars and four Shillings.

W 4. this [*morn*] Clear & Cold / Snow about 6 Inches hig[*h*] / Set off from providance / came to Seconk lower fery / it being full of Ice I could not cros went to the uper fery ware I crost / then pushed on in the Snow / very bad traviling / came to Swanzy ware I put up at a privat house / this day spent six Shillings.

T 5. this morn very pleasan and cule / came from Swanzey / Crost Slaids fery then pushed on as far as acoxet in Dartmth.

F 6 to W 11. Continuing in Dartmouth till ye 12. very cule wether / Implying my Self in making a westcoat / got a pair of Shoes tapt / 2 dollars for a goat Scin for taping a pair of Shoes[23] / 18 Dollars left at home &C.

T 12. this morn thick fogey wether / Set off from acoxet / came about 5 mild / got a mug of cyder: then pushed [*on*] a mild & dined / then came to little Compton ware I put up all Night att Mr. Shaids &C.

F 13. this day thick clowdy weather / Continuing in Little Compton till 2 oClock / then went to ye Squire's after a power for Capt Shaws Cloath &C[24] / then pushed on as far as acoxet ware I put up at Mr. Woods.

S 14 to T 17. this morn fogey wether / came a bout 5 milds to my home ware I continued till ye Wednesday the 18[*th*].

W 18. this morn from Dartmouth very warm & pleasant / came as far as free town / made a small halt / then pushed on as far as taunton.

T 19. Continuing in taunton / the wether very pleasan / Implying my Self in walking around the town / got a pair of Shoes tapt / pay'd eight Shillings.

F 20. this day very pleasant and warm / Continuing in taunton traviling around / Nothing very Remarkeble &C.

S 21. this morn very blowing and blustering wether / Set off from taunton came to Rehobuth[25] ware I made a small halt / then pushed on as far as providance ware I put up / So end this day.

S 22 and M 23. this morn very pleasant & blustering & cold / Continuing in providance / Nothing more Remarkeble [*cipher*].

T 24. this morn from providance Crost Seconk fery / came

to Barrington ware I made a small halt / then pushed on as far as warren ware I crost a fery and dined / then pushed on as far as Birstol[26] / from thair to Slaids fery ware I crost / went five mild put up in freetown.

W 25. this morn start'd from freetown / traveled six milds to acoxet in dartmouth ware I put up all night. Lay'd out two Shillings for traviling expenses.

T 26. this morn from acoxet crost Slaids fery / then eat my brakefast / then pushed on / Crost Seconk Lower fery / came to providance ware I dined [*and*] ware I heard we was to go in soon for ye army.[27] about three oClock it bigan to snow very vast indeed.

F 27. this morn we peraded our Slaves for to march to Grinage[28] / Eight or ten Serjeants of us went down in a fery Boat ware we was fir'd on by a battery at petauxet & rounded two / then we came about two milds / got a ground ware a Conew [canoe] carri'd fore of us a Shore at Warwick / then we pushed on as far as Grinage ware thare was no orders for us / then we pushed on as far as Johnson[29] / from thence came to providance ware put up.

S 28. this morn thick clowdy wether & warm / came from providance / came to Swansy ware I dined / then crost Slaids fery / came to acoxet in Dartmouth / one Shilling.

S 29. Continuing in Dartmouth / went about fore mild at Night / Return'd home agn.

M 30. Continuing in Dartmouth / Nothing very Remarkeble.

T 31. thick clowdy weather / No v Rem.

APRIL 1778 ACOXET

W 1. Wednesday April ye first / Continuing in Dartmouth / went up as far as Waterparponds[30] / at Night return'd again.

T 2 and F 3. Continuing in Dartmouth / very Blustering & Cold Wether / Nothing Very Remarkeble.

S 4. Continuing in Dartmouth / this morn very pleasant / In the after part of ye day Snow & Sum Stormy &C.

S 5. this morn thick clowdy wether & sum wrain / in the after noon clear'd away / Nothing very Remarkeble.

M 6. this morn very pleasant / Set off from acoxet / came

to Slaid fery ware I crost / then pushed on as far as Swanzy ware I stop a few moments / then pushed on 12 milds to providance / ariv'd about 3 oClock / 1 Shilling & six[*pence*].

T 7. this morn very pleasant and warm / Continuing in providance / this day a Number of officers set out for camp after diner / went down ye river in a cannou wich liked to sunk with us before we got a Shore a gain / Nothing more Remarkeble this day.

W 8. this morn very pleasant / Set [*out*] from providance / came as far as petwaxet ware made a small halt / then pushed on as far as grinage ware I dined / then proceeded on as far as Northkingstown ware I ariv'd about 4 oClock / about ten oClock it snowed very fast but it soon clear'd away again.

T 9. this morn thick Clowdy Wether & Sum Small Spits of Snow / Set off from Northkingstown / came as far as little rest / then pushed on as far as Southkingstown ware I ariv'd about Eleven oClock ware I taried all Night.

F 10. this morn very pleasant / Continuing in Southkingstown / Nothing Remarkeble.

S 11. this morn thick hasey wether / came from Southkingstown / came to northkingstown ware I dined / then pushed on as far as Grinage ware our Rec[*r*]utes was ware a party of 25 men was sent down towards ye enemy on ye Shore Side.

S 12. this morn thick hazey wether / Continuing in grinage till 9 oClock then set off for providance / arived about 2 oClock / very hot & pleasant fixed my pack / Send [sent] it down to grinage by a Soldier.

M 13. this morn very pleasant / came from providance / came to Grinag ware I ariv'd about 3 oClock ware we live very mery &C / this Day spent fifteen Shillings.

T 14. Continuing in Grinage exersis[*ing*] our Recrutes / thick Clowdy Wether / in ye after part of the day turn'd out our black [*troops*] / rec'd sum orders picked out a guard of 20 men & a sub.[31] then marcht down to Quidneset ware we made a guard house [*out*] of a dweling house half a mild from ye Shore ware we set 5 Sentinals / at day Light took off our Sentinals / march[*t*] up to Grinag.

W 15. ware we got our Guns draw'd[32] / Sum small showers of wrain / this evening betwen nine and ten oClock we was alarmed by Sum boats that landed at Quidneset point: ware we had a guard of 12 men & a Serjt: we turn'd out our men / Sent a party of men down toward ye enimy / I went up a mild or two to see if I could see any of ye enemy / none heaving in Sight I return'd to my Quarters again / Small showers of wrain &C.

T 16. the biger part of this day wraining and misty wether / one of our men had his arm blowed off firing an alarm gun / in the evening went on Guard att the fort jest below my Quarters.

F 17. this morn very pleasant / after dismising my Guard exersised our men / the biger part of our men marcht to Quitneset on Guard / So end this day &C.

S 18. Continuing in Grinage / Nothing very Remarkeble / So end this day.

S 19. Continuing in Grinwich till Sun down / then marcht a guard of 12 men down to Quitneset point ware we set 4 Sentinels / rain & sum cule / Nothing more Remarkeble.

M 20. this morn at day light marcht my guard up to Grenwich & dismised them / this afternoon our rijmt turn'd [*out*] under arms and the Independance Company[33] that belong'd to the town to wate [*wait*] on Genl Sullivan in to town[34] Nothing more Remarkeble this day.

T 21. Continuing in East Grinag / we are all order'd to be in Readyness to march to Quitneset / at one oClock got leave to go to providence / at half after one oClock sett off from East Grinwich / ariv'd att providance about 4 oClock ware I heard that a Ship had ariv'd at boston from france & further hear that the enemy hath sent for a Sesation of arms. the town fir'd 13 rounds of Cannon hearing that ye french & Spanyards hath declared us [*our*] Independancy &C.[35] then heard we was all order'd to Camp that belong to Colo Angells Rijt.[36] I got leave to go home / Set off from providence at Sun Set / Crost Seconk fery / came about 9 milds / put up to pearces tavern ware I ariv'd about ten oClock / eight & six pence.

W 22. this morn from parces came as far as browns tavern ware I got breakfast / then pushed on / Crost Slaids fery & pushed on as far as acoxet in Dartmouth / Six & three pence / in ye after noon Sum Small Showers of wrain. So end this day.

T 23 to M 27. Continuing in Dartmouth / blowing blustering wether / Nothing very Remarkeble / got a pair of Shoes tapt &C / two Shillings / very warm & C / in the after part of the day wint about 2 milds & return'd home &C.

T 28. this morn thick clowdy wet. from Dartmouth came to Slaids fery ware I crost / then pushed on as far as Rehobuth ware I stay'd all Night / for forage one shiling.

W 29. this morn came from Rehobuth 6 milds to providance ware I ariv'd about 9 oClock. went up on ye hill ware a few Cannon was scailed[37] / thick wether / Nothing very Remarkeble / 9 pence.

T 30. Continuing in providence / very thick clowdy raining weth / Lay'd out six and eight pence. [*illeg.*] Six pence for a Comb [*illeg.*].

MAY 1778. PROVIDANCE

F 1. this day thick wraining wether / Continuing in provid'e / Nothing very Remarkeble.

S 2. Continuing in providance till one oClock / then set off from providance / came as far as Cranstown ware I got a bowl of punch / then set off / came to Grinwich ware I continued all night / 20 Shillings.

S 3. Continuing in E Grinwich till ten oClock / then came from thair with a waggon load of Cloath / came as far as petwaxet ware made a small halt / then came to providance / Sum Small Shower of wrain ware we onloded our bagage / order'd to be in reddyness for a march.

M 4. Continuing in providance / Squaly wether / fitting to march / ten Shillings for mending Sum Shoes &C.

T 5. Continuing in providance / very pleasant / making ready for to march to the westward / Nothing very Remarkbl.

W 6. Continuing in providance fixing our Selves for to march to the westward / drawed all our things out of the Stowers.

T 7. this day about 12 oClock lift providance with the waggons / pushed on as far as Cranston ware oated our horses / then pushed on as far as furnis woods[38] ware our waggon got sat[39] / then I pushed on as far as watermans tavern.[40] the waggon not coming up I return'd back for the waggon a gain but we stay'd in the woods all night.

F 8. this morn rain & cule / hir'd 2 pair of oxen to git on our waggons / we pushed on as far as watermans tavern ware we got our waggons mended & continued all day in Coventry / thirteen and six pence for board.

S 9. this morn started from waterms tavern in Coventry / came about 3 mild oated our horses / then pushed on as far as Dixon[*'s*] in Vollingtown[41] ware we oated our horses / then pushed on as far as plain field ware we put up.

S 10. this morn we was detain'd by two of our horses wanting to be shod / then we set off / came to Canterbury ware we oated our horses / then we pushed on as far as Scotland ware we oated our horses again / then pushed on as far as windom ware we put up.

M 11. this morn started from windom / came to Lebenan Crank ware we oated our horses / then proceeded on as far as andervour ware we gave our horses sum hay [*and*] ware a man over took me from providance & had orders from Colo Green to take Charg of ye Wag[*gons*].

T 12. this morn from andervour came as far as bolton ware we oated our horses. then we proceed[*ed*] on as far as hartford ware we draw'd three days provision ware we tarri'd all night / then we pushed on as far as falmingtown ware I left the waggons & pushed on two or three milds from thare ware I put up.

T 14 and F 15. this morn from farmington pushed on as far as Bethelem in Woodbury ware I ariv'd about two oClock ware I continued till Satterday 16[*th*].

S 16. this morn from bethelem came to Southbury in woodbery ware I ariv'd about 12 oClock but No News of the waggons / Stay'd in town till Sun Set / then rode 5 milds into waterbury ware I put up.

S 17. this morn traveled in to waterbury / I heard Nothing of ye waggons pushed on towards farmington as far as Southingtown ware I made a small halt then pushed on to farmington ware I dined / then pushed on within fore mild of Litchfield ware I put up.

M 18. this morn very pleasan / pushed on about 1 mild to the Eastward of litchfield ware I got breakfast / then pushed on to Newpreston ware I dined / then pushed on as far as paulings precinct ware I made a small halt / then pushed on to the top of the mountain ware I put up &C.

T 19. this morn pushed on / overtook the waggons / then pushed on as far as fishkills ware we drawed sum provision / then we pushed on to fishkills landing ware we tari'd all Night.

W 20. this morn crost the North river / landed at Newbury[42] / then we proceeded on as far as New Winsor ware we drawed sum provision. then we pushed on as far as Bethelem ware we put up all Night ware I got Sum Cloaths wash'd [*and*] ware I got a Shirt & Sum Stocks[43] burnt up—

T 21. this morn from Bethelem came to bluming grove[44] ware we taried a Small Space of time / then proceeded on as far as Chester ware we taried till our horses eat / then we pushed on within two milds of warwick town ware we tari'd all Night in orang County.

F 22. this morn we drove into town ware we halted a few moments / then pushed on into hardy town ship in Sussex County ware we stoped two owers / then pushed on seven milds ware we put up.[45]

S 23. this morn from hardyton pushed on fourteen milds to Newtown in Sessex County ware we put up and drawed three days provision.

S 24. this morn from Newtown came to hardwick wich was 5 milds ware we made a small halt. then pushed on 5 milds to a place cal'd Log Jayl[46] ware we made a halt for three howrs / then pushed on to a small town cal'd hope / Inhabit'd by Moravins.

M 25. this morn set off from hope / pushed on twelve milds to oxford ware we put up / very dry Sultry Wether.

T 26. this morn thick cloudy wether / Set off from oxford / pushed on to Greenwich township wich was five milds ware we oated our horses / then we crost ye Deleware at Eastown ware we drawed 4 days provision / then pushed on 6 milds to bethelem town ship ware we put [*up*].

W 27. this morn thick raining wether / pushed on two milds towards bethelem ware we halted 3 howers / then pushed on to Bethelem town, a small town inhabited by Moravins / hear we drawed two days provision / then crost a small river by bethelem cal'd, lahio,[47] then push'd on two milds to Salsbury in Northamton town Ship.[48]

T 28. this morn cule & pleasant / Set off from Salsbury. pushed on six milds / came so a small town cal'd emus inhabited

183 June. 1778. Valey forge

M 1st Continuing att Valey forge Stormy Wether. holding our Selvs in readynefs for to march every man orderd to pack up every thing to march in the morning.

T 2 this morn. thick faggey wether towards Noon Clear'd away very hot this day our Rigements pass'd Muster. orderd to hold our Selves in Readyness to march.

W 3 this morn very pleasant we was peraded marcht down to the perade with our packs then was Desmissed ord to be in readyness att a moments warning to march in ye afternoon expected &c.

Entries from Greenman's encampment at Valley Forge during the summer of 1778.

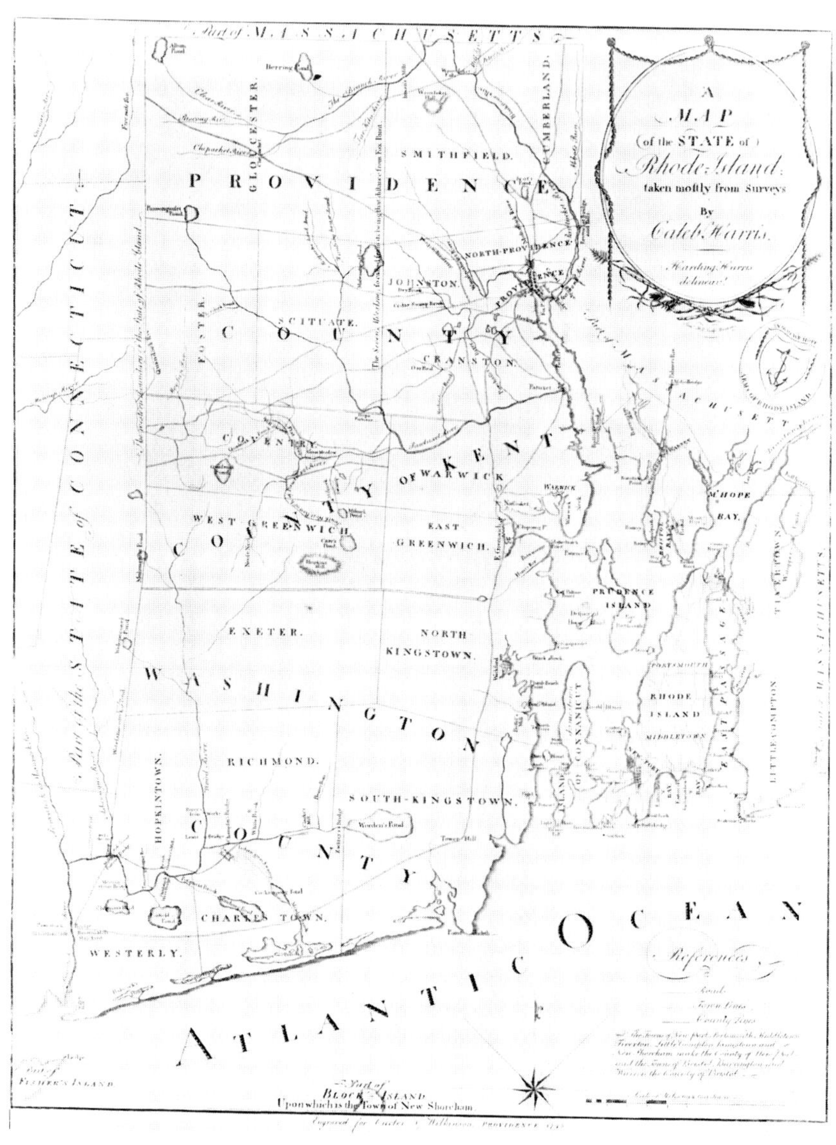

Map of Rhode Island in 1795, from surveys by Caleb Harris. Courtesy of The Rhode Island Historical Society.

by duch Moravins[49] / we hear washed all our Cloaths. then pushed on 3 milds to uper milford ware we put up.[50]

F 29. this morn toock sum provision in a hankerchife / left the waggons to uper milford / pushed on 35 milds to valey Forge ware I joyn'd my Rejiment.

S 30. Continuing att Valley Forge / the biger part of ye Rijt. moved into their huts / very sickly in camp / a new exersise caried on by the prusand general.[51] this after Noon I took a waggon / went out to meet the bagage 8 milds to a place cal'd the trap.[52] at Night return'd to camp again—the waggons taking another road got into camp before me and deliver'd the Cloaths out to the Rijemt. and every man order['*d*] to be in readyness for to march att 3 oClock in the morn.

S 31. Continuing att Valleforge / rain & cold. order'd to hold our Selvs in readyness for to march / all ye Rijtm draw'd froks hats & overhalls, we hear that the enemy is a moving out of phi[*la*]delphia[53] / very cold & raw for the time of year—

June 1778. Valey forge

M 1. Continuing att Valey forge / Stormy Wether. holding our Selvs in readyness for to march / every man order'd to pack up every thing to march in the morning.

T 2. this morn thick foggey Wether / towards Noone Clear'd away very hot / this day our Rijement pass'd Muster. order'd to hold our Selvs in Readynes to march,

W 3. this morn very pleasant / we was perad'd / marcht down to the perade with our packs / then was dismised ord. to be in readyness att a moments warning to march / in ye aftrnoon exersised &C.

T 4. this morn thick wether / Continu'd in Valley forge. this day thare was a man executed for, a Spy[54] / Nothing more Remarkeble.

F 5. this morn thick clowdy wether / in the afternoon, clear'd up warm—order'd to hold our Selvs in Readyness for to march / washed all our Cloths and so forth.

S 6 and S 7. Continuing att Valley forge—Nothing very Remarkeble / Sum Small Showers of wrain / in the afternoon clear'd away warm, and then draw'd alowance of prayers.[55]

M 8. Continuing att Valey forge / we hear that the enemy

is got all thair Sick on board and thair heavy Cannon, & agoing to incamp on the jarsis [Jersey] Shore.

T 9. Continuing att Camp att valey forge / Nothing Remarkeble.

W 10. this morn at the beat of the Genl. struck our tents. marcht about a mild over Schoolkills River & Piched our tents in a field in providance town Ship[56].

T 11 to S 14. Continuing in Camp in providance town Ship. Sum Small Showers of wrain / Nothing more Remarkeble / we hear that thare is a general exchge of prisoners to be very soon. and that fore men is gone to the Congress to try to settl a peace.[57]

M 15. this day a Number of prisoners came from philidelphy who informs us that the enemy is gitting every thing in readyness to go to New York & we hear that the french is proclamed war againts great britton.

T 16 to T 18. Continuing in Camp near chalkiss, a Number of prisoners came out of philedelphia. Continuing in Camp / Nothing very Rem'bl / this day we hear that the ennemy is left philidelphia and a Capt of our train been in to phidelphia.[58] last night about twelve oClock att the beet of the Genl. struck our tents / marcht about 4 milds & incampt in a large field.

F 19. this morn att the beet of the Genl struck our tents / marcht fore or five milds / Stopt a few moments then pushed on as far as Newbriton ware we halted about one oClock & piched our tents in a larg field ware we taried all day.

S 20. this morn the genl beet att two oClock / we Struck our tents / marcht a bout 7 milds & made a halt at a small town cal'd green town / then pushed on in the rain / Crost the dilliware / pushed about 5 milds to Amwell ware we piched our tents in a field / we hear that the enemy is bound for brumswick.[59]

S 21. this morn att the beet of the Genl struck our tents. march about a mild then was order'd to march back in to the field ware we incampt ware we continued all day. Exspecting Genl. Washington to cros the dilliware. very hott whether. order'd to be in readyness for to march in the morn.

M 22. Continuing in amwell / wraining wether / Genl Washington crost the river with a large Number of troops[60] / thare is 4 hunderd of the enemy desrt'd with two comissoned officers.

T 23. this morn started from amwell / the hole army marcht toward prince town / marcht about ten milds & stopt [*at*] hopewill.[61] then the Rijmts marcht off / Left part of our division on the Ground wich was command'd by Genl Lee / then we marcht in to a field ware we fixed our arms, & lay on the Ground in the field / misty wraining wether.

W 24. this morn thare was a detachtmt of 5 thousan men sent toward the enemy[62] / Continuing in hope will / holding our Selvs in readyness for to march / we hear that the enemy is gone to South amboy.[63]

T 25. this morn the Genl. beet / we peraded the Rijt. & slung our packs marcht as far as rockey hill ware made a small halt / then pushed on as far as kingstown ware we made a halt and sent out a large guard. very hot & sultry wether / we have Intiligence of the enemy being about fourteen milds off & the Militia clost [close] after them,[64] we hear that a Number of hassans[65] left the enemy. att Sun down marcht into a field ware we grounded our arms & order'd to stay by them ware we stayed about half a Nowr / then marcht 5 milds and halted in a flax field at a place cal'd long Bridge.[66]

F 26. this morn started very early / pushed on 6 milds as far as a small town cal'd Crambury[67] ware we made a halt ware we heard of the enemy being about 18 milds a head & the enemy a pushing on for Sandy hook.[68] hear we stayed three owers & drawed sum provision / our Division was order'd forrid [forward] under the Command of Genl Lee[69] / we went about 6 milds & made a halt / Sum very heavy Shower of wrain & Thundr.

S 27. this morn turn'd out from amung the wett grass. from [*illeg.*][70] pushed on 6 milds near Englishtown ware we draw'd 40 rounds of Cartireges / then marcht into the wood ware we heard a Number of Cannon fir'd toward the Surthurd of us / then we march'd about half a mild to the left of the army ware we stopt a Nower / then we ware order'd to sling our packs / we marcht half a mild into a Medow almost to the wright whare I took quarts. under a huckel bury buch. for it was very hot indeed / in the Night it wrain'd & cold.

S 28. Englishtown / this morn att two oClock we slung our packs[71] / advanc'd towards the enemy about 3 milds from ware we lay / part of the militia & light hores that was on the wright engag'd the enemy / then our Division under the Command of Genl Lee advanced towards the enemy[72] / thay form'd in a Sollid Collom then fir'd a voley att us / thay being so much Superier to our Number we retreated / thay begun a very heavy Cannading / kil'd a few of our Rijmt. then we form'd again under a fence ware the light horse advanced on us / we began a fire on them very heavy / then the footmen rushed on us / after firing a Number of rounds we was obliged to retreat. a Number of our men died with heat a retreating. a Number of troops form'd in the rear of us and sum artilira wich cover'd our retreat.[73] thay began a fire on the enemy, then thay [the British] retreat'd / Left the Ground with about a thousand kil'd & wounded. on our Side about two hunderd kil'd & wounded & died with heat.[74] after We retreated we went back to the ground ware we left in the morning att English town ware we buried sum of our officers. here rec'd a ball in my left thy.[75]

M 29. Continuing in English town. this day we buried all the dead / the enemy gone off intirly / very hott indeed so that the men that wan [went] on a march retreating yesterday throy'd away thay packs & so forth and a Number dyed before ye enemy retreated back.

T 30. Continuing in a field near to English town / water very scarce indeed / Such a Number of Solders that water is almost as scares as Liquor & what is got is very bad indeed / we hear that the enemy is got to Statton Island.[76] this afternoon we draw'd two days provision & fit for a march.

JULY, 1778 ON A MARCH

W 1. this morn att two oClock the Genl beet / we fix'd our packs marched off about 9 milds & stop'd in a pine woods about a Nower / then we slung our packs / marcht about a mild near to a brook about half a mild from Spotswood ware we continued till 12 oClock att Night.

T 2. this morn at 12 oClock A.M. ye Genl. beett / we fixed our packs / at one the troop beet / we marched off from Spots wood town / marcht ten milds / came to brumswick. marcht about a mild & grounded our packs / very hot wether indeed / our bagage came to us / we pitched our tents. rain & very squaly.

F 3. Continuing near brumswick / rain / very hot sultry wether.

S 4. Continuing in a field about a mild from brunswick / in the afternoon the hole of the army perad'd and form'd two lines ware they fir'd thirteen peases of Cannon & the hole of the army fir'd the [*three*] rounds and gave 3 chears in memory of Independance.[77]

S 5. Continuing in our tents / every man order'd to hold him Self in readyness for to march.

M 6. this morn the genl beet / we struck our tents / My Self being poorly I came with the bag'e waggons / came as far as quibeltown ware we made a halt till 5 oClock. then pushed on to Scoch plains ware we lay all Night.[78]

T 7. this morn at the genl. beeting we struck our tents / marcht as far as west field ware we made a small halt / then we pushed on as far as Spring field ware we made a halt for all Night / very hot wether indeed.

W 8. this morn the Genl. beet at 3 oClock / we marcht to the hi[*g*]hts of New work ware we halted a Nower / then we pushed on about 4 milds from Newwork ware we made a halt all day / Genl. Lee being under an arest we was commanded by a prusan Genl. nam'd Barron d[*e Steuben*].[79]

T 9. Continuing in Camp in Newwork town Ship / washing our Cloaths / order'd to be in readyness for to march in the morn.

F 10. this morn att two oClock struck our tents / marcht about 8 milds ware we forded Second river[80] & pushed on a bout a mild to a place cal'd Slarterdam ware we pitched our tents and stayed all day / att Night it rain'd.

S 11. this morn from Slawterdam marcht within about two milds of peramam[81] ware we made a small halt / then pushed on a mild from peramam ware we pitched our tents / very raining wether & very squalley.

S 12. Continuing near peramus / went into the Country 3 or fore mild / toward Night return'd to Camp again / Nothing more this day.

M 13. Continuing near peramus / this day our rigement pased muster / order'd to hold our Selvs in readyness to march.

T 14. this morn the Genl beet / we struck our tents marcht as far as kearkeart ware we made a halt all day.

W 15. this morn from kearkreat came to haver Straw ware we made a halt about two milds from the North river in a field / very hot indeed / hear we pitched our tents & continued all day.

T 16. this morn the Genl beet / we struck our tents slung our packs / marcht down to kings fery ware we crost the North river[82] & marcht about a mild & pitched our tents by a thick woods ware we continued all day.

F 17. Continuing near kings phery ware we hear that thare is a french fleat ariv'd at Sandy hook & a Number of Cattle sent on board to them[83] / we ware order'd to hold our Selvs in readyness to march att two oClock P.M. / att 3 we sett out / we marcht up to peekskills ware lay in a field on our tents / Sumthing cold for ye time of year.

S 18. this morn very foggey / Started from peekskills / came 7 milds to Crumbpond ware we made a small halt / then we pushed on 6 milds to Cotlins Manah[84] ware we made a halt and washed our Cloaths. pitched our tents in a wheet field.

S 19. Continuing att Cootlins Mannar / Clowdy wether.

M 20. this morn rain / all the rest of ye division & brigade marcht off / left our Rijt. on the ground alone.

T 21. Continuing near Crotons bridge[85] / we had orders to to be in readyness to march to the eastward.[86]

W 22. this morn about 5 oClock the G beet / we struck our tents / march about 16 milds ware we pitched our tents again in an orchard in Salem[87] about 12 milds from Danbury.

T 23. this morn from Salem proceeded on to rigebury[88] ware we made a small halt / then pushed on to danbury ware we drawed sum provision & piched our tents & continued all Night.

F 24. this morn the Genl. beet att 3 oClock / we struck our tents / marcht to New town wich was ten milds from danbury. hear we made a halt about nine oClock & continued till about eleven / then we proceeded on to kinsmans phery ware we crost / then we came about 3 milds & piched our tents in South breton in woodbury township w. draw'd prov.[89]

S 25. this morn the G beet at 3 oClock / we struck our tents put them in the waggons / it began to wrain / we pitched our tents again / at 6 the genl. beet again / we struck our ten / Marcht as far as South bury ware we made a small halt / then we proceeded on within 5 milds of Waterbury ware we made a halt. hear we continued till 12 oClock / then we peraded & marcht thro waterbury 3 milds ware we incampt in a medow & draw'd provision.

S 26. this morn started very early / proceeded on about 4

milds to Southingtown ware we washed our Cloaths & pitched our tents on [a] plain on the Roade / at 5 oClock pm struck our tents / marcht 5 milds & piched our tents within 2 milds of farmington on the side of the Road.

M 27. this morn started about day light / proceeded on thro farmington about 5 milds ware we stopt & cooked sum provision / then we proceeded on to hartford ware stopt till 3 oClock & cooked sum provision / then we crost the phery & proceed'd on 5 milds ware we piched our tents.

T 28. this morn thick clowdy wether / ye Genl. beet about day light / we struck our tents / we proceeded on our rout as far as bolton / it wraining we put up in bolton meattinghouse. 8 milds from ware we started from, ware the troops was order'd to cook up all thair provision / at 4 oClock in the afternoon we marched off as far as andervour ware we halted & picht our tents.

W 29. this morn started from andervor / proceeded on 5 milds to Lebenon Crank ware we stopt 2 howers / then pushed on to windom ware we draw'd sum provision ware we stayed till 4 oClock / then we pushed on to New Scotland ware we piched our tents.

T 30. this morn started from Scotland / came to canterbury ware made a small halt / then pushed on to Plain field wich was about 11 mild from whare came from in the morn / hear we continued till 4 in the afternoon / was order'd to clean all our guns / then we marcht 4 milds furder to vallington ware we piched our tents and continued till the next day.

F 31. this morn started from Vallington / proceeded on our rout as far as Co[*v*]entry about 18 milds from providance ware we grounded our arms / it began to wrain / we took up our arms and put them in a Shed / about 4 oClock we peraded marcht 6 milds to Scituate to angells tavern[90] ware we piched our tents & was order'd to wash all our Cloaths & clean our arms.

August, 1778 on a march

S 1. Continuing in Scituate washing our Cloaths / two Rij't joyn'd us Colo Shurburns & Colo Webbs[91] & sum artilira / we hear that the french fleet is alround Newport, & took sum frigates[92] / was order'd to hold our Selvs in readyness to march in the morning—

S 2. this morn from Scituate push'd 4 milds to Johnson[93] ware we made a small halt / then pushed on 4 milds father ware we pich'd our tents in a medow.

M 3. this morn we was order['*d*] to make a return of what guns & amunition was wanting to compleat [*illeg.*] / this day went to providance / at night return'd again with sum acuterements that was for the Company / this Night rain wet us & our Cloaths.

T 4. Continuing in Johnson / this day in the afternoon the brigade form'd and went thro sum of the exersises, then return'd to our tents again and order'd to hold our Selvs in Readyness to march in the morn at two, oClock.

W 5. Continuing in Johnson / Clowdy misty wether till 10 oClock / then we marcht into providance ware thare was a Number of boats made for to go on to the Island with a Number of french prises ariv'd at providance[94] / order'd to hold our Selvs in reddyness to march in the morn at 5 oClock.

T 6. this morn the G beet / we struck our tents / marcht thro providance / proceeded on to petucket[95] ware we halted about a Nower / then we pushed on to Rehobuth about 6 mild from petucket ware we piched our tents.

F 7. this morn the G beet at two oClock / we struck our tents / marcht down to Slaid phery[96] ware we crost / then pushed on to free town near fall river ware we halted two or 3 howrs / then we pushed on to tiverton 4 milds from howlands phery ware we piched our tents & draw'd sum provision.

S 8. this morn from ware we incampt proceeded on our march as far as howlands phery ware we halted and piched our tents clost to ye river / a very brisk Cannading to the west of Rhode Island & Sum thing sot on fire but we dont hear what it is[97] / this after Noon order'd to draw 3 days provision & 50 rounds of Cartirages to be ready to imbark in the morn for Rhode Is.

S 9. this morn about 7 oClock we imbarked very chearfulley for Rhode Island[98] / landed our troops / marcht up on the Island about a mild & made a halt near one of the enemies forts & form'd a line / then we marcht about a quartir of a mild & form'd a line a gain ware we lay all Night in the wrain without tents clost to a Nother of the enemys forts.[99]

M 10. this morn turn'd out very wet & rub'd our arms and continued on ye hill nigh the fort / a very heavy firing towards the town / ye Shiping againts ye batterys / we hear ye Shiping is gone out & further hear that thare is a fleat off but don't hear what it is.[100] NMR.[101]

T 11. Continuing in portsmouth / we peraded ye Rigmt. marcht about a half a mild towards the enemy & then return['*d*] to our ground again. order'd to cook three days provision and hold our Selvs in ready to march in the morn att 6 oClock towards town.[102]

W 12. this morn wrain / Continuing in Camp / Nothing Remarkeble.

T 13. Continuing wraining & blowing very hard indeed all day / this Night we was alarmed but prov'd to be a false one / we continued on perade drawing Cartirages & fixing our guns for thay was in very bad order by the storm blo[*w*]ing down allmost all our tents.[103].

F 14. Continuing in portsmouth / Cle[*a*]ning our guns / draw'd 3 days provision / order'd to hold our Selvs in readyness to march in the morn. So ends this day.

S 15. this morn about 4 oClock ye Genl. beet / we struck our tents / marcht about 5 milds to Middletown & picht our tents in Sight of the enemy about a mild & a half from thair Lines / turn'd out a larg pequit & a larg body of fatiague men, order'd to lay on our arms.

S 16. Clowdy morn / Relv'd the fatigue party / Sent on a Nother to build batterys againts ye fort. building a fort before our brigade[104] / the enemy very still / Ye heavy Cannon mov'd down towards ye lines / fogey thick wether.

M 17. this morn thick wraining W / Sum Cannon fir'd from ye enemy to our piquits. implying our Selvs in building baterys. N.M.

T 18. thick fogey wether / a Number of Cannon fir'd at our batterys / holding our Selvs in readyness for an atack / So end this day.

W 19. this morn fogey / ye enemy began thair fire in the batterys again / very fogey again at Night.

T 20. Continuing in Camp / a Number of Sail seen off / Sed to be the french fleat / the enemy & our people keep [*up*] a continual fire of Cannon / the french fleat it prov'd to be wich came to off ye Southward the of Island ware thay keep very still / we exspeckt them in very soon / our people heft in a Number of Shells in to thair lines / So end this day.

F 21 to S 23. Continuing in Camp / Cannading & bumbarding each other Night and day / holding our Selvs in readyness for an atack at the first Notification.

M 24. Continuing in Camp / we hear part of ye french fleat is gone to Boston to be repair'd[105] / both sides keeps up a Constant bumbarding and Canonading all ye fore Noon / in the after noon our people got thair heavy Cannon down toward ye North end of ye Island / we exspect to move that way very soon. ye french fleat leaving us.

T 25. Continuing in Camp / ye french fleat all gone to boston[106] / we hear we are agoing to ye North end of ye Island. the Genl. order'd all the bagage to be mov'd to the North end of ye Island / ye enemy keeps up a very brisk fire.

W 26. we hear the enemy is left New york, & all the Troops is bound for New Port[107] / in the after noon ye enemy fir'd a very plenty of bums & a very Constant Cannading / in the evening about 14 of our Rijt taken prisoners and sum officers.[108]

T 27. Continuing at middleton / very warm, a few vessels seen off in Newport harbour / Supposed to be sum of the transports that had scutteled and got them up again[109] / Sum of our Sentenels wounded and one killed by the enemy.

F 28. this day very still on both Sides / we hung a man that was a going to ye enemy one we kecht over the lines / about 7 oClock we ware order'd to strike our tents and be very still in doing it / we stay'd on the ground till 9 oClock at Night / then we marcht off about 4 milds ware we form'd a line ware we continued about 2 owers / then we marcht off again to butses hill[110] ware we continued till Sun wrise.

S 29. we marcht a small distance to the write / two Ships that was beating up the river fir'd a few Shot at us / we continued hear a Nower or two, the hasans made up towards a fort that was on butses hill / Nobody being met we preceed'd thair move / we set out for the fort & jist made out to geet into it before thay come up the hill / then the enemy made back again to a small hill a bout a mild from this fort[111] ware thay mad a stand / at Night our rijement went on the Lower Lines.[112]

S 30. this morn about 6 oClock we marcht up on the hill to the northward of the fort ware we draw'd sum provision / then we mov'd into a field jist below the fort again / ye militia heaving up a line of breast work a crost the Island / a very brisk Cannading / in ye evening we was peraded counted into plattunes & order'd to lay on our arms / about 12 oClock we was peraded / marcht down to howlands phery & crost / then we marcht up to the ground ware we incampt before we crost the river.

M 31. this morn clowdy / we hear a fleat is ariv'd into Newport harbour & 6 thousand troops / we are order'd to hold our Selvs in ready to imbark on bord ye flat bottom boats to go to bristol.[113]

September 1778 on a March

T 1. this morn imbarkt on board of the boats / row'd up to kickmuet river[114] ware we landed & took out all our bagage / hear we continued till ye after noon / then the waggons came / caried off our bagage up to warren ware we piched our tents.

W 2. Continuing near warrin till the after noon / then the Genl. beet / we struck our tents / marcht to bristol ware we piched our tents on a hill[115] / very strickt orders given out for no Solgers to go from Camp without a pass—

T 3. Continuing near Bristol / the Ships that was to this end of ye Island is gone and the enemys tents struck that was pich'd at this end of the island / Nothing more this day Remarkeble.

F 4. Continuing in Camp near Bristol / about 9 oClock ye G. beet / we struck our tents / mov'd about 8 rods fathur to ye left[116] / we hear by a desarter that a Number of the enemy is left Newport & what is left on the Island is making fasheans[117] & putting them on board of the Transports.

S 5. Continuing in Camp / Clowdy wether / draw'd new arms for the Rijmt. So ends this day / in this Night we heard a Numbr. of Cannon fir'd to the eastward.

S 6. this morn very pleasant / thee Cannon we heard fir'd was to bedford / we hear thay landed 2 thowsan & burnt the town and was intrenching.[118]

M 7. Continuing in Camp / Nothing Remble. at Night we heard a Number of Cannon fir'd to the Southward.

T 8 and W 9. Clowdy wether / we hear that ye enemy is

come back to Newport again / raining wether / Nothing remark'l.

T 10 and F 11. this morn very plasant / ye enemy seem to be very still / Nothing sturing of Nary Side.[119]

F 11 and S 12. this morn cule / in the after noon the Brigade peraded / went to bristol / thare thay exersised sum & return'd to Camp. Nothing more [*interesting* ?] olney [only] Sum Small Shower of wrain—So end this day.

S 13 and M 14. this day the Troop all went to Meating to bristol[120] / we hear the french fleat lays in boston very peasful & not coming this way till a Nother fleat arivs wich is exspeckt'd every day.[121]

T 15. Continuing in Camp near bristol / all the boats order'd to howland fery with Speed.

W 16. we hear that thare is an English fleet exspected in every day, order'd to hold our Selvs in readyness to march in the afternoon &C—

T 17. Continuing in Camp near bristol / wraining Wether / we hear that thare is two brigades on thayr march from the grand army for this Quarter / exspecting the enemy will move this way.

F 18. this morn cule / about 8 oClock the G beet / we struck our tents / marcht about 3 milds from whare incampt about a mild from warrin ware we piched our tents in a medow by the river Side[122] / Sum wrain in ye evening / Clear'd off pleasant—

S 19 and S 20. Continuing in Camp near warring. the enemy very still / Nothing sturing oney [*illeg.*] &C &C.

M 21. Continuing near Warring / we hear that the french Spannards & english has had an engagement in ye bay of bisquay & ye english defeeted &C.[123]

T 22 and W 23. Continuing in Camp / Nothing Remarkelbe oney floging a few men at the post, wraining wether & blowing very smart / toar all our tents down &C.

T 24 and F 25. this morn went a crost the river to Warwick ware continued all day & in the morn row'd acrost the river again to warrin to the Camp / we hear that thare is a fleat ariv'd into Newport harbour / So end this 24th.

S 26 to M 28. Continuing in Camp near Warring / Sum

Small Wrain / NMR. this day attended divine Service &C / a very heavi Cannading in too Providance / Nothing Remarkeble.

T 29. we hear that the enemy has had two packets taken with orders in them for to leave america & the firing to providance [*was*] a Rejoysing att the News but we dont know the truth of it yet / NMR—

W 30. Continuing near Warren / we hear two Regements is left Rhode Island and gone to the West Indias & further hear that part of the fleet is ariv'd that had an Ingagemen in the bay of bisque.

October, 1778, Warrin

T 1 to M 5. Continuing in Camp near Warring / Nothing Remarkeble / holding our Selvs in readyness for the first word of Command.

T 6. this morn from Camp went to providance / a Number of tories taken [*and*] braught into town that was in a boat been a plundering at tiverton.

W 7. this morn from provid. pus'd to Swansey ware I din'd / then pushed on to the Camp at Warrin / Nothing M Remle.

T 8. this day we had a Genl. Revew and a Sham fight / fir'd a Nom of Cannon &C / So end this day.

F 9 to S 17. this morn the Rigt past muster / Continuing in Camp / Nothing Remarkeble oney holding our Selvs in readyness to march at the first Notiss / No thing seems to be sturing on the enemys Side.

S 18. this day we all struck our tents & let the ground dry & clean'd out our camp / we hear that Genl. Washington has had a very Smart Ingagmt. near the North River but we dont hear how it went.[124]

M 19. we hear that thare is ten Regmt. left Rhode Island.

T 20. we hear that thare is a Nom of Ships sail'd from New york and lays down to Sandy hook & a Nomr. gone for the west Indias.[125]

W 21 and T 22. Nothing Remarkeble—this day we fir'd a Number of Cannon and small arms & buried the image of Colo Dunap in memory of the 22 of Oct. 1777.[126]

F 23 to T 27. Continuing in Camp / Nothing Remarkeble olney we hear that the enemy is about leaving New York & holding our Selvs in Readyness to march at the first word—

W 28. this day got a furlough / went to Dartmouth ware I continued till the Second of November / then return'd to Camp again / Nothing.

NOVEMBER, 1778, WARRINE

W 4 to T 12. November / turn'd out at 12 oClock to call the Roll / Cal'd / No Movement of the Enemy / very still on both Sides / the Regt very bare of Cloath / raining weth &C.

F 13. fixing up Stores and bords in warring to make barraks.

S 14. we hear a very heavy firing towards Rhode Island / we hear that thay are about to leave it.

S 15. very blowing blustering wether / Sum Small Spits of Snow / Continuing in our tents / Nothing very Remarkeble / a flag a truce came up from Newport with a Nom. of famelies.

M 16 to W 18. very pleasant wether / fixing our barraks in warrin as fast as posabil / Nothing more Remark.

T 19 to M 23. Sum Small Spits of Snow / very Cold blustering Wether / the other Regt. that belon'd to ye brigade mov'd off into Winter Quarters / Nothing sturing more.

T 24. this morn at the beet of ye genl struck our tents / marcht down to warrin ware we took up our Quarters in Sum old Shops & barns prepar'd for us near the Shore.

W 25 to S 28. Continuing in our Quarters / duty very hard / a main guard of 60 men keep in town to take up every Stranger, hearing thare was 6 Spies out from Newport. went to barranton[127] ware I stay'd an hower or two / then crost the fery & came back to my Quarters again / this day past muster.

S 29 and M 30. Continuing in Warrin / Nothing Remarkeble—

DECEMBER, 1778, WARRINE

T 1. this morn set out from Warrin with a boat / ariv'd to providance ware draw'd sum provision / Hear that a Nom of Solders been a stealing powder from the Magezeens.

W 2. this morn loaded my boat with board / then proceeded down the River to Warrin / NMR.

T 3. this morn traveled up to providance ware I continued till Sun Set / then proceeded on down to warrin to my quarters / Nothing More Remark.

F 4 to T 10. Continuing in Warrin / this day past Muster, Continuing in Warrin in our Quarters / Nothing Remarkeble oney duty very hard, we see a very Great Smoke on the Island of Conanicut which was surposed to [*be*] the enemy setting housan on fire &C, Raining Wether &C. at Night snow'd and blowed very hard.

F 11. we hear that ye Rigt is a going to move to Providance.

S 12 to S 26. Continuing in Warrin / Nothing Remarkeble / laying in our barracks wich is very bad indeed, & cold snowy wether / two or three men fros'd to death[128] / we hear no stur of the enemy / we hear that thay have no stores of provision only what thay bring from New York as thay want to yose [*use* ?] it wich gives us Reson to think thay are agoing off in the Spring—

S 27 and M 28. this morn set out to go to provid. very bad traviling / pushed on to Rehobouth / it being very bad traviling we ware oblig'd to put up ware we continued till morn / then pus'd on to the fery / Crost / went to providance ware I continu'd all day / N M Remark'e.

T 29 to T 31. this morn started from providance / Crost the Lower fery / push'd on as far as hunts ware we stopt a few moments / then push'd on to kelleys fery ware crost / came up to the Barraks / N M / So end this year in Warrin.

January, 1779 Warrin

F 1 to S 31. Continuing in Warrin, Nothing very Remarkeble / we hear ones [once] in a great wile from the weston Army / we hear thay are in great Confusion thare Concerning ye pay, being so Depriciated,[129] times very dull indeed / we hear no Stur of the enemy / Thay seem very still / hear that Genl. Washington is gone to the Congress to try to get the Solders pay made up to them[130] / we he[*ar*] a party of the enemy land['*d*] at and went to George doing a great Deal of Damage[131] / part of ye Regt this Evening peraded under arms under pertence of giting thair rights / Soon dispearst by ye Genl on perad.[132]

February 1779 Warren

M 1 to T 11. Continuing in Camp / Nothing RMB / this morn about five oClock we was alarmed by sum of the enimy that landed on Poppaqua wich we supposed was come to plunder[133] / we exspect sum of them will be off before long.

F 12. this day went to Slaids ferry with a letter from Colo Angells & return'd towards Night / Very Pleasant Wether.

S 13. Continuing in Warrin till Second March / then travil'd to Dartmouth.

MARCH 1779, WARREN

T 2 to T 18. Continuing in Dartmouth till the 18th March / this morn from Dartmouth came as far as Slaids ferry ware I sleapd half an Hower / then pushed on as far as warrin ware I continued all Night.

F 19. this morn Snow / Set off from Warrin / came to Swanzey ware I stayed all Night.

S 20. this morn clear and Cold / Set off from Swanzey / came as [*far as*] Diton[134] ware I made a small halt / then I pushed on to Taunton ware I continued untill Tuesday ye 23rd.

[*T 23*]. this morn from Taunton / came as far as Swanzey ware I dined / then I pushed on to warren ware I joyned my Rigm't.

W 24 to S 28. Nothing Remarkeble oney a flag came from Newport NR.

M 29 to W 31. we hear that thare is a No of Ship ariv'd into Newport & further hear a large [*fleet*] layeth in the Sound.

APRIL 1779

T 1 and F 2. this morn set off from warren in persute of a Diserter / went as far as Freeton ware I made a small halt / then pushed on as far as Middlebury ware I found him / put him in Irons / went to taunton with him ware I tarried all Night / NR.

T 3. this morn from taunton came as far as Reboboth ware I dined / then pushed on / came to Swanzey ware I stop'd a few moments / then went to warren ware I delivered up the Deserter.

S 4 to T 22. Continuing in Warren. past Muster / we hear the enemy is defeated at Carrolina[135] we soon exspect to have the campa'n oppen / we exersise the prusan way left of the 64th. intirely[136] / we hear the enemy is left Georgey / we was alarmed by a bacon or a light we see toward providance at which we was order'd to lay on our arms. we have News that the french fleet is bound for this Coats / we have Intiligence of a fleet coming into New York / Sum Spits of Snow.

F 23. this day went to bristol ware I heard thare was a pachut [packet] arrived into Boston from France who informs us a French & Spannish fleet is bound for the American Cost.[137] this Evening about ten oClock the biger part of the Regt. turn'd out in Muterny under arms / paraded & took Comm'd of the artillery ware they stayed about two Hours / gitting No Answer from the Colo. to satisfy them thay push'd off for providance / marcht within two milds of the ferry ware thay halted & sent to Genl. Gates. Genl. Glover came to them / Sum Incurrigement being given them thay return'd back to warren in the morning at Nine oClock and disband'd / thay informed us that had sent a Commity to Providance to make a proper Complaint.

S 24. thay return'd this after Noon [*and*] inform the men thay was to be paid off by the 1st May / the Regt. when paraded at Roll Call this evening behaved as well as hear to fore / two of the Mutiners deserted / NMR.[138]

S 25 to F 30. Continuing in warren / Nothing very Remarkeble / went to barrington. Removed my Quarters to Mr. John Childs.[139] So end this month.

May 1779

S 1 to W 5. Continuing in warren / mounted the main Gua[*r*]d / Nothing Remarkeble during my tower [tour].

T 6 to S 8. this morn was relieved from Guard / came home to Dartmouth ware I continued untill Satterdy the 8 / Nothing Remarkeble / then return'd to warren / at Night was a larmed.

S 9. we hear that the enemy landed at point Judith / took off a No. of Sheep &CC / NMR.

M 10. this Evening went about 3 milds to an owt Guard neer ye River that lead[*s*] to Newport which was commanded by a Serjeant in ye day time / an officer sent every night to remain till day light,[140] Nothing Remarkeble oney a few cannon fired during my tower.

T 11. this morn about day light left ye Guard / went to warren / mounted the main Guard.

W 12 to M 31. Continuing in Warren / Nothing Remarkeble oney duty very hard / Sum Cannon fired over on the Weston

Shore / we are informed sum of Colo. Greens men was taken off by the enemy / we are informed that the french is retaken Sant Luzey.[141]

June 1779

T 1 to T 10. Continuing [*in*] warren untill ye 4th. then at Revalie Beeting we marcht about a mild from warren on [*a*] hill cal'd Graves Hill ware we clear'd off the Stones &C to pich our tents. in the after Noon we march out and piched our tents / went on piquit at the Narrows at ye Serjts. Guard before mentioned / Nothing More Remarkeble.

F 11 to F 18. this day got Liberty to be Absent from the Regmt. till Munday ye 14 Inst.[142] came to Dartmouth / N Remarkeble during my Continuance hear—ye 14th went back to camp / Rain / NMR.

S 19. we have News that ye enemy is lost 15 hunderd men at Georgia[143] / this evening went on pequit at the Narrows / order'd to march from thair to Mount Hope to take Command thair for a week.[144]

S 20 to W 23. this morn according to orders I proceeded to Mount Hope ware I took Comm'd at that post and a Small Guard at bristol point / very pleas't / we hear that Genl. Lincon has captured 7 thousand of the Enemy at Georgia, went to bristol to vizit my guard / thair I tarried a few howrs / then return'd to the Mount again ware I received orders to dismiss my Guard and repair for warren for the Regt was to march on Fryday next.

T 24 to S 27. this morn dismised my Guard / went to warren ware I was order'd to return again and take Com'd untill I was Relived by Some of Colo. Jacksons men as thay was coming to take our post[145] / Continued at Mount Hope untill Sunday 27th. then was reliev'd by Lt. Hills / I then went to bristol with my men / took a flatt bottom Boat / push'd off for Newton on ye Narriganset Shore[146] / the wind blowing hard we was obliged to put on Shore at Warwick Neck ware I continued two Howers / then pushed on for Newton ware I arrived in the evening / tarried in town all Night.

M 28. this morn at four oClock we set out for boston Neck ware the Regiment was staysoned ware I arriv'd about 8 oClock ware I found the tents piched on a height cal'd Barbers Height a very pliasant Situation in plain Sight of Newport & the movements of the enemy[147] / Sum Shower of Rain.

T 29 and W 30. Continuing at Barbers Hill in North Kingston / the duty very hard oney our Regt. being hear and for Safty of this Shore we are obliged to form a line of Sentinels from obdikes New town to point Judith / a man deserted from ye enemy on Jameston.

JULY 1779

T 1 to S 11. Continuing at North Kingstown / Nothing Remarkeble oney alarmed by a few of the enemy that land'd on Quidneset Neck / did no damage.

M 12. this morn clowdy wether / at two oClock set off from camp / came to Greenwich ware I made a small halt. then pushed on as far as warrick ware I tarried all Night—

T 13. this morn from warwick came to petwaxet which was about 5 milds ware I got breakfast / then pushed on to providance ware I continued all Night.

W 14. this morn got a passage to go to obdikes Newton in a boat but She got on a rock [*in the* ?] Providance river / I was put on Shore / proceeded by land as far as warwick ware I dined / then I pushed on to camp / the Sun about an Hower High.

T 15 to M 19. Continuing at Barbers Height / we hear that the enemy is burnt Stratford and part of two or 3 more towns.[148] went down to point Judith on a Court of Inquiry / at Night return'd again N M R.

W 20. this morn we had hand bills which informs us that Genl. Wain with his Infintry stormed a fort at ye North River on a point called Stoney point and captured all the men that was in it with a Loss of but a few men.[149] we see a Small fleet off point Judith.

W 21 to W 28. this day we fired a futie Joy[150] of thirteen Cannon for the News heard of Genl. Waines Victory at Stoney point / went into Newport Harbour 37 Sail of Shipping / hot sultry wether / a prisoner that had deserted and under the sentince of Death got away from the Guard[151] / this day a man deserted from the enemy on the Island of Jameston / braut no new[*s*] Remarkeble.

T 29. this morn rain & cold for time of year / I was detached with a party of men to the South ferry ware I continued till

2 oClock in the after Noon.[152] came an Express from camp / Informed me that the biger part of the Regement had turn'd out in Muterny / I received orders to march with my men to camp all exsept 3 which was [*to*] keep Guad / I then pushed on for camp as fast as posable ware I arrived about 4 oClock ware I joyned my party to sum more Capt. Humphry had[153] / then marcht in persuit of the Mutiners which had marcht off for Greenwich to take a man from the Guad that was under Sentince of Death for Muterny / we marcht within two milds of Greenwich ware we was informed thay was coming back. We faced to the right about to move for camp / I took my Com'd / went down to the South ferry again ware I arriv'd about two oClock at Night / about two oClock a Sloop went down the river. I order'd her to send her boat on Shore / She would no[*t*] which ocasion'd us to fire at her / She [*passed* ?] by us & went out.

F 30 and S 31. Continued at ye South ferry / two or thre boats came hear that was from Stonington with Corn bound for Bristol. Raing & stormy wether.

August 1779

S 1. this morn Smart Showers of rain / at 5.oClock I was relieved by Ensn. Masury[154] / marcht my men up to the Regt. at camp & dismissed them. the Mutiners all return'd to camp / all pardined and marcht thru the Colours exsept one—Geor[*g*]e Milliman by Name[155] / he was sent to providance.

M 2 to T 19. this day thare was a boat that was staysoned at the mouth of the Narrow river took a barg & twelve men that belonged to the enemy / mounted ye main guad in camp / a man diserted from the enemy brings us No News worth Remarking [*illeg.*][156] / the men order'd to pack up all their things [*at* ?] Night which we sarch to see that thay had no unnecessary Baggage & to be in Readyness to march at a moments warning / at 8 oClock marcht down to ye South ferry with a party of men ware I relieved Ens. Wheaton[157] / a Nom. of cannon fir'd on the Island of Jameston & small arms / about Eleven at Night a Small Schooner & sum boats came and lay hear all Night who informed me thay had heard that the french fleet had been seen off Sandy hook / NMR.

F 20 to F 27. Continuing at the South ferry untill the 22nd /

then was relieved NR—we hear that a Capt of our light Hores with about two hunderd men stormed a fort belon[*g*]ing to the enemy at powlers Hook and took it with about two hunderd prisoners.[158] we are informed that part of England is blocked up by the french and that Briton has declared us our Independancy / NMR.

S 28. pleasant / Continuing at North Kingston / we see a very large Smok arise towards providance which made a very large Report.

S 29 to T 31. the Smook & Report we see yesterday was a powder-mill blowed up which killed one man & wounded sum more / we hear that the french is had a smart battle in the west India Islands and took Grenadia[159] / we hear that Comodore Whipple has sent in to Boston eight prises[160] / went to tower hill[161] / Nothing Remarkeble / thirty first Mounted Guard in camp / in the after Noon four of our men diserted / 37 Sail of the Enemys Shipping came into Newport harbour consisting all of small craft[162] / NMR.

September 1779

W 1. Nothing Remarkeble.

T 2 and F 3. this morn mounted the main Guard in camp / was reliev'd by Ensn. Masury / this day was officer of the day.

S 4. this day went to duches Island a fishing[163] / at Night return'd / Clear'd away cule and blow'd very hard / So No MRM—

S 5. this morn cule / order'd to see our mens arms cleen to march in the morn to be reviewed by Barron Stuban, a Major Genl. who hold the Rank of a inspector Genl. of the American army / he is a prusan / first brought the prusan Exersise into our army.

M 6. this morn at eight oClock we paraded our men with thair packs &C / marcht [*for ?*] the ground picked on for [*to*] be reviewed which was eight milds from Camp ware we was reviewed by Barron Stuban / Differant from as before[164] / then marcht back to Camp / in the Evening mounted the M Guard in Camp—[*illeg.*].

T 7. this morn was relieved from Guard / we hear that Count D'Estaign is bound on [for] this Cost & was Spock [spoke] with in Lat. 22.Long.70 / we have the News that Congress has given every officer an 100 Dollars for every Ration retained & ten Dollars for parts of Rations that can be got to every Non Commis'd officers and Solders[165] / a small fleet arrived into Newport Harbour consisting of two or the Square Rig'd Vessels & Sum Small Craft / this Night one of the Enemies vessels seen crusing off Duches Island.

W 8 to S 11. this after Noon Seven Sail of ye Shipping went out of Newport / this day was officer of the day / about twelve oClock went out 41 Sail of Shipping from Newport steering up the Sound / SNMR.

S 12. Continuing at barbers Hill / this day set on a court Martial / try'd a Corpl. for Stealing / found Guilty and Sentenced to receive 60 Lashes / at the Same Court tryed a Soldier for Selling Cydar Contrary to orders / Found Guilty and Sentinced to receive 20 Lashus.

M 13 to S 18. very blowing blustering wether / 3 men deserted from us this Night / went down to the South ferry / took Comd. of Ensn. Hubbarts Guard[166] / Sum boats came hear that was bound to Conanicut.

S 19. this morn was relieved by Ens. Green[167] / Marcht to Camp NMR.

M 20 and T 21. this day went a Sailing in a small cuder [cutter] boat to duches island ware we see a man on Conanecut / he gave Several Signals he wanted to come off / a small fish boat that was their went and feched him off / he proved to be one of Col browns Core belonging to Danbury. the Wind Contin'g at NE which has continued as afore said twelve day exsept part of one day.

W 22. the Wind Continuing at NE / this day was officer of ye Day / a Small Sloop that was bound out to seek for the french fleet with pilots on bord / a Ship being off coming in to Newport Harbour spy'd Hir and chased hir into a small bay by the bonet[168] / I was detacht with the Infentry / went down as far as the bonnet / the Ship seeing men coming down and a field piece fus'd off, went into Newport Harbour / two men belon[*g*]ing to the Ship that went out in a boat to kech sum fish blowed a Shore to point Judith ware sum of our men took them. brought them to our people.

T 23 and F 24. the Winding Continuing at NE / this day went a Sailling / the Sloop that went out with pilots returned no[*t*] seeing the fleet.

S 25 to W 29. Continuing in camp / Nothing Remarkeble

/ went as far as little rest / at Night return'd to camp again / went a fishing / NMR—

T 30. this day set on a court martial / tried 4 prisoners for abusing an inhabitant / found Guilty and sentinced to receive 100 lashes each one worse than ye rest / order'd by the court to be piquited 15 moments,[169] two hasans deserted from the Island of Conannicut by a fishing [*boat*] / thay inform us thay had heard in Newport that the french fleet had arrived at Sank Hook / NMR.

October 1779

F 1. this morn the Court meet according to adjurnment / try'd 4 more prisoners / found them Guilty and sentinced them to receive 20 Lashes.

S 2 to T 7. Sum rain / we hear that the french fleet is arrived to Georgia and land'd six thousand men & Count D'Estaing has sent an Express to hold them Selvs in Readyness to make an atack on the Enemy and the fleet was bound for sum of the Northan ports of ye United States.[170]

F 8. this morn set off from camp in a small boat for warren. came as far as Warwick point ware I was brought two by a four pound Shot / Shoed my pass / then proceeded on to warren ware I arrived the Sun about an houer high / I then went up to Rehoboth ware I continued all night.

S 9. this morn from Rehoboth came to Kelleys ferry[171] ware I got put acrost / then went to warren / took my load and proceeded to boston Neck ware I arrived about ten oClock ware I heard thare was an English fleet in the Sound.

S 10. we hear that the french fleet is off Sandy hook / this Night we heard a No of Cannon fired off in the ossen [ocean] / Sum Shipps seen off / NMR.

M 11. this morn we see about 50 Sail of Shipping bound into Newport which came from New york / as they pased by Maccoral Cove[172] we took down wat thay was / proved to be 32 Ships 8 briggs 5 chooners & eliven Sloops. our people borded one of the Sloops / it being cam could not git hir away & by Reason of two barges coming from sum of the Shipping / She informed us thare was no troops on board & the biger part of the Transports had anings on board[173] / NMR.

T 12. this morn blustering / got liberty to go to Dartmouth

/ Set off from camp / came as far as Newton ware I got a passage in a boat for warren ware we arrived about 8 oClock / then pushed on for Swanzey ware I arrived about Eliven oClock.

W 13 to T 19. this morn set out for Dartmouth ware I arrived about 11 oClock AM & continued thare untill Tuesday ye 19th. N M R more than went to Warren where continued the Remainder of the day—

W 20. this morn set out from Warren in a small boat & came to Warwick where landed from where pushed on to Greenwich where I dined after which push'd on to Obs Dikes Newtown where I tarried all Night.

T 21. this morn went to Camp / are informed that the enemy is about leaving Newport & have burnt the Lighthouse, a No. of Ship that lay up the River fell down to the Southward of the fleet.

F 22. this day we had a very fine diner &C—in memorandum of the action of Read Bank on the 22nd. of Octr. 1777[174] / a No. of fires seen in Newport.

S 23 & S 24. Sum Small Showers of wrain / we hourley expect the Enemy to leave Newport as we are informed that they have got all their bagage on bord / eight Sail of Transports went into [*the harbor*] this after noon.

M 25. this day went on to the Island of Jamestown with a Serjt. & twelve men / Reconighted the Island as far as a small fort that the Enemy had evacuated / on my return I took Mr. Tears a Prisoner[175] & braught him off—in the evening went on again / found the Enemy had all left the Island and Newport, I returned to Camp / Sum boats was sent immediately to Newport—

T 26. this morn the Regt. all imbarked for Newport exsept my Self & a few men which was left for a Guard to take care of the tents & other Camp equipage—

W 27. this morn cule / Continuing in Camp / the Ships seen off which we supposed to be sum of the enemies a Reconighting the Cost / this after Noon receiv'd orders to Stricke the Tents & fix for Moving to Newport—

T 28. this morning sent all the bagage to the Regt. to Rome's point[176] where boats was waiting for the Purpose to transport them to Newport / myself set off in a ferry boat / arrived to Newpor about 2oClock / I found the Regt Quartered on the Point.[177]

F 29 to S 31. Continuing in Newport fixing the North battery on the point which the enemy had layed almost level[178]—ordered to hold our Selvs in Readyness to march for the Grand army[179]—

NOVEMBER 1779

M 1 to F 5. this day ordered to be in Readyness to embark to go to East Greenwich / the wind blowing to exsessive hard we postpon'd it till further orders.

S 6. this morning according to orders we embarked in Vessels precured for the purpose / Sailed for East Greenwich where we arrived at Sun Set / marched our men up into the Town where we barracked them in the Court house & other houses—

S 7. this morning we march'd our men about two miles to warwick, where we incamped near a Small Woods—N M R—

M 8. Continuing in Warwick fixing our Selvs for the March—&C

T 9. this day received our marching order & arrang'd in the following order Viz, 1st Division consisting of Colo. Webbs Jacksons & Livingstons to march to Morrow morning at Sun rise for hartford[180]—2nd Division to consist of Colo. Greens Shurbands & Angells to march Thursday next for the Same Place—

W 10. Continuing in Warwick holding our Selvs in readyness to march—

T 11. this morning the Regt. marched for hartford / I obtained Liberty to tarry behind a few days, came to East Greenwhich where made a small halt / then pushed on to obsdiks New Town where I got a pasage for Newport where I arrived about Sun Set.

F 12. Continuing in Newport purchaseing Trimmings for my Cloathing &C—

S 13 and S 14. this morn set off from Newport for Dartmouth / came as far as howlands ferry where made a small halt / then pushed on to Dartmouth where I arriv'd at Sun Set & continued till the 15th.

M 15 and T 16. this morn set out for Newport where I arriv'd about 5.oClock, the Commanding officer their ordered all the forrage &C moved off as their was an Exspectation of the Enemies coming back as they met orders Countermanding their evacuation of the Island but had got so far forward they prodeeded on for New york[181]—but the Inhabitance being afraid of their return giting off what of their Efects thay can—

W 17. this morning very blustering / Set off from the Point ferry for Conanicut where arriv'd in 15 minnits, then march'd acrost the Island / got a Passage for the Sout[*h*] ferry where arriv'd at 2 oClock PM / then went two miles to Mr. Barbers where continued all Night.

T 18 . this morning set off from barbers Hight / came to East Greenwich where Continued all Night—

F 19. this morning set out from East Greenwich / came to W Greenwich where I dined, then pushed on to Vollington where put up / hear meet Colo. Greens Regt. on the Return back to Newport—N M R—

S 20. this morn from Vollingtown came as far as Canturbury where I dined / then push'd on to windom, where put up.

S 21. this morn from Windom / thick raining wether & came to andevour where dined after which push'd on to bolton where put up.

M 22. this morn from Bolton came to hartford where I dined / then pushed on to farmington where mad a small halt / then pushed on about 5 miles where halted all Night.

T 23. this morn started very early / came to Harwington[182] where breakfasted / then proceeded on to Litchfield where made a small halt from where came to bethelem where put up & continued 'till ye 25th.

T 25. this morn from Bethelem went about two miles where made a halt for an hour / then went to a small town cal'd washington, from where went to ye oblongs in the State of New York where continued untill the 27th Inst.

S 27. this morn came as far as Washington where made a small halt / then came to Bethelem, where continued till ye 29th.

M 29. this morning set out from bethelem, came to Newmilford where mad a small halt from where pushed on within 3 miles of Danbury where put up—

T 30. Started this morning very early & came to Danbury where I join'd my Regt. N M R.

DECEMBER 1779 ON A MARCH

W 1. Continuing in Danbury / Shoeing our horses & fixing for a March 'till Sunday 5th.

S 5. this morn receiv'd orders to march immediately / we

agreable to order set off & came 6 miles / it snowing very hard we made a halt at Cortlands manner.

M 6. this morning set out from Cortlands manner / Came as far as Peekskills where we made a halt in a Woods without any Provision & continued all Night—

T 7. this morn set out from the Woods & marched to the Landing / Crossed our Troops & marched to Kearkearate[183] whare put up.

W 8. Set off this morn from Kearkeareate / came to Pumton where we drew Provision &C—

T 9. Continuing in Pumton untill ye 14th. where drew Provision & got a few Shoes for our men &C—

T 14. this morn marcht from Pumton / very bad Traviling & came to Hannover where put up—in housen.

W 15. this morn proceeded on to Morristown where we was to build huts for to winter in—

T 16 & F 17. this morning marched about half a mile to a thickit of Woods where we was ordered to build our huts but the N York Brigade being their & not a Suffient. of Wood we was ordered to hut about a mile off / Laid out the Ground & fell a few trees.

S 18 to F 31. Continuing near Morris building our huts / very cold & almost Starved for Want of Provision & as the mens huts was near compleated moved up into one of the Serjeants Huts, puting them amongst the men till our Hut could be fit to move into / at the same time to work on my hut when the wether would admit of it / Send out Guard to Elisebeth Town & C—No Camp Duty.

NOTES TO DIARY

1. The changes in the Rhode Island regiments are discussed above in the introduction to this part of the journal.

2. Worcester, Pa., was located just north of modern Norristown (Faden, *NAA*, "A Map of Pennsylvania . . .").

3. Probably the area then known as Franconia, south of modern Quakertown (ibid).

4. Not the modern Pennsylvania town of Richland, but the area just north of Quakertown (ibid.).

5. These areas were more generally called Upper and Lower Saucon (ibid.).

6. Perhaps the Lehigh River, which was also known as the west branch of the Delaware (Lester Capen, ed., *Atlas of Early American History* [Princeton: Princeton University Press, 1976], p. 4; hereafter cited as *AEAH*).

7. The Moravian Church, or *Unitas Fratrum*, though directed from Germany, had its colonial center in and around Bethlehem, Pa. "Strongly pietist in religion, they were friendly, tolerant and practical in their communal enterprises" (Evarts Greene, *Revolutionary Generation, 1763–1790* [New York: Macmillan, 1943], pp. 104–5). And though the Moravians were pacifists, they readily extended their hospitality to American soldiers, as Greenman discovered when he stopped at their settlement in Hope, N.J. (14 January 1778).

8. Now Easton, Pa.

9. Modern Newton, N.J.

10. The journal entries from the fifteenth through part of the twentieth are missing. The fact that the entry for the twentieth partially survives indicates that Greenman did indeed cover these days but that the leaves were subsequently lost. When the text resumes, Greenman and his fellows are in Dutchess County, N.Y., north of New York City, and are about to cross into Connecticut. "Pauling's Precinct" is the modern town of Pawling, N.Y.

11. "Raw mug" is Greenman's phonetic guess at "Waramaug" (also "Raumaug"), a lake and woods near New Preston. The Indian name means "good fishing place" (Florence S. M. Crofut, *Guide to the History and Historic Sites of Connecticut* [New Haven: Yale University Press, 1937], 1:445).

12. Judea and Bethlehem, Conn. The route to Rhode Island is the reverse of the one traversed by the troops on their way to join Washington's army at Morristown, N.J., in April 1777, and place-names not here noted were identified in that section of the journal.

13. Greenman apparently visits his relations in Bethlehem, as he does whenever he is in the area (see part 1, entry for 16 October 1776).

14. Andover, Conn.

15. Lebanon Crank was the name of an inn within the old township limits of Lebanon, Conn. The word "crank" had the meaning of "crooked or devious" and probably referred to a sharp turn in the road (Marian D. Terry, *Old Inns of Connecticut* [Hartford, Conn.: Prospect Press, 1937], pp. 234–36). Chastellux stopped there in November 1781 and thought the house had an "indifferent appearance," but his translator, George Grieve, following the same route, was pleased with the green tea and sugar loaf he was served (*Travels*, 1:71, 256n.).

16. Voluntown, now Sterling Hill, Conn. (Chastellux, *Travels*, map, 1:64).

17. Waistbands.

18. Rhode Island place-names not identified here were noted in parts 1 and 2 of the journal.

19. Ascedince: accidence, a fortuitous circumstance (*OED*, s.v. "accidence").

20. Pawtuxet, R.I., also spelled by Greenman "Petauxet."

21. This place, subsequently known as Knightsville, is within the village limits of Cranston. When the French army under Rochambeau marched through it in 1781, they variously wrought it in their maps and diaries as "Monkey Town," "Mont Kitown," and "Among Town" (Rice and Brown, eds., *Rochambeau's Army*, 2:21).

22. The Olney Tavern was located at the corner of North Main and Olney streets (more generally Olney Lane) and had been originally operated by Epenetus Olney. "It was near the highway from Boston, and had the best traveling patronage; the town mill was hard by, and the site was eminently the commercial center of these Plantations. Its neighborhood, as the most public location, was made the scene of penal discipline, and the town stocks were set up there. The property passed . . . through several generations . . . [and] continued its successful career as a hostelry" almost into the nineteenth century (Richard M. Bayles, ed., *History of Providence County, Rhode Island*, 2 vols. [New York: W. W. Preston, 1891], 1:305). The tavern house has been described as standing "at the top of Constitution Hill, a large old-fashioned, two-story, low-studded house, with a large yard in front" (Edward Field, *The Colonial Tavern*, [Providence, R.I.: Preston and Rounds, 1897], p. 235). And on this tavern green stood a large and stately elm, dedicated on Monday, 25 July 1768 as Providence's Liberty Tree by tavern owner Joseph Olney, with a discourse by Rhode Island Son of Liberty, Silas Downer. See Carl Bridenbaugh, *Silas Downer: Forgotten Patriot* [Providence, R.I.: Rhode Island Bicentennial Commission, 1974) for the text of this discourse. At the time of Greenman's stay there, the tavern was being run by the late Joseph Olney's heirs—including Col. Jeremiah Olney and his mother, "Widow Olney."

23. "Tapping" (not "taping") shoes involved putting a new layer of leather or some other material on the worn soles or heels (*OED*, s.v. "tapping").

24. Power: written permission or authority.

25. Rehoboth, Mass.

26. Bristol, R.I.

27. Col. Christopher Greene published the following notice in the Providence *Gazette* of 28 March 1778: "The Commissioned Officers and Sergeants, belonging to the two Continental Battalions raised by this State, are hereby directed to meet at Major William Arnold's, in East Greenwich, on Friday next, to make Returns of the Recruits, and account for the recruiting Monies they have received. They are also to hold themselves in Readiness to march to join their Cores immediately after that Day, as they will receive Orders at that Time when to go forward."

28. East Greenwich, R.I., the training ground for the new recruits.

29. Johnston, R.I.

30. Watuppa Pond, near Fall River, Mass.

31. Subaltern: a commissioned officer below the rank of captain; distinguished from field-officer (above) and noncommissioned officer (below).

32. That is, they drew guns for the coming campaign.

33. Greenman refers to the Independent Company of Kentish Guards, chartered in 1774 and active to this day. "This militia unit rejected Nathanael Greene as an officer because of his stiff knee, but he suffered the rebuff and joined as a private." Greene's good friend James Mitchell Varnum was commissioned a colonel in the Guards—but it was the humble private who became a Continental major general and who went on to prove himself one of the Revolution's greatest leaders (Boatner, *Landmarks*, pp. 430–31).

34. Maj. Gen. John Sullivan had been appointed commander of the Rhode Island department in March 1778 (Ward, *War of the Revolution*, 2:588).

35. Americans had eagerly anticipated the entry of France into the war ever since Burgoyne's surrender at Saratoga (October 1777) had so dramatically shown the world that American resistance to the British was potent indeed. The treaties of alliance between France and the United States were signed on 6 February 1778, but Spain, contrary to American expectations, did not officially enter the war until June 1779. For a concise discussion of the diplomacy of the Franco-American alliance, see John Alden, *The American Revolution, 1775–1783* (New York: Harper & Row, 1954), chap. 12, "The Bourbons Enter the War."

36. Not to the training camp at East Greenwich this time, but back to Washington's encampment at Valley Forge.

37. To scale a cannon was to clean its bore by firing off a charge of powder (*OED*, s.v. "scale").

38. Here begins the journey along the familiar route taken almost annually by the Rhode Island troops when they began a new campaign. All places not noted here have been previously identified. "Furness Woods" is perhaps so called because of nearby Hope Furnace (near modern Hope, R.I., in Scituate Township).

39. From the context, probably "sat" (set) in the sense of sunk into the muddy ground.

40. Waterman's Tavern was a popular inn on this much-travelled road, about halfway between Providence and Plainfield, Conn. (Rice and Brown, eds., *Rochambeau's Army*, 2: map 15). The tavern has been restored as a private residence (description and photograph in Alan Forbes and Paul F. Cadman, *France and New England*, 3 vols. [Boston: State Street Trust Co., 1927–29], 1: 164–68).

41. Voluntown is now the village of Sterling Hill, Windham County, Conn., "not to be confused with the present village of Voluntown, some 9 miles to the south . . . in New London County" (Rice and Brown, eds., *Rochambeau's Army*, 2:22). The French itinerary of 1781 notes that "Voluntown is a small group of houses, two of which are taverns. Dorrance's Tavern . . . is the better one; the other . . . is called Dexter's" (ibid.). Greenman apparently refers to the latter place.

42. Newburgh, N.Y.

43. Stocks in the sense of stockings; Greenman apparently had some difficulty with his laundry.

44. Blooming Grove, N.Y., village and township in Orange County.

45. Hardyston Township, Sussex County, N.J.

46. Log Gaol, N.J., about 8 miles south of Sussex Courthouse (modern Newton) (John Hills, "A Collection of Plans in the Province of New Jersey," 20 maps on 15 leaves, photostat [Library of Congress], map 15a).

47. Lehigh River (see note for entry of 12 January 1778).

48. Salisbury, Pa., west and south of Bethlehem (Faden, *NAA*, "A Map of Pennsylvania . . .").

49. Emmaus, Pa.

50. Upper and Lower Milford were undeveloped, mountainous regions between Emmaus and Quakertown (ibid.).

51. This was Greenman's first encounter with Friedrich Wilhelm Augustus von Steuben, popularly known in America as Baron von Steuben; Greenman had been in Rhode Island when the "prusand General" had begun drilling the troops at Valley Forge (February 1778).

52. Trappe, Pa., across the Schylkill and north of Valley Forge (Capen, ed., *AEAH*, p. 51).

53. The British, however, did not evacuate the city immediately, and so long as they remained in Philadelphia, the Americans stayed put in Valley Forge (Boatner, *Encyclopedia*, p. 716). Hence the oft-repeated formula in this section of the journal: "Order'd to hold our Selvs in Readyness for to march."

54. This was one Thomas Shanks, formerly an ensign in the Tenth Pennsylvania Regiment (cashiered 12 October 1777 for theft). "Thomas Shanks on full conviction of his being a Spy in the service of the Enemy before a board of Genl. Officers held yesterday by order of the Commander in Chief, is adjudged worthy of Death. He is therefore to be hanged tomorrow morning at Guard mounting at some convenient Place near the Grand Parade" (Washington, *Writings*, 12:10, 14).

55. Greenman may be joking: the routine of public prayers for the army, especially on Sunday, was well-established and assiduously fostered by Washington himself, but to draw prayers as a soldier would draw provision or powder appears to be the stuff of which camp humor is made. Still, it is worth noting that Congress had voted on 11 September 1777 to import twenty thousand Bibles for the troops, and it is just barely possible that Greenman is speaking of the distribution of these or of some other sort of religious hand-out (Bolton, *Private Soldier*, pp. 158–59).

56. Greenman's regiment (a part of Varnum's Brigade) was at this time under the command of Maj. Gen. Charles Lee (Ward, *War of the Revolution*, 2:572). Providence Township was an area almost directly opposite Valley Forge across the Schylkill. For an explanation of "the beet of the Genl." see note accompanying the entry for 14 June 1777 (part 2).

57. The diarist may be referring to the *three* peace commissioners dispatched to America by the North Ministry: Fredrick Howard, Earl of Carlisle; William Eden; and George Johnstone (Washington, *Writings*, 11:307).

58. Washington received intelligence of the British evacuation the morning of 18 June (*Writings*, 12:82–83). As soon as he was certain that British Commander in Chief Clinton's movement was to be by land (northward through New Jersey to New York City), he sent word to General Lee to move eastward into New Jersey: "Be strict in your discipline, suffer no rambling, keep the Men in their Ranks and the Officers with their divisions, avoid pressing Horses & ca. as much as possible and punish severely every Officer or Soldier who shall presume to press without authority. . . . Begin your Marches at four oclock in the Morning at latest and that they may be over before the heat of the day, that the Soldiers may have time to cook, refresh, and prepare for the ensuing day" (*Writings*, 11:489–90).

59. Brunswick, N.J. The place called Green Town has not been identified.

60. The American army, including Lee's Division, crossed the Delaware at Coryell's Ferry, now Lambertville, N.J. By the twenty-third the entire army was in New Jersey (Ward, *War of the Revolution*, 2:572).

61. Hopewell, N.J. On the twenty-third Washington opened his headquarters here in

a Baptist meetinghouse and began analyzing "intelligence reports that were arriving in considerable number and in extensive detail" (Freeman, *Washington*, 5:15).

62. Greenman greatly exaggerates the number of men sent by Washington " 'to act as occasion may serve, on the enemy's left flank and rear' " (quoted in ibid., p. 16). The decision to send some 1,500 men on this mission was a compromise reached in the famous council of war of 24 June 1778. At that meeting General Lee argued against an engagement, with Generals Lafayette, Nathanael Greene, and Anthony Wayne pressing warmly in favor. Lee prevailed for the time being. This council provoked the memorable remark from aide-de-camp Alexander Hamilton, "'the result . . . would have done honor to the most honorable body of midwives and to them only' " (quoted in ibid., pp. 16–17).

63. Camp rumor reflects the concern of the general staff over the exact route the British would take to New York. For an excellent map of the alternatives see ibid., p. 13.

64. The British were near Monmouth Courthouse, N.J., with Gen. Philemon Dickinson and his New Jersey Militia—a thousand strong—threatening the enemy's left (ibid., p. 22). These same militia soon had the honor of fighting the opening skirmish in the Battle of Monmouth: William S. Stryker, *The Battle of Monmouth* (1927; reprint ed., Port Washington, N.Y.: Kennikat Press, 1970), p. 122.

65. Ward cites the German desertion figure on the march from Philadelphia as 440 men (*War of the Revolution*, 2:585).

66. Long Bridge was an area between Cranbury and Monmouth on the south and Brunswick on the north (Faden, *NAA*, map 20).

67. Cranbury, N.J. Roads and places in this part of New Jersey may be clearly seen on Freeman's map (*Washington*, 5:22) of the area.

68. Washington was convinced that the British were rushing toward some New Jersey embarkation point, with Sandy Hook the most likely place (ibid.).

69. On the twenty-sixth Washington ordered Lee "to march towards the Marquis [de Lafayette] with Scot's and Varnum's Brigades. Give him notice that you are advancing to support him, that you are to have the command of the whole advance body" (*Writings*, 12:120). For a discussion of Washington's command problems in the Monmouth campaign see Freeman, *Washington*, 5: chap. 2; and Smith, *Monmouth*, pp. 5–6.

70. Matchaponix Brook (also "River"), which flows through Englishtown (Smith, *Monmouth*, map, p. 4).

71. According to Smith, "This day the sun rose about 4:30 A.M. and was to set about 7:30 P.M., a day with one of the longest periods of sunlight during the year, 15 hours" (ibid., p. 9). Greenman's regiment, part of a detachment under Col. William Grayson, marched early (3:00 A.M.) toward Monmouth Courthouse (Freehold, N.J.) They numbered 600 men and carried four pieces of artillery (Stryker, *Battle of Monmouth*, pp. 117–18).

72. Greenman here collapses a great deal of time: The engagement he describes did not actually begin until after 12:00 noon, the intervening time having been spent alternately marching and halting, while Lee tried in vain to get accurate intelligence of the British movements (Smith, *Monmouth*, p. 11).

73. Lee's infamous retreat—which so aroused Washington's wrath and led to a court-martial—remains a controversial matter even today. Greenman's reasoning—there were more of them than of us—reflects the direct experience of the common soldier who sees the trees but must necessarily remain ignorant of his commander's desperate attempts to glimpse the forest. Lee had most of his troops in full retreat by 1:30 P.M. Greenman's regiment (now under Lt. Col. Jeremiah Olney) was among the first to be met and reformed by Washington (ibid., pp. 16, 18).

74. Greenman is careful to distinguish the direct battle casualties from those who collapsed and died from sunstroke or heat exhaustion. Stryker's figures for American losses are 69 killed, 161 wounded, 93 missing, 37 dead from sunstroke (*Battle of Monmouth*, appendix 5).

75. An examination of the actual journal page indicates that Greenman inserted this sentence at some later date. He means, of course, that he was wounded in the battle and not at Englishtown. Neither Stryker (*Battle of Monmouth*) nor Smith, (*Monmouth*) however, lists Greenman among the wounded.

76. The British safely reached Sandy Hook on the thirtieth and soon after embarked (Boatner, *Encyclopedia*, pp. 724–25).

77. The great pomp surrounding the anniversary of Independence is engagingly described in the general orders for 4 July 1778. But even in the celebration of so great an occasion, certain economies were to be observed: for the running fire of musketry (*feu-de-joie*) "the officers will be careful that their men charge their pieces with their worst Cartridges after having taken the balls out of them, and that the Balls thus taken out be delivered to the Regimental Quartr. Masters . . ." (Washington, *Writings*, 12:154–55).

78. Scotch Plains, N.J.

79. Greenman characteristically refers to Germans and German-Americans on his side as "Prusans." All other Germans are "Hasans." Washington's general orders for 5 July 1778 state that "The Right Wing of the Army is to march at three o'Clock tomorrow morning under the Command of Majr. General Baron de Steuben" (*Writings*, 12:160). It should be noted, however, that Major Gen. "Baron" De Kalb was also commanding a part of the army and may be the person to whom Greenman refers.

80. Both a town and a tributary of the Passaic River, north of Newark (Freeman, *Washington*, 5: front endpaper map).

81. Paramus, N.J.

82. King's Ferry crossed the North, or Hudson, River between Haverstraw and Parsons Point (Nebenzahl, *Atlas*, pp. 88–89).

83. Admiral Charles Hector Theodat, Comte d'Estaing, arrived off Sandy Hook on the fourteenth with "twelve ships of the line and four frigates, mounting 834 guns and carrying 4,000 soldiers" (Ward, *War of the Revolution*, 2:587). Washington immediately asked the commissary to send as a present to the admiral "Fifty of your best Bullocks" (*Writings*, 12:182).

84. Greenman refers in garbled fashion to "Courtland Manor" (Nebenzahl, *Atlas*, pp. 88–89), the estate of Philip Van Cortlandt and his father, Pierre. The younger Van Courtlandt was a radical patriot and a lieutenant-colonel in the New York Continental Line (Boatner, *Encyclopedia*, pp. 1137–40). The manor house has been restored and is now overseen by Sleepy Hollow Restorations (Boatner, *Landmarks*, p. 325).

85. Croton Bridge spanned the Croton River in the North Castle District of Westchester County (Nebenzahl, *Atlas*, pp. 88–89).

86. When it was discovered that the French ships of the line drew too deeply to get across the bar between Staten Island and Sandy Hook and thus could not engage Admiral Howe's fleet (Ward, *War of the Revolution*, 2:587–88), Washington and D'Estaing determined to confront the British by land and sea in Rhode Island (ibid., p. 588). The French fleet accordingly sailed northward, and Washington sent Varnum's Brigade to reinforce Sullivan in Rhode Island (Washington, *Writings*, 12:195–96).

87. Now Salem Center, N.Y.

88. Ridgebury, Conn.

89. South Britain, Conn.

90. That famous traveler the Marquis de Chastellux stopped at Angell's Tavern on

13 November 1780 and pronounced it "a rather bad inn." The place was at this time being kept by Jeremiah Angell (1707–1786), but "the site was inundated when Scituate Reservoir was built in the 1920's" (Chastellux, *Travels*, 1:67 and note).

91. The regiments were two of the sixteen Additional Continental Regiments, authorized by Congress in December 1776. They were not individually numbered but were known by the names of their commanders. This has often confused students of the Revolution, for, as is the case with one of the officers here—Col. Samuel Webb—the commanders were frequently not with their regiments. Webb was at this time a prisoner of war under parole. Col. Henry Sherburne apparently did accompany his regiment to Rhode Island (Heitman, *Historical Register*, pp. 24–27, 578).

92. D'Estaing and the fleet had arrived off Newport (at Point Judith) on 29 July. While waiting for Sullivan's army to assemble, the French harassed the British shipping continuously, and though no enemy ships were taken, eight frigates and several transports were scuttled and sunk (Ward, *War of the Revolution*, 2:588–90).

93. Johnston, R.I.

94. By the "Island" Greenman means Rhode Island itself, with Newport situated at its southern end.

95. Pawtucket, R.I. Greenman does not distinguish carefully between this town and Patuxet.

96. The troops marched first into Massachusetts, then into Tiverton, and finally to the edge of the Pocasset River (see Nebenzahl, *Atlas*, pp. 94–95) at Howland's Ferry, which crossed to the northernmost part of Rhode Island (see Caleb Harris, *A Map of Rhode Island*, facing page 119). General Sullivan, after agreeing with D'Estaing that a joint landing should be attempted on the tenth, went ahead and ferried his troops over on the ninth—Ward says to secure the fortifications on the northern end of the island that had been abandoned by the British (*War of the Revolution*, 2:590). The map accompanying Edward Field's *Revolutionary Defences in Rhode Island* ([Providence, R.I.: Preston and Rounds, 1896], opp. p. 142) has a notation to the effect that the American landing began at "half after six" on the ninth.

97. None of these engagements (through 18 August)—admittedly very minor—are listed in Peckham's *Toll of Independence*, though they do qualify under his definition of an engagement: an incursion which meets some resistance.

98. The preliminaries to the Rhode Island operations were attended with the highest sort of optimism (see the introduction to this part of the journal): Washington mentions Sullivan's being "in high spirits" and entertaining "the most flattering hopes of success in the intended Enterprise" (*Writings*, 12:277). This attitude must have been infectious at first, but as the days progressed one senses a growing disillusionment—even in the dispassionate prose of Sergeant Greenman.

99. Greenman refers to the works built and then abandoned by the British (see note 96 above).

100. This was Adm. Lord Richard Howe, who showed off Rhode Island on the ninth with an imposing fleet of 20 vessels mounting 914 guns (Ward, *War of the Revolution*, 2:590). D'Estaing was now forced to contemplate a sea fight rather than an amphibious assault.

101. Abbreviation for "nothing more remarkable."

102. That is, towards Newport.

103. On the night of 11–12 August a severe gale blew up that was to last forty-eight hours and confound the ships and armies of both sides (Boatner, *Encyclopedia*, p. 790; and Ward, *War of the Revolution*, 2:591).

104. Before: in front of. The Americans had taken up positions in Middleton, to the east and a little north of the British lines (Ward, *War of the Revolution*, 2: map, p. 589;

and Henry B. Carrington, *Battles of the American Revolution* [New York: Promontory Press, n.d.], map, opposite p. 456).

105. The Americans continued to expect aid from the fleet and the French soldiers, despite the alienation between D'Estaing and Sullivan and despite the storm damage to many of the French ships.

106. D'Estaing, refusing to cooperate further, left for Boston with the remainder of his fleet at midnight on the twenty-first (Ward, *War of the Revolution*, 2:591).

107. Washington had written Sullivan on the twenty-second, warning him that British transports were active near Frog's point (Long Island Sound) and were perhaps designated to carry troop reinforcements to Newport (*Writings*, 12:350).

108. Compare Angell's account (27 August 1778) in *Angell Diary*, p. 6.

109. See note above for entry of 1 August 1778.

110. Butts Hill (in Portsmouth). See Field, *Revolutionary Defences*, map opposite p. 142 and photo opposite p. 140; also *Angell Diary*, p. 8.

111. The Germans, under Gen. Baron von Lossberg, took possession of Quaker Hill (*Angell Diary*, p. 8; Field, *Revolutionary Defences*, map opposite p. 142; and Ward, *War of the Revolution*, 2:592).

112. When Angell's Regiment was assigned guard duty after the battle, its commander remarked: "I had not Slept then in two nights more than two or three hours / the Regt. had eat nothing during the whole day / this was our sittuation to goe on guard, but we marched off Chearfully and took our post" (*Angell Diary*, p. 9).

113. *Angell Diary*: "Rec'd orders . . . to Embark on board our Boats and Land near Warren as Genl Varnums Brigade was to be stationed Between Warren and Bristol" (p. 11).

114. Also Kickemuet or Kickamuit River, one of the inlets of Mount Hope Bay (Nebenzahl, *Atlas*, pp. 94–95).

115. Identified by Angell as "Bradfords Hill" (*Angell Diary*, p. 12).

116. One might expect Angell or even the laconic Greenman to comment on this extraordinary march of some 130 feet. But both remain silent on what must have been the shortest formal movement of an army in the Revolution.

117. Fascines: bundles of sticks used to construct batteries or fill in muddy places, etc.

118. The raid on New Bedford, Mass., was conducted by Gen. Charles Grey. The British destroyed "about seventy sail of vessels . . . burned the magazine, stores, warehouses," and many of the residences (*Angell Diary*, p. 13n.). The British commander in chief, Sir Henry Clinton, had ordered the raid "to convince these poor deluded people that that sort of war, carried to a greater extent and with more devastation, will sooner or later reduce them" (quoted in Willcox, *Portrait of a General*, p. 251).

119. The word is clearly "of," but is obviously a lapsus for "on."

120. The chaplain of the Second Rhode Island Regiment at this time was the Rev. Charles Thompson, a Baptist and a member of the first graduating class of Rhode Island College (Brown University). He had succeeded Ebenezer David, who had decided to take up medical studies in preparation for military hospital work but had died soon after leaving his chaplaincy (19 March 1778) (*Angell Diary*, p. 19 and note; *Rhode Island Chaplain*, pp. xxivff., 77).

121. Greenman's irony reflects the anger of the New Englanders toward D'Estaing and the French for abandoning the Americans on Rhode Island. Feeling is said to have run so high as to make certain observers doubt whether the Boston shipwrights would consent to repair the gale-ravaged ships (Ward, *War of the Revolution*, 2: 593).

122. This one inlet into Providence Bay goes by three separate names, depending on what part of the waterway is involved: the Warren River flows by the town, the Swan-

sey above Warren, and the Barrington below (Nebenzahl, *Atlas*, pp. 94–95). Greenman indifferently spells the name of the town "Warrin" and "Warring."

123. This engagement is generally referred to as the Battle of Ushant, for the French coastal town off which it was fought. The British under Adm. Augustus Keppel met a French fleet commanded by the Count D'Orvilliers, and although Washington wrote Lafayette calling the battle a "glorious defeat" of the British, the action was in fact indecisive (Ernest R. Dupuy and N. Trevor, *Encyclopedia of Military History* [New York: Harper & Row, 1970], p. 717 [hereafter cited as *EMH*]; *DNB*, 11:39–41; Washington, *Writings*, 12:502).

124. There was no "smart Ingagmt.," but the British were active around Dobbs Ferry, necessitating "a general alert" and dictating "the opening of a field headquarters at Fishkill." The situation "gave Washington an uncomfortable two weeks before the Redcoats withdrew" (Freeman, *Washington*, 5:77–78).

125. The arena of the sea war between France and Britain now moved for the time being to the West Indies, where D'Estaing and the fleet met the British in a number of indecisive engagements (Boatner, *Encyclopedia*, p. 350).

126. Carl Emil Ulrich von Donop died after the German attack on Fort Mercer, 22 October 1777 (see part 2).

127. Barrington, R.I.

128. Col. Angell reports in his diary that "two . . . men froze to death two nights past on Prudence Island / they got lost in a boat bound to Bristol in a snow storm. . . ." And, "if I ever saw one storm worse than another this was the worst it being Extream cold, never known Colder." The diary's editor notes that this storm is known by local tradition as the "Hessian snow-storm," because of the many German and British soldiers on Rhode Island who are said to have perished in it (*Angell Diary*, pp. 32–33 and 33n.).

129. The monetary inflation of the Revolution, owing largely to the enormous printings of Continental and state paper monies, is a familiar fact, though still astonishing in its magnitude. By September 1779 Congress had authorized the printing of over $200,000,000 in paper money with metal backing (Don Higginbotham, *The War of American Independence, Military Attitudes, Policies, and Practice, 1763–1789* [New York: Macmillan, 1971], p. 293). Depreciation, continuous from the opening of hostilities, accelerated in 1779. According to Trevelyan, "in June of that year $50 were paid in Philadelphia for two pair of shoes, and $60 for two silk handkerchiefs. Fish-hooks, in that piscatorial city, cost half a dollar apiece. In October 1780 beef sold in Boston for $10 a pound, and butter for $12. . . . Samuel Adams, who was not a dressy man, paid $2,000 for a hat and a suit of clothes" (*American Revolution*, 5:299–300).

130. In fact, Washington had been summoned to Philadelphia to discuss the campaign of 1779. He arrived in the city late in December 1778 and remained in almost daily conference with the delegates throughout January (Freeman, *Washington*, 5:90–95). One of the themes he reiterated time and again was that "the great impediment to all vigorous measures is the state of our Currency." The question of the depreciation of the soldiers' pay, while admittedly crucial, was but one among a complex of economic problems that seemed well nigh insoluble (Washington, *Writings*, 14:7).

131. On 29 December 1778 a British expeditionary force under Lt. Col. Archibald Campbell, supported by a naval squadron commanded by Com. Hyde Parker, attacked and captured the city of Savannah, Ga. (Boatner, *Encyclopedia*, p. 980; Peckham, *Toll*, p. 56).

132. The series of mutinies in the Rhode Island Line is discussed in the introduction to this part of the journal.

133. Poppasquash Neck, across Bristol Bay from the town of Bristol (Nebenzahl, *Atlas*, pp. 94–95).

134. Dighton, Mass.

135. Unfounded camp rumor.

136. The reference here, perhaps to a method or technique of drill, is obscure.

137. The Americans watched the sea expectantly throughout the year 1779, but despite the ubiquitous rumors of their imminent arrival, the French fleet did not come (Willcox, *Portrait of a General*, p. 260).

138. Maj. Gen. Horatio Gates had taken command of the Rhode Island department in March, when Sullivan was ordered on his expedition against the Indians (Washington, *Writings*, 14:199–201, 200n.). Brig. Gen. John Glover (of Massachusetts) had been in Rhode Island with his brigade since the beginning of operations there and was at this time second in command.

139. Greenman was now a commissioned officer (an ensign; see the introduction to this part of the journal), and perhaps this is why he was able to procure better quarters in a private dwelling house.

140. This place, which Greenman also calls the Narrows, overlooked the middle passage and Providence Bay. A contemporary British map shows a battery on Poppasquash Neck commanding the ship channel between Providence and Newport, and Field indicates that the place was fortified with an earthwork and a battery of six eighteen-pounders (Nebenzahl, *Atlas*, pp. 94–95; and Field, *Revolutionary Defences*, p. 124).

141. Saint Lucia, Windward Islands, West Indies. The British had routed the French in a combined army and navy attack 12–28 December 1778, and at the time of Greenman's entry were still in possession of the island, later reoccupied by the French (Boatner, *Encyclopedia*, pp. 965–66 and 1184ff.).

142. Abbreviation for "instant," meaning of the current calendar month.

143. As so often proved the case, the facts of a battle were radically different from camp rumor: neither of the operations in Georgia and South Carolina here mentioned (and again mentioned in the entry for 20–23 June 1779) was an American victory. The former was a raid only, with light casualties (Boatner, *Encyclopedia*, pp. 214–15; and Peckham, *Toll*, p. 60). The latter, Maj. Gen. Benjamin Lincoln's supposed capture of "7 thousand of the enemy," never happened at all, giving rise to a remark by Colonel Angell in his *Diary* that he thought it "all most impossible that Lying could be Carried to such a pitch" (p. 64).

144. Mount Hope (in Bristol) is an eminence which commands the bay of the same name (Nebenzahl, *Atlas*, pp. 94–95).

145. Col. Henry Jackson, commander of one of the sixteen Additional Continental Regiments.

146. Newton (now Wickford, R.I.) was also known as "Updikes's Newton" (Greenman's "Obdikes") or "Updike's Harbor" (Nebenzahl, *Atlas*, pp. 94–95).

147. Field describes Barber's Height as "a commanding eminence in North Kingstown two hundred feet above the sea level; from its highest point a view can be obtained of the whole lower bay (Narragansett) and for many miles off to sea" (Angell, *Angell Diary*, p. 56n.). The Lieutenant Hill mentioned is probably Jeremiah Hill (Massachusetts) of Colonel Jackson's regiment.

148. Several Connecticut towns were attacked, sacked, and burned during these large-scale British raids (4–11 July 1779), but Stratford was not one of them. New Haven was plundered and Fairfield and Norwalk virtually destroyed by a British force

of 2,600 under General Garth and Governor Tryon (Boatner, *Encyclopedia*, pp. 260–61).

149. Brig. Gen. Anthony Wayne and his crack brigade of light infantry made this daring bayonet attack on Stony Point (Hudson River) on 16 July 1779. They took the fort in half an hour of hard fighting, and though it was not held for long—the requisite troops were not to be spared—the victory had "an inspiriting effect upon the American army and upon the people in general" (Ward, *War of the Revolution*, 2:598–603). The British lost 63 killed, 71 wounded, and 442 captured (Peckham, *Toll*, p. 62).

150. *Feu-de-joie*: though strictly a running fire of musketry, the term obviously was extended to cover other forms of military celebration.

151. Angell identifies the man as John Deruce (*Angell Diary*, p. 67).

152. The South Ferry crossed the inner channel of Narragansett Bay between the southern part of Conanicut Island (Jamestown) and the mainland at South Kingstown Nebenzahl, *Atlas*, pp. 94–95).

153. William Humphrey, of the Second Rhode Island Regiment, a veteran of the march to Quebec (see part 1). He was at this time Greenman's captain.

154. Joseph Masury, whose career paralled Greenman's in several respects (he, too, had been commissioned an ensign on 1 May 1779). Masury became a long-time friend of Greenman's and was for a time his business partner after the war (see the biographical essay in the introduction).

155. George Milliman, though tried, convicted, and sentenced to die by a general court-martial, was never executed and lived on until 1832—apparently drawing a United States pension. (Louise L. Lovell, *Israel Angell* [New York: G. P. Putnam, 1921], p. 147 and note).

156. The final two lines on the ms. page are partly missing and partly blotted.

157. Joseph Wheaton, of the Second Rhode Island Regiment.

158. The "Capt." was Maj. Henry Lee, whose force of 400 surprised and routed the British at Paulus Hook, N.J. (Peckham, *Toll*, p. 63).

159. In the Battle of Grenada (Leeward Islands) Adm. John Byron ("Foul-Weather Jack") attacked a larger French fleet and was beaten, though not badly, since the French under D'Estaing "unaccountably withdrew" (Boatner, *Encyclopedia*, p. 154).

160. Com. Abraham Whipple of Rhode Island. Boatner summarizes the dramatic successes mentioned by Greenman: "In mid-July '79, while his *Providence* was cruising with [John] Rathbun's *Queen of France* and the *Ranger*, he had the good fortune of drifting into a British convoy of heavily laden East Indiamen off Newfoundland in a heavy fog. Thanks largely to the initiative of Rathbun, he cut 11 of the ships out of the convoy and got eight of them safely to Boston. Sold for $1,000,000, they constituted one of the richest single captures of the war" (ibid., p. 1198).

161. Tower Hill is "to the south-west of Barbers Heights and east of Boston Neck, 178 feet above tide water" (Angell, *Angell Diary*, p. 63n.).

162. Although this is precisely the same information as that set down in the entry for 21–28 July, it is probably not a mistake. The British were evacuating Newport in stages. Gates wrote Washington on 25 July that a "considerable detachment sailed from Rhode Island" (Washington, *Writings*, 15:343). From that time until their final withdrawal, the British were assembling their transport fleet. All the troops were out of Newport by 25 October 1779 and in New York on the twenty-seventh (Washington, *Writings*, 17:2 and note).

163. Dutchess (also "Dutch") Island lies midway between Conanicut Island and the mainland.

164. This difficult syntax seems to say that the manner of review under Steuben was changed from what Greenman recalled at Valley Forge.

165. In order to alleviate the acute problems in the Commissary—the necessities of life often were simply not getting to the soldiers in camp—Congress on Wednesday, 18 August 1779, resolved "That . . . officers be entitled to receive monthly for their subsistance money, the sums following, to wit, each colonel and brigade chaplain 500 dollars, every lieutenant, ensign and surgeon's mate 100 dollars. . . . the sum of 10 dollars [shall] be paid to every non-commissioned officer and soldier monthly for their subsistance, in lieu of those articles of food originally intended for them and not furnished" (*Journals of the Continental Congress, 1774–1789*, ed. Gaillard Hunt, 34 vols. [Washington, D.C.: U.S. Government Printing Office, 1904–37], 15:978, hereafter cited as *Journals CC*).

166. John Hubbard, Second Rhode Island Regiment.

167. John Morley Greene, Second Rhode Island Regiment.

168. The Bonnet is a jutting piece of land and small cove opposite the southern end of Conanicut Island on the mainland (Nebenzahl, *Atlas*, pp. 94–95).

169. This unusual form of punishment apparently consisted of hitting or stabbing the victim with sharp sticks or "pickets" (*OED*, s.v. "picket"). As Bolton remarks, even a hundred lashes ingeniously distributed over a number of days (to let the flesh partially heal, only to be laid open again) meant little to a hardened offender. And, as 100 lashes was the maximum allowed by the military code, and next to the death penalty in severity, novel punishments were sometimes contrived—as was done in this case (*Private Soldier*, pp. 170ff.).

170. D'Estaing was planning to attack Savannah, Ga. The attempt proved a "Franco-American fiasco" and completed the discrediting of the admiral which had begun with Newport and continued in the West Indies (Boatner, *Encyclopedia*, p. 982).

171. Kelley's Ferry (also known as Toogood's Ferry and Swansey Ferry) crossed the Warren River (also Swansey River) "where Kelley's Bridge is now," between Barrington and Warren (Chapin and Chapin, *Rhode Island Ferries*, p. 145).

172. Mackerel Cove, on Conanicut across from the entrance to Newport Harbor.

173. The word is undoubtedly "anings," but Greenman's intent is obscure. Possibly the cargo was "awnings," in the sense of tents or other portable shelters.

174. This was the second annual commemoration of the defense of the Delaware (see part 2, October–November 1777). Colonel Angell records that "this Day being the Day that we defeated the Hessians at Red banks in 1777, the officers of the Regiment provided a Dinner and all Din'd together, with a great number of the Inhabitants" (*Angell Diary*, p. 84).

175. This person has not been identified.

176. Field notes that "Rome's Point is north of Barber's Height, at the entrance to Bissels Cove, in North Kingston. It lies nearly opposite the north end of Conanicut Island" (*Angell Diary*, p. 86n.).

177. Probably Coddington's point, just north of Newport.

178. The abandoned and reduced British fortifications may be seen in Carrington, *Battles*, map opposite p. 456; and Field, *Revolutionary Defences*, map opposite p. 142.

179. Gates was to march his troops to Hartford and from there over the familiar route westward into the Hudson Highlands and south to Headquarters at Morristown (Washington, *Writings*, 17:98–99).

180. Col. Samuel Webb (identified above), Col. Henry Jackson, commander of one of the sixteen Additional Continental Regiments, and Col. James Livingston, commander of the First Canadian Regiment. "Shurband" is Col. Henry Sherburne.

181. The rumor of a British reoccupation of Newport was false. Greene's regiment returned to Rhode Island (see entry for Friday, 19 November) not to meet a British

threat but because Gates thought the men would be more useful there than with the main army (Washington, *Writings*, 17:99).

182. Harwinton, Conn.

183. Kakiat, now New Hempstead, N.Y.

PART FOUR

Morristown to the Hudson Highlands, 1780

INTRODUCTION

Though the winter at Valley Forge is unassailable in the book of American mythology, room should also be set aside there for the 1779–1780 season at Morristown. Simply put, it was far and away the worst winter of the war. "Very early that winter the cold came. And such cold! There had been nothing like it in the memory of the oldest inhabitant. Roads disappeared under snow four feet deep. New York harbor was frozen over."[1] And the fact that as late as March snow was still piled twelve feet high markedly increased the seriousness of the provision problem—a perennial dilemma now turned critical indeed. But the physical suffering, acute as it was, did not tell the whole story: the depreciation of the Continental currency had reached the point of absurdity, at least for those who could afford that sort of an attitude toward a problem which affected the soldiery in such a basic way:

> *In May, 1780, De Kalb, for "a bad supper and grog" and a night's lodging for himself, three others, and three servants, without breakfast, paid $850. "An ordinary horse is worth $20,000; I say twenty thousand dollars!" At that time the pay and subsistence for a captain of one certain regiment, $480, was worth about $13, and a lieutenant's $126.60 was worth about $3.30.*[2]

This means, of course, that Ensign Greenman's real wages were something less than three dollars a month, hardly enough to buy meat or meal—should those rarest of commodities miraculously appear in camp for sale! These deprivations were immediate, inescapable, insidious; they were precisely the stuff of which mutinies were made, and the American army was entering its most critical period in this regard. Washington realized the causes and probable consequences of the situation and even sympathized with those soldiers who took to plundering farms and houses in the countryside: "They have borne their distress . . . with as much fortitude as human nature is capable of; but they have been at last brought to such dreadful extremity that no authority of influence of the officers could any longer restrain them from obeying the dictates of their own sufferings."[3]

Perhaps because they had had their season of discontent in 1779, the Rhode Island troops in camp appear to have been little touched by the disturbances of 1780–1781. Greenman's entries detailing his own camp duties reflect only an orderly mode of regimental life: serving on numerous courts-martial and acting as camp police officer or as a surrogate for the adjutant; mounting all sorts of guards, including the personal bodyguard of Washington; and continuing, to be sure, the routine of military drill. The journal for this period gives the impression of the Rhode Islanders as loyal and supportive, while their brethren of Massachusetts, Connecticut, New York, and Pennsylvania were the mutineers. Though they were not essentially better men than their fellows, the Rhode Island soldiers had the obvious benefit of having worked through their greivances the year before.

Militarily, there was little action for the northern army. The principal theater had moved south, and the idle northerners found themselves reduced to speculation about the arrival of the French fleet—always just over the Atlantic horizon—while they waited for general orders or handbills to bring news "from the southward." The only action of note for Greenman and his regiment was at Springfield, New Jersey (7–23 June)—called a "raid" by military historians and a "battle" by those who fought in it and were proud of their stand against a powerful German force. The Second Rhode Island Regiment (the First Rhode Island, under Christopher Greene, was still back home) got to fight at last under "one of their own," Nathanael Greene, and dramatically distinguished themselves at Springfield, further enhancing their reputation as a crack Continental unit. The commander in chief paid tribute to them in a letter to Rhode Island Gov. William Greene: "The gallant behavior of Colo. Angells, on the 23d. Inst. at Springfield, reflects the highest honour upon the Officers and Men. They disputed an important pass, with so obstinate a bravery, that they lost upwards of forty killed, wounded and missing before they gave up their ground to a vast superiority of force."[4] Greenman's account of the battle, terse and accurate, is written from the perspective of a knowledgeable officer in the very forefront of the action. For the second time Greenman is part of a force which drives the British presence from New Jersey, and for the second time he is wounded in the process—a wound which never properly healed and led to an increasing disability in his later life.[5]

The remainder of the campaign of 1780 was spent inactively in a series of camps from the Preakness area in New Jersey to West Point in the Hudson Highlands. The idea was for the Americans to watch the British in New York City, and to this end they settled in all along the Hudson. But the calm of this arrangement was violently shattered with the discovery of Benedict Arnold's treason (25 September) and the arrest of Major André. The treason created an electric sensation throughout the army. Israel Angell called it "the most Extraordinary affair . . . that Ever has taken place Since the war,"[6] and as the truth of the matter unfolded, sympathy began to grow for the unfortunate André, so endowed was the young officer with style, dignity, and elan, qualities very much admired by the Americans. But that he must be executed was clear to Washington.[7] The death of André profoundly moved its witnesses. Fellow Rhode Islander Stephen Olney wrote that "perhaps there never was any other execution in presence of our army that occasion'd so much Sympathy, to see a man in the flower of life who had been in the Pleasant persuit of Worldly honour, in full health, of a Ruddy Complection, Dark Eyes . . . and every feature engaging about to end his life on a Gibbet Gallows (a mode of Death contrary to his wishes, which were to be shot) was two affecting for many to behold without a tear of sorrow. . . ."[8] According to Douglas Freeman the "officers who were returning from the place of execution were talking of what they had seen—were talking, some of them, with a strain and even a choke: it was over; André was dead; every incident of the hanging had increased the respect of witnesses for the young man in the red coat."[9] In view of this welter of feeling, what is one to make of Greenman's spare statement, "this day went to the Execution of Major Andre Adjt. Genl. to the British army, belonging to the 54th Regt. of foot, who was found Guilty of being a Spy"? This was all he permitted himself: formal, succinct, denuded of all sentimentality, really of all emotion of any kind. Nor was there to be any reflection on the treason of his old leader Arnold, the man who had inspired such awe and personal loyalty among the men on the trek to Canada. "Thanks be to god we timely discovered them in their Plot" was all he had to say in judgment.

After following the diarist this far through the war, readers will not expect effusions of any sort from Jeremiah Greenman; they are not his style. But in this "Extraordinary Affair" the characteristic coolness of the prose is more than a little surprising. What he thought about the treason and the execution will never be known. Yet the recitation of André's "name, rank and serial number," and those formulaic facts alone, suggests a refuge from feelings too strong for the words he had at his command.

It only remained in 1780 for the two Rhode Island regiments to comtemplate their being made over into a single battalion. In one of those small but cruel ironies of history, the surviving regiment was to be Christopher Greene's First Rhode Island: the Second had been so depleted by the stand at Springfield Bridge—losing a fourth of its men—that it was no longer viable as a regimental fighting unit.[10] Many of the officers, including Colonel Angell, were to retire to their farms and businesses under the new congressional dispensation of half pay for life.[11] Ensign Jeremiah Greenman was one of those officers retained in the "new arrangement," and the usual winter furlough duly arriving, he journeyed home to Dartmouth to rest and wait for the campaign of 1781.

NOTES TO INTRODUCTION

1. Ward, *War of the Revolution*, 2:612, quoting N. W. Stephenson and W. H. Dunn, *George Washington*, 2 vols. (New York: Oxford University Press, 1940), 2:121.
2. Ward, *War of the Revolution*, 2:614.
3. Washington, *Writings*, 17:366. See also the journal entry for 18–28 January and note.
4. Ibid., 19:96–97. Contrast Washington's plain speaking with the language of the Rhode Island Assembly in praising the troops: "We cannot omit this opportunity of returning our most sincere thanks to the officers and soldiers in general, belonging to the regiment, for that bravery, patriotism, and perserverance, and those military virtues manifested on all occasions so similar to those exhibited by the famous legions of ancient Rome, in the shining periods of the history of that republic; and it gives us the most sensible pleasure to reflect that the historic page of America will not pass over in silence the services of a regiment of ours so meritorious" (quoted in Lovell, *Israel Angell*, p. 169).
5. See the introduction and appendix 2 for Greenman's remarks on his disability.
6. *Angell Diary*, p. 123.
7. Freeman, *Washington*, 5:218.
8. Olney Narrative, Shepley Papers, RIHS, p. 20.
9. Freeman, *Washington*, 5:221.
10. Washington, *Writings*, 19:93.
11. See Lovell, *Israel Angell*, pp. 180–81.

MORRISTOWN TO THE HUDSON HIGHLANDS, 1780

January 1780

S 1 January to T 13. Continuing in building our Huts / Send out Guard at the Lines which is about 20 miles / other Duty very eassy & warned for Command to parade in ye Morn.

F 14. this morn agreable to orders paraded to Mr. Kimbles at 8.oClock under Command Lord Stirling[1] where we tarried about two hours waiting for the Slays which was to be precur'd for the Detachments / about 400 arrived, we distributed our men about 7 or 8 in a Slay after which we proceeded on to West bury where we put up 'till about 11 oClock / then parad'd & proceeded on our march to Elissbeth where we arrived about day. very cold.

S 15. Continuing in Elisebeth town 'till Near Sun rise / then crossed the River on the Ice / came to Staton Island & proceeded on towards the Enemies forts which was 5 miles / hear we manoeuver'd back & forth for two or 3 hours / then we took post on a hill half a mile from one of the forts where the Snow was about two feet deep / hear we dug the Snow off the Ground & built up fires and tarried all Night and very cold with a Number of our mens feet fros'd.

S 16. this morn about break of Day we paraded exspecting we was to storm the works immeadiately, Receiving orders that if any man quit his plattoon he was to be put immeadiately to death / marcht about a Quarter of a Mile & wealed [wheeled] off by plattoons & marched across the river & came to Elisebeth town where we made a small halt & drew provision / at our halt we found that one third of our mens feet was fros'd / after Dividing our Provision we went on 4 miles where made a halt.

M 17. this morn we marcht to Conaticut farms[2] where we made a small halt and took out our Invalids, & proceeded on towards Camp as far as Spring-field where we made a small halt after which we came to Chatham where we drew Provision & push'd on for Camp where we arrived at half after 6,oClock / we found that our men had privately plundered the Inhabitance & order was given out for Sival [civil] and Militia officers to take up every person that offered any articles for Sail—

T 18 to F 28. Continuing in Camp near morristown in which Time we keep out Guards as usal, & received orders to take up all Soldiers after Retreat beating and if they could not precure a proper pass was to receive one hundred Stripes on their Naked Back and if surpsected to have been a plundering the Inhabitance they was to receive from one hunderd to 500 Lashes on ther back at the Descretion of the officers Commanding the Guards.[3]

S 29 to M 31. this morning mounted the Brigade Guard—orders to have a pequit turn'd out of every two brigades to lay in the huts alwais holding their Selvs in Readyness to march at a Moments warning, as we have Sum Exspectation of a Visit from the Enemy.

FEBRUARY 1780 MORRIS

T 1 to F 18. Moved into my Hut which was very Comfertable after fatiaguing our Selvs near two months / we are informed that the Enemy is at Elisebeth town / all the Troops ordered to hold their Selvs in Readyness Compleated with 40 round pr. Man to march at the Shortest Notice—

S 19. this day there was a man executed near the Grand Parade —for Robery & Several other Crimes—[4]

S 20. this day went on his Excellencys Pequit Guard[5] where continued 'till the 22nd. hear we posted (at Night) a Small Guards in the Rooms & a Serjt. & 6 men at the head of his Stairs.

T 22. this day was releived by the Meriland Line / marcht my Guard to Camp & dismis'd them / found that Capt. Hughes[6] had arrived in Camp with the Cloathing.

W 23. this day the Regt. drew a Suit of Cloaths which altered their Condition they being almost Naked for nigh two Months—

T 24. Mounted the Brigade Guard / very heaving Thundering & Lightning.

F 25 to T 29. this morn releived by Lt. Rogers[7] of Colo. Jacksons Regt.—we received a Number of Small Books for the Soldiers to keep their accounts & C. Imploying our Selvs in fixing our hut to make it as compleat as we can considering our Situation. So end this month / NMR.

MARCH 1780 MORRIS

W 1 to M 13. we are informed by Credible Persons that the Irish is Revolted & denigh the Brittish any Subsistance from their Resolving to have a free Trade &C—

T 14. this day mounted the Camp Guard / Nothing Remarkeble during my Tower—

W 15 to F 17. this morn after being releiv'd went on a Genl. Court Martial / Tryed one Prisoner & sentinced him to receive 100 Lashes on his Nacked Back.—then the Court adjrn'd 'till the 18th Inst.—NMR.

S 18. this day met according to adjurment / Proceeded to the Tryal of Ens. Spur of the 3d. N. York Regt.[8] arrested for unjentlemanlike behavour in turning Cap Pell out of a Publick house—the Court adjurn'd 'till to morrow 10,oClock—

S 19 to T 23. this morn meet according to adjurnment & proceeded to the Tryal of Ens. Spur & found him Guilty of the Section & article of the articles of War & sentinced him to be Discharged the Service of the United States—then proceeded to the Tryal of 2 Serjts. of ye 3d. New York Regt., tryed for abusing the [*adg. ? adjutant ?*] / found them not Guilty & acquited them, then proceeded to the Tryal of a Soldier of the 2nd. N York Regt. Tryed for Deserton & aquited him / the Court adjurned till further orders / Nothing more Remarkeble these days / the Court ordered to set again Next Fryday.

F 24 to S 26. this morn the Court met according to orders and adjurned 'till Munday 27th. Inst. this day went over to the N York line where spent the Day very agreable, hear that our People was surpris'd by a party of the Enemy from Powlers Hook,[9] who came to Paramus & took a Sergt. & 14 men & on their Return our People too about the Same Number / N M R—

M 27. this day met according to adjurment / adjurn'd for want of witneses—N M R—

T 28 to F 31. this day the Court meet / try'd a Serjt. of the

2nd N York Regt. for Embisselling Public property / found Guilty & sentinced him to be Reduced to the Ranks / we are informed that the Enemy is very buisey & exspect them to make sum sudding movement & in Consequence of the Same are ordered to hold our Selvs in Readyness to march in a Moments Warning / the Court Martial desolved / a very heavy Storm of Snow NMR—

April 1780 Mount Pleasant

S 1 to T 6. Continuing near morris Town / mustered & inspected / Mounted the main Guard in Morristown / we are informed that ten Ships of the Line & ten Thousand french Troops is arrived at Martineec,[10] ye Merriland Line is ordered to hold their Selvs in Readyness to march to the Sothward.[11]

F 7. this morn releived by Capt. Hunt of Genl. Starks Brigd.[12] marched our men to the Huts where dismesed them / N M R—

S 8. this morn mounted the Brigade Guard / thundered & Lightned very hard / N more R DMT.[13]

S 9 to T 18. this morn was releived by Ens. Galpen,[14] we are informed that the enemy went to storm the works at Georgia & was repulsed & lost a Vast Number of men—the merriland Line marched for the Southern army—we are informed that the enemy was up to Paramus but are not informed the Peticular yet—4 Battalions ordered to parade to receive the French Embasender—[15]

W 19 to S 22. we are informed that the party which was out at Paramus took 7 officers & 40 men, two of the officers belonging to our Brigade. Major Bayl who commanded the party was mortally wounded—[16]went on the Brigade Guard / the french Embasedor arrived at which 13 Cannon was fired where the 4 Battalions was paraded—

S 23. this morning was relev'd by Lt. Jarault—[17] & went to morristown on the Main Guard / we are informed that the Enemy went to cros the Ashley to get to Charlston & lost a Number of men in the attimp.

M 24 to T 27. this morning after being releived went to the Parade where the 4 Battallions was paraded / hear they manoeuvered 2 or 3 hours / then they saluted the Imbasedor after which return'd to Camp / in the evening a Number of Sky Rockets was fired—

F 28 to S 30. this day went on the Brigade Guard / in the

morn was releived by Ens. Meers[18] / Nothing more Extraordinary this month—

MAY 1780 MORRIS TOWN

M 1 to W 3. this day went on a Regimental Court Martial / Colo. Shurbands Regt. was ordered to be reduced & the men turned over to the Defferent States that thay belonged two / Eight or Nine that belonged to the State of Rhode Island was transfired to our Regt.[19]

T 4. this day was mustered & inspected by his Excellincy & barron de Stuban—this after noon warned to go immeadiately on Command / marched about 40 rod from the Parade, & was releiv'd by Lt. Weaton[20] it being his Turn—

F 5 to S 7. this day was Police officer of the Camp. went on the Parad in Liew of the Adjt. of the day, he being Sick.

M 8. this day went on Guard at Morriston / we had a few Small Showers of wrain—

T 9 to S 13. this morn after being releived marched to Camp / are informed that the Marqis Dilefeat is arrived from France[21] & informs us that there is ten Ships of the Line coming from France & it is exspected there will [*be*] an Expidetion formed to Cannada & the Marquis to take Command of the Land forces—are informed that the Enemy surpris'd a part of our Light Hors near Charlestown & took 15 of them & took a Nr. of Waggons—[22]this day went on the Brigade Guard—NMR—

S 14. this morn was releived by Ens. Pratt[23] / the duty very hard, we are ordered to exersise twise a day & two battallions to parade to Morristown twise a Week for the purpose of Exersiseing—

M 15. we hear that the Enemy is a building a block house at Hackensack. & have gone with two or three Ships up the North River / we are informed that our People had posession of Charleston 1st of May—

T 16. we are informed that the Enemy has been out at Paramus & took a Few of our men / we are informed that the Merriland has got as far as the Head of Elk[24] / went on his Excellencys Guard where there was four Log housen built to post the Guard in Case of an alarm—

M 22 to T 25. this morn was releived by the Pensylvany Line / Provision very Short but half allowance issued to the Troops—

we are informed that the French Fleet is exspected in very soon / No Movements of the Enemy—

F 26. this day the Eleven men that was under Sentince of Death for Desertion & other Crimes was ordered to be executed near the Grand Parade / 50 men was ordered to attend to the Execution / after arriving on the Grand Parade they was all pardinoed exsept one who was one[25]—

S 27 and S 29. we have no new from the Sothward / the york Troops ordered to march to Albeny in Consequence of a Number of Indians & Tories that came down to the Frontears & burned a Number of housen / we had a very glumy and dark day / the Sky very Red & C—

M 29. this day 4 Battallion paraded & went to morris town where they fired 14 Rounds of Cartriges & saluted the Committe of Congress which was hear on buisness, setling the affairs of the Army.

T 30 and W 31. went on the Brigade Guard—the Enemy has been out at Paramus, our people hearing thay was coming retreated from their Quarters, the Enemy came out in two parties one of which arrived at the Ground our People left sumtime before, the other, when the other party came up they seeing men on the Ground our People had left, fired upon them & killed 10 men & wounded several others then returned to their Lines with their Victory / we are informed by sum hand bills from New York that Charleston was taken the 12 Inst. Nothing more Remarkebl this month.

June 1780

T 1 to T 6. went on a manoeurvering party where we performed all the Duties belonging to Camp / are informed from an officer from the Eastward that ye French Fleet is arriv'd at Newport Consisting of 16 Sail of the Line & a Number of Frigates with 8 Regiments of Foot[26] / went on his Excellencys Guard / N M R—

W 7. we have New from the Southward as Late as the 14th. Ult[27] informing us Charles[*ton*] surrendered on the 12 May[28] / orders to hold our Selvs in Readyness to march in a Moments Warning as we are informed the Enemy landed at Elesebeth Town / about ten oClock AM we marched from the Left / Marcht as far as Chatham where we made a halt & the army was formed in the following order (viz) the Pensylvania Line on the right, Commanded by Genl. Green, the Connaticut Line on the left, Commanded by the Marquis Delefeat[,] the Centre Composed of Genl. Hands & Starks Brigades Commanded by the Barron La Sutuban[29]— we drew half a gill of Rum for our men & proceeded on towards the Enemy as far as Short Hills near Spring Field in Sight of the Enemy where we halted & formed the Line, where we continu'd in the wrain all Night.

T 8. this morn was ordered away on Detachment with about 5 hunderd men under Command of Genl. Hand, after being paraded proceded toward the Enemy near Elisebeth where made a small halt where found the Enemy had burned a Number of Housen & ravashed one or two weomen cuting oppen feather Beads & strowing the Feathers about the Road—[30] we then pushed on after the Enemy / came up with them near Elesebeth Tow Point where we displayed our Collom to the left & formed the Line / marched forward in this Position to attack the Enemy / fir'd two Rounds at them / found their Number was far Superiour to ours / we filed off to the left th[*r*]o a Wood whear we made a halt & detached a Plattoon to discover their movements / are informed by two Diserters that Gen. Clinton[31] had arrived from the Southward with Seven thousand Troops who had landed on the Point / about two oClock went down on the Lines where continued 'till Evening then return'd to where I left the Detachment / found they had marched off / Proceeded on after them to Conaticut farms where I overtook, & continued in an orchard all Night.

F 9. this morning we marched from Conaticut farms & came to Sprinfield where made a small halt / then pushed on to Short Hills where I join'd my Regt. & continued all Night / we are informed the Enemy is landing more Troops at Elisebeth Town Point—

S 10. Continuing at Short Hills, we are informed the Enemie is advancing from the Point towards Springfield / two Cannon on the approach of the Enemie is to be fired at which the Troops is to hold their Selvs in the Greatest Readyness to form the line &C— this Evening we was ordered to march about two miles near Vauxhall Road where we keep Pequit—[32]

S 11. Continuing near Springfield on the advance Post—

M 12. this day rode as far as Morris Town where I continued all Night / NMR DMT.

T 13. this [*morn*] came from Morristown to Springfield where I join'd my Regt. where [*it*] lay the two preceeding days where continued till Evening / then moved our Quarters about a Quarter of a Mile on a hill where we built up a bush housen & continued 'till Eleven oClock when it began to wrain at which we took post in sum housan and Barns nigh hand—

W 14 to M 19. Continuing near Spring[*field*] abut two miles advanced from the army in which Time we was alarmed twise by the firing of sum of the advance Sentrys / Seven Sail of Ships came into the harbour of New york this afternoon / on Guard / N M R D T Days.

T 20. this day ordered to hold our Selvs in Readyness to march at a Moments Warning—this Night about Eleven oClock the army marched for Pumton except Genl. Maxfields & Starks Brigades—& a few Light Hors & Militia.[33]

W 21. Continuing near Springfield / Genl. Green ordered to take Command of the Troops left hear / his Excellency marched last Night with the Army which marched toward Kings ferry.

T 22. this day a Number of boats & Small Crafts passing from New york to Elisebeth, which we imagine the enemy was reingforsing & their approach might be spedily expected.[34]

F 23. this morn was alarmed by the advance of the Enemy which atacked & drove in Genl. Maxfield's Brigade which was posted at Conaticut farms / we immeadiately marched from our Post (which was about two miles from Springfield bridge)[35] & join'd the Brigade after which we marched into Springfield near the Meating house, from where our Regt. was ordered to advance & take Command of a Small Orchard, the Enemy at the same time advancing sum scattering fires took place & a few Shot from sum of the Enemies field peases was fired into town after which the Enemy retired the firing seased, but we soon found they was again advancing in two Colloms / a New Disposion was made of our Troops / our Regt. was then ordered to take post at a bridge by a Small Brook which we thought was not pasable onley by the Bridge as it appear'd Slowey [sloughy] and Swampy on Each Side, a field peace was posted on a hill jest in our Rear, our Right wing on the Right of the Bridge & the Left wing on the Left of the Bridge (where we thought the Enemy must all pass) / a firing of musquets immeadiately took place by the Enemies Right Collom advancing for the other part of the Town which they approached with but Little Difficulty. we then discovered their Left Collom approaching us very fast / the feald pice back of us played very briskly on them—the Enemy opn'd with 5 field peaces on the one which they compeled to retire[36] with the Los of a Capt. & a few men / they levil'd them at our Regt. & by this time their Infentry was not more than a Musquet Shot from us & advancing very fast for the Bridge / their Light Troops chifeley yaugers[37] advanced for the Brook & each flank which they soon gained / the Musquetry at the same time playing very smartly on the Bridge / they being so far Superiour in Number they crosed it, & sun [soon] [*were*] considerable in the Rear of the Right wing when they retired, the left wing having advantagious Ground fought them on a Retreat forming at every fence & Noll / at one of the halts received a small ball in my Shoulder; retreated to the Short hills where we formed the line again jest back of the Town. the Enemy marched into Town set fire to 21 housen & burned them to the Ground after which they retired very rappidly / we followed after them as fas[38] Conaticut farms but the Regiment being so fatiagued with ye Toyls of the Day we was ordered back to our Quarters near Vaux Hall Road—the Militia followed them very clostly & took a Number of Stragulars—

S 24. this morning are informed that the Enemy had all left the Jersey Shore / this Evening received orders to march in the Morning at 3 oClock to join the Brigade which lay at the Short Hills.

S 25. this morning according to orders the Regt. paraded to join the Brigade / I obtain'd Liberty to go to Morris Town where I arrived about 8.oClock & continued 'till Eleven / then pushed on to Hanover where I made a small halt / then came to Rockaway bridge where I join'd my Regt. & took post by the Sid of the River under an Oak—

M 26. this morn marched at 3 oClock / came as far as beaver Brook where we made a small halt / then pushed on to Pumton where we breakfasted / from thence came to Ramapo[39] / hear we built Bush housen & continued all Night where the Ratle Snake was very Plenty.

T 27 to F 30. Continuing in Rammapo wood until ye 1st. July —in which time we suffered grately for Provision & wrain'g, at which we peal'd the Bark off the Treas & built very Comfortable Housan—ordered to march / the march to go from the Right—

JULY 1780. ON A MARCH

S 1. this morn at 3.oClock parad'd for Guard. went forward one mile where tarried 'till all the army had pased / then fell in, the Rear for the Bagage Guard, came on as far as Pumpton Forge[40] where made a halt two hours / then came to Pacaness where continued all Night & built up bush housen.

S 2. Continuing in Pracaniss Woods / very heavey wrain.

M 3 to S 8. Continuing in Precaness woods 'till Satturday the 8 in which time built up housen out of the Barkes of the Treas & set on Court Martial / Try'd 3 Prisoners all sentinced to receive 100 Lashes / we are informed that the Enemy is left fort Lee, & the work around that Quarter[41] / our housen leak in such a maner that we was obliged to spread our blancoats in the Rom of tents & N R.

S 9. this morn we marched from the Woods about half a Mile where we pitched our Tents on a very pleasant hill, after laying without tents from the 7th June—

M 10 to S 16. Continuing near Pracaness in which time mounted Several Guards &C—we are informed that the French Fleet is arrived at Rhode Island / the Infentry ordered to be imbodied[42] / No movement of the Enemy.

M 17. we are informed that Aml. Graves arrived into New York with 6 Sail of the Line—[43]

T 18 to M 24. we hear that the enemy & French had an Engagement off the Capes of Virginia & one of the Brittish ships received a Considerable Deal of Damage / are inform'd that there is 8 Sail of the Line & a Number of frigates arrived into Newport & about 500 sick & wounded / the officers of the army are desired by the Commander in Chfe to ware black & White Cockades in Emblematick of the exspected union of the Two Armies—

T 25. are informed that Genl. Wain attacked the block house near Bulls ferry & lost about 90 men killed & wounded / K[*n*]ocked off the Top[44] / thats all the Execution we hear that was done / he brought off about two hundred had of Cattle / we are informed that the french fleet left N port a few days ago.

W 26 and T 27. Continuing at Precaniss / this day went on

the Brigade Guard, ordered to hold our Selvs in Readyness to march at a Moments Warning—

F 28. this morn was releived by Mr. Meers / ordered to hold our Selvs in Readyness to march in the morning at two oClock.

S 29. this morn at the beat of the General[45] struck our tents / I was ordered to be left behind with the Bagage that could not be carried for want of Waggons—at 12-oClock received orders to impress Waggons & proceed on after the army as fast as posable—agreable to orders impresed two waggons / came on as far as Wagharell[46] where I put up—and are informed that Adml. Graves had arriv'd with 9 Sail of the Line & was crusing off the Mouth of Newport harbour—[47]

S 30. this morning set off about day light / came to Paramus where made a small halt / then pushed on about two miles to a place called the River,[48] where we made a small halt and got sum horses shoed / then pushed on to Kearkeart where I overtook the Brigade and join'd my Regt. / are informed that 100 Transports went thro hel gate & steered down the Sound,[49] order'd to march in the morning at two oClock.

M 31. this morn agreable to orders paraded and marcht down to kings Ferry where we crosed the North [*River*] and came about two miles where we made a halt, ordered to send away all the heavy bagage to West Point and half the Tents, & half the Officers Tents / ordered to hold our Selvs in the Greatest Readyness to march towards Kings Bridge. we exspect to make an atack on that part of the Enemies Lines to try if we could not dray [draw] back the Enemy from Rhode Island—

AUGUST 1780. PEEKSKILLS

T 1. Continuing at Peekskills / the Infentry ordered to imbody their Selvs, a Company from Each Regiment which Compose 2 Brigades. 1 commanded by Genl. Hand & the other Genl. Poor, the whole commanded by the Marquis Delafeat.[50]

W 2. Continuing near Peekskills / holding our Selvs in Readynss to march at a moments Warning, we are informed that the Enemy has returned from Rhode Island.

T 3. this day ordered to hold our Selvs in Readyness to march to cros the N. River / the following is the order of the Line of battle for the Present—the Right wing commanded by Major Genl.

Green—consisting of two Divisions in the first Line & one in the 2nd. —first line Right wing, will be composed of the first & Second Pensylvania Brigades, which will compose one Division commanded by Major Genl. Sain Clear,[51] the 2nd will be composed of the Newjersey & New york Brigades commanded by, Lord Sterling 2nd Line wright wing will be composed of the 1st & 2nd Conaticut Brigades composing one Division commanded by the oldest Brigadier—the Left wing commanded by Major Gen. Arnold will consist of two Divisions in the first Line & one in ye 2nd / first Line Left wing on the Right, the 1st & 2nd Massachusetts Brigades will compose one Division Commanded by Major Genl. How[52] / on the Left Starks & Poors Brigades composing one Division commanded by Major Genl. Mc Dougall / Second Line in the Left wing, will be composed of the 3d and 4th Massachusetts Brigades composing one Division commanded by the Barron Stuban a Major Genl.

F 4. Continuing at Peekskills / holding our Selvs in Readyness to march.

S 5. this morn receiv'd orders to hold our Selvs in Readyness to march at two oClock AM. the army giting the Baggage acrost the River. at Sun Set receiv'd orders to march at 9 oClock to the ferry—according to orders at 9.oClock we marched down to the River where we continued 'till two / then crosed the ferry and marched about a mile & took post at a Side of hill where we continued till day Break.

S 6. this morn marched about day light about 4 miles & made a halt in haverstraw where we pitched our tents / hear all the bagage that was sent to W. Point came to us. this Evening receiv'd orders to march in the morning at two oClock—

M 7. this morn marched according to Orders. the army paraded [,] myself in the Van Guard / crosed a Large Mounting & came to Greenbush where made a halt & pitched our tents in Sight of the wright wing of ye army.

T 8. this morning the Troops marched at 3 oClock. myself tarreing on the Ground 'till all the army had pased then with Sum other Troops composed a Rear Guard—& pushed on after the army as far as Tappan where made a halt—

W 9. Continuing in Tappan or orrange Town where we are informed that the Enemy had burned the block house Near buls ferry & avacuated the Post.

T 10 to S 13. this day on fateague / having a well dug for the use of the Regt.—an officer killed by a Cannon Ball from one of the Gallies at Darbeys ferry which keep up a very Constant Cannading on that place where our people was building a Battery—[53] we are informed that the other Division of the French Fleet is arrived at Newport[54] / this Evening warned for Guard.

M 14. this day went on Guard about two miles from Camp / Nothing Remarkeble DT.

T 15. this morn after being releiv'd came to Camp / Nothing more RM.

W 16. we are informed by the Secritary of Congress that Genl. Gates had captured 600 foot & two hundred hors & a Large Number of Waggon who was out from Charles[*ton*] on a Forraging Party, this day waited on his Excellency Gen Washington concerning my Rank & a Number more officers of the Regt.—[55]

T 17. Continuing in Orrangeton in the State of Newyork / holding ourselvs in the Shortist Readyness to march / we are informed that a French 74 & a Number of American Privateers fell in with a Fleet of the Enemi that was carr[*y*]ing Provision to Quebec & captured the biger part of them & further we are informed that there is two or three Privateers crusing in the River St. Lawrance & its supposed the Remainder will be captured—

F 18 to S 20. Continuing in Orrangetown 'till Sunday the 20th in which time are informed that a Packet belonging to the Enemy was taken a few days ago & carried into Philadelphia & Sum of the papers on bord informs us that there had been Great Confusion in Engeland by Mobs / Several housan burned & pulled down &C—

M *21.* this day went on the Brigade Guard / Nothing Remarkeble during my Tower.

T 22. No provision this day as there was none in the Store / ordered to hold our Selvs in Readyness to march tomorrow morning at 7 oClock.

W 23. this morning agreable to orders marched at 7 oClock / marched from the Right & proceeded on as far as Closter where we made a small halt for about two hours / then pushed on to Tennick about 4 miles from Fort Lee[56] / Hear we piched our Tents & Nothing to eat but a small Matter of Bread—

T 24. Continuing at Tenick or English Neighbourhood /

this after Noon the Pennsylvany Line marched down toward Powlers-hook / Nothing More Remarkeble TD.

F 25. we hear a Smart Cannad'g toward Powlers-Hook, Still continuing without any Beef—very hungary—& fretful.

S 26. this day the Pensylvany Line returned with a Large Quanterty of Forrage / one man hung wilst on the Expedition for plundering without ye Benefit of a Court [*Martial*].

S 27. this day drawed beef / the first drawed for four or five days / Continuing very still no movement of Either Side of any Consequence, wating for the other Division of the French Fleet, which we exspect in very soon—

M 28. this day went on Guard with a Major from the Conaticut Line at Spikendevils Crik,[57] where one of the Enemies Ships lay. pattrol the Shore in the Night for a mile or two / Nothing more Rem.

T 29. this morning was releiv'd by a Major from the Pennsylvany Line / in the after noon went down to the Infentry which was about two miles from Camp, in ye Evening return'd to Camp—

W 30 and T 31. this day went on Genl. Court Martial, we hear a very brisk Cannading / holding our Selvs in Readyness to march—Nothing more Remarkeble this month.

September 1780 steenrapia

F 1. this day received orders to march / NMR—

S 2 and S 3. this day stormy which prevented our march / Continuing wraining—

M 4. this morn pleasant / Struck our Tents & marcht as far as Hackensack new Bridge[58] where we made a halt about half an hour / then pushed on to Steenrapia[59] where the army halted & piched their tints in a line.

T 5. this day went on the Camp Guard & No Provision / nothing Remarkeble DT.

W 6. we are informed by letters from the Southward that there hass been a very Smart Ingagement at that Quarter with Genl. Gates & the Enemy. Genl. Gates army got drove from the Feald with the Loss of about four hundred killed in the Field & a great porportion of officer.[60]

T 7. this day went down to the Infentry where continued all Night N M R T D—

F 8. this morn came to Camp where spent the Remainder of the day—

S 9 to T 12. this day went on the Brigade Guard, in the morn of the tenth releived / Continued in Camp 'till the 12th & Nothing Remarkeble—

W 13. this day the army was paraded & revewed by his Excellency Genl. Washington and [*a*] Number of Indian Chifes after which sat on a Genl. Court Martial / Tryed a Serjeant for Desertion who was found Guilty & sentenced to be reduced & receive 100 Lashes on his naked back—

T 14 to S 16. Continuing in Steenrapia 'till Tuesday ye 16[61] then went on the Brigade Guard / Nothing Remarkeble D T T—

S 17. this morn was releiv'd / Nothing more Remarkeble this day—

M 18. we are informed by Sum Friends that a Number of the Enemy is gone to the East End of Long Island / this day his Excellency Genl. Washington pas'd by this Camp with a Large Escort of Hors / Suppos'd to be gone to Hartford to meet Count Deroshambo, the Com'd of the army involved [devolved] on Major Gen Green—[62]

T 19. ordered to hold our Selvs in Readyness to march at the Shortest Notice—in the Evening about 9 oClock receiv'd orders to march in the Morning—

W 20. this morning agreable to Last Evenings orders parad'd & marched from the Left for orrangetown where we arrived about 4.oClock, and ordered to incamp on thee Same Ground left the 23 of August Last—Rain—

T 21 and F 22. this morn culer & wrain / we are informed that there is a Ship gone up the N. River—

S 23. this morn we hear a very brisk firing of Cannon towards Virplancks point which we are informed this after Noon was two feald peaces drawed from the fort at Virplanks point down whare the [*ship*] lay that went up the river a few days ago, & there being no wind for her to make Sail She was obliged to be towed away by her boats / went on the Brigade Guard / Nothing more R.

S 24. this day we are inform'd that a party of the Enemy landed from a Sloop and burned a house belonging to Major of the Militia—[63]

M 25. Continuing in Orrangetown, this morning the army was all ordered to be under arms at ten oClock, when we marched from our Incampment about two miles where the whole Army formed a Line, then changed the Froont to the right & marched to our Incampment[64] / this night about 12.oClock we received orders to hold our Selvs in Readyness to march at a Moments warning on hearing that Genl. Arnold was to give up the forts at West Point— & at the same time this part of the army was to be attack'd.[65]

T 26. this day we are inform'd that Mr. Andree Adjt. Genl. to the Brittish Army is taken up on Suspicion of being a Spy,[66] / as soon as the New[*s*] was sent to Genl. Arnold, who coman'd at West Point that Such a Man was taken up, being Consious of his Guilt, he immeddiately ordered his barck to be maned & passed the works at Virplanks Point (under the pretence of a flag) to the Vulture Sloop of War which lay about three Miles from Stoney point / Soon after this his Excellency arrived to West Point and going to Genl. Arnolds Quarters found he was gone & after sum inquiry found he had gone down the River in his barge at the same time the Prisoner Andre arriv'd and was found about him two Letters which Colo. Livingston had sent to Genl. Arnold with the Peticular Cituation of the Posts at Stoney & Virplanks point and a Number other Papers of Consequence,[67] he was immediately confin'd and ordered to be sent to the army at orrange town to have [*h*]is Tryal as a Spy / on the Evening of the 25th we are informed that the plot was to have been put in Execution, by about 6000 Troops, who had been imbarked several days and went to Sandy hook under pretince thay was bound to the Southward, but thanks be to god we timely discovered them in their Plot—[68]

W 27. Continuing in Camp / N.R. this day—

T 28. this day went as far as the Infentry Camp where am informed that Mr. Smith[69] (Inhabitant of the State of N York) was taken up for receiving Mr. Andre & piloting him toward the Enemies Lines—

F 29. this day went on Guard at Lord Sterlings Quaters / Nothing Remarkeble happined during my Tower—

S 30. this morn after being releived came to Camp where am informed that the Enemy had confined a Number of Inhabitance on Long-Island & had executed one or two more that had been friend

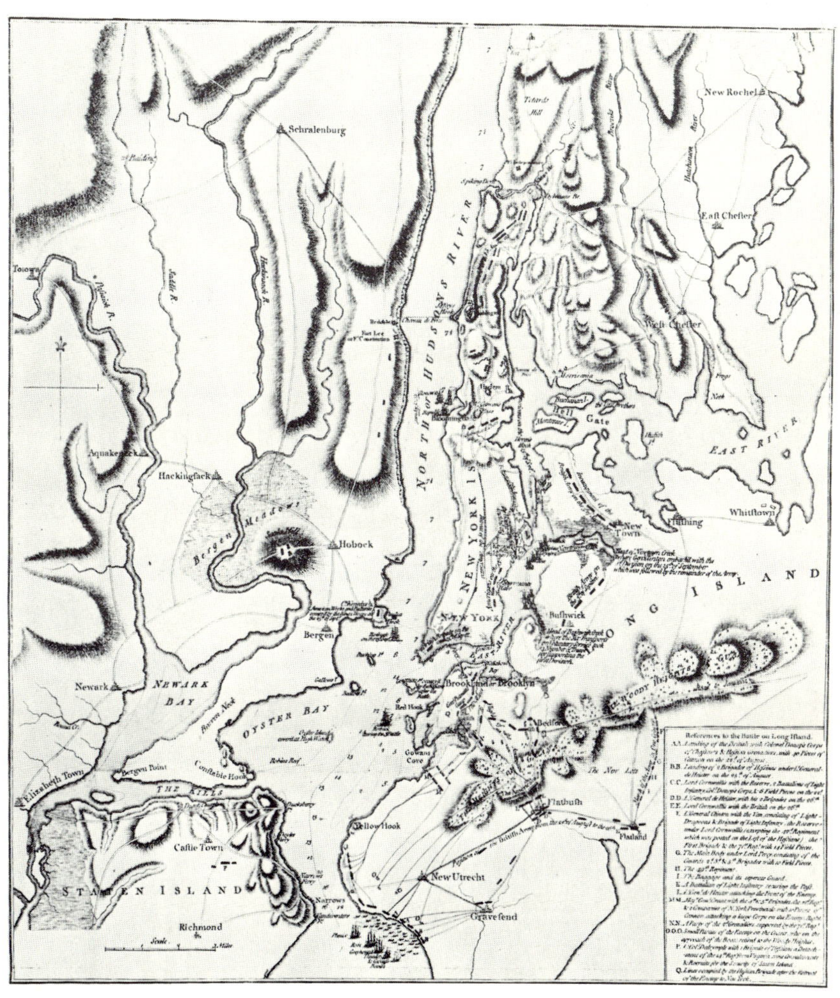

William Faden's map of the invasion of New York in August 1776. Courtesy of The Newberry Library, Chicago.

380 October 1780, 9 Mon

Sat 1 This day on Gen.l Court
Martial Tryed one Sol
for being drunk on his p
& Suffering bread to be St
from the Commissary
found Guilty & Sentenced
to Receive 100 Lashes on his
Naked back—

Mon 2nd This day went to the
Execution of Major
X Adj.t Gen.l to the
army belonging to the
Reg.t of foot who was found
Guilty of being a Spy

Entry recording the execution of Major André.

to us informing us of the Movements of the Enemy / all ocasioned by the Infermation of Gen. Arnold after he went to them.

OCTOBER 1780 ORANGE TOWN

S 1. this day on Genl. Court Martial tryed one Soldier for being drunk on his post & suffering bread to be stole from the Commiserys Stores / found Guilty & sentinced to receive 100 Lashes on his naked back—

M 2. this day went to the Execution of Major Andre Adjt. Genl. to the Brittish army, belonging to the 54th Regt. of foot, who was found Guilty of being a Spy.[70]

T 3. this day went on the Brigade Guard / very Stormy & Nothing but a hut made of bows [boughs] to keep to the rain & wind from me / NMRTD. /

W 4 and T 5. Continuing in Camp these two days & Nothing Remark'le.

F 6. This day receiv'd orders to hold our Selvs in readyness to march at 9 oClock to Morrow morning—

S 7. this day agreable to yesterdays orders the army all marched. the right wing went toward paramus & Newwork, & four Brigades, consisting of Jersey, Newyork, Hamshear & Genl. Stark's under Command of Major Genl. Green marched for west Point, our first halt was at Greenbush where we tarried about an hour / then proceeded on in the rain & cold to Haverstraw where we incamped, and ordered to hold our Selvs in Readyness to march in the Morning.

S 8. this morn the Genl. beet at 5.oClock / the March commenced at 6, I was ordered away on an Escort to the bagage, & Covered Waggons which was to cros the N. River and go to West Point on the East Side of the River, the Troops, all, (except a few Guards) went up the west Side thro the Mountings, crossed the River about 9 oClock & tarried 'till all the Brigades Waggons was over / then pushed on to Peekskills where made a halt but the Town being full of Waggon concluded to push on to the Continental Village, which we effected after fixing Ropes to our waggons to draw them up a very steep hill, hear we continued all Night.

M 9. this Morning drew provision for our Men & pushed on to the landing opposite West Point, where continued 'till Evening / then crossed the River, except a Serj't and twelve men which was left to Guard the Waggons.

T 10 and W 11. Continuing at West Point which I found very much out of repair, & provision short, as no flour or Meet was allowed to be delt out of the Magizens / N M R.

T 12. this day went on Guard at Fort Putnam[71] / are informed that the Infentry has had a Scurmage with the ennemy.

F 13. and S 14. this morning was releiv'd by an Officer from the N. York Brigade, Came to Camp / Nothing More.

S 15. this day are informed that the Enemy had taken Fort Ann & George,[72] the N. York Brigade ordered to hold their Selvs in Readyness to march, & Colo. Gansworths Regt.[73] ordered to embark immedeately for Albeny in Consequence of the above News, ordered for Guard—

M 16. this Morning went on the Main Guard, Genl. Heath arrived, who is to take Command of this Post Vice [instead of] Gen. Green who is ordered to the Southward to take Command as Genl. Gates is Recalled—[74]

T 17. this morning releived from Guard. Sum Small Spits of Snow—N M R T D.

W 18 to F 27. Continuing at West Point 'til Fryday the 27th in which time Nothing Remarkeble happined, more than sending out a Number of Detachments to the Lines & else where.

S 28. this day we have an Extract from Genl. Orders Congratulating the Troops on an important advantage obtain'd in North Carolina over a Corps of fourteen hundred Men, Brittish Troops & New Levies, commanded by Colo. Ferguson, the Militia under Command of Colo. Williams & Shelby, who having colected to the amount of three thousand Men, detached Sixteen Hundred of their Number on hors back, to fall in with Fergisons party which they came up with at a place called Kings Mounting, advantageous posted & gave them a Total Defeat in which Colo. Forgerson with one hundred & fifty of his Men was killed & Eight-hundred made Prisoners / we took 15 hundred Stand of arms, in the atack we lost Colo. Williams & a very few men in proportion to that of the Enemies—[75]

S 29 to T 31. Continuing at West Point / our Men moved into the Barracks / No Barracks being for the officers, we moved our Marques under the Lee of fort Clinton,[76] where we built fire places and sealed it within with boards which made it very comfertable—Nothing More Remarkeble this Month.

NOVEMBER 1780 W. POINT

W 1. we are informed by the arrival of Sum Vessels from the West Indias that the French had captured upwards of 50 Sail of Vessels belonging to the Brittish the biger part of them outward bound—

T 2. hear this [*day*] that the other Division of the french Fleet had arriv'd to Charlestown—& are informed that there was a Number of waggons taken which was privately carreing Stores to the Indians—

F 3. this day part of the N York Brigade imbarked for Albeny, in Consequence of Sum Indians which had been down to the Fronteers & burned about 30 housan / killed 4 Men & carried a Number of Prisoners—

S 4. this day are informed by letters from the Southward that one Mr. Ross (an Inhabitant of Virginia) was taken up with a Brigadear Genl. Commission & a Number of arms & Amunition which he had colected & consealed, which was to have been conveyed to the Convention Troops, which was not far from that quater.[77]

S 5 to T 7. by Deserters are informed that Sir Harry Clinton had sail'd with a Squadron for Virginia, & had arrived there & disembarked his Troops, but on the News of the arrival of the French Fleet he imbark'd & sail'd for Charlestown.[78]

W 8. this day went on Guard at Fort Willis[79] & very cold—ye york Brigade return'd from albeny.

T 9. this Morning releiv'd by an officer from the Jersey Line, then came to Camp / Sum Small Spits of Snow.

F 10. this day we have a Resolve of Congress handed us wherein we are informed the Army is to be reduced & the Supernumera officers to be sent home on half pay for Life, & those which continued during the War was also to have half pay for life and Land agreable to their Rank.[80]

S 11 to W 15. the New york Brigade ordered to imbark for Albeny as they came back thro a Misunderstanding of orders.

T 16. this day ordered for Com'd / went down the River to Haverstraw about tem miles with 24 men to pick up Timber to build Barrack for the officers / arrived at the place about Sun Set; Rain & cold / Traviled about 3 quater of mile thro the wood & came to a house where was kindly used.

F 17. Continuing at haverstraw, very stormy.

S 18. this morn set out with my Schow & came to West Point & onloaded her & continue hear all Night—

S 19. this morn went down the River to haverstraw / Loaded my Schow, at 11.oClock in the Night set off for West Point where arrived at day break—

M 20. we are informed the Grand army sent away all their heavy bagage two or three days ago & exspect to have Sum Suding Movement / a Large Detachment ordered from this post down to the Lines.

T 21. this day the biger part of the Brigade was sent away under Command of Colo. Jackson, & a Battalion from the Jersey Line under Command of Colo. Barber,[81] both of which was under the Command of B Genl. Stark / this day arrived the Adjt Genl to the French Army & a Number more officers.[82] we saluted him with 13 Cannon.

W 22. this morning the French Genl. set off for Head Quarters at which we saluted him with 13-Cannon, are informed that the Enemy hath imbarked a large Number of Troops, we hear that the Grand army is crosing the North River at Kings ferry.[83]

T 23. we are informed by an officer from the Southward that Genl. Smallwood had surround['*d*] a party of the Enemy & that they in provibility fall into his hands.[84]

F 24. this day was adjutant of the day / went in the Grand Parade / Counted off the Guards on the Grand Parade / NR this Day.

S 25. Stormy & Nothing very Remarkeble this day—

S 26. Spent this fore Noon in reading Mr. Witfields Journal,[85] with sontring hours in my bunk[86] / the after part of the day in reading Reflection & Maxims, the Evening in stud[*y*]ing a Geographyeal Sistem of Asia & Africa.[87]

M 27. Spent this morning in reading Mr. Witfields Journal / the Remainder of the fore Noon in fixing my Marque for Winter / this after Noon received orders to march as soon as the Troops arrived from below, the Jersey & Nyork Lines ordered to hold their Selvs in Readyness to march, the Latter to cross the River and build huts / Colo. Hazens Regt.[88] to move to Fish Kills there to winter—Spent this Evening in Stud[*y*]ing a Geographyal Sistem of Asia & Affrica.

T 28. the Detachment return'd from the Lines / braut with them a Large Quanterty of forrage & a few prisoners / one informed that the movement of the Army caus'd the Enemy to debark their Troops, the chife [*object*] the Manoever of the Army was for, this day did the duty of the Adjt. of the day on the Grand Parade / Spent the Evening in Company with Cap. Tisdal who was a Captive with me in Quebeck—[89]

W 29. Spent this morning in reading Reflections & Maxims & the Remainder of the day in draughting a Ship,[90] this Evening warn'd to go on Command at the Lines.

T 30. Spent this Morning in stowing my Portmantua & fixing for Command. at Eight oClock paraded on the Grand Parade with about one hundred & fify men under Command of Major Graham of the Nyork Line,[91] Crossed the N. River about ten oClock / came to the Continental Vilige where made a small halt, in which Time passed about 50 prisoners who had been taken off of Long Island from a Fort which was stormed,[92] came to Peekskills where we put up.

DECEMBER. 1780. DETACHMENT

F 1. this morning started from Peekskills very early & came to Cortlands Manner, near Croten River where we made a halt and detached Capt. Johnson[93] with a Company, then pushed on about 5 miles to Crumbpond, where we put up at Mr. Hortons—and sent out two or three Small Guards—

S 2. Continuing at Crumb Pond, about ten oClock moved our Quarters 4-miles where we posted Guards as usal. Took up my Quarters at Mr. McKuls where spent the Evening very agreable—N—

S 3. Spent this morning in reading the Bible. Capt. Johnson with part of his men joined us, Left a Sub[94] and twenty men at the New bridge on Croton River—[95]

M 4. this morning paraded and marched to Pines Bridge where made a small halt, & left a Subs Guard / then proceeded on our march as far as North Caswill in Queens Street, where made a small halt, & dined / then pushed on about 5 miles to Bedford New-Purchase[96] where made a halt and sent out Guards as Usal.

T 5. this morning marched as far as Bedford where made a small halt / then pushed on to North Caswill where dined /

then pushed on to Pines Bridge where made a small halt / then came to Crumb Pond, at Mr. Mekees where I put up.

W 6. this morning went on Guard about 3 miles from this place to Pines Bridge where I received a flag / Colo. Hatfield[97] from the Enemy desiring sum tory families might have the Liberty to move within their Lines—

T 7. Continuing near Croton River where the flag continueth waiting for the famelys / Spent the Evening & Night with Colo. Hatfield.

F 8. this day the flag was discharged, in the Evening went down towards the Enemy 3 miles, & return's about 9 oClock, NMR.

S 9. this morning rode about 3 miles into the Country where continued all day / in the Evening returned to my quarters / are informed that a party of the Enemy in Disguise came up within Sight of the House where I quartered and plundered an Inhabitant—

S 10. Continued near pines Bridge, NR.

M 11 and T 12. this morning was relev'd by Capt. Fogs Company[98] / marched about two miles & took my quarters at Mr. Davenports.

W 13. this morning at day light received orders to march about 15 miles toward the Enemies Lines, in persuit of Several Prisoners which had made their Escape from the Provost at Fishkills / Came acrost two of them at bedford / one proved to be a Schoole mate. and [*at*] Night returned to my Quarters again at Mr. Devenports—

T 14. Continued at Croton / this Evening about 7 oClock a Detachment arrived at this post to releive us / I marched the Company about two miles and took up my quarters at Mr. Wittnys where spent the Remainder of the Evening very agreable—

F 15. Spent this morning with Capt. Dillivan[99] after which returned to Mr. Witneys / took my leave of them and proceeded to Camp near Roberson Mills[100] where I found the Regt's huts all most compleated, except the officers who lived in their Marques.

S 16. Continuing near Robersons Mills, building our huts N M R—T—D.

S 17. this day received a Furlough / in the evening was alarmed by a party of the Enemy (which was out towards the white plains) consisting of 100 hors & two hundred foot—

M 18. this morning set off from Camp / Came about ten

miles & made a small halt / then pushed on to Fredricksburrough,[101] which was about 16 miles from Camp, are informed that there was a fleet off of Fairfield with 4000 Troops commanded by the Infamus Arnold—

T 18. this morn traviled as far as the Oblongs where made a small halt / then pushed on to New-milford where I crossed the ferry and went on about 3 Miles & made a halt.

W 20 and T 21. this morning started very early and came to Bethelem where continued 'till Fryday morn.

F 22. this morning set off from Bethelem / came to Northbury where made a small halt / then pushed on thro Cambridge and came to Farmington where made a small halt / then went within 5 Miles of Hartford where put up.[102]

S 23. this morn Snow and cold / Traviled into hartford where I crossed the Ferry / then pushed on to Bolton where made a small halt / then pushed on 12 Miles to Land Lord Hills[103] where put up with in 6 miles of Windom—

S 24. this morn came Eight Miles to land lord Carys where I made a halt from where pushed on to Canterbury where made a Nother small halt from where pushed on to Vollington where overtook Capt. Allen[104] & two other officers which set out from Camp the same day I did, from hear traviled to Cituate where made a halt & very tired it being muddy—&C—

M 25. this morn started from Landlord Greens[105] & traviled 5 Miles where we breakfasted / then pushed on to Johnson at Colo. Angells where made a small halt. from where pushed on about 3 miles / it raining very hard we made a halt where continued half an hour, then Mr. Green[106] & my Self pushed on to Providance in the Mud & Rain where put up—

T 26. Continued in Providence / Nothing very Remarkeble this day.—

W 27. this day selebrated the Antient St. John[107] / NMTD.

T 28 and F 29. Continuing in Providence / took a walk at the Lower End of the Town. NMR.

S 30 and S 31. this morning from Providance came to fall River where made a small halt from where came to Dartmouth where continued till the 9th January—

NOTES TO DIARY

1. "Lord Stirling" was Brig. Gen. William Alexander. The exploit noted by Greenman involved, according to Ward, "2,500 men in 500 sleighs." The object was a surprise attack on the British garrison on Staten Island. "But the enemy were not surprised; they retired to their strongholds, and nothing came of the effort beyond the capture of a handful of prisoners, some tents, arms, and other loot." The price was 6 men killed and 500 "slightly frozen" (*War of the Revolution*, 2:614–15).

2. Connecticut Farms, now Union, N.J. (Boatner, *Encyclopedia*, p. 1045).

3. Washington's general orders for 29 December 1779 had addressed this problem in no uncertain terms, but the men, perhaps driven to it by the harshest of winters, continued to plunder the countryside for food and clothing. In the general orders for 28 January 1780 Washington confesses himself "astonished and mortified" that his earlier directive had not been heeded. Again he admonishes the officers to "exert themselves and take effectual measures to prevent" the marauding, though the extreme remedy of 500 lashes is not explicitly endorsed (Washington, *Writings*, 17:331–32, 459–60).

4. Both James Hammell and Samuel Crawford (of the Fifth Pennsylvania Regiment) were convicted of robbery on 18 February and sentenced to be hanged the next day (ibid., 18:22–23).

5. That is, the personal guard for General Washington.

6. Thomas Hughes, of the Second Rhode Island Regiment.

7. Samuel Rogers.

8. The defendant was John Spoor; "Cap Pell" was Samuel Treadwell Pell, Second New York (Washington, *Writings*, p. 184 and note).

9. Paulus Hook, N.J.

10. French Admiral De Guichen reached Martinique late in March with large army and navy reinforcements and took command of all French operations in the West Indies (Boatner, *Encyclopedia*, p. 1185).

11. Maj. Gen. "the Baron de Kalb" was ordered by Washington to march to the south with the Maryland Line and the Delaware Regiment to give "further succor to the Southern States" (Ward, *War of the Revolution*, 2:712–13; and Washington, *Writings*, 18:198–99).

12. Brig. Gen. John Stark and [Thomas ?] Hunt.

13. That is, "nothing more remarkable during my tour."

14. Amos Galpin of Sherburn's Continental Regiment.

15. The new French ambassador to America was the Chevalier Anne-César de La Luzerne, who arrived in camp in Morristown on 19 April, and whose entertainment,

so filled with military pomp, Washington found "expensive and irksome" (Freeman, *Washington*, 5:157–58).

16. Maj. Thomas L. Byles, commanding the Third Pennsylvania Regiment (Peckham, *Toll*, p. 69).

17. Dutee Jerauld, of the Second Rhode Island Regiment.

18. Possibly Samuel Mears, though Heitman (*Historical Register*) says that he was by this time already a 2d lieutenant in Webb's Additional Continental Regiment.

19. General orders for 2 May: "The Noncommissioned Officers and privates of Colonel Sherburne's regiment who belong to the State of Massachusetts are for the present to join Colonel Jackson's Regiment; those belonging to the State of Rhode Island Colonel Angell's and those belonging to the State of Connecticut Colonel Webb's . . . (Washington, *Writings*, 18:319).

20. Joseph Wheaton, of the Second Rhode Island Regiment.

21. Lafayette reached Morristown on 10 May and soon told Washington the good news: "six French ships of the line and 6000 well-trained troops were to have left France for America early in April and should call at Rhode Island early in June." The proposed expedition was not, however, to be against Canada but against New York (Freeman, *Washington*, 5:161).

22. Gen. Issac Huger's cavalry were surprised before dawn by a corps under Col. Banastre Tarleton and completely routed. Besides the loss of many men, forty wagons and almost two hundred horses were taken (Ward, *War of the Revolution*, 2:702; and Peckham, *Toll*, p. 69).

23. William Pratt, of the Second Rhode Island Regiment.

24. So called because the town was at the head of the Elk River. The modern town name is Elkton, Md.

25. Greenman fails to say who the man was or what happened to him, but Fitzpatrick notes that all were pardoned (Washington, *Writings*, 18:422 and note).

26. Dispatches from General le Comte de Rochambeau, commanding the newly arrived French force in Newport, indicated only eight ships of the line with 5,000 troops, but also hinted at autumn reinforcements from France (Washington, *Writings*, 19:211).

27. Abbreviation for "ultimo," meaning the previous calendar month.

28. On the morning of 12 May Maj. Gen. Benjamin Lincoln capitulated to Cornwallis, losing over 5,000 men, almost 6,000 muskets with five rounds of ammunition for each, and many other military stores. "The surrender was one of the greatest disasters suffered by the Americans during the whole war" (Ward, *War of the Revolution*, 2:703).

29. Gen. Nathanael Greene, Brig. Gen. Edward Hand, and Gen. the "Baron" von Steuben (other officers previously identified). This movement of the American army in response to the British landing initiates what Boatner has termed the "Springfield Raid" (7–23 June), undertaken by the British under Gen. Wilhelm von Knyphausen, to take advantage of what they thought was seething discontent with the American cause among the populace in New Jersey. About this they were entirely wrong, and the attempt to organize a Tory uprising was soon abandoned in favor of wanton depredations (see text and note below) that were not checked by the Americans until after the "Battle of Springfield" on the twenty-third (Boatner, *Encyclopedia*, pp. 1045ff.).

30. The incident on the eighth which most aroused the Americans' ire was the killing of Mrs. Caldwell, wife of the Rev. James Caldwell, who was sitting with her children when British soldiers fired through the windows of the Caldwell house, killing her. They then burned the house, the church, and almost every other building in Connecticut Farms (Ward, *War of the Revolution*, 2:621).

31. Sir Henry Clinton, the British commander in chief.

32. Vauxhall Road, along with the other features around Springfield, may be seen on the map prepared by Carrington to illustrate the battle (*Battles*, opposite p. 502).

33. Washington had heard of renewed British activity on the Hudson near Verplancks Point, and he felt the necessity of redeploying his forces "so as to meet an attack against West Point and also to watch for a main effort in N.J. So he moved his main body to Pompton . . . within 16 miles of Springfield." To keep an eye on Knyphausen he left behind 1,000 Continentals under the command of Nathanael Greene (Boatner, *Encyclopedia*, p. 1046). The general called Maxfield by Greenman is Brig. Gen. William Maxwell.

34. For a complete catalogue of the British and American units engaging, see Boatner, *Encyclopedia*, pp. 1046–47.

35. Leaving Elizabethtown at 5 A.M., the British advanced in two parallel columns along the Vauxhall and Springfield roads. The first position of Angell's Second Rhode Island Regiment (really two slightly different deployments, as Greenman indicates) was near an orchard along Vauxhall Road, commanding the bridge over Rahway Creek. Here the Rhode Islanders stood, with their sole cannon, and held up Knyphausen's column for some forty minutes before being forced to retire. According to Carrington, Angell lost fully one-quarter of his men in this action (Carrington, *Battles*, pp. 500–501; and Boatner, *Encyclopedia*, p. 1047).

36. That is, they forced the artillery out of the action.

37. Greenman's rendering of "Jägers," (literally "huntsmen") crack guerrilla-type light infantry from Germany (Boatner, *Encyclopedia*, p. 549).

38. Abbreviation for "as far as."

39. This is the area of the Ramapo Mountains and the Ramapo River in northern New Jersey, leading into Smith's Clove in New York (see entry and note for 4 July 1777). The route surveyors for the French army soon to be scouting this area remarked, "This is one of the most beautiful and most agreeable parts of the Jerseys. The country is well watered, open in all directions, and cultivated with care" (Rice and Brown, eds., *Rochambeau's Army*, 2:54).

40. Near the village of Pompton, N.J. (see Freeman, *Washington*, 5: front endleaf map). "Pacaness" and "Pracaness" refer to the Preakness area just east of Pompton.

41. Fort Lee (also called Fort Constitution) was on the west bank of the Hudson, opposite Fort Washington (see Boatner, *Encyclopedia*, front endleaf map right).

42. General orders for 16 July: "As the ensuing Campaign will in all Probability be peculiarly Interesting the Commander in Chief is desirous of having a well composed Corps of Light Infantry which cannot fail to be extremely useful in our operations: He therefore determines that one Company shall be drawn from each Regiment which shall finally be proportioned to the general strength of the Regiments . . . " (Washington, *Writings*, 19:188).

43. Thomas Graves arrived in New York on "13 July, three days after a French squadron under de Ternay appeared with Rochambeau's expeditionary force off Newport" (Boatner, *Encyclopedia*, p. 446).

44. Brig. Gen. "Mad" Anthony Wayne led his force against the British position "in a reckless manner" on 21 July, losing in the process 64 men (Peckham, *Toll*, p. 73). Greenman is derisive about the results of the affair: only the top of the block house knocked off—rather different from Wayne's sensational success at Stony Point just over a year perviously (see entry for 21 July 1779 and note).

45. See the note for 14 June 1777 (part 2).

46. This place has not been identified.

47. Washington thought there would be a large-scale British attack on Rhode Island

once again and decided to counter with a demonstration against New York City—thinking Clinton would be vulnerable with so many troops on board transports bound for Newport. Greenman notes the strategy in his entry for 31 July and apparently it worked: the British transports returned to New York early in August. The commander in chief believed the return due to his movement across the Hudson (Freeman, *Washington*, 5: 181–83; for Clinton's plans for and problems with the operation, see Willcox, *Portrait of a General*, pp. 326–36).

48. Possibly the village of Saddle River, N.J., on the river of the same name.

49. Hell Gate was the name of the channel between two islands which joined the lower and upper branches of the East River and led into Long Island Sound (see map, facing page 182).

50. Brig. Gen. Enoch Poor.

51. Arthur St. Clair.

52. Robert Howe. Greenman copied this rather confusing order of battle from the general orders for 1 August (Washington, *Writings*, 19:302).

53. Greenman means Dobbs Ferry, which crossed the Hudson between the Manor of Phillipsburg on the east and the area north of Orangetown on the west (Nebenzahl, *Atlas*, pp. 88–89).

54. Once again the reality of the situation was far less sanguine than camp rumor: a single French frigate made port in Boston and reported that the anticipated second division of the fleet was blockaded at Brest and could not possibly reach America until October (Freeman, *Washington*, 5:187).

55. Although Greenman had been mustered as an ensign to rank from 1 May 1779 (see part 3), he and several other Rhode Islanders had not yet got their commissions from the state. On 3 June 1780 Israel Angell wrote Washington asking his intercession with the Rhode Island Assembly, and the commander in chief on the same day wrote Gov. William Greene in behalf of Greenman and six others. Later in the month the Assembly authorized the Board of War to issue commissions (John Russell Bartlett, ed., *Records of the Colony of Rhode Island and Providence Plantations in New England*, 10 vols. [1856–65; reprint ed., New York: AMS Press, 1968], 9:89–90). Greenman's ensign's commission, preserved in the National Archives, is dated 12 July 1780, but he must not have received it by 16 August and was asking Washington why.

56. Teaneck, N.J.

57. English-speaking folk called it "Spiking Devil Creek," as witness the British map of the Hudson River area by Sauthier (himself an Alsatian), published by William Faden in 1777 and included in Nebenzahl, *Atlas*, pp. 88–89. But the Dutch knew this tributary of the Hudson as "Spuyten Duyvil" ("Spite the Devil"). It constituted the northern boundary of Manhattan Island and was crossed by the Boston Post Road over King's Bridge, a place of primary strategic importance throughout the war (Boatner, *Encyclopedia*, p. 1048).

58. Two bridges, called the Old and the New, crossed the Hackensack River north of Hackensack, N.J. (Freeman, *Washington*, 5: front endleaf map).

59. The Army's headquarters was at Steenrapie, N.J., for the first half of September (Washington, *Writings*, 20:1–74). Fitzpatrick notes that the place was also known as "Kendekamack" (ibid., 19:554); Field, citing a newspaper source, maintains that the name "Steenraupie" is a local signification for "Stony Arabia" (Angell, *Angell Diary*, p. 111n.).

60. Ward bitterly remarks that while De Kalb lay bleeding to death on the field of battle, which he refused to leave, Gates was riding away from Camden as fast as his blooded charger would carry him and was soon "sixty miles from the field of honor" (*War of the Revolution*, 2:730). The defeat of 16 August has been described as "the most

disastrous defeat ever inflicted on an American army" (ibid., p. 731, quoting John Marshall's *The Life of George Washington*, 2 vols. [New York: Walton Book Co., 1930]). Peckham estimates the American losses at 250 killed and 800 wounded (*Toll*, p. 74).

61. This is one of the rare occasions on which Greenman confuses his days and dates, for the sixteenth was a Saturday, not a Tuesday. Mistakes in the marginal dating have been corrected.

62. At Hartford, Conn., on the twentieth Washington met Rochambeau, Admiral de Ternay, and other French officers (Freeman, *Washington*, 5:192).

63. Israel Angell records that the "Enemy landed . . . a little below haverstraw and bunt Majr. Smiths hous and all the Grain and hay he had [*in*] his barn . . ." (*Angell Diary*, p. 122).

64. The year and a half of rigorous drill under the methods of Steuben was evidently paying off for the army. General orders for 26 September: "The truly martial appearance made by the troops yesterday the order and regularity with which they made the different marches and the ease and facility they performed the several manoeuvres does them the greatest Credit and affords the most flattering prospect of substantial service reputation and military glory" (Washington, *Writings*, 20: 94–95).

65. See the introduction to this chapter for a discussion of the Arnold treason, and, of course, see the definitive analysis of the subject: Carl Van Doren's *Secret History of the American Revolution* (New York: Garden City Publishing Co., 1941), especially chaps. 12–15.

66. John André, though ranked as a major, was adjutant general to Sir Henry Clinton (this differed from the American system, wherein all adjutant generals were either colonels or brigadier generals) (Boatner, *Encyclopedia*, p. 12). André was "entrusted with handling Clinton's correspondence with his secret agents and informers," and thus became steadily and inextricably involved in the Arnold defection (Van Doren, *Secret History*, p. 125). Willcox, however, claims that André lacked formal confirmation of either his major's rank or the adjutant generalship (*Portrait of a General*, p. 341n.).

67. Col. James Livingston commanded the works at Verplanck's and Stony Point (Van Doren, *Secret History*, p. 287).

68. "The Highlands had a particular appeal to Clinton. Three years earlier he had argued passionately for opening them, had done so on his own initiative, and had been recalled like an errant schoolboy. Now he had the chance to demonstrate to the world how right he had been, to prove that the Hudson was the key to the war" (Willcox, *Portrait of a General*, pp. 339–40).

69. This was one Joshua Hett Smith, who was later acquitted by a court-martial (from lack of evidence), then arrested by the New York civil authorities, only to escape into New York City before he could be tried (Freeman, *Washington*, 5:225n.; Washington, *Writings*, 20:262n.; and Van Doren, *Secret History*, pp. 352, 391, 428).

70. The dramatic hours before André's execution by hanging are recounted in Willcox, *Portrait of a General*, pp. 341–43; Freeman, *Washington*, 5:214–22; and Van Doren, *Secret History*, chap. 15).

71. A work on a hill west of West Point, named for Israel Putnam (Carrington, *Battles*, map opposite p. 512).

72. Fort George was on Lake George (north of Albany, N.Y.), and Fort Anne was just east of it (Boatner, *Encyclopedia*, map, p. 175). The latter was attacked on 10 October and the former the following day, both times by a British force under Maj. Christopher Carelton (Peckham, *Toll*, p. 76).

73. Peter Gansevoort, colonel and commandant of the Third New York Regiment.

74. Maj. Gen. William Heath, who took over the command at West Point after Washington conferred the southern command upon Nathanael Greene (Washington

to Heath, 14 October and to Greene, 14 October, *Writings*, 20:180–82). The commander in chief was also asked by Congress to open a court of inquiry into Gates's conduct at Camden (ibid., pp. 181–82).

75. The action was not in North Carolina but at King's Mountain, S.C., although the Patriot militia were drawn largely from North Carolina and Tennessee. On 7 October 1,550 Patriots under 7 colonels "swarmed up the mountain to annihilate more than 1,000 Loyalists under Maj. Patrick Ferguson," who was killed along with 150 of his men (160 wounded and 700 captured). The Patriots lost 28 killed—among them Col. James Williams (South Carolina)—and 62 wounded (Peckham, *Toll*, p. 76). The bloody fight showed the conflict in the South for what it really was: a civil war. "Ferguson was the only British soldier in the ensuing battle, one of the most important of the war. On both sides, all the rest were Americans" (Ward, *War of the Revolution*, 2:741).

76. Marquees were officers' large field-tents, and the lee side is the sheltered side of anything.

77. The "Convention Troops" were the British prisoners (some 5,000 in number originally) from Burgoyne's surrender at Saratoga (17 October 1777). For the greatest part of the war they were quartered around Charlottesville, Va. (Boatner, *Encyclopedia*, pp. 275–76), and now and again there would arise rumors of some conspiracy or other by loyalists or the British to free them. This particular plot by "Mr. Ross" was discounted by Washington and indeed turned out to be mere rumor (Washington, *Writings*, 20:358).

78. See Willcox, *Portrait of a General*, chap. 9.

79. Fort Wyllis was another of the outworks around West Point, this one on the Hudson to the south (Carrington, *Battles*, map opposite p. 512). It is described by Chastellux in the *Travels*, 1:93–94.

80. The full resolution of Congress concerning the reorganization of the American army was announced in the general orders for 1 November 1780. The new system was to take effect 1 January 1781 and involved the consolidation of the two Rhode Island regiments into one; the command was to go to Col. Christopher Greene, thereby occasioning the retirement of Israel Angell. Greenman was retained as one of the "two subalterns to each company" of the regiment (Washington, *Writings*, 20:277–81).

81. Francis Barber, lieutenant colonel of the Third New Jersey Regiment.

82. The distinguished visitor was François-Jean de Beauvoir, Chevalier (later Marquis) de Chastellux, Maréchal de Camp of Rochambeau's army and the author of the delightful *Travels in North America*. The Chevalier was mightily impressed by everything he saw at West Point—including the regiment of invalids who managed to carry themselves with dignity though they lacked even a stitch of clothing. Besides the salute by 13 cannon, Generals Heath and Stark formed some of the troops for his excellency's review: "I passed before the ranks, being saluted with the spontoon by all the officers, and the drums beating a march, an honor paid in America to major generals, who are the first in rank, though it only corresponds to our Maréchal de camp. The troops were ill clothed, but made a good appearance; as for the officers they left nothing to be desired either in their bearing or in their manner of marching and giving commands" (*Travels*, 1:89–90).

83. Washington was making his winter headquarters (with only a part of the army) at New Windsor, N.Y. (Freeman, *Washington*, 5:232).

84. Maj. Gen. William Smallwood of Maryland.

85. George Whitefield (1714–1770), Anglican evangelist and an associate of the Wesleys. He had had considerable impact in the colonies in the 1740s through a series of evangelistic tours (Clifton E. Olmstead, *History of Religion in the United States* [Englewood Cliffs, N.J.; Prentice-Hall, 1960], pp. 158, 164–65).

86. Greenman is using "sauntering" in the old sense of being in a state of reverie (*OED*, s.v. "saunter").

87. Greenman is reading an English version of La Rochefoucauld's *Maxims and Moral Reflections* (1665). The scientific treatise is probably Charles Middleton's *A New and Complete System of Geography . . . of Europe, Asia, Africa and America* (London, 1777–78).

88. Moses Hazen, colonel, Second Canadian Regiment.

89. James Tisdale, who was an "Engineer" on the Quebec Expedition in the same company as Greenman (Samuel Ward's)(Roberts, *March to Quebec*, p. 38). At this time he was serving in the Thirty-second Massachusetts Regiment.

90. This particular drawing does not survive, but a fine example of his ship-drawing is reproduced in this volume.

91. John Graham of the First New York Regiment.

92. Maj. Benjamin Tallmadge (on 23 November) led a force of sixty men against Fort St. George on Long Island, "dismantled the fort, burned forage, and captured 46" (Peckham, *Toll*, p. 77).

93. Possibly John Johnson of the Fifth New York Regiment.

94. Abbreviation for "subaltern."

95. Also known as "Croton Bridge," crossing the river of the same name (Nebenzahl, *Atlas*, pp. 88–89).

96. Bedford was in northern Westchester County, on the so-called upper road to Connecticut (Nebenzahl, *Atlas*, pp. 88–89). "North Caswill" is a Greenmanism for New Castle in Westchester County, N.Y.

97. This British officer has not been identified.

98. Jeremiah Fogg of the Second New Hampshire Regiment.

99. Possibly Daniel Delavan, a captain in the New York militia.

100. On 12 November Washington had written Heath detailing the various winter quarters for the Northern Army. The Rhode Island Line was to encamp "at the gorge of the Mountain near the Continental village; and to furnish a detachment more to the left; say, about Robinsons Mills" (*Writings*, 20:337). The mills were in the area of Col. Beverly Robinson's house on the east side of the Hudson. Robinson, "a wealthy Tory artistocrat," was a British secret agent and deeply involved in Arnold's treason (Boatner, *Landmarks*, p. 295; *Encyclopedia*, map, p. 531).

101. Fredericksburg, N.Y., was east of Fishkill, on the way to Danbury, Conn. (Colles, *Survey*, plate 12). The places Greenman mentions on his way home on furlough have, except where noted, been identified in previous parts of the journal.

102. No village or township by the name of Northbury has been identified for this area in Connecticut.

103. This is the Lebanon Crank Tavern (see part 3, entry for 29 January and note).

104. William Allen, of the Second Rhode Island Regiment.

105. Greenman will stop at "Land Lord Greene's" again in 1781, on his way back to camp, but no such tavern in Scituate has been identified.

106. John Morley Greene, lieutenant in the Second Rhode Island Regiment.

107. This is the earliest indication in the journal, or from any other source, of Greenman's involvement with Freemasonry (see the introduction), for the "Ancient Feast of St. John" (the Evangelist) is regularly celebrated in America only by Roman Catholics, Episcopalians, and Freemasons. And, of course, his membership in the former two groups is highly unlikely.

PART FIVE

Captive, 1781

INTRODUCTION

THE MOMENTOUS year of 1781 began no differently from the past several for Jeremiah Greenman. The winter months were spent at home, as the furloughed soldier waited for the onset of the campaign. The French army and navy were in Newport, had been there since Rochambeau's Expeditionary Force arrived in July of 1780; but if this exotic presence made any special impression on the diarist he did not record the fact. Greenman gave the French activities an occasional bare mention and allowed only one brief entry for Washington's visit to Newport in March. His own days were being spent in new forms of self-improvement: the journal for 1781 hints at an awakening interest in religion, reflected both in Greenman's going more often to church than in previous years and in his devotional reading. But more important is the study of "the Marriners Art." Here is the initial indication that he was preparing for a career beyond the military—perhaps from a young man's realization that this war, after all, could not go on forever, nor would the army's legion of officers be needed once the independence of America was assured. What the young nation would require, however, was shipmasters, and for this eventuality Greenman began a preparation that would continue at odd times throughout the remainder of the war.

Early in the spring he was recalled and made the familiar trek across Connecticut to the Hudson Highlands, where he rejoined his regiment—now the one and only from Rhode Island, commanded by Col. Christopher Greene. Late in April he was sent to command the guard at Pines Bridge, one of the two bridges spanning the Croton River, and the northern barrier of the "neutral ground" of Westchester County, New York.[1] This was an area of almost daily confrontation between loyalist and patriot, the scene of guerrilla warfare bitterly fought in what might now be called a demilitarized zone, where the fact that America's revolution was a civil war was known to all. The novelist James Fenimore Cooper has described the "neutral ground" as well as anybody:

> *The County of Westchester, after the British had obtained possession of the island of New York, became common ground, in which both parties continued to act for the remainder of the War of the Revolution. A large proportion of its inhabitants, either restrained by their attachments, or influenced by their fears, affected a neutrality they did not feel. The lower towns were, of course, more particularly under the dominion of the crown, while the upper, finding a security from the vicinity of the continental troops, were bold in asserting their revolutionary opinions. . . . Great numbers, however, wore masks. . . .*[2]

Greenman's duty at the Pines Bridge barrier consisted largely ot meeting flags of truce from the British, checking their bona fides, and then either complying with or refusing their requests—usually to move a loyalist family closer to the city of New York. Now and then one of these "flags" would turn out to be a sharp-eyed spy who would note the strengths or weaknesses of the guard. Vigilance had to be maintained by the Americans, for if they nodded for even a moment they could expect a visit from "De Lancey's Refugees," the most active Loyalist military force in Westchester County. The guard duty was an important assignment and should not have lulled the Rhode Islanders to sleep, as it soon unfortunately did.

Greenman's guard was on duty the morning of 14 May when a party of the loyalists—variously estimated at between 150 and 300 men—forded the Croton two and a half miles from Pines Bridge and moved north to surprise the headquarters of Christopher Greene, then commanding the Continental detachments on the "Lines." The facts of the attack are quickly told: Greene and Maj. Ebenezer Flagg, along with twelve of their men, were killed after a few minutes of vicious, hand-to-hand fighting. But the traditions surrounding the affair speak only of the cruelty of the "Refugees": Greene hacked and wounded time and again, Greene asking for his parole after being disabled but being denied, Greene forced to ride behind one of the dragoons in their retreat, Greene falling from the saddle and being left by the roadside to die.[3]

On their way back to New York City, the loyalists met the

Pines Bridge guard with equal surprise, but unaccountably offered Greenman and his men quarter. The luckless Greenman found himself a prisoner again—and on the very day he had been promoted to 1st lieutenant![4] But as he soon discovered, New York was not Quebec, and a lieutenant was not a private: parole was soon granted, along with billeting privileges and the freedom of the Gravesend area of Long Island. This time he was in a prison without walls, but time would weigh no less heavily on the prisoner for that.

The five months spent on Long Island were, in Greenman's own words, "tedious" and "sedentary." There was little to do but walk around Gravesend, listen to the gossip about the war—loyalist in cast for a change—and "imply" himself in sewing and reading. Reading—here was an unequalled chance to further the taste he acquired in 1780. His sources for a diversity of titles he did not confide, but books seem to have been plentiful, and Greenman was not at all selective. When he was not with a book, he was getting the semi-official news of the war's prosecution from James Rivington's consortium of New York newspapers—most importantly the New York *Royal Gazette*—which was pouring forth information and loyalist propaganda on virtually a daily basis.[5]

Greenman's eyes were open; he was actively reading the newspapers; he received guests now and then. All these told him that great things were stirring in the summer and autumn of 1781. His regiment, with most of the American army and the French under Rochambeau, marched "to the southward," but the ponderous and highly litigious mechanism of prisoner exchange worked slowly. He could only watch as the "great concentration" began and matured. In short, it was his fate to miss the triumph at Yorktown.

When freedom finally did come, it was much too late for him to join the troops before Yorktown (the surrender actually took place a few days before his exchange), and so he and his fellow officers "belonging to the northward," returned to the Highlands, there to finish out the year and wait for orders. Then followed a winter holiday with friends in New York and Connecticut, "keeping Chrismas" with a certain "Mr. Butts," and then the return to winter quarters and the news that he was to journey to Philadelphia—for there the Rhode Island regiment was to spend the winter.

NOTES TO INTRODUCTION

1. The two bridges across the Croton River, with the town of Crompond (now Yorktown, N.Y.) and the topography of the area may be seen on the French map reproduced in Rice and Brown, eds., *Rochambeau's Army*, 2: map 146.

2. James Fenimore Cooper, *The Spy*, (New York: Dodd, Mead, and Co., 1946), pp. 1–2.

3. The traditions surrounding what was known as the "Massacre of Col. Greene and Major Flagg" have been collected by Marcius S. Raymond and are included in his article, "Colonel Christopher Greene," *Magazine of History* (September–October 1916): 138–49.

4. Greenman's lieutenant's commission, preserved in the National Archives, authorizes him to take rank on 14 May 1781.

5. See Boatner, *Encyclopedia*, p. 936; and Greene, *Revolutionary Generation*, p. 296.

CAPTIVE, 1781

JANUARY 1781

T 9 to T 16. this morning from Dartmouth came to Portsmouth where mad a small halt / then went to Newport where continued 'till the 17th. In which are informed by an Express from the Grand army that the Pensylvania Line had muternied & marched to their State on account of thier Provision being Short & their Depreciation not being made up to them—[1]

W 17 to S 20. this morning from Newport came to portsmouth where made a small halt / Crosed Howland Ferry and came to Dartmouth where continued 'till the 20th. Inst.—

S 21. Took a small walk into the uper end of Dartmout, where continued 'till munday the 22d which Time spent very agreeably / N M R.

M 22 to T 25. Continuing in Dartmouth / Implying my Self in draufting Sum Emplements on an apron[2] / this Evening went about 2 miles from this place, where spent ye Evening agreably in hearing a Sermon delivered from Mr. Danl. Rogers—

F 26. and S 27. this day implying my Self in learning the Marriners art. Spent this Evening in reading a History called the purity of Heart.[3]

S 28. Spent the fore part of this day in reading the Bible, in the afternoon went about 2 miles where contined the Evening—

M 29 and T 30. Continuing in stud[y]ing Navagation, Nothing more Remarkeble these two days—

W 31. Spent this day in hearing a Sermon delivered, by Mr. Rogers.

February 1781 Dartmouth

T 1 to S 25. Implying my Self in Studiing Navigation 'till Satterday the 4th. then went about 4 miles where continued 'till monday the 5th. then came to Acoxet where continued, 'till the 26, in which time are informed that there is great Confusion in the army to the Westward, further are informed that Genl. Green had captured a Large Number of the Enemy near Georgia—with Sum Bagage—[4]

M 26 and T 27. this morning from Dartmouth. Came to Fall River where made a small halt from whare came to Slaids ferry whare crossed & came to Swanzey whare continued till the 28th.

W 28. this morning from Swanzey came to Providance where am informed that the French Fleet that went out a few days ago had returned, & brought with them the Romulus carring 44 Guns & several other armed vessels, with about 500 Prisoners, which they captured whilts gone from Rhode-Island[5]—are informed that the Jersey line had muternied, but was quelled by Genl. How, & two of their Lead. hung—[6]

March 1781 on a March

T 1 and F 2. Continuing in Providance at Mr. Greens[7] / are informed of the glorious Victory of Brigadeer Genl. Morgan, over a superiour body of Brittish Troops, commanded by Colo. Tarleton wherein the Enemy lost upwards of one hundred killed in the field, & between 2: & 3 hundred wounded & above 5 hundred taken prisoners, with two field peases, two Stand of Coulers, 800 Stand of arms, & thirty five Waggons, with the Loss on our Side 8 men kil'd 60 wounded—[8] this after Noon went to Rehoboth where continued 'till Satturday the 3d. which time spent very agrably.

S 3. this morning came to Providence, where are informed that the Militia is ordered to be called in, to guard the French Stoors at Newport as they are bound on Sum Expedition—N M this day.

S 4. this morn are informed that a Number of the Inhabitance of Newport & this town is taken up on Suspition of Trading with the Enemy, breakfasted this morn with Mr. Green, after which came to Taunton.

M 5 to T 8. Continuing in Taunton 'till Fryday the 9th. which time spent agreably / the Militia are ordered from hear for forty day / Nothing more these days.

F 9. this morn from Taunton came to Sonet[9] where made a small halt from where came to Dartmouth about 4 miles from the head of the River, where continued all Night—

S 10 and S 11. this morn came four miles to the Head of acoxet river where continued 'till Monday.

M 12. this [*morn*] came to howlands ferry where crossed & came to Portsmouth where made a Small Halt / then came to Newport where am informed that the English Fleet had left Gardners Bay & gone in persuit of the French Fleet—[10]

T 13. this day his E[*x*]cellency Genl. Washington went from this Town, at which 2 Battalions of the French Troops ware paraded & saluted him as he pased & was escorted out of Town by a Number of French Officers—[11]

W 14. this day are informed that the French had arrived to Cheasapek Bay and landed part of their men.

T 15 to T 20. this morn from Newport came to Portsmouth where made a small halt from where came to Howlands Ferry where crossed and came to Dartmouth where continued 'till Tuesday the 20th. then left Dartmouth & came to Slaid Ferry where I crossed & came to Swanzey where stoped about an hour, then proceeded to P. where put up—&C.

W 21. Continuing in Providence 'till the afterpart of the day / then went about a mile out of Town, in ye Evening return'd to Providence again—

T 22 to S 24. are informed that Genl. Green had surrounded part of Conwallesses Army, and that he had burned all his heavy bagage, are inform'd that the Light Infentry of the Grand army had marcht for the Southward,[12] buying Sundry articles & setling my buisness & preparing for a March to join my Regt.—

S 25. this morning from Providence / came to Cituate to Land Lord Green where dined, from where came to Vollington where put up—

M 26. this morning went about a mile & a half to Canturbury where breakfasted / then pushed on to windham where dined & continued all Night—

T 27. this morning came to Lebanan where breakfasted / then pushed on to Bolton where stoped, about half an hour, then came to Hartford where I crossed the Ferry & push'd on 5 miles where put up—

W 28 and T 29. this morn set off early / came 8 miles where breakfasted / then came to Northbury where made a small halt, from where pushed on to Bethelem where halted & continued 'till the 30th it being Stormy, &C.

F 30. this morning from Bethelem came to Washington where made a small halt / then proceded on to Newmilford where I crossed the Fery & came to Newfairfield where put up & continued all Night—

MARCH–APRIL 1781 RHODE ISLAND VILLAGE

S 30 and S 1. this morning from New Fairfield came to Fredricksburgh where breakfasted / then pushed on 8 miles & dined, from where came to Camp, and are informed that the biger part of the Regt. is gone to the Lines—[13]

M 2. Continuing at the Huts which I found Compleat'd and very Comfertable. are informed that Genl. Green has had a very smart action with Conwallis & that Genl. Green was oblig'd to quit the field with the Loss of two or three hundred men—[14]

T 5 to M 9. are informed that the Enemy is out from Newyork with 90 hors & 50 foot, this Evening saw too Large Fires at the Westward, this afternoon went about two miles into the Country / at Night returned to Camp.

T 10. this day passed Muster / the 4 men that deserted a few day ago was braught back—

W 11. a Serjt. & a few Recruits came into Camp & 3 Diserters which deserted two & three years ago,[15] Spent the morning in reading the Spectator[16] the After Noon in making out Sum muster Roals—

T 12. Nothing Remarkeble T D.—

F 13. this day set on Genl. Court Martial of which Major E. Flag was President, Tryed Jack Champlin for stealing. Benjn. Buffington for Desertion & Mathew Henly, Corlinius Driskill, Charles Stevens, & James Singleton, all of which plead Guily and was sentinced to receive 100 Lashes—Tryed Cuff Roberts for Stealing and was sentinced to receive 100 Lashes—Nathan Gale was tryed by the Same Court for repeat'd Desertion, plead Guilty & threw him Self on the Mercy of ye Court, the Court having considered the Prisoners Genl. Carracter, in the Regt. do sentince him to suffer Death—[17]

S 14 to T 19. Nothing Extraordinary happined / Implying

myself in reading the Spctator, this day 2 officers joined us from Furlough.

F 20 and S 21. fixing and preparing to go to the lines.

S 22. this morning from camp came 6 miles where made a small halt / then pushed on near Pines Bridge where put up at Mr. Griffens—in the Evening warned to go on Guard—

M 23. this morn went two Miles from my Quarters to Pines Bridge, where mounted Guard with a Serjt. Corpl. & 18 Privates / two Deserters came to me from the Enemy. at 3 oClock receiv'd a Flag which was after families & was discharged in an hour.[18] NMRTD—

T 24. this morn thick raining wether, after being relieved went about 2 miles where spent the day, after which came to my Quaters, which was a Quaker Minnesters—

W 25. this morning went about 2 Miles, after spinding an hour or two returned to my Quaters where continued the Remainder of the day NM.

T 26. Continuing near Pines Bridge / took a Walk a mile or two into the country, in the Evening returned to my Quaters / NMDTD.

F 27. this morning mounted Guard at Pines Bridge where received a Flagg from the Enemy, which was after famelies—

S 28. this morning dismised the Flagg, came to my Quaters after being releived / NMR.

S 29. Continuing at quaters, this day set on Court Martial / adjurned for want of paper.

M 30. this Morn mounted Guard at Pines Bridge / Received a flagg from the Enemy—this afternoon 19 Waggons, with Tory families went to the Enemy by Order of the Sevil Athority / NMRDTD.

May 1781 On the Lines

T 1. this morning dismised the Flagg, after being releived came to my Quaters—went about two miles then return'd to my Quater again—NMR.

W 2. this day went about two Miles to Pines Bridge where all the officers of the Detach't assembled & dined. Spent the Even agreable / NMDTD—

T 3. this morn went on Guard at Poins [Pines] Bridge where received a flagg from the Enemy, desiring leave to move a famely from Terry-Town to New York.

F 4. this morning at 8 oClock received a flag, which was after famelies—at ten oClock was releived / came to my Quaters, where continued all day very sedentaryly—in the Evening a few small arms fired which ocasion'd a small alarm, in Consequence of which ordered to hold myself in Readyness to march to Pines Bridge.

S 5. this day rode to the huts at the Rhode Island Village where continued 'till the afternoon / then came to my Quaters, 50 Men reingforced us from the Hamshire Line.

S 6. this morning went on Guard at Pines Bridge. a Small Detachment went below two or three Miles / in the Evening return'd & NMR.

M 7 to W 9. Raining / continuing in my quaters / NMR DTD.

T 10. went on Guard at Pines Bridge / Nothing Remarkebl DMT.

F 11. this morning after being releived came to my Quaters / two Deserters came to me at my Quaters, belonging to the 54th. [*British*] Regt—

S 12. Nothing Remarkeble.

S 13. went on Guard at Pines Bridge—

M 14. This morning was alarmed by the appearance of a party of Cavalry supported by Infantry, which proved to be Delancey's Corps of Refugees[19] / they soon surrounded me and being vastly superiour in force—& having no prospect of escape, I thought it most adviseable to surrender myself and Guard prisoners of War—They informed me they had taken two officers from the Colo. Quaters[,] that he was Mortally Wounded & Major Flagg killed[20]—A party of the Infantry took charge of me & the Men—marched ous over the bridge where we halted a few moments and then proceeded to Morrisenia, from which place was carried to York Island & delivered over to Capt. Fefiat who treated me very politely—[21]

T 15. this morning after breakfast, was paraded & marched into New York—my Men all put into the Sugar house[22] myself paroled to Mrs. Wheatons in Clefts Street a house prepared for the reception of any Officer that migh be made Prisoners 'till they got their parole.

W 16. this Morning went to Mr. Lorings office where received a parole to go on Long-Island—Came to the Ferry where crost / hear hired a hors & Chair / rode about 9 miles to Mr. Voorhiees, Graves End Neck where was billit'd[23] having Liberty of the Town Ships where the prisoners was billeted, which was these—Graves End, New Utrich, Flatlands, Flatbush,—

T 17. this day went about 3 miles to Flat lands where spent the day / in the Evening returned to My Quaters NM.

F 18. This day went a mile to Graves End where continued an hour / then returned to my Quaters.

S 19. this morn went to Graves End where continued an hour or two / then returned to my Quaters—and went two miles to the Shore and got a Mess of Clams / then return'd & spent the Remainder of the day at my quaters—

S 20 and M 21. Continuing at my quaters all these days sedantaryly & Condoleing my Misfortune of being a prisoner, it being the first days since my being captured, of having an oppertunity to reflect on My Misfortune.

T 22. this Morning went to Graves End / got a pair of overhalls cut out, then returned to my Quaters & implyed myself Remainder of the day—

W 23. Implying myself in making my overalls—

T 24 and F 25. This morning took a small walk about a mile then returned to my quaters & made a pair of Socks—

S 26. this afternoon rode a mile to a Naibouring House where spent the after Noon very agreably—

S 27 and M 28. Nothing happined worthy Remarks—

T 29. this day are in form'd by people from Newyork that there is New Preposals to the United States for peace, what they are can't yet learn, but am quite sure Nothing Short of Independancey[24] / this day Major Hayse arrived,[25] who went out on parole a few days ago, by which Reasons I am obliged to change my Billet (as this Billet formely belonged to him) and go to Graves End Town to Mr. Cornelious Striker, a great Villen a Tory—[26]

W 30. this day the officers on the Island meet at Flat Lands where spent the after Noon—

T 31. this day went a Mile to my former Quaters at Mr. Voorhises where made a Linning Vest with the assi[*s*]tance of my Land la[*d*]y—

June 1781 Graves End

F 1. continuing at my quaters / are informed that the French Fleet is arrived—

S 2. went 2 miles to Mr. Garrisons where spent the after Noon / in the Evening came to my quater NMR.

S 3. took a walk about a mile this fore noon—the after went to New Utrek after which came to my quaters.

M 4. this fore noon went to church / heard a Sermon in duch, did not under stand a woord—Spent the afternoon in Walk & NMR.

T 5. Spent the fore noon in reading the adventures of Capt. Boyle[27] / the after in walk & C—

W 6 and T 7. Spent in reading Capt Boyls adventures except the after Noon of the 7th when went to Flat lands [*to*] a hors race—

F 8. Continuing at my Quaters / the forepart of the day in reading Military Instruction for officers—[28] the after part of the day went to Graves End Neck & implying myself in making two linning night Caps / NMR—

S 9. Spent the forenoon in reading Military instruction / the after—went to Flatlands. in the Evening return'd to my Quater—

S 10 to W 13. Continuing at my Quatr., Sedentary—& Nothing worth Remark happened.

T 14. Nothing Remarkeble during the day—in the Evening a party of men landed on the Island commanded by Capt. Hylar / Took off a large quantety of Goods & C—No prisoners tho it lay in their power too took [have taken] off a hole gua'd [guard].

F 15. this morng. took a walk half a Mile / then returned to my Quater whare continued, till the after Noon, when went a mile to Graves End Neck where spent the after noon & part of the Evening, then came to my quaters / Nothing MR—

S 16. continuing at my quatrs all day—[*cipher*].[29]

S 17. Continuing this day at my quaters reading the History of ye Heathen Gods and Goddesses—[30] NMRDTD.

M 18 and T 19. continuing at my Quaters / Implying mymyself in reading a History of the Heathen Gods & Goddesses.

W 20. The fore part of this day spent sedentary / in the after Noon went to Graves End Neck where drank tea / in the Evening returned to my Quaters [*cipher*].

T 21. the fore part of this day spent in reading Tom Jones,[31] the after part in walking & recreating myself as well as posable for my Cituation—this Evening received my Bagage—the few articles I had on the Lines with me—Consisting of a Shirt or two & Some other Small Articles which rendered my Cituation more agreable than before as it was near six weaks, sinc[*e*] my Capture and not heard from my Regt.

F 22. we are informed a party of the Enemy was gone into the Jerseys / we saw a Small Fleet go around Staten Island & saw several Smooks on the Main which we imagined to be Ho[*u*]ses the Enemy was burning, to have Sumthing in Retalliaton for the Victory gained by Genl. Green at the Southward in taking a fort with 400 men and two other small ones in the whole (we are informed by some of our friends) consist of about 800 Men,[32]

S 23. Spent the fore part of this day in reading Tom Jones—in the after noon received a letter from Mr. Winslow D Coms'y Prisoners and 37 Dollars 4 Shillings and 8-pence—at the Same Time informing me that I had Some Cloathing coming on the Road, & as soon as they arrive he would send them [*cipher*].

S 24. this day traviled 5 miles to Flatt Bush, where continued 'till Evening / are informed that the party of the Enemy which was out, are returned / Made but a poor Manoever of it, lost Several Men—plundered a few old Horses, & plundered several helpless famelies as usual when out from their Den.

M 25. Continuing at my quaters all the forenoon, reading Tom Jones's 2nd. Vollum / in the after noon took severall small walks / NMRDD.

T 26. this morning a Fleet went up to New York consisting [*of*] 30 sail, which we are informed came from South Carolina / Implying myself in reading 2nd. Vollum of Tom Jones.

[*W 27*]. fore part of this day led very sedentary / the after part went to New Utreck where spent the biger part of [*it ?*] then came to my Quater again / all the refugees from the Est End of the Island we hear are on the March in consequence of Some Movement Genl. Washington is making,[33] we are informed they are going on to Staten Island, the 2nd Battallion of New Jersey Vollentiers lay in town this night on their way for Staten Island.

T 28. Raining, continuing at my quaters reading the 2nd. Vollum of Tom Jones / NMRTD.

F 29. Continuing at my Quaters reading the 3d. Vollum of Tom

Jones, the after noon took a walk about two miles then returned to my Quaters NMRtd.

S 30. Pleasant / continuing at my Quaters NR—

JULY 1781 GRAVES END

S 1. this morn took a small Walk, Spent the other part of the day sedentary.

M 2. This morn about 3 oClock there was an alarm in Town ocasioned by the landing of a party of men from, the Jersys who plundered, a famely &C—

T 3. we are informed that there hath been a Smart Ingagement above Kings Bridge and by information of friends are informed that our people got the better,—and that all the Enemy was inside of Kings Bridge—

W 4. This day all the officers that are presant on the Island assembled, to commamorate the 4th. July it being the anniversary of Independancy and drank the 13 following 1st. United State of America may they ever be free Independant & Suvering [sovereign], 2nd. the King of France / 3d. the King of Spain, 4th the United State of Holland / 5th. the Continental Congress / 6th. Genl. Washington / 7th our American ambassador in Europe / 8th. the French Ambassador in America—9th. the French Adml. and Navy in America, 10th. Genl. DeRochambeau & the French Army in America / 11th. the American Arms / 12th. a Speedy Releasment to the Allied Prisoners, 13th what we have gained by our arms may we support by our Virtue—and spent the remainder of the Day in Jolletry & Mirth under a Flagg which had the Figure of his Excellency Genl. Washington on it.

T 5. Received my portmanteau & some of my things—are informed by my Landlord if I dont pay my bord monthly he will not keep [*me*] & informing me he hath the Commesery of prisoners had given him orders to turn me away—

F 6. Continuing at my Quaters implying myself in writing a letter to the Coms'y of Prisoners—concerning my bord &C—

S 7. Spent this day very sedantary.

S 8. are informed by Capt Sullivan,[34] a prisoner, who hath been to Philadelphia on parole, that there is a great movement thro the Country with Military Stores, by that and the Movement of the Enemy (of late) we expect there will be an attack on New York—

M 9. the fore Noon spent in my quaters / the after went to Graves End Neck / the Evening return'd, this night my Landlords Negro & a Couple of Lads Inhabitants of this Town run away, to the Jerseys being disgusted with Colo. Lott the Commander of the Militia of Kings county, at the same [*time*] resolving to come back with a party before the Expiration of a Month and Carry him to our Lines.

T 10. Continuing at my Quaters / the fore noon in reading the Tragedy of Jane Shaw,[35] the after went to Graves End Neck where received an answer to my Letter from the Commesery of Prisoners informing me I should tary at my quaters &C—&C.

W 11. Fine pleasan / rain / NR.

T 12 to S 14. Nothing Worthy except a heavy firing heard toward the east end of the Island.

S 15. this day are informed the firing heard the 13th. Inst. was at Loids Neck or asinord [?] by 4 French Frigates which covered the landing of a Number of Men at that place—&C—

M 16. Cloudy & Sum pleasant Showers of rain—

T 17. Nothing worthy Remark.

W 18. this fore noon continued at My Quaters reading the History of the Heathen Gods and Godesses / after noon took Several Small Walks &C—[*cipher*].

T 19 to S 21. the Whole day spent sedentary—20th & 21st NWRM—s.

S 22. this day the Fleet which lay off againts this place went to Sea—a [line ?] officer & a Doctor belonging to the Massachusetts Line was brought in prisoners, was taken by a Frigate, when comeing down the N. River in. [*cipher*]. about 20 citisans & Masters of Vessels was brought in prisoners, they was taken going to France, on their way from Cape Fransway—

M 23. this day went to Flatt Bush where tarried, two or three hours, then came back to my Quaters / NMR.

T 24. Continuing at my Quaters very sedentary all this day.

W 25. Continuing at my quaters the fore noon,—in the after went to Graves End Neck / heard that the firing last Sunday was ocasioned by a party of our people—which was down to Morrissinia—and that all the Refugees had left that post & retired onto York Island—NMRTD—

T 26. Nothing Worthy Remark TD—

F 27. are informed by a letter in the New York Gazette from a Brittish Captain at Giberalter, that the Spanish draw very nigh to their work and that a fowl feched two dollars & without a Speady Relief must fall to the arms of Spain—[36]

S 28 to T 31. Continuing much in my Quaters & very sedentary—except some few hours reading Some old Books.

August 1781 Graves End

W 1 to F 3. Nothing worthy remarks—

S 4. This Evening a party of Men from the Jerseys landed on the Island, made prisoner of Lieut. Colo. Lott, and plundered him to the Vallew of 100 pounds—

S 5. this day we are informed that the party which was on the Island last Night was Capt. Hyler, with the Two Stillwils & my Landlords Negro, who went off, the 9th of July last.—and now return'd agreable to their Resolution and take Sattisfaction of their Colo.—[37]

M 6. this day went to Flatt Bush where continued till Evening / then came to my Quaters.

T 7 to F 10. Continuing at my Quaters sedentary & Nothing Worthy Remark.

S 11. this after Noon 25 Sail of Shipping went up to New York—

S 12 to W 15. Continuing at my Quaters / Implying myself in Drawing Several Ships &C—Nothing W R—

T 16. Adml. Graves return'd with his Fleet—[38]

F 17 to S 19. Nothing Worthy remar.

M 20. went as far as Graves End Neck, in the Evening return'd to my quaters / NMRDd.

T 21. this day went to Graves End Neck / picked a few cucumber, from a friends field and sent to the prisoners in the Sugar house [*cipher*].

W 22. Continuing this fore Noon at my quaters—the After went to Mrs. Ryders bur[y]ing a Widdow much lamented by the officers, for her godness & Benovolence shewn to Prisoners Quatered at her house.

T 23. Continuing at my quaters implying myself in reading Cato's letters—[39]

F 24. Reading 2nd. Vollum of Guil Blas—[40]

S 25. this day implying myself in Drawing a Ship.

S 26. this day the Enemy seem to be in a Move as tho Sum Expidition was a foot, in crossing a Number of Men to Staten Island & Cannon & C.

M 27. we are informed by the New York Gazette that Genl. Washington had left his Camp at white plains & with the French crossed the North River and marched towards Newark, Springfield & that Neibourhood, and it was exspected by the Manoevers' an attack would be made on Staten Island, Calling for all trew Loyallist now to turn out / Sir Adml. Hood arrived with 13 Sail of the Line from the West Indias—[41] we are informed the French Fleet hath left Rhode Island.[42]

T 28. this Evening a Number of Men from our lines came to My Quaters plundered the house to the Vallue of about 20 pounds, made Prisoners of my two landlords, after which Retir'd off without the Los of a Man / three of the party was persons [*who*] went off hear a few weeks ago one my landlords Negro [*cipher*].

W 29 to F 31. we are informed that Genl. Washington hath gone to the Southward with part of his Army & are informed that the French Fleet had arrived at Chesopeak Bay,—by Some of our Friends & 35 Sail of the line.

September 1781 G. End

S 1. Major Haize a prisoner was exchanged & went out and are informed that we are all to be soon exchanged.

S 2 to W 5. Implying myself in Drawing Some Ships &C—Nothing More Remarkeble / [*cipher*].

T 6. this day are informed to be in readyness to go out at the Shortest—Notice, as we was all exchanged by the Carteal setled the 3d. Inst. on Staten Island by the Commsaries of Prisoners—[43]

F 7. we are informed by the Newyork Gazette that 17 Sail of French line of Battle Ships lay in Chesapeak.

S 8. we are informed by a Frigate which arrived a few days ago that Shee fell in with a French Fleet of 12 Sail of the line and in a few days after fell in with two or three more French line of Battle Ships—

S 9. Continuing at my Quaters fixing to go out but are informed we are not to go 'till the like Number of Brittish officer comes in.

M 10 and T 11. Continuing at my Quaters very Sedentary, the Brittish Fleet returned to Sandy hook and appeared very much shattered, we are informed thay had an Ingagement, and the Brittish claim Victory but by the appearence lost it.

W 12. Continuing at my Quaters in Drawing Ships &C to pass away the tedious hours.

T 13. Lieut. Macomber an officer of our Regt.[44] arrived / informs me the Regt. is gone to Virginia—at the same time informs us of very agreable News, that Lord Conwallis is like to be the Second Vollum to Genl. Burgoine.[45]

F 14. the Fleet all moved up towards Newyork to repair, an then to return to Cheasapeak to try their fortunes with the French again.

S 15. Continuing at my Quaters / are informed the Troops which imbarked some time past, are very unhealthy on board of their Shiping—

S 16 to F 21. Continuing at my Quaters implying myself in Reading Drawing &C / are informed that the 74 which went out a few days [*ago*] after Adml. Graves hath not been heard of, since and it is suppos'd Shee fell in with the French Fleet and is captured.

S 22. this day & Night attended Capt. Sullivan who is Sick.

S 23. fore part of the day spent in reading / the after went to Graves End Neck. Capt. Sullivan died—[*cipher*].

M 24. this day attended the Funeral of Capt. Sullivan / Nothing More R D D—

T 25. Spent the day sedentary—this Evening Sum Shipping appeared off Sandy hook two of which appeared to be Ships of the Line—

W 26. this day went about 4 miles to New lots, where spent the day &C / N M R.[46]

T 27. this day are informed that Genl. Clinton has gone into the Jerseys with a Large Detachment of Troop,[47] the Fleet which appeared off the Other Evening arrived which proved to be Adml. Digby, who it sed hath Six Sail of the line & Prince William Henry with him,[48]

F 28. we hear a Cannonading in Newyork which we suppose to be on the Arrival of this Boy of a Prince—this Evening a party of Men from the Jerseys landed on the Island with an Intent to make Prisoner of Capt. Stillwil (a Capt. of the Militia) but their plan failed them—by the Militia being alarmed and firing on the party.

S 29. are informed by a Friend that the Capt. of the party, which was on hear last Evening is wounded and secreated in a barn in the Center of the Town.—

S 30. this morn found Mr. Stillwil (a yong lad who whent off from this Island a few weeks ago) in a barn, he informed Me had sprained his ancle & the party had left him behind,—he desired my assistance to help him off but being on parole it did not lay much in my power to help him but with Sum Small Assistance of some other officers & my self we got him safely landed on Jersey Shore—[49]

OCTOBER 1781 G. END

M 1 to F 5. Continuing in Graves End at my Quaters very sedentary till 6th. Nothing worthy Remark happened.

S 6. this day a Fleet appear'd off at Sandy Hook Consisting of about 40 Sail which proved to be Adml. Graves in a Most Shatter'd Condition, Sum with their Masts gone others with yards &C—and to compleat without part of the French Fleet which they was to bring with them when they returned—[50] Nmr—

S 7. are informed that ye Enemy lost two Ships of the Line one the Terible of 90 Guns—

M 8. are informed by Some of our Freind from New York that the Enemy are [doing ?] Buisness as fast as posable to repair their Ships &C—Intending to go to the Southward to try their Fortunes once more with the French Fleet.

T 9 to T 16. Continuing at my quaters very sedentary and much discontented waiting with Impatience to have orders to prepare for to go in the Next Flagg—

W 17 to F 19. the English Fleet under command of Adml Graves left the hook with 24 Sail of the Line, with Genl. Clinton on Board with a large Detachment of Foot from the Army—[51]

S 20 to M 22. we are informed to be in readyness to go out the 1st. of next week.

T 23. this day are informed to come to Vanbrunts warf to Morrow Morning—as there will be a Flagg of truce ready for our reception / the most agreable news I could hear—the Evening spent in Company with some of our peticular friends in drinking a Bottle or two of wine & c—

W 24. this Morning at Day break, all the prisoners convened agreable to the orders received last Evening at Mr. Vanbrunts warf, where we all, most chearfully imbarked, for the Jersey Shore where we reached in about 4 hours with a pleasant gale / Disimbarked, in the Evening had a Supper to gether—

T 25. this Morning all the Officers belonging to the Northward hired three Waggons to Transport our Selvs and bagage to the North River,—took leave of our fellow prisoners, and proceeded to Newark, to Colo. Wards (a late Prisoner)[52] where breakfasted, from where proceeded to Cranistown twelve Miles from Elisebeth Town, hear made a Small Halt to refresh Our Selvs and horses—then pushed on 24 miles to Pumton where put up at Mr. Deboes.

F 26. this Morning raining & Stormy, from Pumton came to New Entrum 12 miles from Pumton where made a halt on account of the Storm, and hear the Most Glorious News Confirmed of Conwalleses being taken by our Illustris Commander in Chief and the French army—[53]

S 27. this morning set off by day light / came 9 miles to Judge Coes, at Kearkeart where borrowed sum money to pay for the transport'g of myself & bagage to this place / Mr. Macomber & my self leaving our bagage hear set off for Kings Ferry where arrived about Sun set, crossed and came to the Connecticut Line where tarried all Night.

S 28. this Morning went to Genl. Heaths Quaters, ware tarried till 3 oClock in the Afternoon, received orders from the Genl. to colect what men we had in the Vecenity of West Point &c (which had been left behind when the Regt. marched for the Southward) and join one of the Connecticut Regmts. till we had heard from Colo. Olney—[54] at 4 oClock set off for Crumb Pond where quatered last Winter where arrived at Sunset at the Widdow Brewers.

M 29. this Morning breakfast'd with Doctor Cornelius formely, Surgints Mate of the Regt.[55] then set off for Pines Bridge where taken last Spring where arrived at 2 oClock—& spent the Remainder of the Day & Evening in the Neibourhood—

T 30. this Morning forded the River above the Bridge / went to Mr. Matrosses where breakfasted / then crossed Pines Bridge and proceeded to Crumbpond where arrived at Sun set & continued at the Widdow Brewers—

W 31. Continued at Crumbpond 'till 3 oClock in the Afternoon when set off for Camp, came 3 miles on My Way—when a Man overtook me informing me that an Officer had arrived from Rhode

Island with Recrutes / turned back, where found Ens. Johnson who the State had lately appointed—[56]

November 1781 N. River

T 1. This morning Ens Johnson and My self with Eight Recrutes set off for Camp where we arrived about 8 oClock—when was inform'd all Prisoners in the Vecinety of West Point & its Territory had been liberated by Genl. Heath, on account of the Surrender of Conwalles / the Remainder of the Day Stormy & Cold—

F 2. this Morning went about two Miles to the 2nd. Connecticut Brigade where got a hors and Chair—from where proceeded to Kings ferry where crossed the North River & proceeded to Kearkeart 8 Miles from the river, to Judge Coes, where Mr. Maccomber & my self left our bagage / hear continued all Night.

S 3 to T 6. This Morning from Kearkeart came about 4 Miles towards Kings ferry where made a halt & breakfasted from where proceeded to Kings which crossed and went to the Connecticut line & join'd the 1st Regt. & drew provision & continued till 7th—NR—

W 7. this morn set out for Danbury, (to look amongst sum bagage which was left behind,) amongst which exspected to find some that I left at the Regt. when taken Prisoner—arrived in the Evening / over halled the bagage, but found None of my Own—after which came about a Mile where put up—

T 8. this Morn left Danbury / came to the Widdow Brewers at Crumb Pond, where continued all Night.

F 9 to T 13. this Morning came to Camp where continued 'till the 13th. Nothing Remarkeble.

W 14. Stormy with rain & c.

T 15 to S 17. the 3d. Massachusetts Brigade marched for hutting[57] / all the rest of the Troops ordered to hold their Selvs in readyness to march / Sum partys gone a forraging toward the Neibourhood of West Chester / when they return exspect to go to Winter Quaters—

S 18 to F 23. This day by order of Genl. Heath Lt. Macomber & myself went about ten miles into the Highlands near the Huts of the Connecticut line where picked uppon a place for the Regiment to build Huts the Winter Insuing—in a most dolful place of Rock Stons &c / in the After noon came to the Camp again, where continued in Tents 'till the 23d, when the Connecticut Line was ordered to march to the High lands to repair their Huts / Marched the Men of Our Regt. with them / arrived about Sun set—

S 24. went to West Point after sum [*soldiers*] belonging to the Regiment who was left behind when the Regiment marched for the Southward / in the Evening return'd / NMR.

S 25 to W 28. this Morning moved to the 2nd. Connecticut Brigade nigher where our huts was to be built where continued 'till the 27th. when went to Crumb Pond after sum boards which was on our Old huts but a Guard being there by Order of Genl. Heath could not bring them away / went to the Widdow Brewers where continued till the 29th. when returned to the High Lands to building huts again—are informed that the Regiment is exspected on in a few days —are informed by Ensign Johnson (who hath been into the Country as far as Kent) of the Death of my Father,—[58] Continuing in building our Huts / got two up—

T 29 and F 30. Nothing More Remarkeble than building Huts—

DECEMBER 1781 N RIVER

S 1 to F 7. Continuing in building our huts, 'till the 7th. in which time got two Huts compleated & almost timber enough for the Regiment to build their huts—when heard by Officers from the Southward that the Regiment was to take winter Quaters in Philadelphia—at which News through by building our huts[59] & Ensign Johnson and My self set out for to take a tower in the Country—as far as Connecticut / Came as far as Fish Kill where made a small halt / then proceeded on about 5 miles where put up—

S 8. This morning came to small Town called Hopewill where breakfasted from where went twelve [*miles*] to Dover in Paulings Precient where tarried—[60]

S 9. This day attended Divine Servise, heard Mr. Waldro deliver a Sermon after which came back to where tarried Last Evening, & continued all Night—

M 10 and T 11. this Mornning came about 4 Miles to Mr. Butts's where continued till the 12th [*cipher*].

W 12. this day came about 20 miles to Capt. Chapmans in Bethelem.[61]

T 13. Continuing at Capt. Chapmans where keept Thanksgiving / the Evening went to an assembly.

F 14. Continuing at my Quaters 'till the after noon when rode a copel of Miles in Slay—

S 15 and S 16. Continuing in Bethelem / This day attended divine Servise at Doctor Bellemys[62] / the Evening spent agreable with Sum Gentlem of the place.

M 17. This day rode down to Woodbury in a Slay where continued all Night—

T 18. this Morning rode back to Bethelem, where continued all day, & spent the time very agreable—

W 19. this day rode in a Slay to Letchfield / in the Evening returned to Bethelem again.

T 20. This day continued at Quaters—the Evening spent in Company with Sum Gentlem of the Town—with a fair well Bottle—

F 21. this Morning from Bethelem came a[*bout*] 11 Miles to Washington where made a small halt, oated my hors &c—then proceeded on to the Oblongs where made a halt at Mr. Butt's—

S 22. Continued at Mr. Butts's 'till the Afternoon, when sett off for Camp, Came two miles on My way—when returned back after my Great Coat which I left—Concluded to stay to keep Chrismas.

S 23 and M 24. Continuing at Mr. Butts's where spend the time agreable [*cipher*].

T 25. Spent the day very agreable & the Evening the Same—

W 26. This mornning came 4 miles to an acquaintance where continued all Night.

T 27. This Mornning from Dover came to Fredricksbourrour where made a small halt from where came to Crumb Pond, and put up at the Widdow Brewers—

F 28. Stormy / Continuing at the Widdow Brewers all day —the Evening spent at Mr. Hazzards.

S 29. This day came to the Continental Village where found Lieutenant Macomber who had colected all the Men of the Regt. and keept a Small Guard over the Commeserys Store, by order of Genl. Heath & had orders to tarry 'till sum bagage came from Danbury which was sent there Last Summer, & go on with that to the Regiment which lay at Philadelphia—

S 30 and M 31. Continuing at My Quaters, at the Widdow Marlings, near the Continental Village, Nothing worthy Remarks happeneth—

NOTES TO DIARY

1. The mutiny of the Pennsylvania Line (1–10 January 1781) began in the winter quarters near Morristown, N.J., "about 10 o'clock the evening of 1 Jan. when soldiers emerged from their huts under arms, with field equipment, captured the guns and ammunition, and assembled to march away. Fewer than half the men fell out initially, and probably not more than 1,500 eventually joined the march. During a confused hour before they left camp the mutineers resisted the efforts and the eloquence of [Gen. Anthony] Wayne and about 100 officers to stop them." There was little violence at this time; the men simply wanted to present their grievances directly to Congress in Philadelphia. Besides the issues Greenman mentions, there was the critical one of whether the men's enlistments had been for three years only—if so they were expired—or for the duration of the war. After several days of negotiations, Congress, through their principal agent in the affair, Joseph Reed, agreed to review each soldier's disputed enlistment on an individual basis. The result was the discharge of more than 1,300 Pennsylvania troops. Many of these subsequently reenlisted. Two British spies among the mutineers, sent by Clinton to convince the troops to go over to the cause of the Crown, were surrendered to the American army by the Pennsylvanians and publicly hung on 11 January (Boatner, *Encyclopedia*, pp. 760–65; see also Carl Van Doren, *Mutiny in January* [New York: Viking Press, 1943], chaps. 4–14).

2. Perhaps another indication of Greenman's membership in the Freemasons.

3. *Purity of Heart: A Moral Epistle*, by the English divine, James Scott (1733–1814). This poem of some 190 lines in heroic couplets was published in 1761 and must have had some suggestive sentiments for the ardent young patriot Greenman: "What, PUBLIUS, made they gentle soul despise/ The strictest bonds and dearest charities?/ Rous'd thy young blood to more than civic strife,/ And arm'd thy hand against thy Sov'reign's Life? / The Daemon discord rose in CATO's form, / And blew the trump to freedom's false alarm;/ He caught the sound and mad with patriot pride,/ In faction's cursed cause the rebel dy'd."

4. Gen. Nathanael Greene was at this time fighting not in Georgia but in the Carolinas and was involved in no major engagements during the winter.

5. French Adm. Arnaud de Tilly, while trying unsuccessfully to get up the Elizabeth River (Chesapeake Bay), had captured the *Romulus*, "a British frigate of forty-four guns and, in addition, he had taken 500 prisoners, two privateers and four small transports" (Freeman, *Washington*, 5:262).

6. This second major mutiny in the American army, perhaps in emulation of the Pennsylvanians, occurred 20–27 January at Pompton, N.J. This time, however, Washington himself was on the scene and directed Gen. Robert Howe to extract an "unconditional submission." David Gilmore, John Tuttle, and George Grant were selected

from among the leaders to be made examples of, tried on the spot, and sentenced to be shot (not hung). The former two were executed by a firing squad composed of mutineers, the latter inexplicably reprieved (Boatner, *Encyclopedia*, p. 759; Van Doren, *Mutiny in January*, chaps. 18–20).

7. Not at a tavern, in all likelihood, but at the house of his friend and fellow officer John Morley Greene.

8. On the morning of 17 January 1781, at Cowpens, S.C., Daniel Morgan met a force under the hated Banastre Tarleton, and the "Old Wagoner's" Patriot troops beat the British badly. According to Ward, the battle was important because "it gave a deathblow to Tarleton's reputation as a military leader. . . . In the opinion of John Marshall, 'Seldom has a battle, in which greater numbers were not engaged, been so important in its consequences as that of Cowpens.' It gave Greene his chance to exercise his strategical genius in the conduct of a campaign of 'dazzling shiftiness' that led his opponent by 'an unbroken chain of consequences to the catastrophe at Yorktown . . .' " (*War of the Revolution*, 2:762).

9. Assonet, Mass.

10. Gardiner's Bay, at the eastern tip of Long Island and the Sound, was a British naval base from which they could monitor closely the French in Newport, R.I., and which made the interception of any southbound French fleet an easier matter (Boatner, *Encyclopedia*, map, p. 658; Freeman, *Washington*, 5:262–63). In this particular case the British were out after a squadron under Destouches, which had sailed from Newport (under the admiring eyes of Washington) the evening of 8 March. The British admiral, Marriott Arbuthnot, had gone to sea on the morning of the tenth and hoped to intercept the French before they reached Virginia (Freeman, *Washington*, 5:268). The two fleets met off the Virginia Capes on 16 March, and though the action was indecisive, Destouches decided to return to Newport, thus disappointing for the time being allied hopes of controlling the Chesapeake (Freeman, *Washington*, 5:272).

11. Washington had come to Newport on 6 March to confer with Rochambeau and his staff about combined operations against the British in New York or in the South. It was the first time many of the French officers had seen the American commander in chief. The reaction of Jean-François-Louis, comte de Clermont-Crevecoeur, a lieutenant in the French artillery, is recorded in his journal: "General Washington['s] . . . face is handsome and his expression modest. Although cold, it conveys an impression of kindliness and affability. His uniform is simple and unadorned. He responded to the courtesies shown him in an altogether admirable manner. Our generals gave fêtes and balls in his honor at which he danced indiscriminately with everyone. He was honored and esteemed even by his enemies. His justice, his benevolence, and his courage in the misfortunes he experienced at the head of the army made him even more beloved and respected by his men" (Rice and Brown, eds., *Rochambeau's Army*, 1:25).

12. On 20 February Washington had instructed Lafayette to take command of a detachment of 1,200 men from the northern army and march his men southward into Virginia to oppose Arnold's operations there (*Writings*, 21:253–56).

13. Camp at this time was in the Hudson Highlands, around New Windsor, N.Y. By "the Lines" Greenman means the furthest American positions in the "neutral ground" of Westchester County.

14. Greene did in fact give up the field at Guilford Courthouse, N.C. (15 March) and did suffer nearly 300 casualties in the battle, but Cornwallis's victory has often been called pyrrhic by military historians, gained as it was at the cost of one-third of his army (Peckham, *Toll*, p. 82; Freeman, *Washington*, 5:274–75).

15. This statement is a forcible reminder of just how long the War for Independence has been dragging on.

16. Undoubtedly some of the old—and by then classic—volumes of Joseph Addison's and Richard Steele's *Spectator* from London. In the eighteenth century no literature was more highly regarded as a model for English style, as witness the young Benjamin Franklin: "About this time I met with an odd volume of the *Spectator*. . . . I read it over and over, and was much delighted with it. I thought the writing excellent, and wished, if possible, to imitate it. With that view I took some of the papers, and making short hints of the sentiment in each sentence, laid them by a few days, and then, without looking at the book, tried to complete the papers again by expressing each hinted sentiment at length, and as fully as it had been expressed before . . ." (*Autobiography*, [New York: Modern Library, 1932], p. 17).

17. Of all the soldiers tried in these courts-martial, only Nathan Gale is mentioned in the General Orders. Washington upheld the death-sentence and ordered him executed (*Writings*, 21:459).

18. Pines Bridge, over the Croton River, was one of the principal barriers between the opposing forces in Westchester County (see the introduction to this part of the journal).

19. Loyalists were sometimes known as "refugees" because they had sought refuge under the standard of the King of England. There were three separate corps of "Delancey's Refugees," so called for their commandant, Oliver Delancey. Two of these units served mainly in the South, and it is the third that is involved here (Boatner, *Encyclopedia*, p. 326).

20. About "one hundred fifty dragoons" forded the Croton River about two miles above Pines Bridge, on the morning of the fourteenth, just after Colonel Greene had removed the sentries who guarded the important ford by night. After surprising Greene, Flagg, and their men (see the introduction for more details) they retreated by way of Pines Bridge, where they trapped Greenman and his guard "of colored soldiers." In view of the fierceness of the attack on Greene's headquarters, it is somewhat surprising that Greenman and his men were given quarter (see Raymond, "Colonel Christopher Greene," pp. 143ff.). Rivington's *Royal Gazette* for 16 May reported the capture of "an ensign and twenty privates" at the house of "Widow Griffin," about a mile from the Greene headquarters. The paper also claims that eight men were killed from this guard. Perhaps this report refers to Greenman's contingent, although his journal entry does not mention casualties.

21. Morrisania was a town across Hell Gate from York Island (Manhattan).

22. British prisons in New York City quickly gained an ineradicable infamy as the war progressed. Boatner, without citing any authority, maintains that three sugar houses were used as prisons: Van Cortlandt's, in the northwest corner of Trinity Churchyard; the Liberty Street Sugar House (34–36 Liberty Street), and Rhinelander's (corner of William and Duane streets). Stokes, however, holds that there is evidence only for the Liberty Street building's (also known as Livingston's) having been so used (Boatner, *Encyclopedia*, p. 894 and *Landmarks*, p. 279; Isaac N. P. Stokes, *The Iconography of Manhattan Island, 1498–1909*, 6 vols. [New York: R. H. Dodd, 1915–28], 4:662, 790, 5:1042, 1056). But no matter in which sugar house Greenman's men were imprisoned, the wretched prison conditions are a matter of record, and their commander should have been thankful for his officer's privileges: parole and billeting.

23. Gravesend was the name given to the area around the southwest end of Long Island. The towns of Gravesend, New Utrecht, Flatbush, and Flatlands may be seen on map, facing page 182.

24. Freeman notes that at this time "'peace talk' was in the air, everywhere" (*Washington*, 5:295).

25. Samuel Hayes, of the New Jersey Militia.

26. But apparently Mr. Striker was not villain enough to be listed in Sabine's *Loyalists*.

27. *The Voyages and Adventures of Capt. Robert Boyle, in Several Parts of the World*, by W. R. Chetwood. This popular narrative, which Joseph Sabin says is probably fictitious, first appeared in 1726 and went through numerous editions in the eighteenth century (*A Dictionary of Books Relating to America* [New York: 1867–70], no. 12553).

28. This was Roger Stevenson's *Military Instructions for Officers* (Philadelphia, 1775), said to be the first book dedicated to George Washington and widely read by aspiring young officers like Greenman.

29. Occasionally during the years 1781–82 Greenman writes a line in some sort of code (not like the expense code of 1777–78), perhaps a shorthand. These will be indicated by "[cipher]" but have not been deciphered.

30. This is probably David Watson's *History of the Gods and Goddesses and their Contemporaries* (London, 1753).

31. Henry Fielding's novel of 1749.

32. Greene had beseiged Fort Ninety-Six, S.C., for almost a month before attempting to storm the position (19 June). Contrary to what Greenman heard, the fort was not taken, and Greene was repulsed (Peckham, *Toll*, p. 87).

33. On the night of 2 July Washington attempted to move against the British positions near Spuyten Duyvil; in concert the French under Rochambeau (whose army was approaching New York en route from Newport) were to descend on the area around Morrisania. It is to this operation, a failure, that Greenman refers in his entry for 3 July. The only positive result for the Americans was that all the British forces were driven, as Greenman puts it, "inside of Kings Bridge," that is, on the Manhattan side of the Harlem River (Freeman, *Washington*, 5:298ff.). With both French and American armies concentrating in the area, there was furious activity in New York City and on Long Island: troop movements, militia calls, fleets sailing and arriving almost daily, and, of course, the rumor mill working overtime. All this is reflected in Greenman's entries throughout the summer, as the climactic events of the Revolution approach but are seen through the eyes of a paroled officer with too much time on his hands.

34. None of the Sullivans in Heitman (*Historical Register*) appear to be this "Capt. Sullivan."

35. *The Tragedy of Jane Shore* (1714), a play by the English dramatist Nicholas Rowe.

36. The British fortress, garrisoned by 7,000 troops, was beseiged by French and Spanish ships for over four years. The soldiers were always near starvation, but the fort was successfully defended until the treaty of peace in 1783 (*EMH*, pp. 717–18).

37. This little melodrama being played out at and around Greenman's billet is in four acts: noted in the entries for 9 July, 5 and 28 August, and 28 September. While not without human interest, the action lacks coherence and not all the *dramatis personae* can be positively identified. "Colo. Lott" is Abraham Lott, treasurer of the colony of New York and a well-known loyalist. "Capt. Hyler" is not to be found in Heitman (*Historical Register*), but may be a New Jersey militiaman. The "Two Stillwils" have not been indentified at all. The sort of plundering and kidnapping Greenman describes was typical of the irregular warfare carried on by the "Cowboys and Skinners" during the long period of New York's occupation by the British (see Boatner, *Encyclopedia*, p. 291). Here is Sabine's account of the raid of 4 August: "Some Whigs, in a whale-boat, went to his residence and robbed him of about six hundred pounds, and carried off two slaves. . . . The noted Captain Hyler surprised Colonel Lott in his house at night, and himself and two of his negroes were taken prisoners to New Brunswick" (*Loyalists*, 2:28).

38. Thomas Graves, British admiral.

39. Greenman was probably reading the famous series of pamphlets by John Trenchard and Thomas Gordon, collected and issued as *Cato's Letters* (1721). The authors were "spokesmen for extreme libertarianism" and their work was "a searing indictment of eighteenth-century English politics and society. . . . Trenchard and Gordon ranked in the minds of the Americans with the treatises of Locke as the most authoritative statement of the nature of political liberty and above Locke as an exposition of the social sources of the threats it faced" (Bernard Bailyn, ed., *Pamphlets of the American Revolution, 1750–1776*, vol. 1. [Cambridge, Mass.: Harvard University Press, 1965], pp. 29–30).

40. *The Adventures of Gil Blas of Santillane*, the picaresque classic by Alain-René Le Sage, published 1715–1735.

41. Adm. Samuel Hood made port at Sandy Hook, rather than in the Chesapeake. And although he did not know that Adm. François Joseph Paul, Comte de Grasse, had sailed his entire fleet from the West Indies bound for Virginia, his decision was one more in the series of British naval strategic errors that led to the surrender at Yorktown (Willcox, *Portrait of a General*, pp. 410–13).

42. The Comte de Barras had left Newport with his fleet on 24 August, bound for the Chesapeake (Freeman, *Washington*, 5:316 and note).

43. The American commissary of prisoners was Abraham Skinner (Washington, *Writings*, 22:478); the British, Joshua Loring. The latter was "detested by the patriots for his alleged mistreatment of prisoners" (Boatner, *Encyclopedia*, p. 659).

44. Ebenezer Macomber.

45. This is one of the very few clearly intended jokes in the entire journal. It is interesting to note the casual confidence with which the two junior officers contemplate the blow about to fall on the British.

46. The "New Lots" were in fact just that: a recently laid out subdivision north of Flatlands and Flatbush (see map, facing page 182).

47. This was an unfounded rumor, although Clinton had tried desperately for several weeks to devise some way of relieving the pressure on Cornwallis by land or at least creating some diversion that would stop the allied armies temporarily (Willcox, *Portrait of a General*, pp. 424–37).

48. The report was substantially correct. Adm. Robert Digby had arrived on the twenty-fourth with "a royal midshipman, the first prince of the blood ever to visit America . . . sixteen-year-old Prince William, the King's third son. . . ." Both the low state of British morale and their vast distance from reality during this crucial time are reflected in the comment of William Smith, royal chief justice of New York: "All well, the presence of the Prince may supply our deficiency" (quoted by Willcox, ibid., p. 433).

49. This may have been a violation of his parole, or "word of honor," though technically Greenman was obliged simply not to bear arms until his exchange was effected. But his own doubt about the escape of the young "Stillwil" (who has not been identified) indicates he very well knew that parole extended to such matters.

50. On 5 September Graves had engaged de Grasse in what Willcox calls "one of the least inspired and most decisive naval battles of the century. The French came out of the bay [Chesapeake], and the British, instead of trying to seize their anchorage as they might conceivably have done, fought them in the open sea. Graves made mistakes that he could ill afford," and although the battle was "tactically a draw," Graves spent another week at sea, allowing de Barras's fleet from Newport to slip into the bay and unite with de Grasse's larger force. The combination of the French fleets was the last allied objective in the seige of Yorktown and all but assured their victory. Graves decided to return to New York on the thirteenth (Willcox, *Portrait of a General*, p. 424).

51. The Graves-Clinton expedition had attempted to leave on the seventeenth, but did not get a fair wind until the nineteenth, arriving off Cape Charles on the twenty-fifth, far too late to do the beleaguered Earl Cornwallis any good. For on the seventeenth, while the New York expedition was vainly trying to get out of the Hook and on the fourth anniversary of Burgoyne's surrender, Cornwallis asked for terms (ibid., pp. 438–39).

52. Matthias Ward, who had been a prisoner since 1777.

53. The formal articles of surrender were signed on 19 October. The glad tidings reached Congress in Philadelphia early on the morning of the twenty-second, and "as it spread throughout the country, the news was hailed with rejoicing and celebrations, in the well grounded belief that the war was about over" (Ward, *War of the Revolution*, 2:895). The "Judge Coes" mentioned in the next journal entry (27 October) is probably the proprietor of Coes Tavern in Kakiat, N.Y. (Rice and Brown, eds., *Rochambeau's Army*, 2:51).

54. Lt. Col. Jeremiah Olney had been made commandant of the Rhode Island Regiment upon the death of Christopher Greene. The unit was henceforth generally known as Olney's Rhode Island Battalion.

55. Dr. Elias Cornelius served as surgeon's mate to the Second Rhode Island Regiment, then continued with the combined regiment until May 1781.

56. Heitman (*Historical Register*) reports that Reuben Johnson was appointed ensign on 26 August 1781 and also shows that he deserted a few months later.

57. That is, they marched to the area on which they would build their huts for winter quarters.

58. The Greenman family Bible register page records that "Jeremiah Greenman Senr. died 30th July 1781 at Dartmouth Massachusetts, Ag'd 61 years five Months & nine days,—" But there are several reasons to suspect the accuracy of this death date. In the first place the arithmetic is wrong: if he was in fact born 11 Feb. 1719/20, as the Bible records, then he lived nineteen days beyond his 61 years, 5 months. And surely Jeremiah Jr.—even in prison—would have received earlier news of the event had it occurred in July. And, finally, there is the testimony of Esek Eddy Greenman, who loved to read his grandfather's journal so many years later. Esek Eddy has noted in the margin of the journal page covering this period, "My Great-Grandfather died about Nov. 25th 1781."

59. Through by: threw by, left off.

60. At this point Greenman inadvertently offers evidence of recopying at a later date and then tries to disguise what he has done in order to preserve the realism of time and place. The phrase "to my wife's sister's" has been written and then almost smudged out—as if Greenman realized he was not married in 1781. The same mistake is made in the entry for 26 December where he substitutes "an acquaintance" for the blotted phrase. He was not married until 1784 (see the introduction), and one is led to conclude that at least this immediate section of the journal was redone sometime thereafter.

61. Elijah Chapman.

62. The text appears to read "Bellamy," though it is somewhat smudged. If so, the person intended could only be the Rev. Joseph Bellamy (1719–1790), widely known New England divine. Bellamy had been a disciple and close associate of Jonathan Edwards and helped foster the Great Awakening and New Light theology in Connecticut. He was the first minister of the Society of Bethlehem and continued there for over fifty years (*DAB*, 2:165).

PART SIX

Seeing It Through, 1782–1784

INTRODUCTION

As AN icy January in 1782 closed upon the highlands about the Hudson River near Peekskill, Jeremiah Greenman waited impatiently at the Continental Village for the baggage wagons to get on so that he could set out for Philadelphia to rejoin the Rhode Island regiment. His waiting interrupted by the death of a fellow soldier, he set about "getting a Coffin made," then resumed his watch for the ensign with the baggage. When the ensign arrived, he was hardly allowed a decent rest before Greenman set off for King's Ferry and the well-worn road to Philadelphia. Greenman, an experienced traveler now, was not always forced to stay at local inns; he found "an acquaintance" to visit near Morristown. He was also a wary Yankee who refused to pay the exorbitant fee charged by the Trenton Ferry and demonstrated his independence by marching around the "nose" of the Delaware River and striking out for Philadelphia on the Jersey shore. But not everyone in the army shared Greenman's single-minded determination to rejoin his regiment. Nor was the future of the Revolution entirely clear, despite the stunning victory at Yorktown. Even in hindsight it is easy to forget that Yorktown was not the end, that British armies remained in New York, Charleston, and Savannah, and that as the year 1782 opened it was unknown how they would be dislodged.

In contrast to Greenman's attitude the victory at Yorktown undoubtedly contributed to a growing reluctance to serve among some Virginia officers, who entertained notions of quitting the service. Washington was astonished at their attitude and wondered whether they supposed the independence of America had already been established. Writing Colonel Febiger he asked, "Do they think the remaining force of the enemy is to be crushed by Words or Blows?"[1]

The great danger, Washington believed, was that relaxation would follow success, and thus he was particularly pleased during his stay in Philadelphia to find members of Congress disposed "to prepare vigorously" for the next summer's campaign.[2] As he put it in his Circular to the States: "To bring this War to a speedy and happy conclusion, . . . no means are so likely to effect these, as vigorous preparations for another Campaign." Washington was troubled by the awareness that an erosion of spirit takes place among a people bearing the burden of a prolonged and undecided war. Relaxation of effort might encourage the enemy to "new exertions . . . whereby the War . . . may be protracted to such a length, that the people, groaning under the burden of it and despairing of success, may think any change, a change for the better."[3] These reflections may strike us as unnecessarily grim and gloomy, perhaps because many modern accounts of the war virtually end with Yorktown so that we are unprepared to take seriously the military problems of 1782.

Duty in Philadelphia was not very challenging for Greenman, but it involved a favorable reversal of roles since he spent much of his time as a guard over prisoners of war, though he could hardly have relished it. He appears to have enjoyed walking in the city, particularly after the worst of the winter weather was past; he would walk from his barracks at the upper end of the city out to the hospital or along the waterfront. Duty also required serving as military police and marching with the regiment to perfect maneuvers so that they might pass inspection under the critical eye of Baron von Steuben. Again and again Greenman served on courts-martial, for discipline was at best difficult to maintain in winter garrison. In this instance drunkenness was common no matter what kind of punishment was meted out. One soldier was even charged with a political crime, "damning Congress," though it is doubtful that he was penalized further than being told not to do it again. After all, Congress was frequently far behind in pay, clothing, and provisions and had earned at least a mild epithet or two. Despite the obligations there were compensations for service in Philadelphia. There were taverns and gardens and churches to visit, a Masonic organization to participate in, and young ladies to be met. With Congress there, Philadelphia was a hub from which sprung much real information as well as fascinating rumors, and it drew to itself urgent communications and important people, such as the "French Imbasidor." But for sheer exuberance nothing in the journal surpasses the outing of 1 April, when Greenman, in the company of "Major Olney . . . & Sum other Officers of the Regiment with a few Citesons," made an excursion to Red Bank, the name itself already symbolic of the valor of Rhode Island men, and returned in boisterous good humor. Philadelphia had at least one other delight for the eye, occasional celebrations such as public fireworks upon the arrival of news of the birth of a dauphin in France, or the more stately occasion hosted at the City Tavern by the governor and council. But on 22 March, Washington had left Philadelphia to take up his post on the North River, and it was certain that there would be a limit to the springtime pleasures of the city.

As spring passed, new recruits joined the army, and orders directed the Rhode Island regiment to march to the Hudson Highlands again, where they would help to maintain surveillance over the movements of British forces in and about New York. Before they left, they took time for a second and more elegant celebration (23 May) of the birth of the dauphin, amid the discharge of cannon toasting the zeal of 1776 and liberty and independence from the rule of George III, while they congratulated the French on having an heir to Louis XVI. Whatever the ironies, it was probably the grandest occasion Jeremiah Greenman had ever witnessed, and, as he said, it "ended with all Decorum that possable [can ?] be." Then by easy stages they left the city and proceeded toward the highlands, more watchfully as they drew closer to British lines on the road between Morristown and the plains about Pompton. Finally they passed Ramapo, passed the Hudson, and made camp on 9 June northwest of the Continental Village, almost opposite West Point.

For all his urging of Congress to prepare for the summer campaign and despite Washington's circular letters, consultations, and memoranda about objectives, when the summer of 1782 arrived there was not so much a campaign as a series of maneuvers. The reason for this was partly a matter of resources, both American and French; partly it was a change Washington seemed to discern in April in the British mode of conducting the war—retiring to strong defensive posts—and it was also a matter of developing possibilities for peace.[4] Even as late as 19 July, during a conference with the Count de Rochambeau, Washington was going over three principal objectives—New York, Charleston, and an offensive expedition to Canada to annex it forcibly to the Federal Union.[5] The most important strategic idea that survived was the concentration of Washington's forces on the Hudson River, which is the reason why Greenman spent most of the summer in the Highlands.

Active duty for Greenman this summer amounted to fairly routine patrol and guard duty chiefly in three places—Pines Bridge over the Croton River, Constitution Island across from West Point, and Dobbs Ferry. But for one who has followed Greenman this far the most interesting of these is his service with the light infantry in the vicinity of Pines Bridge, when he substituted for his sick friend, Lieutenant Masury. He does not tell us how he felt as he returned to the place of his capture on 14 May 1781, but this time he was fully alert to the places where the enemy might ford the stream, indeed had forded the stream and bloodily disposed of his commanding officer, Col. Christopher Greene, who had survived Quebec and Red Bank to die unexpectedly and unwarned in an inconsequential action near Pines Bridge. One can imagine that Greenman had gone over the events of that nightmare many times in his head while a prisoner of war and wondered if at some time that night his guard might have detected a sound from DeLancey's Refugees that would have revealed their mission in time to form a defense. He may have wondered why the men who had killed Greene had been willing to spare his life. Without question Greenman was just the man to send out to gather intelligence near the enemy lines in this area. He marched his men sometimes late into the night, when they were forced to lie on their guns in the field; they would wait and watch and filter through woods and listen as though this time to save Colonel Greene, but no opportunity presented. The most his straining ears could detect was the passing of a band of horse thieves in the night.

August brought rumors of peace and increasing evidence that the British might be planning to evacuate rather than fight. The post at Dobbs Ferry, while Greenman served there, was being used as the checkpoint through which persons crossing the lines under flags of truce must come. But if military duty grew less dangerous than before, military drill and discipline were emphasized with new vigor. Washington once found occasion to express his pleasure in obedience to his recommendations even to the "cocking and decorating the hats," but still he thought "some small improvements may yet be made; to wear the hair cut or tied in the same manner throughout the whole corps would still be a very considerable ornament." Not content to rest the matter upon good advice, Washington went on to provide supplies with which the men could dress their hair, "two pounds of flower and half a pound of rendered Tallow per hundred men. . . ."[6] Following such preparation it is not surprising that before the campaign of 1782 was over the army had distinguished itself and won commendations from its commander on two occasions, the parade for the reception of Count Rochambeau on 14 September and the Grand Maneuver performed for Washington on 24 October, which was said to have surpassed all others.

The parade upon the arrival of Rochambeau was without doubt the more unusual and stirring occasion. Orders given 13 September had included parade orders and conveyed the purpose: "to complement his Excellency the Count de Rochambeau; The Troops as he passes them will pay him the honors due the Commander in chief. On this occasion the tallest men are to be in the front rank."[7] While American drums beat a French march,

> [*American*] *troops were all formed in two lines extending from the ferry where the Count crossed, to his quarters. A troop of horse met and received him at King's Ferry, and conducted him through the line to General Washington's quarters, where sitting on his horse by the side of his Excellency, the whole army marched before him and paid the usual salute and honors. Our troops were now in complete uniform and exhibited every mark of soldiery discipline.*[8]

An air of festivity seemed to prevail for a time, as Greenman and others from his company cut boughs and saplings to make a colonnade before their encampment both for the sake of appearance and to shade their tents from the late summer sun. But the mood of this occasion did not reflect the inmost thoughts of the commander in chief.

At about this time Washington was expressing private doubts about the course of the war, perhaps because he was worried about both the position of the British in New York and the state of peace negotiations following the upheaval in the British cabinet caused by the death of the Marquess of Rockingham during an epidemic of influenza.[9] On 12 September Washington had written James McHenry, "our prospect of Peace is vanishing." He went on to mention the loss of Rockingham and then to express a strong conviction: "that the King will push the War as long as the Nation will find Men or Money, admits not of a doubt in my mind."[10] He expressed himself more fully when he wrote Maj. Gen. Nathanael Greene saying that he believed the negotiations were part of a design: "the principal Design was, to gain time by lulling us into security and wasting the Campaign without making any efforts on the land, and in the interim to augment their Naval Force and wait the chance of some fortunate Event to decide their future line of conduct."[11] It added up to an inactive and therefore indecisive campaign, the principal feature of which he told Lafayette was "the junction with the French Corps . . . the Middle of September; . . . We have done nothing more than to keep a watch upon the enemy this Campaign except restraining them from detaching; which I believe has been the consequence of our junction, and lying here."[12] Less than a week after writing this, Washington issued orders for his troops to march to winter hunting grounds, and the Rhode Island regiment set out for Newburgh to await boats that would take them farther north to Albany from where they could make their way to barracks at Saratoga.[13]

Before he marched off for Saratoga, Jeremiah Greenman received the highest recognition for soldierly accomplishment from his superiors that was ever to be afforded him. On 1 October he was named adjutant to the Rhode Island regiment. By this time we know him well enough not to expect a dissertation on its meaning or a long entry expressing the depth of his feelings on this occasion, and he does not disappoint us. He simply put it down: "This day was appointed adjt. to the Regiment Lt. Rogers resigning that office." Nothing remarkable perhaps, but a fitting recognition of his steady devotion to duty never more plainly evident than during this year, when without the motivation of great enterprises or personal rewards Greenman had persevered through guard duty, courts-martial, and the business of managing the regimental baggage on and off boats along the Hudson. The qualities he had demonstrated were those of a superior professional soldier.

For men who had spent the previous winter in Philadelphia one can hardly imagine a more bleak prospect than assignment to the battered and war-worn barracks at Saratoga. It was virtually a

Roman banishment to the frontiers. But Greenman had by this time earned the right to some respite and got it, a leave of absence that would release him from duty at Saratoga from 28 December 1782 to 15 April 1783.[14] He stayed long enough to see the new year in and then set off on the road to Providence, riding at the rate of about thirty miles per cold day, in the company of his commanding officer, Colonel Olney. Even on leave he recorded his short jaunts in Rhode Island as he divided his time chiefly among Providence, Newport, and Swansea, where his mother was living. We may safely assume that he was scouting opportunities for his peacetime employment, perhaps trying to decide what sort of career he should pursue and where to settle. Near the end of his leave, on 30 March, news burst upon Providence of the signing of the Preliminary Peace Treaty, done at Versailles on 20 January and accompanied by declarations of an armistice.[15] At last the end for which all had been risked was within sight, and Greenman allowed the enthusiasm to creep into his journal: "the Glorious Peaces is taken place," he wrote, and perhaps for that reason he set off a little early for his return to Saratoga.

Predictably, nothing much was happening in Saratoga upon his return. Until June, when Greenman began to sign certificates of discharge for Rhode Island soldiers, he did little but make short trips, play a game of skittles when the weather improved, and develop a great curiosity about the Salt Springs near Saratoga. In groups officers and men marched home, their service ended, so that when the fourth of July came to be celebrated, it was Greenman who stepped forward to host as honorable and spirited an occasion as could be mounted in Saratoga, presenting as many toasts (with muskets substituting for cannon) as if they were seated in the City Tavern of old Philadelphia. Later in July both Washington and von Steuben passed through Saratoga, but Greenman had little to record until an intriguing September interlude when he spent two weeks about Lake George and Lake Champlain with Esq. William Gilliland, who had held large land claims and speculations there. The trip recorded by Greenman in detail sounds like a pleasant fall camping trip as they view the ruins of Gilliland's settlements and mills, all casualties of the war, but they also seem to have interested themselves in sites offering speculative opportunities. Whatever Gilliland was planning to reclaim or develop, we cannot help but wonder why Greenman was chosen to accompany him. Was it because he was looking for a new career and perhaps a place to settle, perhaps even a business connection with Gilliland? Or was he performing a secret intelligence mission, trying to detect any possible collusion between Gilliland and the British in their outposts on the northern border? The journal unfortunately affords us no evidence for an answer.

From late September into October of 1783, those remaining at Saratoga waited anxiously for an order to leave the post. Ironically, they finally learned of the signing of the Definitive Treaty and its arrival in New York from two British officers taking advantage of the cessation of hostilities to travel to Canada. Suddenly aware that the end was very near, they discovered how inadequate was the clothing of the men for their return home; little could be procured, however, beyond a pair of shoes for each man. The trip home quite unexpectedly brought Greenman perilously close to the rigors he experienced plunging through snowy forests on the march to Quebec when he tried to pursue a sleigh on foot and missed the road. By going considerably out of his way he managed to arrive in Providence on 6 January 1784 ahead of his baggage, the new year having been all but ignored in a snowstorm on the road.

Until spring Greenman stayed close to home, "implying [himself] in reading a few Historys" and getting ready to open a business in Providence in partnership with Lieutenant Masury. The fate of that venture is briefly stated in the journal and is discussed in the introductory biographical essay. Then follows a brief paragraph in which Greenman records some few highlights of his second career at sea. And then he breaks off his journal in mid-sentence in the year 1788. Ostensibly the reason the sentence was never completed was that his career as a ship's master had not yet ended, but it is also true that the original reason for keeping his journal had ceased to exist. With the same diligence and care that characterized the performance of his soldierly duties he had kept his journal even through the last two years of military service. When he turned to "the Nautical line of business" he undoubtedly kept a ship's log, but not his own journal any longer, except for the brief notes we find here. The record of his part in the great enterprise of independence was complete.

NOTES TO INTRODUCTION

1. 12 January, Washington, *Writings*, 23:443.
2. Ibid., p. 429.
3. 22 January, ibid., p. 460.
4. Ibid., 24:114.
5. Memorandum of 1 May 1782, ibid., p. 197.
6. 12 August, ibid., 25:9.
7. Ibid., p. 157.
8. James Thacher's *Military Journal of the American Revolution* (Hartford, Conn.: Hurlbut, Williams & Co., 1862), 14 September 1782, quoted by Fitzpatrick in Washington's *Writings*, 25:158n.
9. Richard B. Morris, *The Peacemakers* (New York: Harper & Row, 1965), p. 280.
10. Washington, *Writings*, 25:151.
11. 17 October, ibid., p. 265.
12. 20 October, ibid., p. 279.
13. Now Schuylerville, N.Y.
14. Granted by Major General Lord Stirling (William Alexander), "Register of Officers of the Rhode Island Regt. to whom leave of absence has been granted" in the Regimental Book for 1781 &c., the Rhode Island Archives, Providence.
15. Morris, *The Peacemakers*, pp. 408–10.

SEEING IT THROUGH, 1782–1784

January of 82. N. River

T 1 & W 2. Nothing worthy remarks.

T 3. Lieutenant Jencks[1] arrived from Rhode Island, who informed us the Regiments Cloathing was on the Road to Fisk Hills [Fishkill], but exspected they could not cross their in Consequence of so much Ice being in the River, & expected them down to cross Kings Ferry.

F 4. this Morning Lt. Jenckes set out to meet the Bagage (if comeing this way) if not to proceed on with it to the Regimen[*t*] by the upper Rout and go thro Susex &c.[2]

S 5. Continuing at the Contneltal Village / Mr. Jenck not arrived, by which suppose the waggons crossed Kings Ferry. NR.

S 6 & M 7. Continuing at the Village waiting with impatience for Ensign Ennis[3] to arrive, (with the Bagage) from Danbury as we are then to set out to join our Regiment—

T 8. this day a Soldier belonging to the Regiment died with a Putred Fevor—[4]NMR.

W 9. Implying myself the fore part of the day in getting a Coffin made—NMRDT.

T 10. this day morn Ensign Ennis arrived / fixed to move which was effected at two oClock when set off / Came to Kings Ferry where crossed at Sun set & came two Miles to Haverstaw where put up—

F 11. This Morning Sum Small Showers of rain / Set off from Landlord Curtis's [*and*] came about 6 Miles to Judge Coes[5] where impressed three waggons, dismissed our others & proceeded on our way about 8 Miles to Ramapo where put up—

S 12. this morn set off very early / Came to Pumpton where dismissed our Waggons / Stormy weather—with Snow &c.

S 13. this Morning impressed 3 Waggons to carry us to Morristown, where arrived at Dark—went three Miles from Town to an acquaintence where spent the Night—

M 14. this Morning went to Morristown where drew Provision for the Men and impressed 2 Waggons,—then came back to where lodged last Evening / Continued the Remainder of the Day—and Night.

T 15. this Morning came to Bareskinridge [Basking Ridge] where made a small halt then proceeded to Summer sett where over took the Waggons from where came to Hilsburrour, in Summer Set County[6] where put up.

W 16. This Morning came to Pined Town[7] where made a Small Halt, from where came to Trenton where halted & dismissed our Waggons—& left several of our Recruits to be innoculated for the Small Pox—

T 17. This Morning after getting 2 teams proceeded to the Ferry—where could not cross without giving an Extravegent price for the Ferrage / went back & took the Jersy Shore for Coopers ferry / Came 7 Miles to Burdington[8] where made a Small Halt, after which came about two-Miles where put up.

F 18. this Morning from the Square[9] came ten Miles to Burlington where brok[*e*] one of our Waggons which detained us 'till we could get another—then proceeded on to Ranerocus Ferry[10] where crossed and came 5 Miles to Mount Pleasant where put up.

S 19. This Morning came to Coopers Ferry where crossed and came to Philadelphia & joined My Regiment which was quatered in the Barraks at the upper End of the Town—

S 20. Continuing at my quaters—found the Regiment very Sickly, & much reduced with Deaths—

M 12. this day was officer of Police NDMT—

T 22 & W 23. Nothing worthy Remarks—

T 24. This day went on Court Martial—Tryed Robert Dicsion[11] a Soldier in the 2nd Company for being Intoxicated with Liquor when a Sentinel & abusing Mrs. Nicols, found Guilty of abusing Mrs. Nicols & sentinced to receive 30 Stripe on his Naked back, which was put in Execution in the Evening.

F 25. This day took a Walk through the City. NMRDD.

S 26. This morning went on Guard at the New Goal[12] over Prisoners of War / Nothing Remarkelbe happ'd Durring My Tower.

S 27. This Morning releived by Lieutenant Pratt[13] Came to My Quaters where continued all day, NMRTD.

M 28 & T 29. Continuing at my quaters very Sedentary.

W 30. this day went on Regimental Court Martial / Tryed George Blin[14] for being Absent from roll call—acquitted—

T 31. Continuing at my Quater this day—

FEBRUARY, 1782 PHILADELPHIA

F 1. this day went on Police / Nothing happined dureing my Tower—Remarkeble.

S 2. went on Guard at the New Goal, NRDMT—

S 3. after being releived came to the Barraks / Soon after Lieutenant Jencks died— [*cipher*].

M 4. This day attended the Funeral of Lieut Jencks who was attended with a Sutiable Number of Men from the Regiment, agreable to his Rank with the officers of the Regiment and a Number of Officer from Deferent lines, and a Number of Respectable Citicens / was carried to the Presbyterian buring Yard where he was Desently Entered—[15]

W 6. was officer of Police and sett on Court Martial / Tryed 5 Soldiers of the light Company on suspicion of stealing wood from the Publick / all acquitted—

T 7. Set on Court Martial / Tryed 6 Soldiers for being drunk on Duty—and one of the Light Company for Damning Congress—all sentenced to receive 60 Stripes—which was put in execution at evening Roll call except Dyes, which was posponed during his good behavour.

F 8 & S 9. Nothing worthy remarks.

S 10. Went on Guard at the New Goal—Nothing happined during my tower worthy remarks—

M 11. was officer of Police—

T 12. Set on Court Martial / Tryed 2 Soldiers, one for being [*blank*][16] when on Guard the other for beging Money of the Inhabitance of the City. (with the Officer Complements) to by Necessarys for the Sick, the former sentenced to receive 40 Stripes on his Naked back. the Other for Want of evidences, was acquited, [*cipher*].

W 13. This day was Police officer of the Regiment. NRDMT.

T 14. this day went on Guard / nothing remarkeble—

F 15. This Morning after being releived came to My Barraks where continued all Day.

S 16. this day was Police officer of the Regimen[*t*]—in the After noon attended the Funeral of a Brother.

S 17. Continuing in Quaters all day. Nothing Remarkeble—

M 18. This day mustered and inspected. [*cipher*].

T 19. This day went as far as the Hospital[17] / Visited the Sick &c, then returned to My quaters where continu'd all day. & Nothing More R—the Evening spent at Lodge Number 3—[18]

W 20. Continuing at my quaters all day very Sedentary—

T 21. went on Guard at the New Goal. NRDMT.

F 22. Went on Court Martial / Tryed Michael Kelly a Soldir for being [*blank*][19] when warned for duty—found Guilty & sentenced to receive 40 Stripes which was put in exe[*c*]ution at Evening Roll call.

S 23. Nothing remarkeble—

S 24. This day attended divine Servise / Nothing More remark.

M 25. Spent the day in taking up Sum articles at a Store on Account of a Note of hand from the Pay Master Genl. [*cipher*].

T 26. Implying myself this day in making an Apperlet—[20]

W 27. Continuing at My quaters all day very Sedentary—

T 28. Went on Guard at the New Goal over Prisoners of War. Took a walk as far as Water Street after which came to My Guard again. Nothing happined during my Tower—

MARCH [1782] PHILADELPHIA

F 1. this Morning after being releived came to my quaters where continued all day.

S 2. Nothing worthy remark.

S 3. Went on Court Martial / Tryed two Soldiers for being Out of Garrison without Leave, & one for attempting to steal a Wach. the latter sentenced to receive 80 stripes & the two former 20 stripes Each.

M 4. Continuing in Camp all day. [*cipher*].

T 5. Continuing in Camp all day / Nothing worthy Remarks—

W 6. Continuing in quaters all day very sedentary. [*cipher*].

T 7. went on Guard at the New Goal—15 Pr[*i*]soners dug through a flower [floor] of one of the Rooms and got in to a bomproff (or one of the Dunjand) where they dug a hole under the foundation of the Prison. 4 of them made their escape before the Sentinel discovered them—Took the Remainding 11 & put into one of the Dungons.[21]

F 8. this Morning after being releived came to my quaters where continued all day—

S 9 to T 14. Nothing Worthy remarks.

F 15. Received orders to be in readyness to exersise to Morrow on the Commons—

S 16 & S 17. Raining & Stormy / Continuing in quaters all day.

M 18. this morning Clowdy / went on Guard at the New Goal / hear that Charleston is avacuated—[22] The hand bill arrived renounceing the Capture of Nevis & Saint Christopher, with the articles of Capitulations, which was on very honourable Terms alowing them Every Priveledge, or More than they had under Brittish Goverment.[23]

T 19. After being releived came to My Barracks / went on Court Martial / Tryed Sergt. Hail[24] for Disobedince of Orders / found Guilty & sentenced to be reduced—then tryed Beriah Clarke, for being Drunk on Duty, found Guilty & sentenced to be confined 14 day in the Guard House & to do Police duty during that time—

W 20. Continuing in my rome [room] very Sedentary—

T 21. This day went as far as the Hospital after which came to My Quaters & Nothing More re.

F 22. This day paraded with the Regt. agreable to order to go through Sum Manoeuvers which is to be performed Next Monday.—[*cipher*].

S 23. this Morning parade with the Regiment & went through Sum Manoeuvers in presents of the Barron—[25] in the afternoon went through a few more.

S 24. This day was officer of Police. [*cipher*].

M 25. This day paraded with the Regiment / went on the Commons in the rear of the Town where went through a Number of Manoeuvers in presents of the President of Congress,[26] after which came to our Barracks when was dismised—Soon after came on Guard at the New Goal.

T 26. This Morning was releived by Mr. Pratt, after which came to the Barracks where continued all day. [*cipher*].

W 27 to S 30. Nothing worthy R.

S 31. this day was officer of Police / Nothing Remarkeble.

April, 1782, Philadelphia

M 1. This day Major Olney Myself & Sum other Officers of the Regiment with a few Citesons went down the River in a Boat about 7 Miles to Read Bank, (the Place where Fort Mercer formely stood) where had a Dinner & spent the day very agreabelly, from hear proceeded to the City, with Coulars flying & Our Musick playing, landed at the upper end of the City / Marched to the Barracks & spent the Evening agreabelly—[*cipher*].

T 2. This Morning went on Guard at the New Goal / Nothing happined worthy remarks.

W 3. This Morning after being releived came to my quaters where continued the day / the Evening spent in Company with Capt. Harrison—[27]

T 4. This day was officer of Police / Nothing remarkeble happined during My Tower.

F 5. Continuing in Barracks / Nothing happined. RMDD—

S 6. this day muster'd & inspt'd.

S 7. This fore Noon attended Divine Service at Christ Chuch—[28] the Afternoon went to the Upper end / Returned in the Evening to the Barracks where continued 'till Eleven oClock when was called to releive Lt. Hubbard who was on a Flagg of Truce Guard, & had order'd Sum of his Men to fire uppon a boat which would not bring too, & wounded two persons, at which he was ordered to be confin'd to his Rome—[29]

M 8. This Morning the officer of the Flagg & Capt. of the Brigg went on Shore / Continued with the Flagg 'till 12 oClock when was releived by Ensign Welch[30] after which came to my quaters where continued the Remainder of the Day very Much Indsposed, by a Cold cetched in lying on the Vessels Deck all Night.

1775

ab

the Carring plases on Cannek River from fort Hallefax to ye Great Carring place

~~hallefax fals~~	Caring	miles	Rod
hallefax fals	1	..	110
Cowhigens	1	..	100
ner Brigwalk	1	1/4	..
tentucket	1	..	86
hole Number	4	4 1/2	56

from Cannebeck to ye ded river with ye ponds &c

One of several tables of "carrying places" on the rivers crossed by the American army (see Appendix 1).

474 July 1781 G. End
brought in prisoners, was
taken by a Frigate, when
comeing down the N. River.
in [cipher]
about 20 citisans & Masters
of Vessels was brought in
prisoners, they was taken
going to France, on their way
from Cape Fransway —
23d this day went to Flatt
Bush where tarried, two or
three hours, then Came
back to my Quarters [illegible]
24th Continuing at my Quarte
very sedentary all thing

An example of Greenman's more complicated cipher, which he began using while he was a prisoner of war for the second time.

T 9. Continued in Barracks 'till 4 oClock in the After Noon when was ordered to releive Ens. Welch—arriv'd at the Flagg where continu'd all day—This Evening was sent up to the City (by the Hydore-ally) the Genl. Monck a Sloope of War mounting 18 Guns 12 9 Pounders & Six 6 pounders—

W 10. This Morning was releived by Lt. Wheaton / Came to the Barracks where continued all day very Sedentary. [*cipher*].

T 11. This day was police officer of the Regt. Nothing More remark'le.

F 12. Went on Regimental Court Martial / Tryed a Soldier for being drunk. when on Guard / found Guilty & sentenced him to receive 60 Stripes—

S 13. This morning the Sentence was put in Execution / Continuing in Barracks all day very much indisposed—

S 14. do—do—

M 15. Spent Sedentary & 16th.

W 17. This day was police officer of the Regt. Nothing Remarkeble happined during my Tower—

T 18. Continuing in Barracks / 70 Recruits for 9 Months came in to Garrison under Command of adj. Rogers.

F 19. raining / Continuing in Barracks—

S 20. The fore noon spent in playing wicket ball / Continuing the Remainder of the day in Barracks.

S 21. This day was police officer of the Regt. Nothing worthy remarks during my Tower.

M 22. This day went on Guard at the New Goal, went to the Hospital visited the Sick &c return'd to My Guard where continued the Remainder of the day. NMRTD.

T 23. Received a pettition from a Prisoner of War desireing the benifet of his Excellencys Genl. Washingtons pardon, for the comeing in of Visiters—waited on the Secratery at War concerning the Pettition & other Prisoners—after being releived came to Barracks—took a ride through the City &c &c—hear of the arrival of the Marqus Deli Fayett—[31] [*cipher*].

W 24. this day was police officer of the Regt. Nothing Extraordinary happined during my Tower—

T 25. this day went to Kings Centon[32] where spent the After noon agreable—

F 26. this morning Lt. Peckham[33] arrived with 56 recruits / Set on Court Martial—

S 27. This day was Police officer of the Regiment. NRDMT—

S 28. This Morning went on Guard—Visited the Sick in Hospital / Nothing More Remarkeble during my Tower.

M 29. This morning was releived by Lt. Pratt, came to the Barracks where continued all day—

T 30. went on Guard at the New Goal for Lt. Peckham / Nothing Remarkeble happined during my Tower—

MAY 1782. PHILADELPHIA

W 1. This morning was releived by Lt. Hubbart [Hubbard] after which came to the Barracks / at one oClock went out of Town with Sum Laydes [ladies] to the Schuilkills on a party of Pleasure from there to German Town—from there to Philadelphia—

T 2. This day was officer of police / Nothing Remarkeble happined during my Tower—

F 3. This fore noon continued in the Barracks. the after noon went through Sum Manoeuvers with the Regt—we are informed by the New York Gazett that Genl. Arnold hath had a Confirence with the King of Engeland & it is advised to send over 16 Thousand more Troops which will subdue the Americans—[34] not yet done.

S 4. went on Guard at the New Goal / Nothing worthy Remarks happined during my Tower—

S 5. after being releived came to Barrack where continued all day.

M 6 & T 7. Nothing Remarkeble.

W 8. This day went on Police.

T 9. This day set on Court Martial / Tryed Sergt. Crandal[35] for Disobedience of Orders & a Soldier for forging Major olneys Name / both acquited—

F 10. N R.

S 11. went on Guard. NRDMT—

S 12. Continuing in Barrack all day Sedentary—

M 13. This day the Regiment paraded with the City Ligh[*t*] hors & artelery & fired a fude Joy on the Be[*r*]th of the Dauphin of France—the Evining a very Ellegant Fireworks was displayed in the State house yard—[36]

T 14. Continuing in Barracks till 12-oClock when was sent to

Gloster,[37] on board of the Ship Genl. Washington after Deserters—

W 15 & T 16. Continuing in Barracks very much indisposed.

F 17. Nothing Remarkeble—

S 18. this day 13 recruits arrived from Rhode Island / Continuing in Barracks all day—

S 19. this day took a Walk as far as South work, [*cipher*] / the Evening returned to Barracks.

M 20. Continuing in Barracks / we are informed by Revingtons Paper that the Brittish fleet is gained a most Signal victory over the French Fleet / took 6 Sail of the Line and took the Adml. Ship & killed or badly wounded Count De. Grase.[38]

T 21. This day received orders from the Commander in Chife to march immeadiately for the North river, at the same time Major Olney received orders to have the Brittish Capt. carefully conducted to the Jersey Line, at Elisebethton where he is to be executed in Retalliation for Capt. Huddy who the Refugees had hung.[39]

W 22. Mounted Guard at the New Goal / Visited the Sick in Hospital &c—the After Noon spent in Company with Sum Laydes at Mr. Crispens Garden.

T 23. this day agreable to a ticket received from the Govener & Counsell of this State to dine with them went to the City Tavern[40] where was an Elegant Dinner prepared for all the Officers of the Continental Army which was in Town & the Imbasidor & Minnister at war &c &c &c / at entering the Dining rome was fired thirteen Cannon / after Dinner drank the 13 following Tosts (viz) United States, 2 King of France, 3d the Duphin, 4th Queen of France & the Royal Family 5th King of Spain, & all Friendly Powers 6th Genl. Washington & the Army 7th Count Rochambeau & the French Army 8th Genl. Green & the Southern Army 9th Count De Grasse & the allied Fleet 10th Perpetual alliance betwen France & America 11th May the Year 82 be annimated with the zeal of 76. & obtain the Sucseses of 81, 12th Dependence to all wether Princss or Private Men who wish the Dependency of America 13th A peace astabelished our Independency, Liberty, Safety Honour or no Peace—after which wass fired 13 more Cannon, & ended with all Decorum that possable [*can* ?] be— [*cipher*].

F 24 to S 26. Continuing in Barracks till the 26th in which time nothing happined worthy remarks.

M 27. took a small walk through the City.

T 28. are ordered to hold our Selvs in readyn[*e*]ss to march in the Morning / Prepareing for the March.

W 29. This Morning left Philadelphia at 10, oClock / came as far as Frankford[41] 5 Miles from the City whare made a halt an hour, & parted with Sum of Our friends who came here wit[*h*] us from the City. from here proceeded to Bensalem where incamped, [*cipher*].

T 30. This Morning the General Beat at day Break when the Tents was struck and loaded into the Waggons, went on the rear Guard. in half an hour the Genl. beat when the March commenced from the right. Came as far as Shameny Ferry[42] where crossed & made a small halt, from here came to the Cold Springs 6 Miles from the Ferry, where halted 4 hours after which proceeded on our March to Trenton Ferry where crossed the Delaware, when 6 Companys incamped. the other 3 in barns &c, for want of Tents—

F 31. This Morning the Genl. beat at day break / Struck our tent / in half an hour the Assembly, when the March commenced from the right. came as far as Maidenhead[43] (6 Miles from Trenton) where halted an hour then counter march'd / Came to Prince Town [Princeton], where halted an hour from where proceeded to Rockey hill[44] where incamped by Millstone River.

June, 1782 On a March

S 1. This Morning the General beet at half after 3 the Assembly at 4 when the March commenced from the right. Came 5 Miles to Summer set where halted a few Moments, then proceeded on to Rariton[45] 3 Miles whare breakfasted / then proceeded to Stials Gap whare halted 'till 3 oClock then came to Bareskinrdge whare halted & incamped.

S 2. This Morning the General beat at half an hour before Sun wrise the Assembly at the Sun 3 Quaters of an hour high, when the March commenc'd from the right / Came 4 Miles where halted then came to the half Moon Tavern where breakfasted—from whare proceeded to Morris Town halted & incamped on a hill in Front of the Town, [*cipher*].

M 3. Continuing in Morris Town—whare drew Provision & our men washing their Cloaths &c fiting for the March—

T 4. Continuing in Morris Town prepareing for Our March / Sat on Court Martial the fore Noon, in the After Noon order'd to

Seet again / Proceeded to the Trial of Sergt. Amstead[46] for Neglect of Duty. adjurned the Court for want of Evidince.

W 5. This Morning the Genl. beat at 5, oClock / at half after 5 the assembly when the March commenced from the right / Came as far as Troy[47] where made a small halt & breakfast'd / then counter marched and came to Pequaneck[48] whare halted 'till half after 4 when came 2 Miles & incamped / had a very Severe Squall of rain & wind.

T 6. This Morning drawed Provision from the New York Lines Contractor[49] then proceeded on our March to Pumpton Plains where made a small halt / very warm, a Number of Men fainted & fell in the rear that could not keep up. Came to Pumpton whare continued 4 hours, then proceeded on our March to the Pond Meatingho[*u*]se,[50] whare incamped—myself having Command of the Rear Guard plased out a Sergt. with a Guard, as it was thought Dangerous at this place.

F 7. This Morning the Genl. beat at 4 oClock. Soone after the Assembly when the March comminced from the Left / Came as far as Ramapo where halted & breakfasted / then proceeded on our March as far as Kearkeart, where incamped & the Court which adjurned from Morristown assembled & proceeded to the Trial of Sergt. Amstead, who was found Guilty of the Charges alledged againts him, and ordered to be reduced to a Private Sentinal which Sentince was approved of. [*cipher*].

S 8. This Morning the Genl. beat at day break [*and*] in half an hour the Assembly when the March commenced from the right—Came 7 Miles to Haverstaw where halted 2 hours, after which came a Mile and a half & incamped in Order to wait General Washingtons Orders wether to cross the River or tarry the West Side—at two oClock received Orders to cross the river. at 4 oClock the Genl. beat when we struck our Tents & proceeded on Our March to Kings Ferry where crossed the North River. Sent our Bagage up by Water / came one Mile & lay in the Woods / very Cold—

S 9. At day break the Revally beat [*and*] in half an hour the Assembly when the Troops paraded and marched from the right / Came to the Continental Village where breakfasted after which proceeded on our March as far as the N Battery where halted an hour, then came to the Connecticut huts where halted two hour, after which received orders to incamp / came one Mile below the Mountain Nigh the North River where incamped—

M 10. Continuing Incampt Near opposited West Point. we are informed by an officer from the S[*o*]uthward that a Conspirecy had been in adjutation by the Sergeants of the Army under Command of Genl. Greene—they was to indevoar to have the armey surprised & make Prisoner of Genl. Greene & all the Officers, but by a Sergeants wife it was brought to Light / the head was immeadiately shot & in two days after a Nother hung, & Some More confined whose fate was not yet known[51]

T 11. Continuing in Camp / Nothing worthy remark—

W 12. This day went to West Point where dined, after which crossed the River and came back to the Regimt.—are informed that 22 Sail of Shipping suppos'd to be Ships of forse went through the Sound, and was thought was bound for Rhode Island—

T 13. Mustered and inspected by the Barron De Stuban. NMR TD—

F 14. This Day was put through a Number of Manoeuvers by the Barron & fired a Number of blank Cartriges—

S 15 to S 23. Nothing happined worth Remarks / laying incamped waiting the Movements of the Enemy—

M 24. The Light Infentry Company ordered from the Regiment to go on the Lines—

T 25 to F 28. Spent Sedentary at Camp—

S 9. this day Lieut. Masury came from the Light Infentry Sick—in consequence I was ordered to join the Light Infentry—the after noon implyed myself in puting up Sum Bagage to carry to the Lines. [*cipher*].

S 30. This Morning at day break sett off from Camp with a Soldier to carry my Bagage for Pines Bridge[52] where arrived at 4 oClock in the afternoon when join'd Capt. Allens[53] Company who commanded the Light Company from our Regiment—the whole Detachment under Command of Major Knap[54] from the Massachusetts Line tarried near the River 'till 8 oClock in the Evening when marched half a Mile & took post oposite a ford a Mile & a half above the Bridge laying on our Arms—

July, 1782 Pines Bridge

M 1. this Morning about half an hour before Sun wrise was alarmed. we immeadiately took Post on a hill jest in our rear where continued a quat[*e*]r of an hour, when marched back to our former Post. The Alarm was ocasinoed by a party of hors theives who was fired uppon by Some Militia—at 8 oClock A.M. the Detachment or the two Companys who was staysoned at the Visenetys of Pines Bridge marched to that place where our Men went to washing their Cloathing, order'd to take a party of Men and go down towards the Enemies lines to get what inteligence lay in my Power—at 5 oClock the after noon set off / came as far as Sing-sing where made a small halt from where proceeded on to Tarry Town Meating House where arrived at 12 oClock at Night, put out a Small Guard, and lay on our arms.

T 2. This Morning at Day break proceeded on my March towards Kings Bridge as far as Tarrytown where made a small halt, from where took a Cross road towards the White Plains, came to Phillips burrough[55] where halted half an hour, then came 4 Miles where halted and dined / from where countermarched & crossed to Turkeho[56] where made a small halt then proceeded towards the Plains and came to Phillipsburrough where made a halt / from where came 6 miles & took post in field nigh the Road laying on our arms where continued all night—

W 3. this Morning at day break marched towards Pines Bridge 5 Miles when made a halt and breakfasted after which came to Pines Bridge where join'd my Company and continued 'till Evening. when went a half a Mile and took post on a hill in froont of the Bridge half a Mile on a hill in a thicket of woods.

T 4. This Morning at the Sun an hour high marched out of the woods, & came near the River where sent out Small Guards and continued 'till Sun set when marched to the Bridge—the Detachment crossed myself tarryed (being on Guard) 'till 10. oClock at Night when marched over the Bridge and took Post on a hight a half a Mile from the Bridge where continued all Night & Nothing Remarkeble.

F 5. This Morning marched my Guard back to the Bridge where continued 'till 9. oClock when join'd the Detachment which was one mile up the river from the bridge where tarryed (laying on our arms) till 8. oClock in the Evening when took post on a Hill in a thicket of woods on the North Side of the River, where continued (laying on our arms) all night / Nothing happined Worth Remark.

S 6. This Morning marched to the Bridge where continued till 10 oClock when went 3 quaters of a Mile where made a halt, (on account of a sivear squall of wrain) till 2 oClock when marched toward the White Plains about 12 Miles where the Other 3 Companys of the Detachment join'd us / hear put our Men into barns and made a halt on account of the rain.

S 7. This Morning paraded and marched to the White plains where halted & breakfasted & sett on Court Martial / tryed 3 Soldiers for plundering the Inhabitance,[57] all found Guilty 2 sentenced to receive 50 Stripe Each & one 60 on their Naked backs which was put in Execution after which came 4 Miles to Harlesons Precient,[58] where halted two or there [three] hours, from where proceeded to North Caswell[59] where took post in an Orchard—

M 8. this Morning paraded the other two companys [*which*] whent to their Stayson at Bedford & we proceeded on for pines Bridge where arrived at 8 oClock / put our Men into a Barn on account of rain, where they continued till Sun set, when came 3 miles up the road towards Crumbpond Meatinghouse, where we took post in an Orchard but in [it] began to rain, was alarmed by the fire of a Musquet—

T 9. the Detachment continuing at the same post 'till the evening when came half a Mile & took post in an orchard, was alarmed by a mans approching the Centry, who hail'd him, but gave no answer & made his escape—NMR.

W 10. Continuing in the Orchard all day & nothing Metireal hap'd / in the Evening marched a quater of a Mile & took post on a hill in a thicket of woods when lay on our arms NR—

T 11. this Morning came one Mile towards Crumbpond where halted and breakfasted / Major Darby[60] from the Massachusetts line came with a Detachment to releive us. after being releived proceeded on our march towards Camp as far as Crumb Pond where halted & lay in an Orchard.

F 12. This morning proceeded on our march as far as the Continental Village where made a halt for our men to wash—here continued till 2 oClock when proceeded on our March 6 miles where one company was dismised from the Detachment after which proceedet on to [*4th* ?] Massachusetts,[61] where we was all dismissed to our Regiments / came to our Regiment in the after noon when joined my Company.

S 13. This day was officer of the Police, nothing happined during my tower.

S 14. Nothing remarkeble—

M 15. was Police officer of the Regiment / NR—

T 16. This day went on the Brigade Guard / Nothing remarkeble happined during my tower.

W 17. This morning after being releiv'd came to Camp where continued all day sedentary, the Evening receiv'd orders to go on Guard, for a week / as duty was done by Regiments all the Interiour Guard was furnished from our Regt.—

T 18. this morning went with 12 men a Sergt. & 2 Corporals on Constitution Island, oposite West Point, where took Command of Several Small Redouts & Some Cannon—

F 19. Continuing at my hut all day Sedentary—

S 20. This day went to Nelsons Point where dined with Some Officers of my acquaintenc of the Massachusetts Line, where spent the day, in the evening came back to the Island—

S 21. Spent this day in reading the History of Sir Charles Grandison, in a Series of letters.[62]

M 22 to W 24. Spent in reading Sir Charles Grandisons History and amusing my self in walking around the Island, an unhabit'd one excep the Guard, and Nothing to bee seen except sum old Redoubts, rocks &c—

T 25. This Morning was releiv'd by an Officer from the 10 Massachuseets Regt. came with my Guard in a boat oposite the Regt. where landed and join'd it. NRR—

F 26. This day was officer of Police—

S 27. fixing for inspection—

S 28. Continuing in Camp / Nothing remarkeble—

M 29. This day morn was put through a number of Manoeuvers by Order of Colo. Stewart after which was mustered and inspected by him, who is Inspector to the Northern army.[63]

T 30. This day went on the Brigade Guard / are informed that the United State of Holland hath declared the 13 State of North America Independant & resolve to take an active part in the War—[64] nothing happined during my Tower worthy remark—

W 31. a New Resolution of Congress came to hand derageing all Lieutenants above ten to a Regiment of Infintry to go home on the Establishment that the Officers went home in Novr. 80—[65]

AUGUST 1782 N RIVER

T 1 to S 3. N R.

S 4. we are informed by a Gentleman from Philadelfe that 13 Ships of the line had arrived into the Chesapaek and we hear that the Duch hath taken 4 Ships of the line from the Brittish.

M 5. Nothing remark.

T 6. we hear that there is a packed [packet-boat] arrived, from Great Briton to New York, with Despaches to Congres—

W 7 to S 10. went to West Point from where went to Nelsons Point where continued the Biger part of the Day—after which came to the Regt. again / Nothing more remarkeble till the 10th when we hear that Rear Adml. Digbey & Sir Gui Carleton, had sent Letters to His Excellency Genl. Washington informing him that there is a prospect of peace, as Mr. Greenvele, had gone to France to settle the Preliminary but on his first arivance in France he was to d[*e*]clare the 13 Colinys of America Indipendant & had power invested in him to settle a Peace with all Powers at War.[66]

S 11 to T 20. nothing happined worthry remark / laying very still incampt on the Banks of the Hudson.

W 21. this day received orders for the Regiment to relieve the Troops on the Lines at Dobbs Ferry, Stonny and Virplanks Point, the Infintry ordered to be imbodyed / Major Dexter[67] of our Regiment ordered to take Command of one Battallion—

T 22. this morning agreable to yesterdays Orders the Regt. paraded to go on the lines / the Genl. beet at 4. oClock when the Tents were struck and carried to the Shore to be put into a Vessel which I pr[*o*]cureed yesterday to carry the bagage down the river in —the Assembly beet at 5 & soon after the March commenced [*and*] came as far as the Continental Village, where made a small halt, from where proceeded on to Kings Ferry, where we left two Companys one at Virplanks & the other at Stonny Point. we then proceeded on with 6 companys as far as Kearkiat where halted & put our men into Barns.

F 23. This morning the Genl. beet a[*t*] 5. oClock / Soon after the Assembly when began our march, came as far as Green bush where halted four hours then proceeded on our march within a half a mile of the Block house[68] where halted & lay in an orchard all night—

S 24 to M 26. This morn the Genl. beet at 4 oClock at half after 4 the Assembly when the march commenced & came to the Block house at Dobbs ferry, where releiv'd the 1st. Connecticut Regiment and went on Guard in the Block house where continued 'till the morning of the 25th when the Same Guard was order'd to be in readyness to go on Pequit at night—we hear the Light Infentry hath moved to Peekskills & the Grand Army ordered to hold them selves in readyness to march. two flags arrived from the Enemy one with letters for Genl. Washington & the other with Medicins & a Doctor to go to Philadelphia to take care of their Sick. the Evening went on Pequit in Froont of the works on a hight where continued 'till the morning of the 26 when came to camp & mounted the camp Guard & nothing happined during my Tower worthy remarks—

T 27. This morning was reliv'd by Lt. Pratt / came to Camp, Colo. Olney arrived, (by which Capt. Hughes,[69] who command the Regt. did duty as a nother Capt.[)] / we hear that there is 18 Ships of the Line expected into New york as they had been spoke with in a Certain Lattitude nor far from bermud[*er ?*] / we are informed that Savannah is evacuated by the Brittis & Gen. Wain is taken possession & that the Georgia battalion on his marching in was almost compleated, without any expence—[70]

W 28. Continuing in Garrison sett on Court Martial, tried a Soldier of the 7th Company [*for*] neglect of Duty when on sentry / found Guilty & sentinced to receive 60 Stripes on his naked back, the Evening went on Piquit in froont of the Works / nothing happined during the night—

T 29. This morning at sun wrise came to camp where continued all day & Nothing worthy remarks.

F 30. This day mounted the Camp Guard / Nothing remarkeble during my Tower. [*cipher*].

S 31. This morning was releived by Lt. Pratt. Soon after went with a Flagg of Truce to the Enemies advance post on the Hudson with two weomen & a letter, returned at 3 oClock in the after noon, nothing MTD.

SEPTEMBER 1782 DOBBS FERY

S 1–M 2. This day Lt. Pratt went with a Flagg, to carry Lt. Wheaton of our Regt. on board of the Guard ship, who had Liberty from his Excellency Genl—Washington to go to New York to see his Father.[71]

T 3. This morn a flagg came from the Enemy with one of the [*women*] I carried who could not obtain Liberty to go into Newyork / we hear that the Enemy is about evaucating South Carolinia and we have hopes from the series of conduct of the Enemy at New York, that they are about to evaucate that place / we hear that the 17th Regt. of horse is advertised to be sold at Publick Vondue— this after noon two flaggs came from the Enemy one with Lt. Wheaton who could not obtain Liberty to go into Newyork, the other with a Merchant from Philadelphia with Books for the Library of that City which had been contracted for whilst the Enemy lay at that Place.

W 4. this day went on the Camp Guard / one Deserter, (a yorger)[72] came to us from the Enemy, he informeth us the Enemy hath got a large Number of Boats colected in readyness for some secret expidetion—

T 5. This morning was releived by Lt. Pratt / came to camp / hear that 22 Saile of the line had arrived at Newyork & it was imagined that part of them would go to New Engeland.

F 6. Continuing in Camp / Nothing worthy remark happined during the day.

S 7. This day a flagg came from the Enemy with letters &c. &c. this Evening went on piquit in froont of the work / nothing happined during ye night.

S 8. this after noon 2 Company of Light Infentry, belonging to the Jersey line came to relive what men was hear belonging to our Regt. the Troops after releiving, the Guards &c marched out of the Garrison / I was ordered to go with the Bagage by water in flat bottom boats, the wind blowing so high & tide againts us could not get but 6 miles where halted—[*cipher*].

M 9. This morning set off very [*early* ?] & proceeded up the River to Verplanks Point, where landed the Bagage of the Regmt. & had it carried to the ground alloted for the Regmt. to incamp on & spread the Tents &c. at 3 oClock the Regiment arrived & piched the Tents on the ground assigned them. the whole Armys Incampment [*is*] in one right Line with elegant bowers built before the Tents.

T 10. this day received Orders to be in readyness to inspect & muster—

W 11. This day mustered and inspected agreable to yesterdays orders—

T 12 & F 13. Implying ourselves in making a Colonade before our Regiment.

S 14. This day the whole Army paraded to receive the Count Rochambeau, Commander in Chief of the French Army.

S 15 & M 16. Implying ourselves in compleating our Colonade.

T 17. This day the Regiment went on Guard—myself detached with a Capt. & 48. Priv'ts on the right of the Chain of the army, Nothing happined during my Tower worthy remarks—

W 18. this Morning was releived by the Jersey line / came to camp where continued all day—

T 19. Implying my self this day in superintending the Company, in the woods who was a cutting their qoto [quota] of wood for the Garrison of West Point.

F 20. Continuing in Camp sedentary all day.

S 21. This day the Army paraded for a Genl. revew / appear'd in exceeding good order—

S 22. we hear that the Enemy hath imbarked a Number of Troops & halled their Transport down to Sandy hook.

M 23. this day was officer of ye Police / nothing worthy remarks happined during my Tower—

T 24 & W 25. Continuing in Camp / hear by Mr. Cornhill a Member of Congress,[73] that the Brittish Court, on hearing of the Success of Adml. Rodny & their Fleet in taking Count De Grase that they seemed not to be so anxious for making a peace as heretofore, & he informs us that the French Court would not agree to any preposals 'till Engeland had first declared America his Independance for the first Preliminary—

T 26. This day went on Guard / nothing remarkeble during my tower.

F 27. This day was releived by the Connecticut Line, after which came to Camp & went on Police / are informed Genl. Washington & Count DeRochambeau with the Light Infentry Sheldons Hors & the French Legon had gone down to Morrissinia,[74]

S 28 to M 30. to the End of the Month, nothing Remarkeble—

October, 1782, [*illeg.*] Point

T 1. This day was appointed adjt. to the Regiment Lt. Rogers resigning that office—[75]

W 2. This day was Adjutant of the day / nothing more Remarkeble.

T 3 & F 4. Nothing Remarkeble—

S 5. This day the Regiment furnished ye Guards on ye left of the Chain.

S 6 & M 7. Nothing worthy remarks—

T 8. The Armey ordered to hall down the Colonade in froont of our Tents—as the wethe[*r*] grew Cule & they could be of no further Utilety.[76]

W 9 to M 14. Continuing in camp and nothing worthy remark—

T 15. a Detachment ordered out from ye Armey to Manoeuvre on ye 17th Inst.

W 16. rain & cold.

T 17. rain—

F 18. N.R.M.

S 19. this day the Detachment ordered out / ye 17th paraded & went through a Number of Manoeuvres—

S 20 to W 23. Nothing worthy Remark except the whole armey order'd to manoeuvre tomorrow.

T 24. This day agreable to yesterdays orders the whole armey paraded & went th[*r*]ough Several Manouvers which was, thought by his Excellency Genl. Washington to surpass all of the like kind since the commencement of the present War.[77]

F 25. This Morning the Armey ordered to march by wings, by the left, the left wing to march tomorrow morning at 7 o'Clock, & the right wing to march the Next day at the Same Hour—[78]

S 26. This day wrain which provented our marching.

S 27. This morning agreable to wing orders, by Genl. Gates struck our tents & put them in Vessels procured for that purpose—at 10 oClock the March commenced, from the Left our Regt. in froont, (as it was the left of the right wing) / came as far as Peekskills where made a small halt, from where proceeded to Nelsons Point, from where crossed the North River, went on west Point / went about two miles up Butter Hill[79] & very much fatigued, halted & built fires—

M 28. This morning at day break paraded & marched over the Mountain, where gained the Massachusetts Line who had marched the 26th Inst. here halted a few monts [moments ?], from where proceeded on our march to the ground alotted for the Troops to build their Huts on—no ground being alotted in peticular for our Regiment, we counter marched & came betwen Newbury & Newburgh where piched our tents, & received order to march for Albeny.[80]

T 29 to T 31. Continuing at Newburgh (rain & stormy) waiting for Vessels to transport our Troops to Albeny.

NOVEMBER, 1782

F 1. This day pleasant, the 1st & 4th companies imbarked for Albeny.

S 2. Continuing Near Newburgh—this after noon, the 6th Company imbarked.

S 3 & M 4. this morning the 3d and 7th Companies inbarked on board of a Sloop for Albeny, in the after noon the 5th & 8th imbarked on board of a Sloop, on which I went on board, came up about 30 Miles / the wind halling a head we came two, 'till the Morning tide w[*h*]en came about 8 miles, & came two, till the Evening time when came 6 miles & came two,—

T 5. At this morns morning tide waid anchor & proceeded on our passage about 5 miles, wen a Southerly breas took us and came about 50 miles and came too about ten oClock at Night—at the South Side of the Bar—distance 3 miles from Albeny.

W 6. this Morning wai'd Anchor at 6 / came about half a Mile & came to anchor, at 1 .oClock waied anchor, came within half a Mile of Albeny & went a Shore on the East Side of the River were stoped a half an hour with Capt. Tenicke,[81] (formely of Colo. Livingstons Regimt.[)] where drank a glass or two of wine then crossed the River & came to Albeny City. which I found contrary to my expectation, a very eregular town & exceeding muddy &c—

T 7. This morning after the Bagage of the 8th Company & my own, was loaded into a battau to transport to the half moon which was 12. miles I sett out on hors back came 12 miles & crosed the Mohawk River, from [*where*] proceeded on three miles to the widdow Peoples, Nigh the half moon, where put up—[82]

F 8. This morning wrode down the North River about two miles where Capt. Peckham[83] lay with his company, & breakfasted, from where came to Still water where dined, and had my bagage put

on board of a battau* which was brought, after which came about 3 miles, & made a halt.
*the bagage belonging to Capt. Peckham & my self was traut[84] in waggon from the half moon to Stile water.

S 9. This morning wrode to Saratoga Garrison[85] where companies of the Regiment had arrived & took posession of the Barracks which was very poor.

S 10. Continuing at Saratoga fixing our Barrack &c—During the Remainder of the Month Nothing happined worthy of remarks excep a flagg of Truce from Cannada—

DECEMBER 1782

M 1 to T 31. Continuing at Saratoga fixing our barracks &c, nothing hapined worthy remarks.

JANUARY, 1783, SARATOGA

W 1. Continuing at Saratoga fixing to go on furlough.

T 2. This day sett out in company with Colo. Olney Majr. Dexeter & Doctr. Tenny for Providence, proceeded on our Journy after a great deal of fateague to find the road as far as St. Caiak where oated our horses, from wher proceeded on to Pownel where halted 38 miles from Saratoga.[86]

F 3. This morn wrode 22 Miles to New Providence where made a halt about two hours at Colo. Staffords from where proceeded on 14 miles to comeington where put up at Lt. Mitchels—[87]

S 4. This morning proceeded on our rout 18 miles to Northhamton to Major Pomeroys where halted & breakfasted, from where proceeded on 14 Miles to Belchertown where halted at Mr. Dwights—[88]

S 5. This morning wrode 12 miles to Mr. Chadwicks at Westtown where breakfasted after which proceeded on 5 miles to Bruck field, where put up on account of the Storm of Snow—at Capt. Rices—[89]

M 6. This morning wrode 20 miles to Wocester where halted at Lt. Stowers, & took breakfast, after which came to Grafton where parted with Colo. Olney & Major Dexter / Doctor Tenny & myself proceeded on to Upton.[90] (12 miles from Wocester,) whe[*re*] halted at Mr. Perrums.

T 7. This morning wrod 18 miles to Cumberland[91] where took breakfast after which came 12 miles to Providence where arrived at

3 oClock, and reconing all the Stages maket it 186 miles from Saratoga.

W 8. Continuing in Pro[*v*]idence until ye. 16th in which time nothing happined worthry remarks—

T 16 to S 18. wrode 6 miles into the country to Rehoboth[92] where continued the 17th & untill the Evening of the 18th when came to Providence where continued all Night—

S 19 to M 27. This morning went to Rehoboth where continued all day—20th / this day came 6 miles to Swanzey[93] where continued all day—21st / wrode to Newport, where continued visiting my friend &c, until the 27th when came to Swanzey.

T 28. this day wrode 2 miles to a Friends house where continued all day & Night.

JANUARY–FEBRUARY, 1783

W 28 to M 3. Returned so my Quaters where continued untill the 4th Feby, in which time Nothing worthy Remarks.

T 4 to T 20. whent to Providence where continued untill 6th when came to Swanzey again where continued untill 8th when went to Dartmout[*h*] where continued 'till 11th where came to Swanzey where continued untill the 20th / went to Providence and returned the same day.

F 21 to T 25. Continuing in Swanzey and nothing transpir'd wor they [worthy] remarks—

FEBRUARY–MARCH 1783 FURLOUGH

W 26 to W 26. This morning wrode 6 miles to Slaid's ferry (to get a passage for Newport) where continued 'till the 28th when got a passage in a row boat as far as Bristol ferry[94] where landed & came a foot to Newport, where continued untill 13th March when got a passage to Slaid ferry where my hors was brought to me, from where came 6 miles into Swanzey where continued till 19th when went to Providence where continued 'till 22nd when returned to Swanzey where continued untill 26th when went to Taunton where continued all night.

T 27 to S 30. this [*day*] came back to Swanzey where tarried 'till 29th—when wrode to Providence where continued half an hour then return'd to Swanzey, where continued all night—30th This day went to Providence where am informed that the Gloreous Peaces is taken place, that the Prelimenary Articles where [were] signed at

Parris on the 20th Day of November last[95] / in consequence all hostilitys was to seas, in Urope on th[*e*] 3d day of Feby & in America on the 3d day of March—

MARCH–APRIL 1783 FURLOUGH

M 31 to M 7. This day came to Swanzey where continued untill the 4th when came to Providence, where continued untill 7th when Capt. Hughes Lt. Greene and myself set off for Camp / came 16 miles to Glocester where put up—[96]

T 8. This morning from Glocester came 22 Miles to Woodstock,[97] where halted two hours from where proceeded to Sturbridge 12 Miles where made a small halt after which came 8 miles to Brimfield, to Blisses where put up.

W 9. This morning from Brimfield came 18 miles to Belchor town, to Dwits [DeWitt's] where dined after wh[*i*]ch came to Northhamton 15 miles where halted one hour / from here proceeded on to Williams Town[98] 9 miles where put up at Doctor Pains.

T 10. This morning came 9 miles to Comeington to Mr. Mitchels where breakfasted from where came to Adams 21 Miles where halted at Mr. Levingsworth.

F 11. This morning proceeded on our rout 12 m[*iles*] as far as Mr. Brown in Pownnell where breakfasted from where came 18 miles to Cambridge[99] where made a small halt at Mr. Cowdens, from where came 7 miles to Esqr. Palmers,—where put up—

APRIL–MAY 1783 SARATOGA

S 12 to S 17. This morning from Esquire Palmers proceeded on to Saratoga 8 miles where joined my Regt. and nothing happined 'till 18th when read the order for a ceassation of Arms, from the commander in Chief.[100] Continued in Garrison very Sedentary 'till 7th May when went, to Albeny where continued one Night—

MAY–JUNE 1783 SARATOGA

S 18 to M 2. This morning from Albeny came 14 Miles to the half mon[101] where tarried 'till 5 oClock when set off for Garrison where arrived at 9. oClock at Night, where continued till 23d when wrode about 4 miles into the country & return the same day—& continuing in Garrison 'till 3d Joune / Nothing happing worthy remarks, implying our selvs in a skettle & ball Alle[*y*]—[102]

T 3 to T 10. this day Lt. Pratt and myself wrote [rode] about

12 miles to the Northward of this place to the Salt. Springs (a great curiosety) see page 619—where continued one hour.[103] The mineral Springs near Saratoga—are five or Six in number situated in the Margin of a Marsh, formed by a branch of Kiadarossa Creek[104] about 12 miles W[*est*] from the confluance of Saratoga Creek and Judson River—the water is strongly impregnated with salts, which operate as a cathartic on those who make use of it—Besides the salt which predominates in the taste of the water, there is an acid very simelar to that of Stale beer—These springs rise perpendicular from the earth, through the apertures of a rock of a pecular kind formed by the water—In most of these apertures there can be no bottom discovered by sounding—they are all circular, & one is eighteen inches diameter, the others less; yet there is very little water flow from any of them excep at certain periods—This periodical efflux is observed to be monthly, after which the waters settles to a certain degree and there remains untill the time of the next discharge—The rocks through which the springs rise, are considerable higher than the serface of the earth and the water which flows out soon petrifies, so that they are constantly growing larger, but the matter so petrifyed exfoliated (altho hard) may be disolved & when the water is disdate there remain a greyish sand—one of those rocks is more remarckable than the other. it rises from the ground, six or seven feet high, in the form of a pyramid—The aperture in the top which contains the water is perfictly cylindrical, of about nine inches diameter—In this the surface, of the water is about twelve inches from the top, except at the time of its menstrual discharge—It always appears to be in the same agitation as water boiling in a pot, altho it is excessive cold.

This phenomenon of the waters as well as the acid taste is attributed to the large quantity of fixed air contain'd in its composition, the ferment action is so great, it will soon burst any tight vessel it is put into—the same properties and appearance are found in the waters of all the Springs—

Near these are excelent springs of fresh water.—besides the fixable air there is a large Quanterty of calcanous earth contain'd in the waters—it is partly combin'd with an acid & partly with the fixed air / it is probaly supplyed with this Substance by hapning there a bed of lime ston or earth after being imprignated with ye Acid—

[Spent one hour at the Salt Springs] when return'd to Garrison again

—and continued very sedentary 'till 10th when order came for all the officers, excep a few to tarry with the three year men, to retire on Furlough till the arrival of the Definitive Treaty, and all the Non Commissioned officers & Privates was [*to*] be discharg'd with a Proviso that the Definitive Treaty arrived & till then it was to be considered as a Furlough. The Same as the Commissioned officers.[105]

W 11 & T 12. 11th and twelvth continuing in Garrison / nothing remarkbl.

F 13. This day implying my self in signing a certificate of the Men Discharges. Capt. Hughes[106] marched off with a party for the State.

S 14 & S 15. Capt. Holden march off with a party / 15th / Capt. Humphrey marcheed off.[107]

June–July 1783 Saratoga

M 16 to T 3. Capt. Dexter & Lt. Rogers marched off with the 4th and last Detachment leaving behind Capt. Allen & Capt. Brow[*n*], with Lieut's Wheaton, Shearburne, Pratt, and Ensign Kirbey.[108] and myself to tarry with the theree year men untill further orders—17th / implying myself in making a Register of the officers this day—18th / to the 4th day of July / Nothing Material happined.—

F 4. This day had all the officers of the Regement to dine with me, after dinner drank the following Toasts, with a Discharge of a Volley of Musquets at the end of each—[109] 1st The Day / 2nd The United States & their congress, 3d the Genl. & Army of the United States, 4th the Congress of the year 1776 & common Sence,[110] 5th Louis the 16th & the French Nation / 6th May, the Brave ever enjoy the Smiles of the Fair—Given by a lady / 7th May the Fair ever have the Protection of the Brave / 8th All those who have been instremental in establishing our Independance—9th The memory of those who have sacrificed their lives in the cause of American liberty—10th May the characture of america never be sullied by Ingratitude to her deliverers. 11th May the Justice of America forever preserve her from deserving, and her Resorcess from fearing an Enemy—12th May Purity of Morals & dignity of Deportment ever characterize the citizens of the United States—13 Perpitual Friendship among ourselves & Peace will [with] all the world—

S 5 to M 21. to the 22nd of the month Nothing transpired worthy remarks, continuing very sedentary at my quaters.

T 22. his Excellency Genl. Washington passed this place on his way for crow[*n*] Point to review those Northarn work as he never had been that way, during the War—[111]

W 23. Barron, Stuban, the Inspector General passes through this place bound for canada, at the same time had orders to take cognisance of the Post, which belonged to the United States, but not evacuated by the British & to desire Genl. Alderman to deliver them up—[112]

August, 1783, Saratoga

S 23. this day the Barron return'd from visiting the Northward Posts—the Barron Stuban return'd from canda, & informs us Genl. Alderman saith the Season is to far advanced to deliver up the Posts this fall—[113]

S 24. Nothing worthy remark during the Month—

September [1783] On a March

M 1. Continuing at Saratog—

T 2. this morning sett off in company with Majr. Scott. & Esqr. Gilleland[114] for lak champlain / came as far as Fort Edward 14 miles from Saratoga where halted and took a small review of the old works which [*were*] built in the year 1756[115] after which proceed on to the half way brook 7 miles from Fort George where we put up—[116]

W 3. this morning came to Fort Georg at the head of Lake George a very beutifull lake which contain'd upward of two hundred small Islands—here we repaired a Publick boat, reviewed the old works which was very much Demolished / at 12 oClock set off to go dow[*n*] the lake / came 14 miles and made a halt at a Small Island, which we called Waterburys, on account of his making a halt here on his retreat from Tianteroga[117] in 1776. we piched out tent & built up a fire & pased the night very comfortable—

T 4. This morning at sun wrise we departed from the Island and arrived at the landing place at 12 oClock. 24 miles from the Island, where [*we*] came from in the morning—had our boat & bagage drew acrost the land one mile & a half then put her into a creek which led into lak champlain & proceeded on to Tianteroga 3 miles where halted and had our boat mended.—[118]

F 5. this morning with a South wind proceeded 15 miles to Crown Point where halted 4 hours then came 12 miles to a Small

Island called button Island where we halted, (on account of two Guns being fired,) found them to be a Flagg from canada with 64 Prisoners, the officer commanding it wanted to enquire where he could be received at our lines, after making a halt a quater of an hour we proceeded on our rout 2 miles to Bason harbour[119] in Farys Burrough where piched our Tent as usal—

S 6. Proceed'd on 5 miles to groog harbour wher whent a Shore and whent 2 miles, when got in the boat again & came 2 miles to the mouth of Gillelands crick, in wills burrough (about 90 miles from Saratoga) where was a great plenty of sand suitable for to make Iron / here halted an hour when proceeded up the crek 2 miles where Esqr. Gilleland House, mills, &c. formely stood before they where burnt by the enemy—[120] ketched 20 Salmon and piched our tent—

S 7. this day continued at Willsburrough. which is an exceeding good tract of land belonging to Esqr. Gilleland which he vallis at one Gunia pr. acre—[121]

M 8. this morning at 9 oCloc[*k*] set off for Salmon River,[122] proceeded on 12 miles when was meet with a severe squall of wind & wrain from the Northward which ocasioned us to land on Schuylers Island[123] where tarried half an hour and the wind lulling a little we proceeded on within half a mile of salmon River, where halted and piched our tent on a Beach opposite the Island—Valcort[124]— an Island containing one thousand acres of land, on the W. Side of this Island, the infamous *Arnold* lay with his Fleet, in October 1776, & was defeated.

T 9. This morning Esqr. Gilleland Major Scott. & my self whent, on foot. to Salmon River, (a small stream suitable for Mills &c) after which came to our boat. Set Sail with the wind at the Northward came about ten miles the wind blowing so excessive hard carried away our Sail and lost one of our ors, by which mean we had like to have been overset. got before the wind, run into a small bay called ligeneer,[125] fixed our sail again and proceeded on to Gillelands crick, where halted. the last two day almost a continual storm of wrain & wind—

W 10. This morn at ten oClock left Gillelands crick / came 3 miles to Point Pleasant[126] where incamped—

T 11. This morning rowed acrost the lake to Hills, or Burch Bay[127] where we halted 2 hours & breakfasted after which proceeded on to Bason harbour, where halted half an hour after which proceeded. to Hospital Point,[128] whe[*re*] incampt a mile & a half from crown Point.—

F 12. This morning came to crown Point where halted two hours, when we made an attempt, to go up the lake but the wind blowing so hard at the southward was obliged to turn back again to Crown Point, where tarried 4 hours, when proceeded on within 5 miles of Tianteroga where we put up—

S 13. This morning proceeded to Tianteroga where made a small halt, after which proceeded on to Lake George Landing where piched our tent and got a passage in a nother boat & left Esqr. Gilleland.

S 14. This morning we proceeded on 10 miles to Long Point where made a halt. & breakfasted after which proceded on 2 miles to Sabbothday Point. know[*n*] by that name on acct. of a battle fought there by Rogers last war.[129] here halted two hours on acct. of a heavy squall of wind & wrain, the winds lulling we proceeded on 6 miles, where halted & piched our tents—

M 15. This morning came ten miles when made a halt & breakfasted after which came 6 miles to Fort George where arrived at one oClock and tarried 'till 4: when took our horses and came to Fort Edward 14 miles where arrived 3 quaters after 4 & continued all night.

T 16. This morning set off for Saratoga where arrived at one oClock—

W 17 & T 18. fixing for to muster & inspect.

F 19. This day mustered & inspected—

S 20 & S 21. wrain—

M 22 to T 30. to the end of the month. nothing remarkeble.

October, 1783 Saratoga

W 1. —NR

T 2. we here that a fleet is arrived at New York to carry away Trops—[130]

F 3 to S 12. Continuing in Garrison very sedentary as there is only a few Troops to take up our attention. imply our leisure time in reading or at some divertion. to drive away the Dull hours.

M 13. This day with the officers of the Garrison (Except Capt Brown) set off for albany to attend the court of enquiry as evidences againts Lieut. Wheaton,[131] arrived at dark in albany—

T 14. This day attend the Court. nothing more remarkable—

W 15. This day set off for camp, came 14 miles as far [*as*] the widdow Peoples where tarried all night.

T 16 to S 18. This day arrived at Garrison, where continued till the 18th & Nothing more remarkable than raining almost every day, which had been the case sinc[*e*] 1st of Sepr.

S 19. This day a very severe storm of Snow—

M 20 to F 31. Continued at Saratoga very sedentary the remainder of the month,—

November [1783] Saratoga

S 1 to T 6. have nothing worthey remark.

F 7. we are informed that the British is to leave New York on the 15th Inst.—[132]

November–December [1783]

S 8 to [F] 5. This Evening we are informed by two British officers (on their way to Canada) that the Definitive Treaty had arrived at New York[133] / Continuing in Garrison waiting anxiously for Order to leave this post, our men in a Miserable Condition / Some of then [them] not a Shoe or a Stocking to their feet and the climate at this place much sevearer, than in the Estern States—Continuing at Saratoga / no thing of consequenc happin'd till 5th Decr. when we r[*e*]cieved orders for Discharging our men. & the officers permission. to return home which order had laid in the post office at Albany sinc 18th of Novr.[134]

S 6. Continuing in Garrison fixing to make our Exit from this place.

S 7 to W 24. Fixing to discharge our men and waiting for the Muster Master and Lieutenant Wheaton, who had gone to Head Quarters. to endevour to procure Some Shoes and other Cloathing for our naked men—but returned with only a pair of Shoes for each man—

T 25. This morning all our men had their discharges, in the evening set off with the Bagage & crosed the North River & put [*up*] at Mr. Deriders.

F 26. This morning from the East Side of the River Hudson proceeded on 8 miles to Cambridge where halted—

S 27. This morning from Cambridge came to St. Coick where

breakfasted then proceeded on to Pownell at Browns where halted in froont of the Slay with the Bagage.

S 28. This day Mr. Kirby and myself set off from Browns in persuit of the Slay. (which had gone a head) / came to Williams Town where made a small halt and parted with Mr. Kirby. then proceeded on after the Slay, took a wrong rout which ocasioned me to cross Husick River[135] (on a Bridge made by myself) / after a great deal of Trouble and Danger found I had only crosed an arm of it and was o[*b*]liged to recross the same way, after which endevoured to cross in siveral places on the ice but the water being so rapid had not fros'd it sufficient to bare, after trying (and all to no purpose) an hour or two came to a narrow place in the River where a Tree leaned from the opposite Side & by the help of that and a long plank got a thought / came 6 miles to Adams and put up 17 miles from Brown[*s*].

M 29. This morning came 5 miles to Colo. Staffords in New Providance where continued till Sun down waiting for the bagage which had been in the rear, ocasioned by the Slay having got one of its runers broke, after the Slay came up. Came 5 miles to winsor at Mr. Saffords where put up.

T 30. This morning came 11 miles to Werringham[136] where dined, from where proceeded on within 5 miles of North Hampton. where put up at Mr. Allens—

W 31. This morning came to Pumroys in North Hampton. where made a small halt, from where cam[*e*] 5 miles to Hadly, in a very severe Storm of Snow and wind, made a small halt after which came 3 miles and dined from where came 3 miles to Major Dwits [De Witt's] in Belchor Town where halted 11. mil[*e*]s from Allens.

JANUARY 1784

T 1. This morning from Dwits came 3 miles in a very severe storm when we was obliged to make a halt an hour or two after which came 7 miles to Chadwicks in Westown[137] where halted—

F 2. This morning came to Breckfield[138] 6 miles and the Snow very deep and No track / we halted an hour, from where came to Walkers 4 miles, made a small halt. then proceeded on 4 miles fa[*r*]ther the Snow so drifted & No track / we halted within a mile of a Tavern but so many Slays had halted on the same acct. we went forward to the Tavern in Spencer, and put [*up*] at Mr. Witmores—

S 3. This morning proceeded on to Wocester [Worcester]. 10 Miles / the Snow very deep & much drifted / made a small halt / when we went about 3 miles on Providance road but the Snow being so high was obliged to turn back and take the Bostown Road / came 2 miles and put up.

S 4. This morning sett off very early / came 5 miles to Shrewsbury [*and*] made a small halt. from where proceeded on 8 miles to Malbro where breakfasted, then went through Sudbury & Weston into Walthham and put up.

M 5. This morning drove into Roxbury where we breakfasted, from where proceeded on in the rain and bery bad traveling, thro Dedham and Walpole into Wrentham where put up—

T 6. This morning it wrain'd and the road excessive bad / left the bagage and came on a Foot. and in many places the water over the tops of my boots / came to Attlebourrough[139] where breakfasted, from where came 18 miles to Providance—

W 7. Continuing in Providance / my bagage arrived—Continuing wraining.

T 8. Continuing warm & sum wrain which carried off all the Snow, which ocasioned the Bridge at the North End of the Town to be carried off and seven buildings—[140]

F 9. Continuing in Providance / we are informed that the freshet hath carried away all the bridges within 20. or 30 miles & a Number of Mills—

S 10 to F 16. Continuing in Providance untill the 16th when came to Swanzey.

S 17 to F 23. Continuing in Swanzey 'till the 23d when whent to Providance after my Bagage and return'd / in the Night a very severe storm of wrain and wind.

JANUARY–FEBRUARY 1784

S 24 to S 28. Continuing in Swanzey, 'till Wednesday 11th of Febuary when whent to Providance & returned ye same day to Swanzey where continued very Sedentary till the 25th when whent to Taunton / Nothing happined worthy remark til Satturday 28 when it was very Cold and in the Night a Small Earth Quake was felt. by Some of the Inhabitants of the Town.

S 29. This morn severe Cold thought to be the Coldist day had the [this] winter / on the Greene & several ajasent from Taunton was to be seen a number of cracks in the Ground ocasioned by the Earth Quake on Satternight—

MARCH 1784

M 1. this day came to Swanzey.

T 2 to T 31. Whent to Providance, where continued untill the 3d when came to Swanzey where continued. 'till 9th when whent to Warren where continued one hour and came to Swanzey / during the remainder of this Month Nothing happined worthy remarks / Implying myself in reading a few Historys & whent to Providance several times from the 9th to the last of March—

APRIL 1784

W 1 & T 2 . Continuing in Swanzey—

F 3. whent to Providence where continued a day, and entered into a contract with Mr. Masury [(]formely an officer of the Regt.)[141] to put our small Interest togeth[*er*], (which we had been fighting, bleeding, and all most dying for,—for the Space of 8 long years in the Army of the United States,) in order for to trade and try for a livelyhood.

S 4 & S 5. Continuing in Swanzey fixing for to move my mother & Go[*o*]ds to Providenc—[142]

M 6. Moved to Providence into Decon Richmonds house[143] and Mr. Masury and myself began our Shop and whent into traid, & setled my-Self for an Inhabitant of Providenc.

APRIL 1784 TO JUNE 1788.

Continued in Trade with Mr. Masury 'till 1st Sepr. when buisness grow'd very dull / parted and trid a Shop and took my part of the stock and continued in the Mercantile line till Septr. 1785—when I took to the seas. Shiped on board of the Active at Boston. whent to the Caneries & Cape Verd[*e*] Islands and landed part of our Cargo in Newyork. then proceeded to Boston. 12th June 1786. from where came to Providence. & 10th July shipped on board of the America for the coast of Guin[*e*]a. arrived in the west Indias in Feby. 1787 where I continued a[*t*] Trinidad 'till 19th May. 1788 when I embarked for the United States. and arrived in Providence on the 21st June—& continued in the Nautical line of buisness to gain a lively hood untill[144]

NOTES TO DIARY

1. Oliver Jenckes, an experienced soldier commissioned a 2d lieutenant in the Second Rhode Island on 1 January 1777, was promoted to 1st lieutenant the following June and had served in Olney's Rhode Island Battalion since May 1781.

2. He refers to an upper route to Philadelphia that connected the Hudson Highlands in the vicinity of King's Ferry, or Haverstraw on the west bank, with the Delaware by a route running through Sussex County in New Jersey. Greenman's own route, not quite so far north, would take him through Ramapo, Pompton, and Morristown pretty much as the army had marched to Yorktown; that route with a few variations is clearly drawn on a map in James T. Adams, ed., *Atlas of American History* (New York: Scribner, 1943), p. 80.

3. William Ennis.

4. "Putrid fever" referred to a fever caused by typhus (*O.E.D.*, s.v. "putrid"), but in popular usage it was apt to be employed as a label for a wide variety of illnesses exhibiting somewhat similar symptoms.

5. This is the same Coe's Tavern in Kakiat, N.Y., where Greenman stopped on 27 October and 2 November 1781 (see Part V).

6. Hillsborough in Somerset County, N.J., is shown on a map in Lundin, *Cockpit of the Revolution*, facing p. 6. It was located north of Princeton on a road which went to Pluckemin and then turned northeast for Morristown. Very helpful for understanding sites in this area is John P. Snyder, *The Story of New Jersey's Civil Boundaries, 1686–1968* (Trenton, N.J.: Bureau of Geology and Topography, 1969), pp. 20, 24.

7. Lying between Hillsborough and Trenton, as "Pined Town" does in his itinerary, one might almost suppose he meant Princeton, but Greenman was too well informed to make that mistake. Probably "Pined Town" was not far from Princeton.

8. Bordentown, N.Y., today, this was Burdenton on Faden's map of 1777 which has been reproduced in Nebenzahl, *Atlas*, p. 93.

9. Probably the site of Mansfield Square on maps today.

10. A ferry across the Rancocas Creek, which he encountered because he was marching toward Philadelphia on the Jersey side of the Delaware. The best and most carefully drawn map of this region is in the series of maps depicting the American colonies ca. 1775 in Capen, ed., *AEAH*, p. 5, where the name of the creek is given as Ancocus, which is apparently its uncorrupted original form.

11. Probably Pvt. Robert Dixon, who is listed in Arnold, *Vital Record*, 12:152.

12. Conditions in Philadelphia's Old Stone Prison had deteriorated so badly that early in 1773 expenditures for a new jail were authorized, but building proceeded slowly, and the jail was only partly finished in January 1776, when it began to receive prisoners.

Known as the Walnut Street Jail, most of the space in this new jail was commandeered for military prisoners during the Revolution (Negley K. Teeters, *They Were in Prison* [Philadelphia: John C. Winston Co., 1937], pp. 13–21).

13. William Pratt had been made a sergeant in the Second Rhode Island Regiment on 22 February 1777 and had advanced in rank since then; he received his commission as lieutenant on 25 August 1781.

14. George Blinn is mentioned as a private in Arnold, *Vital Record*, 12:110.

15. With seeming indifference to any feeling of personal loss in the death of his fellow officer, Greenman records the details of military protocol that attended the funeral, the decencies with which an officer is borne to his grave in the burying ground of the Presbyterian Church on Mulberry Street, which location is easily found on the detailed map of the city prepared by Benjamin Easburn, "A Plan of the City of Philadelphia, . . ." (1776) and reprinted by Nebenzahl, *Atlas*, pp. 120–21.

16. The charge is inadvertently omitted, but drunkenness is very likely.

17. The Pennsylvania Hospital, chartered in 1751 after some controversy and strenuous fund-raising efforts, was built on the outskirts of the city as it then was settled, in the block between Eighth and Ninth streets and bounded by Spruce and Pine (Horace M. Lippincott, *Philadelphia* [1926; reprint ed., Port Washington, N.Y.: Kennikat Press, 1970], pp. 178–79).

18. One of his few nights out appears to have been spent in Masonic activities.

19. Again the charge has been omitted and again drunkenness probably was the offense. Michael Kelly was listed as a private by Arnold, *Vital Record*, 12:198.

20. An epaulet.

21. The main stone building of the Walnut Street Jail, according to an early description, was 184 feet long, with wings at its east and west ends which extended 90 feet south, and "beneath the wings were dungeons, in the basement, . . . partially under ground." (Quoted by Teeters, *They Were in Prison*, p. 18.) Some idea of what those dungeons were like can be formed from looking at the photograph of dungeons surviving from the *Old Stone Prison* published by Teeters, ibid., p. 11.

22. Rumors of the evacuation of Charleston by the British were very premature, but just the day before Washington had expressed to Thomas Paine the belief that "this Post will be given up, . . . unless G: Britain can do more than acquire a momentary superiority in the West Indies and on this Coast" (*Writings*, 24:71). Still they did not evacuate Charleston until December (Freeman, *Washington*, 5: 428n.).

23. The British garrison at St. Christopher, or St. Kitts as it is better known, capitulated to French forces under De Grasse on 12 February 1782 (Boatner, *Encyclopedia*, p. 960), but Philadelphia was just learning about it. Most interesting is the political observation that the terms allowed more privileges than those of the British had, which may have been a welcome indication among men convinced of the need to cast off the British monarch that their ally, the French monarch, showed signs of enlightened policy.

24. James Hale, according to Arnold, *Vital Record*, 12:175.

25. The Inspector General, Baron Friedrich von Steuben.

26. John Hanson of Maryland.

27. Captain Harrison has not been identified, though it is clear from a study of Heitman (*Historical Register*) that if he was still in active service, as seems likely, he must have come from North Carolina or Virginia.

28. Christ Church was the first and most prestigious outpost of the Church of England in this Quaker city (Lippincott, *Philadelphia*, pp. 94–97).

29. Lt. John Hubbard was suspected of acting improperly, and a "Court of enquiry"

was convened on 11 May on a "complaint exhibited by the Citizens of the State of Pennsylvania" which concluded that Hubbard "could not consistently with the orders which he had received have permitted the said Boat to have passed without examination and therefore think his condition Justifiable" (General Orders, 19 June 1782, in Washington's *Writings*, 24:361–62.)

30. John Welsh, quartermaster, was made an ensign on 12 March 1782, but the ranking dated from 1 July 1781.

31. The Marquis de Lafayette had arrived safely in France after a passage of twenty-two days, as Washington reported in a letter of 19 March to Comte de Rochambeau (*Writings*, 24:81).

32. The word is uncertain and perhaps was intended to be "Center," but whether it was a tavern, a park, or something else entirely is unknown.

33. Benjamin L. Peckham in 1777 had been regimental quartermaster of the Second Rhode Island Regiment, was commissioned a lieutenant 15 April 1779, and would be promoted to captain on 21 June 1782.

34. Arnold had sailed for England with his wife on 31 December 1781, hoping that the defeat of Cornwallis at Yorktown might enhance his chances for advancement even to the point of enabling him to gain the command that had belonged to Sir Henry Clinton. The intelligence which appeared in the New York paper may have been fairly accurate, for Arnold had been favored with opportunities to confer with the king in private when he might have made such a proposal, which was known to coincide with his views that with a renewed effort England might ultimately win the war (James T. Flexner, *The Traitor and the Spy* [New York: Harcourt, Brace, 1953], pp. 398–99; John C. Miller, *Triumph of Freedom* [Boston: Little, Brown, 1948], p. 613). The following phrase "not yet done" is an interlined rejoinder.

35. Hosea Crandall was listed as a sergeant in Arnold, *Vital Record*, 12:143.

36. The birth of a dauphin was known on 13 May in Philadelphia where it had been announced to Congress, and a letter had been written to inform Washington of the event (Washington, *Writings*, 24:274). Washington ordered celebrations at the end of the month and hosted an elaborate celebration at West Point, but Philadelphia preceded the rest in celebrating the good fortune of the Bourbons (ibid., pp. 299, 302; Freeman, *Washington*, 5:416). Greenman struggled again with "feu de joie," not much more successfully than he had much earlier in the war.

37. Gloucester, N.J., now Gloucester City, is located just across the Delaware River and a little below Philadelphia, close enough that Greenman was apparently able to return the same day, and yet he records no results of his mission.

38. The Admiral Comte de Grasse, who had sailed from the Chesapeake in November sharing the honors of victory at Yorktown, had met a disastrous defeat in the West Indies, where he surrendered to the British Admiral, George Rodney, on 12 April after a major naval battle, five of his ships of the line, including his handsome flagship *Ville de Paris*, falling into British hands that day (Piers Mackesy, *The War of America* [Cambridge, Mass.; Harvard University Press, 1965], pp. 457–58). According to James P. Perkins, the carnage was so great on French ships that it was said that over a thousand sharks were attracted to the ships as bodies were thrown overboard (*France in the American Revolution* [Boston 1911], p. 399). Admiral de Grasse's reputation was lost but not his life.

39. Washington issued orders on 15 May "to Major Coggeshall Olney or Officer Commanding the Rhode Island Regiment," from his headquarters at Newburgh, N.Y., to conduct the regiment "by easy marches and the most convenient route to, join the Army on the North River." Greenman is correct in reporting that these orders gave

directions for dealing with the British captain to be executed in retaliation for the hanging of militia captain Joshua Huddy, who had been captured by a unit of refugees (Washington, *Writings*, 24:258). The best short account of the Huddy affair is in Freeman, *Washington*, 5:412ff.

40. The City Tavern was a relatively new building completed in 1773, but it was evidently large and important to the business, political, and social affairs of the city, "the successor to the London Coffee House," according to Lippincott (*Philadelphia*, p. 79). The occasion for which they were gathering was a second and more formal celebration of the birth of the dauphin in France.

41. Frankford was located on the road that left the northeast part of the city for Bristol and Trenton, as shown on the map in Nebenzahl, *Atlas*, pp. 116–17.

42. A ferry across the Neshaminy Creek. The place is clearly and beautifully drawn, together with the road from Trenton to Red Lion Tavern in Rice and Brown, eds., *Rochambeau's Army*, 2: plate 56.

43. Maidenhead lies about midway between Trenton and Princeton and is most easily viewed on the large-scale map by Faden in Nebenzahl, *Atlas*, p. 93.

44. Rocky Hill in Somerset County is found on the road from Kingston to Hillsborough on Lt. John Hill's map of New Jersey (photostat in the Newberry Library) and is conveniently shown on the front endpaper map in Boatner, *Encyclopedia*.

45. This appears to be a small community where the road crossed the Raritan River. The exact site of Stial's Gap has not been identified, but there are some likely places where the road to Basking Ridge passes through gaps in the hills.

46. Probably Adam Armstead, who was a private on the list found by Arnold, *Vital Record*, 12:97.

47. Troy was probably the place marked as Troy Forge on Hill's map of New Jersey (photostat in the Newberry Library), rather than the Troy Hills of today.

48. Pequanock River is easily found on the front endpaper of Freeman, *Washington*, vol. 5, but is best drawn on the map showing the Middle Colonies and Quebec about 1775 in Capen, ed., *AEAH*, p. 4.

49. Comfort Sands & Company; see Freeman, *Washington*, 5:405 and Washington, *Writings*, 24:127, 153–55, and many other entries in this volume.

50. Pond's Church and the features of the area around Pumpton are most easily studied on the map printed on the front endpaper of Freeman, *Washington*, vol. 5.

51. The mutiny took place in April among troops who had endured absolutely wretched conditions. Without pay for more than a year and poorly fed, many wasted with fever and dysentery and were so ill-clothed that a description of their condition as one of nakedness, a frequently heard description during the Revolution, was in this instance almost literally true. Historian Francis V. Greene said that a great many "were so ragged that they could not in decency leave their tents" (*General Greene* [New York, 1893], p. 287). One Sergeant Gornell, who had taken part in a mutiny in New Jersey "concocted a scheme to seize [General] Greene in the night and deliver him to the enemy. This was to be followed by a general mutiny of the Pennsylvania and Maryland troops." On 22 April the conspiracy was broken, according to Greene, when Gornell was arrested, tried, and hanged (ibid., p. 288).

52. Pines Bridge across the Croton River, N.Y., it should be remembered, was the place guarded by Greenman when he was captured 14 May 1781.

53. William Allen had served since 1775, when he was an ensign in the Second Rhode Island, had received his commission as captain in January of 1777, was later transferred to the First Rhode Island in 1781, and finally was retained in Olney's Battalion.

54. Moses Knapp's career closely parallels that of Captain Allen, for he was a ser-

geant in the Lexington Alarm of 1775, was commissioned captain in the Thirteenth Continental Infantry in January of 1776, and in 1782 belonged to the Fifth Massa chusetts.

55. Sauthier's early map shows a very large territory known at Philipsburg Patent or Mannor on the east side of the Hudson, but the town Philipsburg to which Greenman refers can be seen just east of the road which parallels the Hudson, south of Dobbs Ferry about four or five miles, on the map in Nebenzahl, *Atlas*, pp. 88–89.

56. Probably Tuckahoe in Westchester County, between White Plains and Mt. Vernon.

57. Washington had foreseen that problems might arise and had included in his orders to Major Olney the admonition to "pay particular attention to the discipline and regularity of the Regt while on the March, seeing that the Men do not straggle from the Corps, destroy fences for fuel, or commit any other outrages whatever against the persons or property of the Inhabitants" (*Writings*, 24:259).

58. Harrison township in Westchester County just east of White Plains is very possibly the area to which he applied this earlier designation.

59. Very likely he referred to North Castle, which was only about six miles south of Bedford (William Darby and Theodore Dwight, Jr., *A New Gazetteer of the United States of America* [Hartford: E. Hopkins, 1833], p. 364) and is now Mr. Kisco (Rice and Brown, eds., *Rochambeau's Army*, 2:142).

60. Samuel Darby, another veteran of long experience, had begun his service in Scammon's Massachusetts Regiment in 1775, but in 1782 he belonged to the Seventh Massachusetts.

61. Greenman seems to have been confused about which Massachusetts regiments were camped there, but he means that they proceeded to the Massachusetts camp.

62. Samuel Richardson's novel, published in 1754.

63. Col. Walter Stewart, who had been transferred to the Second Pennsylvania in July of 1778, had been named inspector for the Northern army on 11 February 1782- and was, according to Washington, "now setting off to inspect the York and Jersey Brigades" on 7 May (*Writings*, 24:230), so he must have shortly afterward directed his attention to the Rhode Island Battalion.

64. "The Intelligence from Holland is indeed very important," wrote Washington on 22 July, but with characteristic caution he added: "I wish however to be ascertained what Exertions those States will make on this Occasion" (ibid., p. 437). In Congress it served to encourage and strengthen those who felt Americans were in danger of domination by France (Edmund Cody Burnett, *The Continental Congress* [New York: Macmillan, 1941], p. 548). In fact, as Alden wrote, "as belligerents they had no strength to strike, and their ships and their colonies were exposed to attack" (*The American Revolution*, p. 192).

65. The general situation that confronted Congress was the need to maintain the army in strength while peace negotiations were being conducted, yet at the same time to reduce to whatever extent possible the financial burden of paying for the army. Part of the answer was the resolution Greenman refers to which would reduce the number of lieutenants to ten per company, a process referred to unhappily as "deranging," or as Greenman said "derageing," the lieutenants above ten. The text of this resolution dated 11 July is printed in full in the general orders of 30 July (Washington, *Writings*, 24: 445). Washington had many problems with the plan even before he received the text: "it is an irksome and disagreeable business to derange the Lieutenants," he wrote the secretary of war (ibid., p. 392).

66. The letter from Adm. Robert Digby and Sir Guy Carleton reached General Washington on the evening of 4 August, and he immediately dispatched a copy of it

to Congress for an official response. The letter did say that Grenville had been sent to Paris "invested with full powers to treat with all parties at war," and that "the independency of the thirteen Provinces should be proposed by him in the first instance, instead of making it a condition of the general treaty. . . ." (Quoted by Freeman, *Washington*, 5:420).

67. John Singer Dexter was a trusted veteran to whom promotions had come with some regularity. A lieutenant in the First Rhode Island from 3 May 1775, an adjutant the first of the next year, he was promoted to captain on 1 January 1777. He later served for a time as assistant to the adjutant-general and was promoted to major on 25 August 1781.

68. The Block House at Dobbs Ferry, as the following entry makes clear.

69. Thomas Hughes, a veteran who had served as an ensign in the Third Rhode Island in 1775, was made a 2d lieutenant with the Eleventh Continental Infantry in January 1776 and wounded during service that year on Long Island; he was promoted to captain 23 June 1777.

70. Gen. Anthony Wayne began an expedition to Georgia in January 1782. He drove the British back into Savannah, staved off an attack from their Creek allies, and kept up the pressure until on 11 July the British pulled their troops out of Savannah for Charleston (Boatner, *Encyclopedia*, p. 421).

71. Washington had written to Col. Jeremiah Olney on 29 August, telling him to provide Lieutenant Wheaton with a passport to go behind enemy lines (*Writings*, 25: 92n).

72. A German jäger, member of a specially selected corps of light infantry armed with rifles and trained to be marksmen but usually detached from their companies for "special missions as reconnaissance, headquarters security, advance guards, and to occupy the front trenches at sieges to snipe at the American defenses" (Boatner, *Encyclopedia*, p. 549).

73. Ezekiel Cornell, who had served as a lieutenant colonel in Hitchcock's Rhode Island regiment during the siege of Boston but left military service in 1780 to serve as a delegate to the Continental Congress until 1783 when he retired to his native Scituate. (*Biographical Directory of the American Congress, 1774–1971* [Washington, D.C.: U.S. Government Printing Office, 1971], p. 786).

74. Morrisania, N.Y.

75. "Lieutenant Greenman of the Rhode island regt. is appointed Adjutant to the same from the 1st of september last vice Lieutenant [John] Rodgers resigned that office" (General Orders, 2 October 1782, Washington, *Writings*, 25:226).

76. General orders of this date mention leaves and rubbish and a danger of fire (ibid., p. 247).

77. Washington observed that "the last Grand Manoevre that will be performed this Campaign surpassed every other exhibition of the kind that has been made in the American army" (ibid., p. 293).

78. As adjutant Greenman has a very accurate idea of the detailed marching instructions Washington sent them in the general orders (ibid., pp. 298–99).

79. Butter Hill is very clearly marked on the detailed map of the Highlands, northwest of West Point, in Adams, *Atlas*, p. 73.

80. Two days later Washington expressed to Lord Stirling his desire to send the Rhode Island Regiment to Saratoga "that Colo Olneys Regt. may be kept in as collected a State as circumstances will admit" (*Writings*, 25: 305). He then reassured Governor Clinton that he was providing for defense of the northern frontiers, replacing the New Hampshire Line with state troops and Olney's Regiment, which he called "a strong one" (ibid., p. 308).

81. John D. P. Ten Eyck, who had retired from service 1 January 1781.

82. Mrs. Elizabeth Peebles, Chastellux informs us, was the widow of a Dutchman who kept "a handsome inn" in the town of Half Moon, now Waterford, on the Hudson River (*Travels*, 1:221). Francisco de Miranda, who stopped with Mrs. Peebles in June of 1784 remarked that he found there "very good tea, supper etc., and a conversation with the daughter of said widow, about sixteen years old, to whom I offered to send some books from New York" (*The New Democracy in America* [Norman: University of Oklahoma Press, 1963], p. 100).

83. Benjamin L. Peckham had just been promoted to the rank of captain on 21 June 1782.

84. Probably he meant to write "brought," or as he used to write it "braut."

85. Schuylerville, N.Y., is the location of what was then called Saratoga, where they seem to have spent a good part of their time just fixing the delapidated barracks.

86. Greenman's distinguished traveling companions as he begins the trip home on furlough are his commander, Col. Jeremiah Olney, Maj. John Singer Dexter, and Dr. Samuel Tenney, a Harvard graduate of 1772 who later studied medicine and began to practice in Exeter, N.H., just before the Revolution. Upon the outbreak of hostilities Tenney joined the army as a surgeon's mate in Gridley's Massachusetts Artillery Regiment, but in 1777 joined the Second Rhode Island Regiment with which he saw a great deal of action at Red Bank, there attending the wounded Hessian Count von Donop (see Greenman's description in part 2). After the Revolution Tenney gave up medicine for politics; see the brief notice in *Appletons Cyclopaedia of American Biography*, ed. James G. Wilson and John Fiske, 6 vols. (New York: D. Appleton, ca. 1886–89), 6:63.

St. Caiak here and St. Coick in the entry of 27 December 1783 are Greenman's phonetic renditions of the name of a very small community about 12 miles west of Bennington, Vt., and perhaps 7 miles south of Cambridge, known as Sancoick's Mill, where action began in the famous battle of Bennington (Boatner, *Landmarks*, p. 229). Henry B. Carrington says this place was also known as Van Schaick's Mills (*Battles* p. 330).

These eager travelers, heading for Northampton, Mass., spent the night in the town of Pownal, in what is now the extreme southwestern corner of Vermont.

87. A strenuous day's travel through very hilly country from Pownal to Cummington, Mass. Both Stafford and Mitchell appear to be retired soldiers who have turned to tavern keeping. A search of Heitman, *Historical Register*, suggests that Mitchell may have been 2d Lt. Rotheus Mitchell, who served from 1775 to 1781, when he resigned. No Stafford of the rank of colonel from this part of the country is listed in Heitman. Closest in rank would be New York militia capt. Joab Stafford, wounded at Bennington in 1777.

New Providence in Massachusetts, mentioned here and again on 29 December 1783, is not to be found on any maps to which we have had access or in Hayward's *Gazetteer of Massachusetts*. The entry of 29 December places it almost midway between Adams and Windsor.

88. "Major Pomeroys" bore the name of the family of the prosperous gunsmith and distinguished patriot, Seth Pomeroy of Northampton. This is the first of three stops in Belchertown, Mass., for Greenman in 1783, each time at "Dwights" or "Dwits" as he later spells it (9 April and 31 December). The last entry refers to it as "Major Dwits," suggesting that the man in question is Thomas DeWitt, who resigned as a captain in the Third New York in January 1780, but "served subsequently as Major New York Levies" (Heitman, *Historical Register*, p. 196).

89. Greenman's "Westtown" was the town of Western, known by that name from its incorporation in 1742 until it was changed to Warren in 1834, to honor Joseph Warren promising patriot leader who died in the Bunker Hill battle (Hayward, *Gazetteer of Massachusetts*, p. 294).

90. Stowers was probably Lt. John Stowers of the Fifth Massachusetts, who served until April 1781; the town in which his tavern was located was Worcester. Both Grafton and Upton appear on modern maps of Massachusetts, southeast of Worcester.

91. Cumberland, R.I., lies in the extreme northeast part of Providence County in the territory northeast of the Blackstone River.

92. Rehoboth, Mass.

93. Swansea, Mass.

94. Instead of crossing the Taunton River at Slaid's Ferry, Greenman waited for a boat to take him to Rhode Island, to the place where the ferry from Bristol landed, known as Bristol Ferry.

95. A letter from Elias Boudinot, president of Congress, to General Washington on 12 March 1783 brought word that the text of the preliminary treaty of peace had arrived in Philadelphia as signed by the commissioners in Paris on 30 November (not the twentieth as Greenman thought) (Washington, *Writings*, 26:237n.). Britain proclaimed an end to hostilities on 4 February, and Congress issued a similar proclamation on 11 April. Peace negotiations are briefly summarized by Boatner, *Encyclopedia*, pp. 847–49. For a more detailed account, see Richard B. Morris, *The Peacemakers*, chaps. 14–16.

96. Greenman's return trip to Saratoga with Capt. Thomas Hughes and Lt. John M. Greene takes them west of Providence and slightly north to Gloucester, R.I. From Gloucester, they will cross a corner of Connecticut and strike out to the northwest for Northampton, Mass., from which point their journey will retrace in reverse much of the route taken in January.

97. Woodstock, Conn.

98. Williamsburg, Mass., nine miles northwest of Northampton must be the town to which reference is made here (Hayward, *Gazetteer of Massachusetts*, p. 310).

99. Cambridge, N.Y., east of the Hudson River.

100. General orders of Friday, 18 April, stated: "The Commander in Chief orders the Cessation of Hostilities between the United States of America and the King of Great Britain to be publickly proclaimed tomorrow at 12 o'clock at the Newbuilding, and that the Proclamation which will be communicated herewith, be read tomorrow evening at the head of every regiment and corps of the army," Washington, *Writings*, 26:334.

101. Half Moon, now Waterford, N.Y., named according to the traveller Francisco de Miranda, because "the river forms exactly this figure there. . . ." (*New Democracy*, p. 100.)

102. Skittles or ninepins (*O.E.D.*, s.v. "skittle").

103. Greenman copied a treatise on the mineral springs at Saratoga into his journal beginning on ms. p. 619, though his visit to the Salt Springs, as he called them, is described on p. 613 of the manuscript. Moreover, his visit only lasted an hour, so this description must have been copied at some later time, possibly in August, for each of the copied pages of description is headed by the date "August 1783." The author of this description may have been Dr. Samuel Tenney, Greenman's traveling companion of the previous January, who is said to have contributed "to the 'Memoirs' of the American academy . . . an account of the mineral waters of Saratoga. . . ." *Appletons Cyclopaedia*, 6:63.

104. "A Map of the Province of New-York . . ." engraved by William Faden and published in London in 1776 is reprinted in Nebenzahl, *Atlas*, pp. 158–59 and there shows the course of Kayadrossera Creek.

105. The order to grant furloughs originated in a resolution of the Congress conveyed to the army by Washington in the general orders of 2 June; he was instructed "to grant furloughs to the non-commissioned officers and soldiers . . . inlisted to serve during the war, who shall be discharged as soon as the definitive treaty of peace is concluded, together with a proportionable number of commissioned officers of the different grades. . . ."These men were to be conducted home in an orderly manner and "allowed to take their arms with them" (*Writings*, 26:464). In a dispatch of 4 June, Washington conveyed to Colonel Olney blank discharges "which, under the restriction of the Endorsement are only to be considered as furloughs until farther Orders . . . and the Men permitted, . . . to retire to the State immediately" (ibid., p. 468).

106. Capt. Thomas Hughes, who had accompanied Greenman on his return from furlough in April.

107. Capt. John Holden and Capt. William Humphrey, who had been a member of the expedition to Quebec and like Greenman had spent most of that winter in jail.

108. The officers mentioned here are: Capt. Daniel Dexter, Lt. John Rogers, Capt. William Allen, Capt. Zephaniah Brown, Lt. Joseph Wheaton, Lt. Benjamin Sherburne, Lt. William Pratt, and Ens. Ephraim Kirby. Each one had served more than three years.

109. It cannot be allowed to pass unnoticed that on this occasion Jeremiah Greenman was the host of the regimental celebration and apparently carried it off in the grand tradition, despite the serious depletion of their numbers since so many had marched off on terminal furloughs.

110. It is worth noting how closely linked in the consciousness of these men were Thomas Paine's *Common Sense*, which first appeared as an anonymous pamphlet during January 1776 in Philadelphia, and the Continental Congress that declared independence.

111. Greenman became confused about the dates on this page of his journal, and the dimness of this one indicates that he may have tried to rub it out. 22 July fits rather well, however, with what little we know of Washington's schedule and itinerary. Freeman says that Washington set out from headquaters at Newburgh on 18 July, planning to visit Ticonderoga and Crown Point and perhaps other posts in the north (*Washington*, 5:450). Two of Washington's letters sent during the trip were dated "Saratoga, July 26, 1783," but these were probably sent on his return from the northern posts (*Writings*, 27:27). Thus his passage northward on 22 July is plausible.

112. Baron von Steuben had been recommended to Congress by Washington in a letter of 30 June as the logical person to negotiate with Gen. Frederick Haldimand (Greenman's General Alderman) for possession of the frontier posts (Washington, *Writings*, 27:39). Washington issued orders to von Steuben for this mission on 12 July, but it is quite possible that the inspector general did not move north until the day after Washington's departure, as Greenman's journal seems to suggest.

113. Without warning Greenman skips a month in his journal, though the headings on the five preceeding pages, this, and the following page all indicate "August." However, the notice of Steuben's return is the only August incident actually reported, and it is corroborated by Steuben's report to General Washington written from Saratoga on 23 August saying that he arrived "last night" and going on to describe his rather unfruitful negotiations with the difficult Haldimand (Sparks, *Correspondence*, 4:41–43). Haldimand's explanation was that the order for the cessation of hostilities was the only formal instruction he had yet received from his government, so he was

unprepared to negotiate for withdrawal from the frontier positions (Haldimand to Washington, 11 August 1783, ibid., pp. 39–40). A convenient sketch of Haldimand's career is available in *DNB*, 8:900–901.

114. Very likely the Scott mentioned here is Maj. William Scott of New Hampshire, who retired in January 1781. The major mover of this expedition was undoubtedly William Gilliland, a native of Ireland, who served in the British army during the French and Indian War in the vicinity of Lake Champlain, becoming thoroughly acquainted with the region. After the war he engaged in a mercantile business in the city of New York, the ample profits from which he invested in lands on the west side of Lake Champlain and in Vermont. In 1765 Gilliland began to settle lands to the west of Champlain, bringing in laborers, slaves, and cattle and building saw and grist mills as well as a large manor house for himself. He also attracted settlers to Milltown, as his settlement was called, by leasing lands at low rates. During the war this "village of fifty dwellings, forty other buildings, two grist mills, two sawmills, and a 'smithery,' was burned, and the inhabitants dispersed"; he was left with debts and disputed land claims, but not it seems without hope during this tour of recovering his fortunes. The quotation and this account of his life are drawn from the article on him in the *National Cyclopaedia of American Biography*, 55 vols. and supplements (New York: J. T. White, 1922), 8:140.

115. Fort Edward is described by Chastellux, the ruins of which moved him to comment that though it had been much spoken of in Europe it was clearly unable to resist an attack of 500 men supported with 4 cannon (*Travels*, 1:215, 352).

116. The location of Halfway Brook, south of Lake George, may be seen on the map in Nebenzahl, *Atlas*, pp. 158–59, which also marks the site of Fort George. "Fort George was built about a mile S.E. of the ruins of Ft. William Henry (which Montcalm destroyed), and it was the northern link of the overland route to Fort Edward on the Hudson, a straight-line distance of 10 miles" (Boatner, *Encyclopedia*, p. 389).

117. Ticonderoga is also spelled "Tienderoga" on some old maps, such as that in Nebenzahl, *Atlas*, p. 158–59. Perhaps that was what Greenman was aiming at.

118. The narrows at the northern end of Lake George where they went ashore to carry over to the creek flowing into Lake Champlain are shown in some detail with most of the prominent features of these lakes in maps from *The American Military Pocket Atlas* (London, 1776) reprinted in Nebenzahl, *Atlas*, pp. 62–63.

119. Basin Harbor on the east side of Lake Champlain at the narrows above Crown Point. Returning from a visit there on 2 February 1796, William Gilliland was to become lost and freeze to death (*National Cyclopaedia of American Biography*, 18:141).

120. The town as well as the creek were named after Gilliland, who gave the names of several members of his family to towns in the region (ibid., p. 140). The side of the mills marks the area of his settlement on the map in Nebenzahl, *Atlas*, pp. 62–63, and modern maps show what is now Willsboro.

121. Gilliland valued this land at one guinea per acre; a guinea gold-piece was equal to twenty-one shillings, which at exchange rates prevailing in this general period would range in value from a high of about $4.66 in New England to a low of roughly $2.62 in New York (Boatner, *Encyclopedia*, p. 714).

122. The Salmon River appears on modern maps; it flows into Lake Champlain from the west opposite Valcour Island.

123. Schuyler's Island, just off the west shore of Lake Champlain, is clearly labeled on the map in Nebenzahl, *Atlas*, pp. 62–63.

124. Valcour Island. A bay on the west side of the island afforded a good anchorage for Arnold's fleet, and to that place he drew the British ships in the beginning of his brilliant defensive action in October 1776 to stave off a British advance into the Hud-

son valley, probably nowhere better described than by Kenneth Roberts in his novel *Rabble in Arms* (1939), chaps. 36–40. But no consideration of the valor of his former commander softens Greenman's feelings toward "the infamous *Arnold*." The underlining is Greenman's.

125. Ligonier Bay on the west shore of the lake, southwest of Four Winds Islands, is shown on the old map in Nebenzahl, *Atlas*, pp. 62–63. The bay appears to have been a short distance from the mouth of a creek which drained some of the land Gilliland had cleared in the vicinity of his mills.

126. Point Pleasant is not identified on the map in Nebenzahl, but judging from the fact that they are beginning their return south, one must assume that the Point was on the western shore, three miles south of the mouth of what they call Gilliland's Creek. That would just about bring them to Cloven Rock at the north end of the Narrows in Lake Champlain. This seems likely since, according to the next entry, from this Point they row across the lake without attempting to raise a sail.

127. If we are correct in identifying Point Pleasant in the last note with the point that reaches out into the lake from the west at the north end of the Narrows, what they called Hill's Bay or Birch Bay would be one of the several bays on the eastern shore opposite Cloven Rock.

128. Hospital Point is on the eastern shore of Lake Champlain and just above Chimney Point, which stands opposite Crown Point on the west side. These details may be found on a large scale map of the period, "Plan. Lake Champlain from Fort St. John's to Ticonderoga with the Soundings Rocks Shoals and Sands Surveyed in the Years 1778, 1779," photostat in the Newberry Library of an original in the Library of Congress.

129. What Greenman calls Long Point may be one of the two rather prominent points on the eastern shore of Lake George, though Sabbath Day Point is a clearly marked feature of the western shore on the map in Nebenzahl, *Atlas*, pp. 62–63. The battle mentioned was an incident of the French and Indian War in which Robert Rogers, Massachusetts frontiersman, a step ahead of prosecution on charges of counterfeiting, made a reputation for himself as a leader of independent ranger companies in 1756. Rogers served with Sir Robert Abercromby at Ticonderoga in 1758 and the following year with Maj. Gen. Jeffery Amherst at Crown Point. By the Revolution, Rogers was deeply in debt and under suspicion as a spy in 1776, but escaped while under investigation and served for a time as leader of the Queen's American Rangers (Boatner, *Encyclopedia*, pp. 945–46).

130. This was a fleet of British transports that had gone to Nova Scotia, the return of which British commander Sir Guy Carleton awaited so that he could fix the date of his departure from New York City (Washington to Maj. Gen. Henry Knox, 2 November 1783, *Writings*, 27:222).

131. Whatever the charges against Lt. Joseph Wheaton, which do not appear to have survived, they do not seem to have impaired confidence in him, for in December (entry of 7 to 24) he was dispatched to headquarters with the muster master to obtain shoes and clothing. Such duty in supplying the army must have been congenial to him, for in 1813 he was appointed asst. deputy quartermaster-general of the U.S. Army with the rank of captain (Heitman, *Historical Register*, p. 583).

132. Greenman is not far off here, although the earliest date for evacuation from New York City named by Sir Guy Carleton appears to have been 22 November, which he proposed in a letter of 12 November to General Washington (Washington, *Writings*, 27:243). But the withdrawal did not take place until 25 November (ibid., p. 255).

133. The so-called definitive peace treaty, signed at Paris on 3 September 1783, was brought to the United States by John Thaxter, private secretary to John Adams, who

arrived in Philadelphia on 22 November 1783 and delivered the treaty to the newly elected president of the Continental Congress, Thomas Mifflin of Pennsylvania. (Burnet, *Continental Congress*, p. 590.) The arrival of the definitive treaty was the event which proved conclusively that the obligations of the soldiers who had been given furloughs in June were at an end.

134. Perhaps not all the trouble was at Albany, since Washington complained on 2 November that "all my public and private letters written in the Six Weeks preceeding, were lost with the Mail on thursday Night last" (*Writings*, 27:220).

135. Lost somewhere between Williamstown and Adams, Mass., Greenman was trying to cross the Hoosic River.

136. Probably Greenman means Worthington, which is seventeen miles west and somewhat north of Northampton "on the old stageroad from Northampton to Pittsfield," according to Hayward (*Gazetteer of Massachusetts*, p. 318).

137. Warren; see note for 5 January 1783.

138. Brookfield.

139. Now Attleboro.

140. So violent was this "freshet" that it won a place in the work of William R. Staples, one of the chroniclers of Providence: "In the beginning of January 1784, the streets and bridges sustained great damage by a sudden freshet in Moshassuck river. The rain fell in torrents on Monday and Tuesday, the fifth and sixth days of January. The weather being at the same time quite warm, the snow and ice were melted, so that the stream of the Moshassuck was higher than it ever had been within the knowledge of any of the oldest inhabitants. The mill dam of the old grist mill, which stood near where the lowest stone lock of the Blackstone Canal now is, remained undisturbed; by which means, the water overflowed the west bank of the stream, just above the dam, cutting itself out a new channel, carrying away the bridge and eight buildings in the vicinity" (*Annals of the Town of Providence, From Its First Settlement to the Organization of the City Government, in June, 1832* [Providence; Rhode Island Historical Society Collections, vol. 5, 1843], pp. 349–50).

141. Joseph Masury, formerly 2d lieutenant in the Second Rhode Island Regiment and a member of Olney's Rhode Island Battalion from its formation in May 1781 until 3 November 1783. For what is known of their business venture together see the biographical essay at the beginning of this volume.

142. His mother, Amy Wiles Greenman, had been living in Swansea probably since the death of Jeremiah senior in 1781, while they were living at Acoaxet in Dartmouth, Mass.

143. Barzillai Richmond had been a zealous supporter of an awakened Christianity in 1743 and a founding member of Beneficent Church in Providence, where he was the second deacon elected (10 February 1745). Richmond was a hatter with land interests in the vicinity of the meetinghouse where Greenman eventually acquired property of his own. See the introductory biographical essay; material on Richmond has been gleaned from Arthur Wilson's *Weybosset Bridge*, pp. 76, 120, 150, 174, 256.

144. The journal ends in the middle of a sentence because at the time Greenman made his last entry he was still in "the Nautical line of business," and years later he allowed that suspension to stand. His career at sea is described as fully as sources will allow in the opening biographical essay.

TABLES OF THE MARCH TO QUEBEC

The following four tables were drawn by Jeremiah Greenman in an attempt to tabulate distances and numbers of portages encountered along the Kennebec, the Dead, and the Chaudière rivers on the expedition to Quebec. With the exception of a table omitted because it largely duplicates the first in this series, the tables are reproduced here as he drew and inserted them between the entries for 3 and 4 November 1775. The second table below appears in the journal without explanatory captions in a position that suggests it might record the portages and ponds along the Great Carrying Place, but it may refer instead to carrying places along the chain of ponds on the upper Dead River, which led to what Justin Smith called the Boundary Portage (Smith, *Arnold's March*, chap. 11). Ditto marks in the tables correspond to Greenman's indication of a blank entry.

Table 1

The Carring plases on Cannabeck River from fort Hallifax to ye Great Carring place.

	Caring	milds	Rods
hallifax fals	1	〃	110
Cowhigens	1	〃	100
Norigewalk	1	1¼	〃
tintucket	1	〃	86
hole Number	4	2	56

[For identification of places mentioned in this table see the notes to Greenman's entries for the period from 29 September to 10 October 1775.]

TABLE 2

Carring placs	Nom milds	Nom. Rods	Nom Ponds	Nom. Milds
1	4	40	1	½
2	1	"	2	1
3	½	"	"	"
4	3¾	"	3	2
Total	9¼	40	Total	3½

TABLE 3

The No. of Carring places on the dead River with the ponds Leading into Shedore [Chaudière] River, in the province of Cannada.

Carring places	No. Milds	No. Rods	No. Ponds	No. Milds	Total rod M	1	60
1	"	5	"	"			
2	"	10	"	"			
3	"	40	"	"			
4	"	60	"	"	Carring	Milds	Rods
5	½	"	"	"	1	½	
6	"	20	1	3	2		60
7	"	30	2	1	3	½	
8	"	3	3	¾			
9	"	30	4	7			
10	"	4	5	2			
11	¾	"	6	1			
12		8	7	13			
13	¾	"					
14	1	"					
15	4¾	"					
Total	8¾	30	Total	27¾			

Number of Carring places on the dead River & No. Milds and Rods.

TABLE 4

The Number of all the Carring places and pond on Cannabeck River to the dead River & Shedore with the Whole Number of milds and Rods.

Carringplaces	Carring places	Nom Milds	No Rods	No Ponds	No Milds
on Cannebeck River	4	2	56	″	″
to the dead River	4	9¼	40	3	3½
on the dead River	15	8¾	30	7	27¾
on Shedore	3	1	60	–	–
Whole Number	26	21½	26	[?]	31¼
		31¼			
pond Included		52¾			

PENSION DECLARATIONS, LETTERS, AND WILL

1. Original Declaration of Jeremiah Greenman for his Pension Application to the War Department (from the National Archives).

State of Ohio
Washington County
On this sixteenth day of April 1818 before me the subscriber one of the associate Judges of the Court of common Pleas within and for the County of Washington personally appeared Jeremiah Greenman a resident in said County who being by me first duly sworn according to Law doth on his oath make the following declaration in order to obtain the provision made by the late act of Congress entitled "An act to provide for certain persons engaged in the land and naval service of the United States in the revolutionary war:" That he the said Jeremiah Greenman entered the service about the 20th of May 1775 Joined the troops then before Boston and on the 13th of September following joined the troops Commanded by Colonel Arnold in Captain Samuel Wards Company / proceeded with said detachment through the wilderness to Quebec and that on the 31st of December following was made a prisoner of war at the storming of said City under the command of General Montgomery and remained a prisoner nine months after which he on the 23rd day of February 1777 entered again into the service of his Country as a serjeant in Captain Sylvanus Shaws Company, who was killed at the assault of the Hessians at the Red Banks on the Delaware after which he was raised to the rank of Serjeant Major in Colonel Angells Regiment and on the 1st of May 1779 was promoted to the rank of Ensign and on the 14th of May 1781 in the Rhode Island Regiment

commanded by Lieutenant Colonel Olney was promoted to the rank of Lieutenant and was on that day made prisoner of war at the Massacre of Colonel Green and Major Flagg, After being exchanged joined his Regiment at Philadelphia and continued with said regiment until they were discharged at Saratoga on Furlough which was to operate as final discharge on the ratification of the definative treaty, but was retained with the men enlisted for three years being previously appointed by the commander in chief as Adjutant, Here he taried making out returns regularly of the Rigiment permitted to return to their respective homes on furlough as above stated until the 25th of December 1783 all of which services were on the Continental establishment and that he is at the advanced age of 61 Years the 7th day of May ensuing and from his reduced circumstances he stands in need of the assistance of his country for support —Sworn to and declared before me the day and year aforesaid /
Ezekiel Deming

I Ezekiel Deming Associate Judge &c as aforesaid do certify, that it appears to my satisfaction that the said Jeremiah Greenman did serve in the revolutionary war as stated in the preceding declaration against the common enemy for the term of nine months as a Commissioned Officer on the continental establishment—and from the testimony taken and had before me am fully convinced that he is in reduced circumstances and Stands in need of the assistance of his Country for support; and I now transmit the proceedings and testimony taken and had before me to the Secretary for the department of War pursuant to the directions of the aforementioned act of Congress Ezekiel Deming

Wooster [*township*] March 16th 1819

2. Second Declaration of Jeremiah Greenman for his Pension (*The National Archives*).

The State of Ohio
Washington County

On this 24th day of July 1820 Personally appeared in open court being a court of record for the said county Jeremiah Greenman aged Sixty two years 7th May last past resident in said Washington County who being duly sworn according to law doth on his oath declare that he served in the revolutionary war from the 20th May 1775 untill the 25th December 1783 being eight years & seven months in different grades as specified in his Original Declaration in the Rhode Island line commanded successively by Colonells Church, Angell, Green & Olney, and that the date of his Original Declaration was on the 18th April 1818, before Judge Demmons [Deming] One of the Associate Judges of the County of Washington & was certified before said Judge under Oath of one of the Trustees and one of the over seers of the poor for the township of Waterford, State & County afforsaid that he was incapable of supporting himself by labour & that his property was insufficient without the assistance of publick or private aid / And that the number of his certificate signed by the Secretary of War is 9398, And that I do solemnly swear that I was a resident Citizen of the United States on the 18th March 1818, And that I have not since that time by gift sale or in any manner disposed of my Property or any Part thereof with intent thereby so to Diminish it as to bring myself within the provision of an act of congress entitled an act to provide for certain persons engaged in the land and Naval Service of the United States in the Revolutionary War passed the 18th March 1818, that I have not nor has any person in trust for me any property, securities, contracts or debts due to me nor have I any income other than what is contained in the schedule hereunto annexed and by me subscribed— And that my Private and Personal Estate is as follows (Viz) / An upland hilly farm containing one hundred acres with a log cabin & a log barn on the premises, Two horses one of 21 years of age & the other of 24, two cows & one this springs calf, twenty three sheep, One old waggon with the gear for two horses, fourteen years in constant despair [*sic*] One old plow, One Iron tooth harrow, one sand

Shovel, one hoe, one cythe one axe with several articles generally used on a farm [*illeg.*] / My house hold furniture consists of one three feet poplar Table, one Bureau one light stand a portable writing desk, four common chairs, one pair of fire dogs, one pr of tongs & shovell, one looking glass 14 by 20 Inches one Monumental engraving of the memory of Washington 12 by 14 Inches, Six Silver Table spoons, six ditto of Teaspoons 3 old case Knives & forks, Ten volumes of old books and Pamphlets on different subjects, two pewter platters, Six pewter plates, twelve earthen Ditto, two earthen Teapots, one sugar bowl & creampot five china cups & saucers, four Liverpool Ditto, one castor containing four glass pieces, five wine glasses, one earthen pitcher Two Iron Kittels 10 Gals each, one dinner pot, one Cake Oven without a cover one frying pan One Small Skillet One small spider, an old tin bake oven & several other articles too trifling to mention / And [*illeg.*] about Sixty Dollars—

As to my Occupation I have none that I can follow with that prospect which many others can do even if my health would admit of it, altho I have been endeavoring for fourteen years past to till a small portion of the land which I fought for and three different times bled to regain from Brittish Tyrants, having Devoted my youthful days to the service of my country I was deprived of the opportunity, which young men generally possess of acquiring any mechanical art or perfecting my self in any proffession, And where it not for the leasure hours I spent while in the army in the Study of Navigation under the pupilage of Major Genl. Schuyler, at the close of the War I should [*have*] been plunged on the world destitute of employment or been Obliged to have resorted to some business ill becoming a person who for more than eight years had [*merited ?*] the attention and approbation of the best men of his country, After leaving the Army I followed the seas as a Nautical Commander till drove by necessity to the Wilds of Ohio / That I am unable to labour Occasioned by a wound received whilst in publick service in my left side & the small of my back which wound for more than seven year past hath rendered me incapable of doing but trifling manuel business and that it is noted in my former Declaration why I did not make application to be placed on the pention list at the close of the War agrecable to the acts of congress for those wounded and debilitated in the Revolutionary War, and that my wife is in the sixty first year of her age & very much debilitated and that this constitutes the whole of my family, the other branches being three sons and one Daughter being married & large families cannot contribute towards my support without embarrassing themselves and that I have not one Solutary friend or acquaintance, that knows or ever heard of me, except such that has been made prior my migration to this country—

Jeremiah Greenman

Sworn to and Declared on this 24th day of July 1820
before the Court of Common Pleas of Washington County in session

Attest Geo. Dunlevy Clerk

The court doth certify that the declarents Statement as to his wounds, the state of his health and [condition ?] are correct and true

Attest Geo. Dunlevy Clerk

I George Dunlevy Clerk of the Court of Common Pleas within and for the County of Washington in the State of Ohio do hereby certify that the foregoing oath and the Schedule thereto annexed are truly copied from the record of said Court / And I do further certify that it is the Opinion of the said Court that the Total Amount in Value of the property Exhibited in the aforesaid Schedule is two hundred ninety four dollars and twenty eight Cents—

In testimony whereof I have hereunto set my hand and affixed the seal of said Court on this second day of August Anno Domini one thousand eight hundred and twenty.

Geo. Dunlevy, Clerk of the Court of Common Pleas of
the County of Washington Ohio

3. Supplementary Declaration of Jeremiah Greenman, a letter of 14 October 1820 to John C. Calhoun, secretary of war. Underlinings are those of the original. The endorsement added as a postscript by Levi Barber, former Congressman from Marietta, contains the earliest independent reference to Greenman's "voluminous Journal."

Marietta 14th October 1820
Honoured Sir—

At the July term of the Court of Common pleas for the County of Washington State of Ohio, I together with a number of other persons made declarations before said Court in order to obtain pensions as Revolutionary officers & soldiers, under the Act of Congress of March 18th 1818. & the Act amendatory thereto in May. 1820. A number of the Applicants have received their certificates of the continuanc of their pensions, but heard nothing from mine altho forwarded at the same time. On application to Mr. Dunlevy the clerk he informs me a Copy of my declaration was forwar[*d*]ed with the Others, with diffidence I suppose that Eight years & Siven Months service together with three wounds received whilst in that service, & one of them rendering me incapiable of <u>hard</u> labour, that it would have some weight in the decision and further when I made my scheduel, I was not advised that it would be proper to state the amount of my debts, but at the Moment I was about to hand it to the court a friend suggested it & I interlined one debt 60$ (which was on demand) while in fact I owed at that time, one handred & fifty Six dollars & 100/58 which I am now called on for, and agreable to the rule adopted by the court allowing the applicants to introduce their debts it would have reduced my scheduel to Twenty seven dollars & 100/70 / I hope a desissive, determination has not been made in my Case & that upon a strict investigation of my <u>two</u> declarations I trust my pension will be continued, which in my Old age and inabilities to persue my occupation as a farmer, will afford me some degree of support, without thowing myself on the charrity of my Children, which has been the case for five years before I received the bounty of my Country, & that my Sons have large famelies themselves & are not in affluant Circumstancs / at any rate some have had their pensions continued who are in better bodyly health & circumstancs to git a liveing than myself, with due submition I leave the result with your honor and am Sir your Obedient & humble Servant—

Jeremiah Greenman

Honou[*r*]able J. C. Calhoun
Secratery at War—

Marietta Oct. 14. 1820

Sir

I have been many years acquainted with Capt. Greenman; as a man of character and integrity he ranks with the first in this County—

From having perused a very voluminous Journal which he kept during the War I have no doubt of the correctness of his Whole Statement, nor have any doubt but he ought to be continued on the principle which has governed in deciding on others from this County.

Respectfully your Obdt. Servt.
L Barber

Hon. J. C. Calhoun

4. Greenman's Final Appeal, 20 September 1821. This was a letter to an unnamed representative or magistrate, probably Levi Barber, whose testimony to Greenman's character and service is appended to the preceding document. The erasure of the name of one of Greenman's neighbors mentioned in this letter was probably the work of the recipient, who in forwarding this letter to Washington may have wished to avoid opening a case against this man while allowing Greenman's moral outrage full expression. Underlining follows the original in the pension records at The National Archives, Washington, D.C.

Waterford 21th Septr. 1821

Dear Sir— On receipt of the desision of the secratery at War on my declaration, from the pension Office dated the 26th July 1821, and transmited by you, I can say that dureing 8 years & 7. month service in the Revolutionary War & some parts of that time before the enemy of my Country, that dureing that period of time that I never felt my heart recoil or my Spirit more dejected, than on reading the Secrateries oppinion on my schuidel [schedule] or property. My hopes & prospects to a future residence on this Terestiacal Globe, it seams are to be filled up with mortification of spirit & attended with hard labour what few remaining yea[*r*]s I am permited to tarry on it, being prosc[*r*]ibed by the Laws of that Country I had faithfully served 8 years & I might Justly say 12, haveing served it four Years since ye Revolutionry War, under a Commision from Genl. Washing[*ton*], which commison I now have. Three different times has my blood been spilt to help gain her Independance, five Month laying in Irons out of Sixteen a prisoner of War, led a forlorn hope at the Assault on Quebeck, since which time in 10 different Actions, often selected for Extra se[*r*]vice which I preformed, & gave sattisfaction, more than once to the Commander in Chief / And as 'tis allowed for old men to talk about their former exploits I hope you will excuse my Vanity if so it may be called, for robing you of time, you might better be imployed in service of your Country in the high station you now fill. But to return, is it possible that on mature deliberation the Secratery of War will posist in ordering my name to continue struck from the pension list & retain others whose service was of so short a duration, and some of which to my Own Knowledge reced [received] large bounties, on their short term of Inlistments, & ammounted to more money in hand than a Continental solder ever received for three Years or dureing the War, & never saw the enemy dureing their time of Service & many of them in bodyly health & their property far superior to mine but they have sworn! And I am very sensible his honor the Secratery of War cannot deside on any other criterion but the applicants Oath certifyed by order of Court—

Amongst many I could mention, I will take notice of Mr. [*illeg.*], whose farm joins on the one I returned & is called superior to the one I reside on, his service also was of short duration, but long enough to come under the period of time allowed of by Law to intitle him to a pension, but he hath frequently told Me that, he was tired of the Service & that he had hired a substitute, & for all I know both receive the bounty of their Country, & the ammount of the foot of my schaduel was only $3 dollars more than Mr. [*illeg.*] allowing my debts to be reducted, which where [were] not half put in, not knowing that the applicants debts was to be inserted, the Court to their honor after my Declaration had been delivered to the Clerk allowed me to interline $60. which is all that I could recolect when before the Court, but on my return home, calling to mind all my debts I found that I owed $156 & sum od[*d*] cents, which is impossible for me to pay without selling every thing I possess. As you was present you must recolect the laugh it made in Court when my old horses where to be aprised, that the Judges Unanimously said Nothing, but on my observeing they where like their Master worn out in Service but was Yet worth something, the Court then ordered $20 to be put down. More peticularly had I sworn I had no real Estate, which was actually the case, only the writings had never been recorded / of course in law it was mine, but I had gave it to my eldest Son in the Year of 1815, he finding that he could not support himself & family & provide for me, transfered it to my Youngest, who now Occupies it & indevours to support me, which is also out of his power, is it possible that a Magnimanious Country will take advantage of such Circumstances & Keep one of their Old Invalids in almost Actual want of ye necessaries of life, 'tis mortifying beyond description to see & hear of numbers continued on ye pension list, some of which where deserters, retaken & made to serve out their time after receiving the sentance of a court martial. But Sir, I must be silent or draw on my head vengance from many, I cannot dupe to be a Government's informer, 'tis said misery love company, but a genarous heart will not let his neighbours ship split on the rock that Wrecked him. More especially when it will be of no advantage— I am not unawares that there is many that fealt themselves as much disapointed in not being placed on the pension list as myself / my final settelments shared the fate with thousands of others & my Claim on Government is no better on that principle, But Sir with due diffidence, will not actual Service for a series of Years, & my wounds, and an Alarming rupture, together with my reduced Circumstancs, and my never being placed on the Invalid pension list which there is no doubt in my mind but that I might have been 37. Years ago had not my patriotism keept me from imbraceing the laws of Congress passed for wounded & debilitated Officers & solders of ye Revolotinary War, I was at that time master of as good a ship, as sailed from our ports litle dreaming night would overtake me in the Wilderness of Ohio, had I obtained a pension Certificate at ye above mention'd time I should have drawn from my Countrey $5772, The Original Certificate gave me by Colo. Olney in July 1784, is forever lost being destroyed amongst old bills of lading, Invoices, Sea letters, &c., &c., which where burned on my migration to this Country, but there is still liveing a female of a reputable famely from Morristown, New Jersey, who now resides in this County, who told me that 7 Years ago that she very well remembered when I lay wounded at a private house Near Morristown / This I expect is all the proof that can now be obtained, except my Oath will be admitted. On my first declaration, I was obliged to carry forward before Judge Demmings [Ezekiel Deming], One of the Trustees of the Town & one of the Overseers of the poor, who on solem Oath declared that I was incabeable [incapable] of Maintaining myself & that my property was insufficient, This was a Mortifying circumstance, on reflecting on my Cituation a few years ago / this I was obliged to comply with or not obtain my Certificate, You are very sensible, that men in general do not want their poverty Known, I declare to you in confidence that since the stoping of my pension that one solletary pound of Tea hath not entered my Cabbin & many other Articles of the necessaries of life which was the case long before the 18th March, You Sir know me & have for this 15 years past, & I have the Vanity to believe that you know that I am too much of a Patriot to call for assistance from my Country was I as heretofore able to labour / All the circumstances that I have aluded to are stricktly true & [*I*] hope Sir with your friendly assistance on a reveiw of my former declaration & distresing circumstance, that the Secratery of War will condesend to replace my name on the pension list & think my claims Just, when one payment of six months puts those retained, in better Circumstances, than I ever can arrive to—My Declarations I suppose are on file in the pension office there / it may be seen that every article I possesed is enumerated, many of which is but trifeling, but under a solem oath I could not in conscience admit, of not entering them, There is many more circumstance I could insert which in my humble oppinion puts me on a par with many that have been continued on the pension list & receives the bounty of their Country & hope that if I ever merited any gratitude from my Country it will not be with held from me in this my last stage of life, being neither Mechanick or farmer my Cituation is truly distressing—

I cannot stop my pen when I reflect on a number of circumstances that took place dureing an 8 years War, that I could insert / I will pen you one more altho it doth not come under the acts of Congress for granting of pensions, Yet Sir it will shew You that I was a patriot from the begining of the War & was not to be moved from the cause, that I had volunteryly imbarked in—When I was made a prisoner at the Assault on Quebeck, Capt. James Frost formely an intimate with my Farther came into prison with a Number of Brittish officers, he then commanding a Ship in the Brittish Service finding me amongst the prisoners, called me out of prison & made me a present of mony & solicited me to sign the Kings pardon, & that he would have me entered as a Midshipman on board his Ship & put me immeadeately under pay / this I refused telling him I had entered the Cause of my Country & ment to continue in it untill our rights was declar'd, this made some laughter amongst the Officers present some of which said I now had an oppertunity to be made a man of &c. &c— I then was 17 Years Old, howsomever he continued sending me whilst a prisoner, Small Stores & Cloathing, & when I [*e*]mbarked for New York he supplyed [*me*] with small stores sufficient for my pasage.

I mearly insert the above to shew you that amongst many Circumstances that I might pen, that a little merrit where 'tis due might mitigate the Mistaken notion of my being rich because I formely wore desent Cloathing, and put me one that is now almost a beger equal to some of our old patriots

Excuse my lengthry rhapsody. You Sir know my Circumstances & also know my inability to compose a subject fit to go before the Secratery of War—

I am Sir with respect yours &c.

Jere Greenman

5. Jeremiah Greenman's Will, 6 February 1821, transcribed from a copy contained in the Probate Court Records of Washington County, the Court House, Marietta, Ohio. Greenman's authorship of much of the original is suggested by the fairly typical vagaries of spelling and punctuation reproduced by a diligent copyist.

In the name of God Amen. I Jeremiah Greenman of Waterford, County of Washington and the State of Ohio Knowing and considering the uncertainty of this mortal life, and being of sound & perfect memory of mind & in full health and strength according to my years of this transitory life already alloted me by Almighty God & blessed be his name, for continuing me so long a moniment of his goodness. Do make this my last Will and testimony, in manner & form following, (that is to say,[)] First I give and bequeath unto my beloved wife Mary Greenman all my real Estate laying & cituated in the Township of Waterford & State of Ohio, & County aforesd. during her life for her maintainance [*while* ?] she remains my widow under the cultivation of my son Jeremiah Greenman or his heirs or assigns solely for the above mentioned purposes for her maintainance, during life after which it is my will desire & order that my messuage or teniments with all my freehold Estate laying and cituated as above mentioned, I give and devise to my youngest son Jeremiah Greenman his heirs or assigns forever / I also give and bequeath unto my second son Esek Eddy Greenman fifty dollars, to be paid him by my son Jeremiah in stock or mony which may be most convenient in six month after my deceas [when ?] demanded. I also give and bequeath unto my eldest son John Greenman Twenty five dollars to be paid in stock or produce in six months after my deceas. I give & bequeath unto my daughter Mary Dunham twelve dollars, having at her marrage gave her what I could afford, which sum of twelve dollars [is ?] also to be paid her by my son Jeremiah in three months after my deceas. [I] will and order that the above mentioned legases be paid to the said respective legatees agreeable to the above mentioned times & I hereby order & will that my son Jeremiah, pay all my funeral charges & all just debts that I may ow[*e*] at my deceas, and lastly, as to all my residue & remainder of my personal Estate goods & chattels of what kind & nature soever, I give and bequeath the same to my beloved wife Mary Greenman, to her only use during life or whilst she remains my widow, & it is my will & order at her deceas if any personal property be left or remaining in her possession that it shall be equally divided amongst my three children, (their heirs or assigns) viz., Mary Dunham, John Greenman & Jeremiah Greenman leaving to my wife the manner [*and* ?] form she may see fit to make the distribution, and 'tis my farther will that the produce of grain of all kinds that may be in the ground or harvested is not to be considered as my personal property or any part thereof at the deceas of my wife, but the sole property of my son Jeremiah, and I Do hereby appoint my wife Mary Greenman my sole Executrix of this my last will & Testiment, hereby revoking all former Wills by me made. In witness whereof, I the w[*r*]iter of this instrument have hereunto set my hand & seal this six day of February in the year of our Lord one thousand Eight hundred & twenty one.

Jeremiah Greenman

Signed, sealed, published and declared by the above named Jeremiah Greenman to be his last Will & testiment in the presence of Us, who have hereunto subscribed our names as Witnesses in the presence of the Testator.

Cyrus Eddy
John Vincent

The State of Ohio Washington County: Personally appeared before me Ami Lawrence one of the acting Justices of the peace in said county the above signer Jeremiah Greenman & of his own free will & accord acknowled[*ged*] the same to be his last will & testment before me.

Ami Lawrence, Justice of Peace.

OBITUARY FOR JEREMIAH GREENMAN

The obituary for Jeremiah Greenman was published 29 November 1828 in the *American Friend & Marietta Gazette* (13, no. 10) and is preserved in the special collections of Marietta College Library, Marietta, Ohio. In striking contrast to the usually brief death notices appearing in the *American Friend* of this period, Greenman's obituary is a rather lengthy eulogy. Perhaps local interest and filial duty played a part in this departure from form, although its wide departure from several of the substantiated facts of Greenman's life and service recounted in the introductory essay to this volume creates doubt that its author was a member of the family, unless the children had not quite got it straight as to whether their father had been imprisoned on the notorious Jersey prison ship, or even at what age he had for the first time marched off to fight. On 1 May 1779 he was commissioned an ensign at age twenty, not nineteen. But those are stories that might have been improved upon in retelling, and probably his children were not very avid readers of his journal. Most astonishing of all, however, is the assertion that Greenman was "an orphan boy," for it is mentioned in the journal that his father died in 1781 and that his mother was living as late as April 1784 when he moved her to Providence, not long before his marriage to Mary Eddy. Thus there remains the possibility that the obituary may have come from the pen of a friend outside the family circle. The obituary is generally more accurate in dealing with that part of his life that would have been known best by his children, from the time when he turned his back on the sea and headed west.

Another Revolutionary Patriot descended to the tomb!

Soon—*very soon*, will all Columbia's sons who assisted in laying the foundation of her present prosperity and happiness, be numbered with the dead!

DIED, at his residence in Waterford, on the evening of the 15th instant, after thirty hours severe indisposition of a billious colic, Capt. JEREMIAH GREENMAN, in the 71st year of his age.

Capt. Greenman was a native of the State of Rhode Island; he entered the revolutionary army at the commencement of the contest, at the age of sixteen, and was attached to a regiment commanded by the late Jeremiah Olney, of Providence. He continued in it until the close of the war, and until the definitive treaty of peace was ratified. Promotions in the Rhode Island Line, by some reason, unknown to the writer, were very slow. Some who entered the service at the commencement of the war, as captains, left it at the close in the same capacity. But we find by the journal of Capt. Greenman, (which he kept during that time,) that at the age of nineteen he received an Ensign's commission—at the age of twenty-two a Lieutenant's and before the close of the war he acted as Adjutant of the Regiment. Merit alone must have been his passport to promotion, as he was an *orphan boy*, and had no influential connexions. He was in most of the conspicuous battles that were fought. The walls of Quebec, the Plains of Monmouth and Germantown, Red Bank and Fort Mifflin were scenes of his youthful valor. More than once he met the enemy at the point of the bayonet—and more than once he received the personal commendation of the Commander-in-Chief—the immortal WASHINGTON. He received three wounds while in public service—one in his side, which afflicted him during life. He was twice a prisoner: Once in the loathsome prison of Quebec, and once in the pestilential Jersey Ship.—Soon after the close of the war, he received a Commission as Lieutenant on board one of the Revenue Cutters, which were employed by government in protecting the revenue and preventing smuggling. But this employ was too sedentary for his active mind. He soon left it and took command of a ship, in the mercantile employ until our commerce was much depressed by the aggressions of foreign nations, and his small, hard earned property nearly exhausted, when he abandoned the ocean and removed to the State of Ohio. He arrived at Marietta in October, 1806, and soon after purchased a small farm in Waterford, where he resided until his death. He was twice elected a Justice of the Peace by his fellow townsmen. The law of Congress of 1818, for the relief of the Officers and Soldiers of the Revolution extended to him; and he received a pension as an officer during the remainder of his life, with thankfulness and gratitude. Capt. Greenman, as *an Officer of the Revolution*, met with the highest approbation. As a *nautical commander*, he always enjoyed the fullest confidence of his employers. As a *Magistrate*, "he was without fear, and without reproach." As a *Patriot*, he was a warm supporter of that Constitution and government, which he had fought, bled, and labored eight years assisting to establish. So fully persuaded was he of the wisdom of the measures of the present Administration, that he appeared at the polls at the last election and supported the re-election of Mr. Adams with the ardor of younger days—endeavoring to convince the ignorant and confirm the wavering. As a *man*, he was rigidly honest and punctual in all his dealings. As a *husband* and *father*, he was kind, tender, and affectionate. An aged widow, two sons and one daughter are left to mourn a loss which is irreparable.—His funeral was attended on the 17th instant —when, after an appropriate discourse by the Rev. Mr. Pitkin, his remains were attended "to the house appointed for all the living" by mourning relatives, a large concourse of citizens, and the Members of Mount Moriah Lodge, of which fraternity the deceased had been a worthy member of nearly fifty years.

BIBLIOGRAPHY

Reference Works, Atlases, Gazetteers, Maps, Bibliographies

Adams, James Truslow, ed. *Atlas of American History.* New York: Scribner, 1943.

Arnold, James. *The Vital Record of Rhode Island, 1636–1850.* 1st series. 21 vols. Providence, R.I.: Narragansett Historical Publishing Co., 1891–1912.

Boatner, Mark Mayo. *Encyclopedia of the American Revolution.* Bicentennial ed. New York: D. McKay, 1974.

———. *Landmarks of the American Revolution.* Harrisburg, Pa.: Stackpole Books, 1973.

Capen, Lester, ed. *Atlas of Early American History.* Princeton: Princeton University Press, 1976.

A Census . . . of Rhode Island and Providence Plantations . . . Taken in the year 1774. 1858. Reprint. Baltimore: Genealogical Publishing Co., 1969.

Chace, Henry R., comp. *Maps of Providence, R.I., 1650–1765–1770.* Providence, R.I.: N. E. Osterberg, 1914.

———. *Owners and Occupants of the Lots, Houses and Shops in the Town of Providence, Rhode Island in 1798.* Providence, R.I.: Livermore and Knight, 1914.

Colles, Christopher. *A Survey of the Roads of the United States of America, 1789.* Edited by Walter W. Ristow. Cambridge, Mass.: Harvard University Press, 1961.

Cowell, Benjamin. *Spirit of "76" in Rhode Island.* Boston: A. J. Wright, 1850.

Darby, William, and Dwight, Theodore, Jr. *A New Gazetteer of the United States of America.* Hartford: E. Hopkins, 1833.

Dictionary of American Biography. 21 vols. New York: Scribner, 1943.

Dictionary of National Biography. 66 vols. London: Smith, Elder, 1885–1901.

Dupuy, R. Ernest, and Trevor, N. *Encyclopedia of Military History*. New York: Harper & Row, 1970.

Faden, William. *The North American Atlas, Selected From the Most Authentic Maps, Charts, Plans, &c.* London: 1777.

Forbes, Harriette Merrifield. *New England Diaries, 1602–1800: A Descriptive Catalogue of Diaries, Orderly Books and Sea Journals*. Topsfield, Mass.: privately printed, 1923.

Force, Peter, ed. *American Archives*. 4th series. 6 vols. Washington, D.C.: 1837–46.

———. *American Archives*. 5th series. 3 vols. Washington, D.C.: 1848–53.

Harris, Caleb. *A Map of the State of Rhode Island*. 1795. Reprint. Providence: Rhode Island Historical Society, 1969.

Hayward, John. *A Gazetteer of Massachusetts*. Boston: 1846.

———. *A Gazatteer of Massachusetts*. Rev. ed. Boston: J. P. Jewett, 1849.

———. *The New England Gazetteer*. 5th ed. Concord, N.H., and Boston: 1839.

Heitman, Francis Bernard. *Historical Register of Officers of the Continental Army During the War of the Revolution, April, 1775 to December, 1783*. New, rev., enl. ed. Washington, D.C.: Rare Book Shop Publishing Co., 1914.

Index of Revolutionary War Pension Applications. Washington, D.C.: National Genealogical Society, 1966.

Klein, Milton M., comp. *New York in the American Revolution, A Bibliography*. Albany: New York State Bicentennial Commission, 1974.

Matthews, William. *American Diaries: An Annotated Bibliography of American Diaries Prior to 1861*. Berkeley: University of California Press, 1945.

———. *American Diaries in Manuscript, 1580–1954: A Descriptive Bibliography*. Athens: University of Georgia Press, 1974.

National Cyclopaedia of American Biography. 55 vols. and supplements. New York: J. T. White, 1922.

Nebanzahl, Kenneth. *Atlas of the American Revolution*. Chicago: Rand McNally, 1974.

Peckham, Howard H. *The Toll of Independence.* Chicago: University of Chicago Press, 1974.

Rand McNally Commercial Atlas. Chicago: Rand McNally and Co., 1968.

Sabin, Joseph. *A Dictionary of Books Relating to America.* New York: 1867–70.

Sabine, Lorenzo. *Biographical Sketches of Loyalists of the American Revolution.* 2 vols. Boston: Little, Brown, 1864.

Smith, Clifford Neal. *Federal Land Series, A Calendar of Archival Materials on the Land Patents Issued by the United States Government, with Subject, Tract, and Name Indexes.* 2 vols. Chicago: American Library Association, 1972.

Smith, Joseph Jencks. *Civil And Military List of Rhode Island.* Providence, R.I.: Preston and Rounds, 1901.

Stokes, Isaac Newton Phelps. *Iconography of Manhattan Island, 1498–1909.* 6 vols. New York: R. H. Dodd, 1915–28.

Stryker, William S. *Official Register of the Officers and Men in the Revolution.* Trenton, N.J.: 1872.

Terry, Marian Dickinson. *Old Inns of Connecticut.* Hartford, Conn.: Prospect Press, 1937.

United States Geological Survey. *Atlas of Massachusetts.* Boston: 1890.

U.S. Congress. *Biographical Directory of the American Congress, 1774–1971.* Washington, D.C.: U. S. Government Printing Office, 1971.

Wilson, James Grant, and Fiske, John. *Appleton's Cyclopaedia of American Biography.* 6 vols. New York: D. Appleton, ca. 1886–89.

Printed Primary Sources

Ainslie, Thomas. *Canada Preserved, The Journal of Captain Thomas Ainslie.* Edited by Sheldon S. Cohen. New York: New York University Press, 1968.

Angell, Israel. *Diary of Colonel Israel Angell Commanding the Second Rhode Island Continental Regiment During the American Revolution, 1778–1781.* Transcribed and edited by Edward Field. Providence, R.I.: Preston and Rounds Co., 1899.

Bailyn, Bernard, ed. *Pamphlets of the American Revolution, 1750–1776.* Vol. 1. Cambridge, Mass.: Harvard University Press, 1965.

Bartlett, John Russell, ed. *Records of the Colony of Rhode Island and Providence Plantations in New England.* 10 vols. 1856–65. Reprint. New York: AMS Press, 1968.

Brissot De Warville, J. P. *New Travels in the United States of America, 1788.* Translated by Mara S. Vamos and Durand Echeverria. Cambridge, Mass.: Harvard University Press, Belknap Press, 1964.

Brown, Lloyd A., and Peckham, Howard H., eds. *Revolutionary War Journals of Henry Dearborn, 1775–1783.* 1939. Reprint. New York: Da Capo, 1971.

Butterfield, L. H., ed. *Letters of Benjamin Rush, 1761–1790.* 2 vols. Princeton: Princeton University Press, 1951.

[Caldwell, Henry ?]. "The Invasion of Canada in 1775." Manuscripts Relating to the Early History of Canada, Series 1, no. 5. Quebec: Literary and Historical Society of Quebec, 1866.

Carter, Marian Pearce, comp. *Swansea Vital Record Book "B."* Attleboro, Mass.: n.p., 1930.

Chastellux, François Jean, Marquis de. *Travels in North America.* Edited by Howard Rice. 2 vols. Chapel Hill: University of North Carolina Press, 1963.

Clark, William B., ed. *Naval Documents of the American Revolution.* 5 vols. Washington, D.C.: U.S. Naval Department, 1966—.

Custer, Milo, ed. *A Few Family Records, No. 7.* Bloomington. Ill.: privately printed, 1922.

David, Ebenezer. *A Rhode Island Chaplain in the Revolution.* Providence, R.I.: The Society of the Cincinnati, 1949.

[Finlay, Hugh ?]. "Journal of the Siege and Blockade of Quebec by the American Rebels, in Autumn 1775 and Winter 1776." Manuscripts Relating to the Early History of Canada, Series 4, no. 4, Literary and Historical Society of Quebec. Quebec: Dawson & Co., 1875.

Fitzpatrick, John C., ed. *The Writings of George Washington from the Original Manuscript Sources, 1745–1799.* 39 vols. Washington, D.C.: Library of Congress, 1931–44.

Ford, Worthington C., ed. *General Orders Issued by Major-General Israel Putnam, When in Command of the Highlands in the Summer and Fall of 1777.* Brooklyn, N.Y.: Historical Printing Club, 1893.

Franklin, Benjamin. *Autobiography*. New York: Modern Library, 1932.

Henry, John Joseph. *Account of Arnold's Campaign Against Quebec*. 1877. Reprint. New York: Arno Press, 1968.

Jennings, William. "Marriage Record of Washington County, Ohio." *Old Northwest Genealogical Quarterly* 4 (1901); passim.

Journals of the Continental Congress, 1774–1789. Edited by Gaillard Hunt. 34 vols. Washington, D.C.: U.S. Government Printing Office, 1904–37.

Martin, Joseph Plumb. *Private Yankee Doodle*. Boston: Little, Brown, 1962.

Montresor, John. *Journals*. Edited by G. D. Scull. New York: New York State Historical Society, 1882.

Moore, Frank, comp. *The Diary of the American Revolution, 1775–1781*. Abridged ed. by John Anthony Scott. New York: Washington Square Press, 1967.

Rhode Island Historical Society. *Revolutionary Correspondence From 1775* to *1782*. Rhode Island Historical Society Collections, vol. 6, part 2 (1867). Providence: Rhode Island Historical Society, 1843.

Rice, Howard Crosby, Jr., and Brown, Anne S. K., eds. & trans. *The American Campaigns of Rochambeau's Army, 1780, 1781, 1782, 1783*. 2 vols. Princeton: Princeton University Press, 1972.

Roberts, Kenneth, ed. *March to Quebec*; *Journals of the Members of Arnold's Expedition*. 2d. ed. New York: Doubleday, Doran & Co., 1940.

Scott, James. *Purity of Heart*: *a Moral Epistle*. Cambridge: 1761.

Senter, Isaac. *The Journal of Isaac Senter*. Philadelphia: Historical Society of Pennsylvania, 1846.

Ship Registers and Enrollments of Providence, Rhode Island, 1773–1939. Providence, R.I.: Works Projects Administration, 1941.

Sparks, Jared, ed. *Correspondence of the American Revolution*; *Being Letters of Eminent Men to George Washington*. 4 vols. 1853. Reprint. Freeport, N.Y.: Books for Libraries Press, 1970.

Staples, William R., ed. *Annals of the Town of Providence, From Its First Settlement to the Organization of the City Government, in June, 1832*. Rhode Island Historical Society Collections, vol. 5 (1843). Providence: Rhode Island Historical Society, 1843.

Sullivan, John. *Letters and Papers of Major-General John Sullivan.* 3 vols. Concord: New Hampshire Historical Society, 1930–39.

Thacher, James. *Military Journal of the American Revolution.* Hartford, Conn.: Hurlbut, Williams & Co., 1862.

U.S. Congress. *Debates and Proceedings.* 16th Congress, 1st Session. Washington, D.C.: Gales and Seaton, 1855.

U.S. Congress. *Debates and Proceedings.* 16th Congress, 1st Session. Washington, D.C.: Gales and Seaton, 1855.

U.S. War Department. *Pension Rolls.* Washington, D.C.: 1835.

Ward, Samuel. *Correspondence of Governor Samuel Ward, May 1775–March 1776. with a Biographical Introduction Based Chiefly on the Ward Papers Covering the Period 1725–1776.* Edited by Bernhard Knollenberg and Genealogy of the Ward Family, Thomas Ward, son of John, of Newport and some of his descendants. Compiled by Clifford P. Monahan. Providence: Rhode Island Historical Society, 1952.

Secondary Sources

Alden, John Richard. *The American Revolution,* 1775–1783. New York: Harper & Row, 1954.

Arnold, Samuel Greene. *History of the State of Rhode Island and Providence Plantations.* 4th ed. 2 vols. Providence, R.I.: Preston and Rounds, 1899.

Barck, Ocsar Theodore, Jr. *New York City During the War For Independence.* New York: Columbia University Press, 1931.

Bayles, Richard M., ed. *History of Providence County, Rhode Island.* 2 vols. New York: W. W. Preston, 1891.

Berg, Fred Anderson. *Encyclopedia of Continental Army Units: Battalions, Regiments and Independent Corps.* Harrisburg, Pa.: Stackpole Co., 1972.

Bicknell, Thomas W. *The History of the State of Rhode Island and Providence Plantations.* 5 vols. New York: American Historical Society, 1920.

Billington, Ray Allen. *Westward Expansion.* 2d ed. New York: Macmillan, 1964.

Bolton, Charles K. *The Private Soldier Under Washington.* New York: Scribner, 1902.

Bolton, Reginald Pelham, and Calver, William Louis. *History Written with Pick and Shovel.* New York: New York Historical Society, 1950.

Bridenbaugh, Carl. *Cities in Revolt.* London: Oxford University Press, 1971.

———. *Silas Downer: Forgotten Patriot.* Providence: Rhode Island Bicentennial Foundation, 1974.

Bronson, W. C. *The History of Brown University.* Providence, R.I.: The University Press, 1914.

Burnett, Edmund Cody. *The Continental Congress.* New York: Macmillan, 1941. Reprint. New York: W. W. Norton and Co., 1964.

Carrington, Henry B. *Battles of the American Revolution.* New York: Promontory Press, n.d.

Carroll, Charles. *Public Education in Rhode Island.* Providence, R. I.: n.p., 1914.

Chapin, Anna Augusta, and Chapin, Charles V. *A History of Rhode Island Ferries, 1640–1923.* Providence, R.I.: Oxford Press, 1925.

Codman, John. *Arnold's Expedition to Quebec.* New York: Macmillan, 1902.

Commemorative Biographical Record of Dutchess County, New York. 2 vols. Chicago: J. H. Beers, 1897.

Cooper, James Fenimore. *The Spy.* New York: Dodd, Mead, & Co., 1946.

Cremin, Lawrence A. *American Education: The Colonial Experience, 1607–1783.* New York: Harper & Row, 1970.

Crofut, Florence S. Marcy. *Guide to the History and the Historic Sites of Connecticut.* New Haven: Yale University Press, 1937.

Douglas, George William. *The American Book of Days.* New York: H. W. Wilson, 1948.

Duffy, John. *Epidemics in Colonial America.* Baton Rouge: Louisiana State University Press, 1953.

Duis, Edward. *The Good Old Times in McLean County, Illinois.* (1874). Bloomington, Ill.: McKnight and McKnight, 1968.

Field, Edward. *The Colonial Tavern.* Providence, R.I.: Preston and Rounds, 1897.

———. *Revolutionary Defences in Rhode Island.* Providence. R.I.: Preston and Rounds, 1896.

Flexner, James T. *The Traitor and the Spy, Benedict Arnold and John André.* New York: Harcourt, Brace, 1953.

Forbes, Alan, and Cadman, Paul F. *France and New England.* 3 vols. Boston: State Street Trust Co., 1927–29.

Ford, Corey. *A Peculiar Service.* Boston: Little, Brown, 1965.

Freeman, Douglas Southall. *George Washington.* 7 vols. New York: Scribner, 1948–57.

Greene, Evarts B. *Revolutionary Generation, 1763–1790.* New York: Macmillan, 1943.

———., and Harrington, Virginia D. *American Population Before the Federal Census of 1790.* New York: Columbia University Press, 1932.

Greene, Francis Vinton. *The Revolutionary War and the Military Policy of the United States.* New York: Scribner, 1911.

Gruber, Ira. *The Howe Brothers and the American Revolution.* New York: Atheneum, 1972.

Hatch, Louis Clinton. *The Administration of the American Revolutionary Army.* New York: Longmans, Green, 1904.

Higginbotham, Don. *The War of American Independence, Military Attitudes, Policies, and Practice, 1763–1789.* New York: Macmillan, 1971.

History of Washington County, Ohio. Cleveland: H. Z. Williams & Bro., 1881.

Howe, Edgar Watson. *Plain People.* New York: Dodd Mead & Company, 1929.

Jackson, John W. *The Pennsylvania Navy, 1775–1781: The Defense of the Delaware.* 2d ed. New Brunswick, N.J.: Rutgers University Press, 1974.

Kurtz, Stephen G., and Hutson, James H., eds. *Ersays on the American Revolution.* Published for the Institute of Early American History and Culture. Chapel Hill: University of North Carolina Press, 1973.

Lemisch, Jesse. "The American Revolution Seen from the Bottom Up." In *Towards a New Past: Dissenting Essays in American* History, edited by Barton J. Bernstein. New York: Alfred A. Knopf and Random House, 1968.

———. "Jack Tar in the Streets: Merchant Seamen in the Politics of Revolutionary America." *William and Mary Quarterly* 25, no. 3 (July 1968): 371–407.

———. "Listening to the 'Inarticulate': William Widger's Dream and the Loyalties of American Revolutionary Seamen in British

Prisons." *Journal of Social History* 3, no 1. (Fall 1969): 1–29.

Lippincott, Horace Mather. *Philadelphia.* 1926. Reprint. Port Washington, N.Y.: Kennikat Press, 1970.

Lovell, Louise Lewis. *Israel Angell.* New York: G. P. Putnam, 1921.

Lundin, Leonard. *Cockpit of the Revolution: The War for Independence in New Jersey.* Princeton: Princeton University Press, 1940.

Mackesy, Piers. "British Strategy in the War of American Independence." *Yale Review* 52 (1963): 539–57.

———. *The War for America, 1775–1783.* Cambridge: Harvard University Press, 1964.

Marshall, John. *The Life of George Washington.* 2 vols. New York: Walton Book Co., 1930.

Mason, George C. *The British Fleet in Rhode Island.* Rhode Island Historical Society Collections, vol. 7, part 5 (1885). Providence: Rhode Island Historical Society.

Merriman, Charles P. *The History of McLean County Illinois, Containing a History of the County, its Cities, Towns, etc.* . . . Chicago: W. LeBaron, 1879.

Miller, John C. *The Triumph of Freedom: 1775–1783.* Boston: Little, Brown, 1948

Miranda, Francisco de. *The New Democracy in America.* Norman: University of Oklahoma Press, 1963.

Morison, Samuel Eliot. *The Maritime History of Massachusetts, 1783–1860.* Boston: Houghton Mifflin Co., 1921.

———. *Oxford History of the American People.* New York: Oxford University Press, 1965.

Morris, Richard B. *The Peacemakers.* New York: Harper & Row, 1965.

Olmstead, Clifton E. *History of Religion in the United States.* Englewood Cliffs, N.J.: Prentice-Hall, 1960.

Perkins, James B. *France in the American Revolution.* 1911. Reprint. Williamstown, Mass.: Corner House Publishers, 1970.

Portrait and Biographical Album of McLean County Illinois. Chicago: Chapman and Bros., 1887.

Printers and Printing in Providence. Providence, R.I.: n.d.

Quarles, Benjamin. *The Negro in the American Revolution.* Chapel Hill: University of North Carolina Press, 1961.

Ramsay, David. *The History of the American Revolution.* 2 vols. 1789. Reprint. New York: Russell and Russell, 1968.

Raymond, Marcius S. "Colonel Christopher Greene." *Magazine of History, with Notes and Queries* (September–October 1916): 138–49.

Remini, Robert V. *The Election of Andrew Jackson.* Philadelphia: J. B. Lippincott Co., 1963.

Rider, Sidney Smith. *An Historical Inquiry Concerning the Attempt to Raise a Regiment of Slaves by Rhode Island During the War of the Revolution.* Providence, R.I.: 1880.

Shy, John. *A People Numerous and Armed; Reflections on the Military Struggle for American Independence.* London and New York: Oxford University Press, 1976.

Smith, Justin H. *Arnold's March from Cambridge to Quebec, A Critical Study together with a Reprint of Arnold's Journal.* New York: G. P. Putnam, 1903.

———. *Our Struggle for the Fourteenth Colony, Canada and the American Revolution.* 2 vols. New York and London: G. P. Putnam, 1907.

Smith, Samuel Stelle. *The Battle of Monmouth.* Monmouth Beach, N.J.: Philip Freneau Press, 1964.

———. *Fight for the Delaware, 1777.* Monmouth Beach, N.J.: Philip Freneau Press, 1970.

Snyder, John P. *The Story of New Jersey's Civil Boundaries, 1686–1968.* Trenton, N.J.: Bureau of Geology and Topography, 1969.

Stanley, George F. G. *Canada Invaded, 1775–1776.* Toronto: Hakkert, 1973.

Stedman, Charles. *The History of the Origin, Progress, and Termination of the American War.* 2 vols. London: J. Murray, 1794.

Stephenson, N. W., and Dunn, W. H. *George Washington.* 2 vols. New York: Oxford University Press, 1940.

Stevenson, Roger. *Military Instructions for Officers Detached in the Field.* Philadelphia: R. Aitken, 1775.

Stryker, William S. *The Battle of Monmouth.* 1927. Reprint. Port Washington, N.Y.: Kennikat Press, 1970.

———. *The Forts on the Delaware in the Revolutionary War.* Trenton, N.J.: J. L. Murphy, 1901.

Teeters, Negley K. *They Were in Prison, A History of the Pennsyl-*

vania Prison Society, 1787–1937. Philadelphia: J. C. Winston Co., 1937.

Trevelyan, George Otto. *The American Revolution*. 4 Vols. London: Longmans, Green, 1899–1907.

Uhlendorf, Bernard A. ed. *Revolution in America, Confidential Letters and Journals 1776–1784 of Adjutant General Major Baurmeister of the Hessian Forces*. New Brunswick, N.J.: Rutgers University Press, 1957.

Underdal, Stanley J., ed. *Military History of the American Revolution*. Proceedings of the 6th Military History Symposium, United States Air Force Academy, 1974. Washington, D.C.: Office of Air Force History and United States Air Force Academy, 1976.

Van Doren, Carl. *Mutiny in January*. New York: Viking Press, 1943.

———. *Secret History of the American Revolution*. New York: Garden City Publishing Co., 1941.

Vivian, Jean. "Military Land Bounties During the Revolutionary and Confederation Periods." *Maryland Historical Magazine* 61 (1966): 231–55.

Vose, James G. *Sketches of Congregationalism in Rhode Island*. New York: Silver and Burdett, 1894.

Ward, Christopher. *The War of the Revolution*. 2 vols. New York: Macmillan, 1952.

Willcox, William B. *The Portrait of a General: Sir Henry Clinton in the War of Independence*. New York: Alfred A. Knopf, 1964.

Williams, Catherine. *Biography of Revolutionary Heroes, Containing the Life of Brigadier General William Barton and, also, of Captain Stephen Olney*. Providence, R.I.: 1839.

Wilson, Arthur E. *Weybosset Bridge in Providence Plantations, 1700–1790*. Boston: Pilgrim Press, 1947.

Wurtele, Frederick C., ed. *Blockade of Quebec in 1775–1776 by the American Revolutionists*. 1906. Reprint. Port Washington, N.Y.: Kennikat Press, 1970.

Manuscripts

Bloomington, Illinois. McLean County Courthouse. McLean County Land Evidences (Deed Books).

Marietta, Ohio. Washington County Courthouse. Washington County Land Evidences (Deed Books).
Providence, Rhode Island. Rhode Island Historical Society. Shepley Collection of Revolutionary War MSS.
———. Rhode Island Historical Society. Port of Providence Customs House Papers
———. Rhode Island Historical Society. Rhode Island Society of the Cincinnati Archives.
———. Rhode Island Historical Society. Town of Providence Tax Records (Direct Tax List of 1798).
———. City Hall. Town of Providence Land Evidences (Deed Books).
———. State House. Archives of the State of Rhode Island.
Washington, D.C. Library of Congress. "A Collection of Plans in the Province of New Jersey" [by John Hill]. Photostat.
———. Library of Congress, Manuscript Division. Washington Papers.
———. National Archives. Military Pension Records.
———. National Archives. Revolutionary War Records.

Newspapers

American Friend & Marietta Gazette (Ohio), 29 November 1828.
Boston Evening Transcript, 14 March 1921, 6 February 1922, 18 October 1938.
Gazette and Weekly Mercury (New York), 30 September 1776.
Gazette (Providence), 1 February 1777, 14 March 1778, 28 March 1778.
Pilot (Marietta and Washington County, Ohio), January–June 1828.
Royal Gazette (Rivington, New York), 16 May 1781.

INDEX

This book was designed by Gerard A. Valerio. It was typeset and printed by Heritage Printers, Inc. The text face is Caslon Old-style, named for its designer William Caslon (1692–1766). The monotype used here (No. 37) captures many of the qualities of the original typeface. 1500 copies of the book were printed by letterpress on Warren's #60 Olde Style wove.